"Bad" Mothers

"Bad" Mothers

The Politics of Blame in Twentieth-Century America

EDITED BY

Molly Ladd-Taylor and Lauri Umansky

New York University Press

NEW YORK AND LONDON

NEW YORK UNIVERSITY PRESS
New York and London

Library of Congress Cataloging-in-Publication Data

"Bad" mothers : the politics of blame in twentieth-century America / edited by Molly Ladd-Taylor and Lauri Umansky.
p.   cm.
Includes index.
ISBN 0-8147-5119-9 (cloth : acid-free paper). — ISBN
0-8147-5120-2 (pbk. : acid-free paper)
1. Mothers—United States—History.   2. Mothers—United States—Public opinion—History.   3. Blame—Social aspects—United States—History.   I. Ladd-Taylor, Molly, 1955–   II. Umansky, Lauri, 1959–   .
HQ759.B218   1997
306.874'3'0973—dc21   97-21142
                               CIP

New York University Press books are printed on acid-free paper, and their binding materials are chosen for strength and durability.

Manufactured in the United States of America

10   9   8   7   6   5   4   3   2   1

For our children
Disa, Julian, and Timothy
&
Carenna and Wendy

Contents

Introduction

Molly Ladd-Taylor and Lauri Umansky

It was every parent's nightmare. Five-year old Corinne Erstad disappeared. A massive search found only her blood and a few strands of hair in the home of a family friend, Robert Guevara. DNA evidence linked the girl's blood to Guevara's sweatpants. His fingerprints were found on a plastic bag containing her sundress, her barrette, and a blood-soaked pair of her underpants. The prosecution thought the physical evidence against Guevara was overwhelming. But defense attorneys cast him as a pawn in a scam perpetrated by his lover, Corinne's mother. She was "a scheming welfare mother" who sold her child because she was tired of being poor. The jury found Guevara not guilty.[1]

Sarah and James were engaged in a bitter fight for custody of their six-year-old daughter. Although the two had never married, James believed that he was a more fit parent because of Sarah's hippie lifestyle. Consequently, when the trial court ruled in Sarah's favor, he took his case all the way to the state Supreme Court. As evidence of Sarah's insensitivity to her daughter's needs, James listed her midwife-assisted home birth, advocacy of natural food, preference for home schooling, and opposition to immunization. James also worried about Sarah's unconventional relationships—with a couple who had an "open marriage" and with members of a Native American community. While the court acknowledged that Laural had thrived under her mother's care, it found James a more effective parent, because he was stable, mature—and had a conventional lifestyle. It awarded physical care to the father.[2]

Some mothers are not good mothers. No one can deny that. There are women who neglect their children, abuse them, or fail to provide them

1

with proper psychological nurturance. But throughout the twentieth century, the label of "bad" mother has been applied to far more women than those whose actions would warrant the name. By virtue of race, class, age, marital status, sexual orientation, and numerous other factors, millions of American mothers have been deemed substandard.

In the past few decades, "bad" mothers have moved noticeably toward center stage in American culture. The stereotypes are familiar: the welfare mother, the teen mother, the career woman who has no time for her kids, the drug addict who poisons her fetus, the pushy stage mother, the overprotective Jewish mother, and so on. But mother-blaming goes far beyond these stereotypes. It can be found in custody disputes, political speeches, and parent-teacher conferences. It can be found in the glares of disapproval mothers get when their children act out in public. It can be found as well in the guilt feelings of working women who have internalized the "bad" mother label.

The long list of stereotypes and dizzying array of mother-blaming accusations tempt one to conclude that mothers get blamed for everything, pure and simple. Why? Is it just that mothers are *there* at the center of the nuclear family? Is it that no one can live up to the sentimentalized good-mother ideal? Or is mother-blaming merely a symptom of our society's misogyny?

The essays in this volume speak to these questions. They show that mother-blaming has varied widely in content, cause, and consequence over the past century. Moreover, they reveal the extraordinary elasticity of the "bad" mother label. *"Bad" Mothers* analyzes the social, cultural, political and economic purposes of mother-blaming. It examines who has been targeted, by whom, when, and why, and it probes the impact of the "bad" mother label on individual women and their families.

What Makes a "Bad" Mother?

To most Americans, "bad" mothering is like obscenity: you know it when you see it.[3] Everyone agrees that mothers who beat or kill their children are bad. But beyond that? Americans are divided on whether mothers should stay home with their children, and on whether a "good" parent would spank a child. We even disagree about what age a "good" mother should be. Most of us agree it's bad to become a mother too young, but at what age does a new mother become too old?[4] Does allowing your baby to sleep in your bed build a more secure child or an overly dependent one? Is it bad to breastfeed a toddler—or to give a newborn a bottle? The proliferation of consumer goods compounds the problem: advertisers make mothers feel bad if they don't buy the right baby products, while advice givers say a sure sign of a "bad" mother is a woman who buys her child too much.[5]

The fact is that all mothers are "bad" sometimes. Who has never spoken too sharply to her child or been too quick to discipline (or not quick enough)? Yet because most mothering takes place at home, away from public scrutiny, truly harmful mothering is not always easy to identify. Countless numbers of abused children fall through the cracks in the child welfare system because no one recognized the danger signs. At the same time, some women get classed as bad mothers, lose custody of their children, and even face criminal charges on astonishingly flimsy evidence.

We do not mean to downplay real violations of parental duty. However, the "bad" mother label does not necessarily denote practices that actually harm children. In fact, it serves to shift our attention away from a specific act to a whole person—and even to entire categories of people. Thus doctors are far more likely to diagnose fetal alcohol syndrome in the child of a Native American than in the child of a WASP, police and social workers are conditioned to look for juvenile delinquency among the sons of welfare mothers, and the media seem stunned when a likeable white woman like Susan Smith kills her sons, something we think a drug addict more likely to do.

Over the past century, women classed as "bad" mothers have fallen into three general groups: those who did not live in a "traditional" nuclear family; those who would not or could not protect their children from harm; and those whose children went wrong. The first is the most remarked upon, and the most clearly unjust. Women who did not fit the middle-class family ideal of breadwinning father and stay-at-home mother have born the brunt of mother-blaming throughout most of American history. Wage-earning mothers, single mothers, slave mothers—in short, everyone except middle-class whites—fall outside the narrow good-mother ideal.

Yet the "traditional" two-parent, one-income family so celebrated by conservatives today is the historical exception, not the norm. Prior to the Second World War, few working-class men made enough money to support their families. Working-class mothers took in boarders or washing, did industrial homework such as making cigars or paper flowers—or sent their children off to jobs.[6] Only in the 1950s did a significant number of working-class men earn wages high enough to support their families. Nevertheless, the proportion of married women in the work force continued to grow. By 1960, 30 percent of married women were in the labor force, twice the proportion just twenty years earlier but still far less than the 68 percent of mothers with children at home who are labor force participants today.[7]

Class runs through a second piece of "evidence" of failed motherhood: the refusal (or inability) to protect one's child from danger, or even from disease. Mother-blaming abounds when children suffer untimely deaths. The readiness of the jury to believe that Corinne Erstad's mother had a hand in her death is just one example. The media's callous criticism of Jessica Dubroff's mother after the seven-year-old girl died trying to become the youngest person to copilot a plane across North America is another.[8] Mothers are also faulted when babies die of natural causes, especially when child care practices are identified as risk factors. For example, well-intentioned health reformers of the 1910s and 1920s considered the garlic and spicy food immigrant women fed their babies to be a significant factor in infant mortality.[9] Similarly, some researchers in the 1990s claim that putting babies to sleep on their stomachs in a crib (instead of letting them sleep with their mothers in the family bed) increases the risk of Sudden Infant Death Syndrome—despite the fact that the majority of SIDS deaths are not associated with any known risk factors.[10]

A host of diseases thought to have psychological origins also get blamed on mothers. As Jane Taylor McDonnell shows poignantly in this volume, not so long ago the psychiatric establishment considered autism, a neurological condition, to be caused by "refrigerator" mothers who rejected their children. Psychological experts also blamed schizophrenia on maternal rejection; many still associate anorexia with a troubled mother-daughter relationship, describing mothers of anorectics as controlling, perfectionist, frustrated, and nonconfrontational.[11]

Mothers often face blame when their children fall victim to incest or sexual abuse. In some cases, doctors and social workers suspect maternal abuse when a child suffers from a chronic disease. For example, failure to thrive often arouses suspicion of maternal neglect, although it can be caused by a defect in the esophagus. But beware of mothers who seem overly protective of ill children. Medical literature now warns doctors to suspect the mother of a frequently sick child, particularly if she seems "too" versed in medical parlance, of Munchausen's Syndrome by Proxy, a rare psychiatric disorder in which a mother induces illness in her child in order to surround herself with medical personnel and procedures.[12]

Finally, a child "gone wrong" is considered sure-fire evidence of faulty mothering. From the 1890s to the 1950s, independent-minded or overprotective women were thought to have "caused" their sons' homosexuality. Working mothers have long been blamed for juvenile delinquency; black mothers for welfare dependency; and, as Su Epstein's essay shows, mothers of serial killers for the crimes of their sons.[13] Yet women can be at fault even when sons commit no crimes. Conservatives blamed permissive mothers following the advice of Dr. Spock for an entire generation of flower children![14] Fathers, schools, television — and the environment outside the home — get little if any attention in this frenzy of attribution.

Childrearing advice, which gained unprecedented influence in the twentieth century, further narrows the range of good mothering. Moreover, the advice has changed dramatically over the years. In the 1920s, a "bad" mother raced to pick up her baby when he cried. Babies were to be left alone in their cribs for several hours a day, not overstimulated by too much cuddling, bouncing, or noise. Since doctors emphasized the importance of breaking "bad habits" early, thumbsucking and infant masturbation became signs that the mother had failed.[15] By the 1980s, bestselling author Penelope Leach assured mothers that they could not spoil a baby. She encouraged them to breastfeed on demand, pick up crying children, and even get babies to suck their thumbs. Now only "bad" mothers meted out solace by the clock.[16]

To add to the confusion, the experts in a given era don't agree on the measures of "good" parenting. Most now recommend breastfeeding, but they differ over how long. And there is no agreement about whether parents should sleep with the baby, when they should offer solid food, or when a child should be encouraged to read.[17] No matter. No one could possibly follow all the expert advice, because it often conflicts with real women's lives. For example, although advice givers now encourage women to breastfeed their babies, and for a longer period of time, those who do so in public (or even in private — as the Karen Carter case shows) risk public opprobrium and even arrest.[18] Despite the fact that most mothers of infants work outside the home, the childrearing advice continues to assume that they are home — and to insist that this is best for the children.[19] Indeed, with a minority of American families living the two-parents, one-wage-earner lifestyle, we all face a discomfiting question: Do most mothers now qualify as "bad" mothers in one way or another?

"Bad" Mothers for Every Era

Virtually every culture on historical record has had its wicked women, and in many cases their wickedness revolved around the reproductive function. Euripides' Medea, though fictional, epitomizes the evil mother: she slaughtered her own children out of rage over her husband's philandering. Some psychologists surmise that the mysterious power of the womb to bring forth life frightened men, who then projected their fear and aggression onto women in the form of monstrous mythical mothers who abandoned, maimed, slaughtered, or devoured their children (usually sons).[20] Other scholars emphasize the ways "bad" mothers of old threatened the economic status quo. Evil stepmothers, who jeopardized children's inheritance upon the father's death, have populated fairy tales and folklore for centuries.[21] A glance at the "bad" mothers of any age reveals the fate of women who violated the gender norms of their time, whether by choice, by fiat, or by the force of circumstance.

Ultimately, the definition of a "bad" mother intertwines with that of a "good" mother, itself a relatively recent invention. The concept of an instinctive mother love did not exist in the Western world prior to the eighteenth century. Maternal behaviors we take for granted today—such as grieving when your child dies, loving all your kids equally, and physically caring for your own children—were rare, at least among European mothers of the upper classes.[22]

The "bad" mother we recognize today has historical roots in the late eighteenth and early nineteenth century. Her appearance connects to the new ideas about motherhood and childhood innocence that accompanied industrialization, the American Revolution, and Protestant evangelicalism. These historical sea changes continue to inform mothering today: in the beliefs that children are innocent, that good mothering and good government are intertwined, and that nurturing represents woman's essential nature. Vestiges of the Victorian ideal of motherhood persist: the "good" mother remains self-abnegating, domestic, preternaturally attuned to her children's needs; the "bad" mother has failed on one or more of these scores.

Changes in the organization of work provided the basis of the new maternal ideal. As industrialization took hold in North America, "work" was redefined as entrepreneurship and wage earning, and tied to the cash economy. Men went outside the home to "work," while women remained at home, in "woman's sphere," to rear children. The physical differences between men and women supposedly mandated this arrangement.[23]

Political and religious developments, in the form of the American Revolution and Great Awakenings, reinforced the new ideas about women's and children's place. The ideology historians have dubbed Republican Motherhood defined women's place in the new nation and tied "good" mothering to nation building. Women were formally excluded from most rights of citizens (such as voting), but they were assigned informal responsibility for the moral education of their citizen-sons. This education was considered essential to a democracy; citizens' self-control could make or break the American political experiment.[24] In the same years, Calvinism and the belief in original sin gave way to a faith in childhood innocence and malleability. Where children's deaths had once been understood as God's will and their moral failings as the inevitable outcome of innate sinfulness, now the mother could be blamed. She had it in her power to make or break the child.[25]

In many ways, the ideology of woman's sphere signaled an advance for the white middle-class women who most embraced it. Where previously womanhood was associated with sexuality, cunning, and immorality, the Victorian cult of "true womanhood" defined women as pure, pious, domestic, and submissive. Their supposedly superior moral sensibility gave "true" women dignity, increased their authority at home, justified their education, and defined their role in public life.[26]

Yet the sentimentalized Victorian mother perched on a shaky pedestal. The mother who lifted her voice too loudly or attended too diligently to her own needs felt the sting of familial, clerical, and community disapproval. "The care of children requires a great many sacrifices, and a great deal of self-denial," wrote the author and reformer Lydia Maria Child, "but the woman who is not willing to sacrifice a good deal in such a cause, does not deserve to be a mother."[27]

The ambiguous impact of such beliefs can be seen in the enormous changes to custody law over the nineteenth century. Mothers gained new powers as courts came to accept the view that they should have custody of young children. English common law, which dominated the American legal system until the mid-nineteenth century, gave fathers almost unlimited rights to the custody of their minor legitimate children. By midcentury, however, new ideas about childhood innocence and mother love led courts to emphasize the welfare of the child in custody determinations. By the 1860s, a number of states had adopted the doctrine of tender years, under which mothers, unless they were determined "unfit," automatically received custody of young children. At the same time, however, judicial authority gained force. Ideas about parental fitness, combined with ideas about true womanhood, placed all parents, but especially mothers, at the mercy of judicial assessments of their capacity as childrearers.[28]

The idea of woman's sphere—and the equating of maternal presence with "good" mothering—was not only new to the nineteenth century; it was also specific to middle-class culture. In most societies childrearing responsibilities were shared. Even within the United States, Native Americans, African Americans, and many immigrant groups had more communal childrearing practices that automatically defined the mothers in these groups as "bad" by middle-class Anglo-Saxon standards.[29]

Slave mothers, for example, could not possibly exhibit the hallmarks of "good" Victorian mothering. Slaveowners forced pregnant and nursing women to work long hours in fields, unable to protect their children, who were, after all, the property of the slaveowner. Frequently, slave children were sold away from their mothers, and in general they also suffered high rates of disease and death, as a result of poor nutrition, inadequate housing, and lack of health care. Recent research suggests that many infant deaths, previously explained as infanticide by both contemporaries and historians, may have been due to Sudden Infant Death Syndrome. Thus the high mortality rate among slave infants may well have signified, not slave women's inept mothering or refusal of slave status for their children, but the tragedy that can result from poor nutrition, low birth weight, and inadequate health care.[30]

In spite of these conditions, slave mothers did protect and nurture their children in manifold ways. Yet where the maternal ideal for white women dictated that they nurture their own children exclusively and in private, enslaved mothers developed networks to protect and care for children communally. If force or fatality separated a child from his or her parents, other adults stepped in to see that child through to adulthood. Thus, although slaveowners expropriated women's domestic and maternal labor for the use of their own families, slave children could count on the entire black community for everyday care.

Ironically, the image of the mammy romanticized the "mothering" skills of some black women—as long as these skills were directed to white children. Although proslavery ideologues declared black women to be lacking in maternal feelings for their own children, they sentimentalized the mammy, always there to protect and care for her young white charges. In so doing, they reinforced both the slave system and the gender hierarchy of their own households. The mammy, who was a slave and hence subordinate, epitomized for slaveowners the selfless mother figure; in that way, her image bolstered the notion that good mothering of white children involved submissiveness and domesticity. Since caring for slave children required challenging slaveowners, at least to some extent, the black mother of black children became a "bad" mother in comparison to the mammy.[31]

By the end of the nineteenth century, new scientific thinking had changed how people thought about mothering, and just about everything else. While earlier generations viewed mothering principally through a religious lens, middle-class families increasingly saw child nature as a matter to be investigated, quantified, and studied by psychologists, doctors, and others. Every aspect of children's care and development came under scrutiny.

The late-nineteenth century term "scientific motherhood" captured the new mood. "Good" mothers still had to love their children and be there for them, but now they also had to keep abreast of the latest expert advice. Scientific knowledge (usually provided by men) combined with women's mother love to form the ingredients necessary for successful childrearing in the modern age. A "good" mother joined a child study club. She kept a childrearing manual by her bedside, charted her child's physical and cognitive development, and monitored her own behavior.[32]

Evolutionary theory undergirded notions of good and bad mothering in this period, for it established a hierarchy of races in which only women of Anglo-Saxon or northern European origin could be truly "good" mothers. Women of "superior" heredity could ensure not only the well-being of their families but also the future of the nation (since they raised the next generation of citizens) and the progress of their race! Darwinian ideas thus enhanced the authority and prestige of Anglo-Saxon mothers, even as they turned up the pressure on them.

Women at the top of the evolutionary ladder were at least granted the *possibility* of being good mothers. Mothers of the so-called lesser races inevitably produced inferior offspring, no matter what they did. Maternal presence, which was considered crucial to the upbringing of middle-class white children, was thought unnecessary for blacks, Native Americans, and most immigrant groups. Darwin's followers thus provided a scientific justification for a two-track social policy, whereby women of so-called inferior races were compelled to leave their children for outside work, while elite mothers were required to remain at home.[33] Conservatives blamed the New Woman—the middle-class woman who sought education, work outside the home, and perhaps even the right to vote—for a host of social ills. Noting the exceedingly low birth rate among college-educated women, they accused graduates (and women's higher education itself) of contributing to the decline of the race. According to one doctor, writing in the *New York Medical Journal* in 1900, the rare "New Woman" who married was a "menace to civilization" and her child. "The weak, plastic, developing cells of the brain are twisted, distorted, and a perverted psychic growth promoted by the false examples and teachings of a discontented mother."[34]

"Bad" Mothers in the Early Twentieth Century

As millions of immigrants from southern and eastern Europe poured into the United States in the first two decades of the twentieth century, jittery nativists noted the relative diminution of the white Protestant, native-born population and charged elite women who did not produce large crops of children with "race suicide." A good mother was "sacred," proclaimed Theodore Roosevelt, but the woman who "shirks her duty, as wife and mother, earns the right to our contempt."[35]

Three aspects of modern American life exacerbated mother-blaming in the twentieth century: the dominance of childrearing experts, the growth of state power, and the flux in gender roles, manifested in the growing number of women in the work force and in feminist movements. As infant mortality dropped and families gained new hope for the survival of their children, parents began to attribute the deaths or illnesses of their children not to God but to the environment. Infant death was preventable—if the mother kept her home clean and sanitary and followed the experts' advice. With the improvements in infant health and the rise of such professions as psychology and medical pediatrics, the experts' attention moved from physical health to mental development. This shift had dire consequences for the mother.[36]

Prior to the 1920s, childrearing experts told women to combine mother love with scientific advice. By the 1920s, however, they described mother love as a "dangerous instrument" and a "stumbling block" to children's psychological development. Behaviorist psychologist John Watson, who dedicated his influential *Psychological Care of Infants and Children* to the "first mother who brings up a happy child," even wryly suggested that children would be better off never knowing their mothers![37] According to the experts, industrialization—and the resulting removal of production from the home—led to bored mothers who dominated their children. Moreover, mothers who had little experience beyond the home were limited in their ability to teach children the habits necessary to succeed in business. How could stay-at-home mothers who followed no strict schedule rear children to live by the clock?[38]

These experts might have had little clout if their rise had not been broadly interwoven with the growth of state power and the "helping professions" in the first third of the century. Public health programs, compulsory schooling, and the growing influence of the social work profession both provided much needed assistance to families and narrowed the range of acceptable behavior. In attempting to "save" children—and make them "American"—social workers frequently engaged in disputes over childrearing with immigrant and working-class mothers. A good American mother, they insisted, did not swaddle her infant or give her a pacifier. She did not feed her baby garlic or sausage or tortillas (or anything other than milk for the first nine months). When her children were sick, she turned to a doctor. A good mother would not place a talisman around her child's neck to ward off the evil eye.[39]

Feminists both challenged and reinforced the good mother/bad mother divide. In the 1910s and 1920s, middle-class women joined together in millions in the social reform movement historians now call maternalism. They attempted to increase women's status and carve out a space in public life by using the rhetoric of good motherhood. Maternalists such as Jane Addams claimed that motherhood (or potential motherhood) united all women, regardless of class, race, or nationality, and that women were uniquely suited to nurturance and care. Maternalists established parent-teacher associations and mothers' clubs and lobbied for numerous "pro-child" policies, such as publicly funded health education for new mothers, the abolition of child labor, and mothers' pensions (which evolved into Aid to Families with Dependent Children).[40]

In invoking the rhetoric of the "good" mother to build welfare services, maternalists unwittingly fostered a more intense criticism of mothers deemed to be bad. Mothers' pensions, for example, were available only for "good" mothers, mostly widows, who were identified as deserving by social workers who came into their homes. The 1935 Social Security Act, which made mothers' pensions (then called Aid to Dependent Children) into a national program, permitted states to deny welfare payments to mothers who did not provide a "suitable home." Many maternalists, like other American reformers, touted education in hygiene or "mothering skills" as solutions to child poverty. Thus, the nation's first welfare measure, the Sheppard-Towner Maternity and Infancy Act of 1921, provided education in nutrition and hygiene, but no medical care, to pregnant women and new mothers and explicitly prohibited monetary aid.[41]

The most egregious antimother laws of the early twentieth century were those permitting the compulsory sterilization of "feebleminded" and insane people considered unfit to bear children. The Supreme Court upheld the principle of compulsory eugenic sterilization in *Buck v. Bell* (1927), a case replete with tragic irony. Scholars now know that Carrie Buck, the allegedly feebleminded white woman whose sterilization the Court endorsed, was not retarded but merely an impoverished single mother who became pregnant as the result of a rape, and was institutionalized. By 1939, more than thirty-three thousand people—mostly women—had been legally sterilized. Yet, as Steven Noll's essay on Willie Mallory poignantly shows, the definition of "feeblemindedness" was vague. For women, it was tied up with other conditions that made one a "bad" mother, such as having a child out of wedlock, being on welfare, living in poverty.[42]

"Bad" Mothers in the Postwar Years

Mother-blaming of the 1920s and 1930s, however fierce, paled in comparison to that of World War II and the postwar years. Philip Wylie, who coined the term "momism" in 1942, set the mother-bashing tone. To Wylie, "megaloid momworship" was responsible for most problems of modern American society. He and other critics linked the upheaval in gender roles during the war, and American men's responses first to fascism and then to communism, to an apparent crisis of motherhood.[43]

In part this backlash responded to very real concerns that emerged during the war. In the 1940s, war effort propaganda encouraged women to enter the labor force. Real difficulties of combining wage work and family life in the absence of adequate child care or housing combined with hysteria to create media horror stories of juvenile delinquents out of control, children abandoned and uncared for while their mothers worked. Newspapers reported women giving up their children because they could not (or would not?) support them. The Boston liquor licensing board even asked saloon owners to cease serving liquor to women with babies and to discourage the practice of parking baby carriages outside saloons.[44]

Mother-bashers saw the problem as working women's selfishness, not the lack of services. This is partly because of the influence of neo-Freudian thought, which reached its zenith in the 1940s and 1950s, and provided "scientific" justification for mother-blaming. Psychologists believed that in the course of normal development, children had to settle a predictable set of crises as their unbounded inner drives confronted the limitations of real life. To understand the individual, one had to analyze the family of origin. In a therapeutic context, this meant looking for the source of psychic distress in the family configuration. In the renewed craze for domesticity of the postwar economy, the search invariably led to the mother, bound anew to home and children in ideology if not in actuality. And so the question became: What kind of mother led to this person's problems? The answers stretched as far as the variations on the bad-mother theme could go.

The 1947 publication of Dr. Marynia Farnham and Ferdinand Lundberg's *Modern Woman: The Lost Sex* encapsulated the antimother rhetoric of the period. Farnham and Lundberg mentioned the decline of the home, under industrialization, as a contributor to modern problems. But the real culprit was feminism. The proper "feminine mother . . . accepts herself fully as a woman"; that is, she accepted her dependence on a man and sought no fulfillment outside the home. The "good" mother did not need to read books on child care; she knew what to do for her children by keeping attuned to their needs. Yet this "fully maternal" mother was in the minority. A variety of bad mothers—the rejecting mother, the oversolicitous or overprotective mother, the dominating mother, and the overaffectionate mother—produced half the nation's children, and all its delinquents, criminals, and alcoholics.[45]

The bad mother gained a new edge of insidiousness: one could not always tell the difference between the good and the bad at first glance. The overprotective mother might be the model mother of the community whom everyone admired.[46] On closer inspection, one would see that her hovering and intruding ways stunted her children's development. She needed to be pried loose, emotionally. Psychotherapy, and perhaps drug therapy, offered the best solution.

Mother-blaming found its way to Hollywood, as well. Films such as *Mildred Pierce* dramatized the danger and tragedy of the working mother. *Psycho* showed just how crazy a mother could make her son. Women who did not fit the cultural stereotype of passive dependence provided boundless material for comics and caricaturists. The Jewish mother, as the object of derision and ridicule, began to emerge in the general culture as the ne plus ultra of hysterical mothering during this period.[47]

British psychiatrist John Bowlby seemed to provide further "scientific" evidence that a good mother did not venture far from the home. Drawing from studies of war orphans and institutionalized children, Bowlby theorized that maternal absence devastated a child's emotional development. Mary Ainsworth took Bowlby's ideas further, assessing the quality of children's attachment to their mothers by a laboratory test. In this test, conducted on twenty-three mother/child pairs, a year-old child first plays with his mother, then with the mother and a stranger, and then is left for a few moments with the stranger. The child's emotional security is measured by the response when the mother first leaves and then reenters the room: if the child protests his mother's departure, the attachment is secure. The studies of Bowlby, Ainsworth, and others fueled the claim that children's mental health depended on mother love—and that mother-love meant being at home with your child. Numerous investigations "proved" that day care damaged children. A good mother stayed out of the work force. She didn't even hire a babysitter too often.[48]

For black women in particular, mother-blaming manifested itself not just in criticism but in public policy. Daniel Patrick Moynihan's report *The Negro Family: The Case for National Action* saw maternal dominance in the black family as the basis of African Americans' societal problems. Noting that one-quarter of all black births were illegitimate, and that welfare rates had increased sharply, Moynihan decried the "tangle of pathology" tied to the black matriarchal family. The solution, Moynihan argued, was to strengthen men's role in the family: by making Aid to Families with Dependent Children available to male-headed families and redesigning the employment structure so that black women gave up their jobs to black men.[49]

Counterculturalists in the 1960s and 1970s both romanticized motherhood for its earthy physicality and rejected the traditional nuclear family arrangement for childrearing. Second Wave feminists, similarly, defined

1950s-style mothering as stultifying to women and to children, yet simultaneously proclaimed the healing power of liberated motherhood; as maternalists had done fifty years before, many feminists harnessed themselves to a notion that women were united by actual or potential motherhood. But the idea that women are naturally nurturing brings its own downside, its own notion of the good mother. For example, feminist health activists who promoted home birth and breastfeeding sometimes defined these as markers of good mothering, with the implication that hospital birth and bottle-feeding were the choices of not-so-good mothers.[50]

Still, any feminist contribution to the "bad" mother rhetoric of today cannot compare to that of the New Right. The Right consistently takes a narrow view of woman's place. Sociologist Kristin Luker, in a study of abortion politics in California in the 1970s, concluded that the debate over abortion was really a "referendum on the place and meaning of motherhood." Where "pro-choice" activists saw motherhood as one of several roles for women, "pro-life" activists seem wedded to the notion that woman's duty and destiny bind her to home and children.[51]

The battles over good motherhood rage particularly forcefully in the area of new reproductive technologies. The famous case of "Baby M," although not really about the use of new technology, first called attention to the issue. Mary Beth Whitehead signed a surrogacy contract, agreeing to be artificially inseminated by William Stern in return for ten thousand dollars if she gave birth to a healthy baby. When the girl was born, however, Whitehead decided she wanted to keep her. The trial judge terminated Whitehead's rights to the child, but the New Jersey Supreme Court reversed his decision.

Since custody decisions are supposed to be based on the best interests of the child, the Baby M case hinged on whether Mary Beth Whitehead was a "good" or a "bad" mother. Many saw her as good, because she was the "natural" mother and had carried Baby M within her womb. Others saw her as bad, because she had agreed to give away (sell?) her child. Class issues complicated the case. The Sterns had wealth and advanced degrees; the Whiteheads did not. Mother-blaming permeated the trial and Judge Harvey Sorkow's decision: Whitehead was depicted as emotionally unbalanced and "overenmeshed" with her kids.[52] Whatever one's views on surrogacy, it is clear that it taps our culture's deepest notions about motherhood. As legal scholar Carol Sanger puts it, "Surrogacy converts maternal selflessness into profit and transforms maternal devotion into a time-dated offer." In so doing, she says, it undermines the view that motherhood is "natural, sacred, and necessarily long-term."[53]

In the 1980s and 1990s, the battle over mothers' place has been expressed most clearly in debates over "fetal rights." As with mother-blaming in general, science and politics intersect here to provide "scientific" evidence about what is good for children (or fetuses) and the place of a good mother. As Katha Pollitt points out in her essay in this volume, the current clamor to protect the rights of the "unborn child" has much to do with controlling the behavior of pregnant women. Accepting the view that the "good" mother is self-sacrificing, proponents of fetal rights want to get the "bad" mother—especially, but not only, the drug addict—to put the interests of the unborn child above her own. As fetal rights critic Cynthia Daniels points out, the pregnant addict is a metaphor for women's alienation from instinctual motherhood—a powerful metaphor strengthened by the popular assumption that motherhood itself is in crisis. Not surprisingly, poor, unmarried mothers of color—the archetypal "bad" mothers in our society—are the predominant victims of the new vigilance over the purity of pregnancy. According to Daniels, fully 76 percent of 167 documented cases of criminal prosecution of women who used illicit drugs or alcohol during pregnancy involved women of color (mostly African American).[54]

In this age of "family values," however, you don't have to be a drug addict to be a "bad" mother. Despite—or perhaps because of—the fact that more than half of all mothers return to work before their children are out of diapers, working mothers too are blamed for our current social ills. Prior to the Civil Rights Act of 1964, which forbade employment discrimination on the basis of sex, women—and especially mothers—were often openly barred from employment. Beginning in 1908 with the landmark case *Muller v. Oregon,* the Supreme Court regulated the hours and wages of women workers, but not of men, on the grounds that healthy motherhood was an object of public interest "to preserve the strength and vigor of the race." School boards routinely fired women teachers when they married or became visibly pregnant. These practices could not continue unchallenged after 1964, but their cultural legacy still affects the lives of working mothers.[55]

Although most mothers now spend significant amounts of time outside the home, in employment or in higher education, popular acceptance of that trend lags, especially if the children are young and in day care. The much publicized custody dispute of Jennifer Ireland is a case in point. Ireland placed her three-year-old daughter in day care so she could attend classes at the University of Michigan, but a judge awarded custody to the father, a student at another university. The judge not only felt that a single parent attending classes at a school as demanding as the University of Michigan could not be a good parent but also preferred the father's plan to keep the child in the care of her grandmother to the mother's out-of-home day care arrangement. Ireland, like Zoe Baird, the ill-fated attorney general nominee, was a "bad" mother in part because she was smart and successful, and did not stay home to rear her child.[56]

As political mother-blaming intensified in the 1990s, single mothers and welfare mothers took center stage. Just as Mom was blamed for American weakness during the Cold War, conservatives now blame single mothers for crime and the growing divisions in American society. Speaker of the House Newt Gingrich saw in Susan Smith's desperate drowning of her sons evidence of "how sick society is getting" and suggested the solution: vote Republican. In a similar leap of logic, Vice President Dan Quayle attributed the 1992 Los Angeles riots to the breakdown of the family, as exemplified in the decision of television character Murphy Brown to bear a child out of wedlock. Conservative author Charles Murray added statistical "proof" to the charge that single motherhood correlates with child poverty, crime, and a host of other ills. In *The Bell Curve*, he and coauthor Richard Herrnstein identified "low-intelligence" mothers as the propagators of illegitimacy and urged that welfare benefits be taken away as a disincentive to further childbearing. The 1996 Personal Responsibility Act, which abolished Aid to Families with Dependent Children and established work requirements for single mothers, wrote many of Murray's recommendations into law. While more affluent women are "bad" mothers if they do not stay at home, poor women are "bad" mothers if they do.[57] As this book goes to press, mother-blaming unfortunately shows no sign of abating.[58]

Making "Bad" Mothers

This book is the product of our own "bad" mother experiences and many years of discussion. Like most North American women, we have sometimes been labeled "bad" mothers. Both of us are professors whose children are in day care. We juggle, with varying degrees of success, career and childrearing. As we teach and write, we also struggle with homework, with temper tantrums, with getting our children to eat properly, and with getting them to sleep. Both of us are also the children of "bad" mothers, women who divorced and worked outside the home in the 1950s and 1960s, the supposed heyday of the "traditional" family. We come from different backgrounds, yet both of us carry vivid childhood memories of defending our mothers—and, we felt, ourselves—against accusations that children of "broken homes" and working mothers were inevitably neglected and damaged.

Our experiences, we learned, are typical. When we sent a call for submissions over the Internet, we were swamped with almost three hundred replies. Most were from scholars engaged in academic work on the subject, but many women wrote of their own experiences. "I could write this book!" several women said.

"Bad" Mothers: The Politics of Blame in Twentieth-Century America does not claim to be a comprehensive examination. It contains a sample of the scholarship on the subject, with an orientation to our own discipline, history. It is not the end of the conversation but a call for further study. We hope it is also a contribution toward ending the "bad" mother label.

The arrangement is roughly chronological, but four themes run throughout. First is the extraordinary elasticity of the "bad" mother label. Some groups—the poor, the unmarried, women of color—have been portrayed as bad mothers continuously. Others, such as the welfare mothers so demonized today, reflect more transitory political concerns.

A second theme explores the sources of mother-blaming. These essays show that mother-blaming comes from many quarters and cannot be simply explained as a product of patriarchy or our culture's misogyny. The "bad" mother label is applied by the experts and by the state, in the welfare and legal systems. It also comes from family members, and even mothers themselves. As Elaine Tyler May indicates, victims of the "bad" mother label sometimes impose the same label on other groups to ease their own self-doubt.

A third theme in these essays explores how feminism fits in. At different times and in different circumstances, feminists have challenged and employed the "bad" mother label. Much mother-blaming, as Katha Pollitt shows, is a backlash against feminism. But as Annalee Newitz points out, feminism has been unable to fully explain, much less challenge, "bad" mother labeling.

Finally, these essays demonstrate that children as well as their mothers suffer from mother-bashing. Annette Appell argues that women who make bad childrearing decisions can still be loving, committed parents; taking their children away can hurt the kids.

The book is divided into three parts. The first part covers the pre–World War II years. Three articles, by Karen Tice, Steven Noll, and Emily Abel, are case studies of "bad" mothers and the experts who "helped" them. Rosa, an African American working mother, white working-class "prostitute" Willie Mallory, and Mrs. Germani, an Italian immigrant mother whose daughter had tuberculosis, reveal the race, ethnic, and class dimensions of mother-blaming. In each case, professionals brought the explicit or implied power of the state to bear on the "bad" mothers before them. For the Mallorys and the Germanis, the results were tragic.

Women were not simply the victims of mother-blaming experts and authorities, however. Elizabeth Rose and Kathleen Jones show how middle-class women who took their children to nursery schools and child guidance centers came to adopt the "bad" mother label. Having defined themselves as incompetent, these mothers got not only help with child-rearing but time away from their children, trained ears to listen to marital or psychological woes, and status in the community for seeking the most modern forms of intervention.

The book's second part, "The Middle Years," describes the mother-blaming that took shape in midcentury with the dominance of psychology and continues until the present day. The section opens with Paula Caplan's discussion of the pervasiveness of mother-blaming and its therapeutic roots. Ruth Feldstein and Jennifer Terry examine the political uses of psychological discourse. Feldstein's analysis of liberal thought at midcentury shows that liberals employed the familiar trope of mother-blaming as they sought to combat racism in America. Terry's analysis of military psychiatrist Edward Strecker's harsh criticism of "Moms" ties women's alleged overprotection of their children to "treasonous" homosexuals, communists—and national decline.

Betty Jean Lifton, Elaine Tyler May, and Jane Taylor McDonnell examine the pain psychological theories about motherhood caused women who did not fit the "good" mother norm, either because they had children outside marriage, because they could not have children at all, or because they had an "abnormal" child. Lifton, an adoptee, points out that birth mothers and adoptive mothers are both "good" and "bad," depending on one's perspective—and political agenda. May shows how psychological theories about the maternal instinct were used to treat infertile women, despite no evidence that they worked. The cruel power of medical mother-blaming also runs through McDonnell's personal account of her experience as the mother of an autistic child. In these cases, ignorance about the cause of a medical problem (infertility and autism) led to the easy answer: blame the mother.

Cultural ideas about race and sexuality drive judicial understanding of "bad" motherhood, as the articles by Renee Romano and Christine Allison show. Romano studies white women who lost custody of their white children when they married black men. The courts determined these women to be "bad" mothers; interracial marriage not only marked them as sexually immoral but also meant they could no longer be "good" mothers to white children, that is, provide them with the advantages of whiteness and protect them from racism or the stigma of growing up in an interracial home. Where Romano focuses on the legal aspects, Allison's interviews with the daughters of a noncustodial lesbian mother reveal the shallowness of the courts' efforts to protect children and the toll such absurd notions of "bad" mothering have on real families. To some extent, in some circumstances, the "bad" mother label can, by undermining a mother's self-confidence, become a self-fulfilling prophecy.

Su Epstein's essay on the mothers of serial killers also depicts our culture's ambivalence toward maternal sexuality and reveals the ultimate form of blaming: mothers punished and scapegoated when their sons commit a crime.

The book's final part, "Bad Mothering of Late," follows old themes and reveals new ones. Single mothers, wage-earning mothers, and mothers of color remain particularly vulnerable to mother-blaming. But now pregnant women have moved to center stage. Feminism also emerges as a new theme, as several authors tie the intensification of mother-blaming in recent years to a backlash against the women's movement and challenge feminists to take on the "bad" mother label.

For Katha Pollitt, Lauri Umansky, and Diane Sampson, the "bad" mother label masks our society's ambivalence about feminism, class, and maternal sexuality. They write about mothers who were not sufficiently self-sacrificing and consequently were punished, sometimes by themselves. Pollitt shows how new legal theories that set fetal rights in opposition to the mother promote the antifeminist notion that motherhood means self-sacrifice: a woman's health and religious convictions are secondary to the well-being of her unborn child. Umansky shows how the antimother mood intersects perilously with the confessional Twelve-Step

Movement. Sampson explores Zoe Baird's unsuccessful efforts to define herself as both a good mother and a good choice for attorney general of the United States. No woman who earns half a million dollars a year could possibly be sufficiently self-sacrificing to be a good mother!

Norma Coates and Annalee Newitz raise a provocative question: Can women rebel by owning the mantle of the "bad" mother? Coates analyzes rock star Courtney Love, whose motto could be, Bad Mother and Loving It. Love ignores the rules for "good" mothering, gets hammered in the press for her efforts, and emerges defiant. Coates recognizes Love's insulators: money, fame, fans. Nevertheless, she views Love as a radical of some significance. Annalee Newitz, by immersing herself in the tales of America's most notorious killer mothers and identifying with the frustration these women must have felt in a punitively pronatalist culture, provides a rationale for remaining childless. By doing so, she asserts, she has created a space in her life that would not exist if she cowered under the mandate to mother and mother properly.

Annette Appell and Rickie Solinger return our attention to the particular burden mother-blaming places on the poor, and especially on women of color. Appell served as attorney for Chicago-area women and children who struggled with a child welfare system obsessed with punishing the "bad" mother. As she recounts the stories of four women who fit the most common "bad" mother profiles of the 1990s—the battered woman, the drug addict, the mentally impaired woman, and the teen mother— she shows that real-life cases are rarely so cut and dried as they appear in political propaganda. Whatever their faults, and in spite of some bad parenting decisions, Appell's clients are mothers. Removal from their care did not help, and may even have hurt, their children. As Rickie Solinger writes in "Poisonous Choice," the liberal feminist rhetoric of "choice"— the ultimate individualistic marketplace concept—has had a devastating impact on women, especially poor, nonwhite "bad" mothers, who are blamed for making bad choices. We cannot arrive at a full-face confrontation of "bad" mother accusations through the language of individual rights that currently surrounds discussions of childrearing.

Good Riddance to a Bad Label

Many mothers do act in ways that are not good for their children. Through those acts, in those moments, they function as bad mothers.

That we must acknowledge. But we must also learn to recognize unjust extrapolations from the specific acts of individual mothers.

In many ways, "bad" mothers are not so very different from "good" ones. We all struggle under mountains of conflicting advice that cannot possibly be followed in real life. We all must find our way in a society that devalues mothering, sees childrearing as a private family responsibility, and pays little heed to what actually happens to kids. Our point, however, is not that the pervasiveness of current mother-blaming creates a rough equality of suffering. One woman's psychic distress over society's harsh judgments cannot be equated with another's loss of legal custody of her children.

Fundamentally, the "bad" mother serves as a scapegoat, a repository for social or physical ills that resist easy explanation or solution. Scapegoating, as a process, does not engage principles of equity or evenhandedness; it seeks pockets of vulnerability. Unfortunately, some of the most vulnerable—May's infertile women, for example—sometimes use the "bad" mother label themselves. It's a kind of preemptive strike: I'm not the "bad" one, she is!

But the uses of the "bad" mother label go beyond personal confidence boosting. They also have a political purpose. Today that purpose is bound up with government "downsizing." Thus we profess outrage at the death of six-year-old Elisa Izquierdo, allegedly killed by her crack-addicted mother, who got custody when Elisa's father died despite strong evidence that she was abusing the girl. At first glance, Elisa's tragic and well-publicized death highlights the failure of the child welfare system's emphasis on family reunification. Yet it serves another purpose. In deflecting our attention to Elisa's monster mother, it gives us someone to blame for her death, someone not ourselves. Blaming Elisa's death on her mother, and on the welfare agencies that reunited them, allows us to tolerate child poverty and further cuts to the child welfare system. It diverts our attention from the lack of resources for children to a bad mother, an immigrant drug addict.[59]

Blaming Elisa's mother—or at least blaming her exclusively—will not prevent more children's deaths, just as blaming the television show *Murphy Brown* will not prevent more riots in Los Angeles. It is dangerous fantasy to believe that if "they" can be identified and labeled, and then treated or punished, the nation will be somehow purified, made safer for the rest of us. This scapegoating does enormous harm to the women accused of "bad" mothering and serves to intensify already existing social antagonisms, including those of race and class. It also fails as a method of social purification and redounds to the detriment of all women. In other words, the labeling of the "bad" mother narrows for all of us the definition of "good" mothering, while luring us to participate in the limiting of our own options.

We cannot afford to let the cipher of the bad mother stand in for real confrontations with the serious problems of our society. When in fact we need to examine poverty, racism, the paucity of meaningful work at a living wage, the lack of access to day care, antifeminism, and a host of other problems, let us not be diverted by "bad" mothers.

NOTES

1. The trial received wide coverage in the Minnesota press. See, for example, the front-page story, "Guevara Trial Opens with Stunning Assertions," *Star Tribune*, February 23, 1993

2. *James A. Lambert v. Sarah Everist*, No. 86-1854, Supreme Court of Iowa, January 20, 1988, 418 NW 2d, 40–44. The Supreme Court maintained the lower court's ruling of joint legal custody.

3. Justice Potter Stewart made this point about pornography in *Jacobellis v. Ohio*, 378 U.S. 184, 197 (1964).

4. Margaret Carlson, "Old Enough to Be Your Mother: Technology-Assisted Fertility in Post-Menopausal Women," *Time* 143 (January 10, 1994): 41.

5. See Penelope Leach, *Children First: What Society Must Do—and Is Not Doing—for Children Today* (New York: Vintage, 1995).

6. For a general overview of U.S. family history, see Stephanie Coontz, *The Way We Never Were: American Families and the Nostalgia Trap* (New York: Basic Books, 1992). See also Mary Frances Berry, *The Politics of Parenthood: Child Care, Women's Rights, and the Myth of the Good Mother* (New York: Viking, 1993). Books that shed light on the lives of working-class mothers include Eileen Boris, *Home to Work: Motherhood and the Politics of Industrial Homework in the United States* (New York: Cambridge University Press, 1994); Elizabeth Ewen, *Immigrant Women in the Land of Dollars: Life and Culture on the Lower East Side, 1890–1925* (New York: Monthly Review Press, 1985); Linda Gordon, *Heroes of Their Own Lives: The Politics and History of Family Violence* (New York: Viking, 1988). Ellen Ross, *Love and Toil: Motherhood in Outcast London, 1870–1918* (New York: Oxford University Press, 1993) is a brilliant study of the experiences of English working-class mothers.

7. William H. Chafe, *The Paradox of Change: American Women in the Twentieth Century* (New York: Oxford University Press, 1991), 188; Shannon Dortch,

"Moms on the Line: The Share of Mothers in the Labor Force Continues to Grow," *American Demographics* 18 (July 1996): 25. According to Dortch, mothers have a higher labor force participation rate than women as a whole.

8. Mary Kay Blakely, "Jessica's Mom," *Ms.* (July–August 1996): 96.

9. See Molly Ladd-Taylor, *Mother-Work: Women, Child Welfare and the State, 1890–1930* (Urbana: University of Illinois Press, 1994), 88.

10. James J. McKenna, "Sudden Infant Death Syndrome: Making Sense of Current Research," *Mothering*, No. 81 (Winter 1996): 74–80. The author notes that the majority of infants who die from SIDS worldwide have no known risk factors.

11. Theodore Lidz, Stephen Fleck, and Alice R. Cornelison, *Schizophrenia and the Family* (New York: International Universities Press, 1965); Joan Jacobs Brumberg, *Fasting Girls: The Emergence of Anorexia Nervosa as a Modern Disease* (Cambridge: Harvard University Press, 1988), 29–30.

12. Paula Caplan, "Mother-Blaming," in this volume. On this syndrome, see Herbert A. Schrier and Judith A. Libow, "Munchausen by Proxy—the Deadly Game," *Saturday Evening Post* 268 (July–August 1996): 40; Nancy Wartik, "Fatal Attention," *Redbook* 187 (February 1994): 67; and Skip Hollandsworth, "Hush, Little Baby, Don't You Cry," *Texas Monthly* 23 (August 1995): 70. For medical parent-blaming in Canada, see "The Crime of Being the Parent of a Sick Child," *Globe and Mail*, November 30, 1996.

13. Jennifer Terry, "Momism and the Making of Treasonous Homosexuals"; and Su Epstein, "Mothering to Death," in this volume. On juvenile delinquency during World War II, see Karen Anderson, *Wartime Women: Sex Roles, Family Relations, and the Status of Women during World War II* (Westport, Conn.: Greenwood, 1970), 95–102. On welfare dependency, see Daniel Patrick Moynihan, *The Negro Family: The Case for National Action* (Washington: Government Printing Office, 1965).

14. See Spiro Agnew's famous April 1970 comment on permissive parents, cited in Todd Gitlin, *The Sixties: Years of Hope, Days of Rage* (New York: Bantam, 1987), 42.

15. U.S. Children's Bureau, *Infant Care*, 2d ed. (Washington: Government Printing Office, 1921); John B. Watson, *Psychological Care of Infant and Child* (New York: W. W. Norton, 1928); "Child Disobedience Blamed on Mothers," *New York Times*, May 4, 1937, 28: 2.

16. Penelope Leach, *Your Baby and Child, from Birth to Age Five* (New York: Knopf, 1987).

17. Compare the following childrearing books, written at different times but still widely read: Leach, *Your Baby & Child*; William Sears, *The Baby Book: Everything You Need to Know About Your Baby* (Boston: Little, Brown, 1993); Frank Caplan, *The First Twelve Months of Life: Your Baby's Growth Month by Month* (New York: Bantam, 1973); T. Berry Brazleton, *Infants and Mothers: Differences in Development*, rev. ed. (New York: Delta/Seymour Lawrence, 1983); Benja-

min Spock and Michael Rothenberg, *Dr. Spock's Baby and Child Care* (New York: Simon & Schuster, 1985). See also David Elkind, *The Hurried Child: Growing up Too Fast Too Soon* (Reading, Mass.: Addison-Wesley, 1981), 32–34.

18. See Perri Klass, "Decent Exposure: It's Simply Breastfeeding, and as Natural as a Walk on the Beach," *Parenting* 8 (May 1994): 98; and Pete Kotz, "Not for Public Consumption: When Are Breasts Obscene?" *Utne Reader*, No. 76 (July–August 1996): 68.

19. Diane Eyer, *Motherguilt: How Our Culture Blames Mothers for What's Wrong with Society* (New York: Times Books, 1996), 3–7. For a critique of "child-centered moms," see John Rosemond, "Hey, Mom! Get a Life!" *Better Homes and Gardens* 74 (May 1996): 106.

20. Shari Thurer, *The Myths of Motherhood: How Culture Reinvents the Good Mother* (Boston: Houghton Mifflin, 1994); Paula J. Caplan, *Don't Blame Mother: Mending the Mother-Daughter Relationship* (New York: Harper & Row, 1989), 62.

21. Thurer, *The Myths of Motherhood*, 151–52; Louise Bernikow, *Among Women* (New York: Harmony Books, 1980), 26–28. For a fascinating discussion of a particular evil-stepmother myth, see Peter Gossage, "La Marâtre: Marie-Anne Houde and the Myth of the Wicked Stepmother in Quebec," *Canadian Historical Review* 76 (December 1995): 563–98.

22. Elizabeth Badinter, *Mother Love, Myth and Reality: Motherhood in Modern History* (New York: Macmillan, 1980).

23. Sara Evans, *Born for Liberty: A History of Women in America* (New York: Free Press, 1989); Nancy F. Cott, *Bonds of Womanhood* (New Haven: Yale University Press, 1977).

24. On Republican Motherhood, see Linda Kerber, *Women of the Republic: Intellect and Ideology in Revolutionary America* (Chapel Hill: University of North Carolina Press, 1980).

25. Mary P. Ryan, *The Empire of the Mother: American Writing about Domesticity, 1830–1860* (New York: Haworth, 1982); Bernard Wishy, *The Child and the Republic: The Dawn of Modern American Child Nurture* (Philadelphia: University of Pennsylvania Press, 1968).

26. Carroll Smith-Rosenberg, *Disorderly Conduct: Visions of Gender in Victorian America* (New York: Oxford University Press); Cott, *Bonds of Womanhood*; Mary P. Ryan, *The Cradle of the Middle Class: Family and Community in Oneida County, New York, 1780–1865* (New York: Cambridge University Press, 1981).

27. Quoted in Cott, *Bonds of Womanhood*, 91.

28. Michael Grossberg, "Who Gets the Child? Custody, Guardianship, and the Rise of a Judicial Patriarchy in Nineteenth-Century America," *Feminist Studies* 9 (Summer 1983): 235–60. See also Michael Grossberg, *Governing the Hearth: Law and Family in Nineteenth-Century America* (Chapel Hill: University of North Carolina Press, 1985).

29. See Carol Sanger, "Separating from Children," *Columbia Law Review* 96 (March 1996): 375–517.

30. Stephanie J. Shaw, "Mothering Under Slavery in the Antebellum South," in *Mothering: Ideology, Experience, and Agency*, ed. Evelyn Nakano Glenn, Grace Chang, and Linda Rennie Forcey (New York: Routledge, 1994), 237–58. See also Deborah Gray White, *Arn't I a Woman? Female Slaves in the Plantation South* (New York: W. W. Norton, 1985).

31. White, *Arn't I a Woman?* 46–61.

32. On scientific motherhood, see Rima Apple, *Mothers and Medicine: A Social History of Infant Feeding 1890–1950* (Madison: University of Wisconsin Press, 1987); Ladd-Taylor, *Mother-Work*, chap. 2.

33. Sanger, "Separating from Children," 404–5.

34. William Lee Howard, M.D., "Effeminate Men and Masculine Women," *New York Medical Journal* 71 (May 5, 1900); reprinted in *Root of Bitterness: Documents of the Social History of American Women*, 2d ed., ed. Nancy F. Cott et al. (Boston: Northeastern University Press, 1996), 338–40.

35. Theodore Roosevelt, "Address to the Congress on the Welfare of Children," *National Congress of Mothers Magazine* 2 (April 1908): 174.

36. Susan Strasser, *Never Done: A History of American Housework* (New York: Pantheon, 1982); Deirdre English and Barbara Ehrenreich, *For Her Own Good: 150 Years of Advice to Women* (Garden City, N.Y.: Anchor Books, 1978).

37. Watson, *Psychological Care of Infant and Child*, dedication, 5–6; U.S. Children's Bureau, *Child Management* (Washington: Government Printing Office, 1925), 3–4.

38. Ernest Groves and Gladys Hoagland Groves, *Parents and Children* (Philadelphia: J. B. Lippincott, 1924), 118. See English and Ehrenreich, *For Her Own Good*, 205.

39. Ewen, *Immigrant Women in the Land of Dollars*; Ladd-Taylor, *Mother-Work*.

40. Sonya Michel and Seth Koven, eds., *Mothers of a New World: Maternalist Politics and the Origins of Welfare States* (New York: Routledge, 1993); Ladd-Taylor, *Mother-Work*; Linda Gordon, *Pitied But Not Entitled: Single Mothers and the History of Welfare* (New York: Free Press, 1994); Theda Skocpol, *Protecting Soldiers and Mothers: The Political Origins of Social Policy in the United States* (Cambridge: Harvard University Press, 1992).

41. Ladd-Taylor, *Mother-Work*, 175.

42. Philip R. Reilly, *The Surgical Solution: A History of Involuntary Sterilization in the United States* (Baltimore: Johns Hopkins University Press, 1991); Stephen Jay Gould, "Carrie Buck's Daughter," *Natural History* 93 (1984); Molly Ladd-Taylor, "Saving Babies and Sterilizing Mothers: Eugenics and Welfare Politics in the Interwar United States," *Social Politics* (1997).

43. Philip Wylie, *Generation of Vipers* (New York: Rinehart, 1942), 185. See also Chafe, *The Paradox of Change*, 175–93.

44. See, for example, Eleanor Lake, "Trouble on the Street Corner," *Common Sense* 12 (May 1943): 148; "Mother Left Three Children Thirteen Hours to Gamble Her Husband's Earnings," *New York Times*, January 26, 1944, 21; "Soldier's Wife Who Deserted Baby Says Allotment Was Too Small," *New York Times*, February 16, 1944, 34; "Would Bar Liquor to Mothers," *New York Times*, March 30, 1944, 24.

45. Ferdinand Lundberg and Marynia F. Farnham, *Modern Woman: The Lost Sex* (New York: Grosset & Dunlap, 1947), 298–321.

46. Ibid., 308.

47. E. Ann Kaplan, *Motherhood and Representation: The Mother in Popular Culture and Melodrama* (New York: Routledge, 1992); Thurer, *The Myths of Motherhood*, 257, 270. See also Suzanna Danuta Walters, *Lives Together, Worlds Apart: Mothers and Daughters in Popular Culture* (Berkeley: University of California Press, 1992), 49, 86; and David Everitt, "Mom's the Word," *Entertainment Weekly*, No. 274 (May 12, 1995): 70.

48. John Bowlby, *Maternal Care and Mental Health*, 2d ed., World Health Organization, Monograph Series no. 2, (Geneva: WHO, 1951); Mary Ainsworth, M. Blehar, E. Waters, and S. Wall, *Patterns of Attachment: A Psychological Study of the Strange Situation* (Hillsdale, N.J.: Lawrence Erlbaum, 1978). Ideas about attachment filtered into popular childrearing manuals; one recent example is Sears, *The Baby Book*. For critiques, see Diane Eyer, *Mother-Infant Bonding: A Scientific Fiction* (New Haven: Yale University Press, 1992); English and Ehrenreich, *For Her Own Good*, 229–30; and Eyer, *Motherguilt*, 77–80.

49. Moynihan, *The Negro Family*. For the antecedents of Moynihan's view, see Ruth Feldstein, "Antiracism and Maternal Failure in the 1940s and 1950s," in this volume.

50. Lauri Umansky, *Reconceiving Motherhood: Feminism and the Legacies of the 1960s* (New York: New York University Press, 1996). One example of a women's health publication that equates breastfeeding with good mothering is the cover graphic with the words "Stamp Out Bottlefeeding" of the Canadian journal *The Compleat Mother*, No. 43 (Fall 1996).

51. Kristin Luker, *Abortion and the Politics of Motherhood* (Berkeley: University of California Press, 1984), 193.

52. Sorkow's decision is reprinted in the appendix of Phyllis Chesler, *The Sacred Bond: The Legacy of Baby M* (New York: Times, 1988). See Katha Pollitt, "Contracts and Apple Pie: The Strange Case of Baby M," *The Nation* 244 (May 23, 1987): 667.

53. Sanger, "Separating from Children," 453, 464.

54. Cynthia R. Daniels, *At Women's Expense: State Power and the Politics of Fetal Rights* (Cambridge: Harvard University Press, 1993), especially chap. 4.

55. Quoted in Lynn Y. Weiner, *From Working Girl to Working Mother: The Female Labor Force in the United States, 1820–1980* (Chapel Hill: University of North Carolina Press, 1985), 45. See also Alice Kessler-Harris, *Out to Work: A History of Wage-Earning Women in the United States* (New York: Oxford University Press, 1982).

56. Susan Jane Gilman, "A Michigan Judge's Ruling Punishes Single Mothers," *Ms.* 5 (November–December 1994): 92–93.

57. Alison Mitchell, "Gingrich's Views on Slayings Draw Fire," *New York Times,* November 23, 1995, B18; "Dan Quayle vs. Murphy Brown: The Vice-President Attacks the Values of a Television Show," *Time* 139 (June 1, 1992): 20; Charles Murray and Richard Herrnstein, *The Bell Curve: Intelligence and Class Structure in American Life* (New York: Free Press, 1994).

58. Anne Roiphe notes the mother-blaming in four Hollywood films released in 1996. "A Quartet of Monstrous Mothers," *Globe and Mail,* January 4, 1997, C4.

59. Katha Pollitt, "The Violence of Ordinary Life," *The Nation,* January 1, 1996, 9.

Part I

The Early Years

Chapter 1

Mending Rosa's "Working Ways"
A Case Study of an African American Mother and Breadwinner

Karen W. Tice

Maternal wage earning, childrearing practices, and norms for housekeeping, hygiene, and conduct preoccupied caseworkers in the emergent field of social work early in this century. In a quest for professional legitimation, social workers challenged prior approaches to benevolence as unscientific and sentimental, while championing a new constellation of practices for investigation and social diagnosis.[1] The reconstitution of the supposedly weak characters of "bad" mothers became a key component of this new social work.

The case of Rosa, an African American mother in Minneapolis forced into wage earning to provide for three children and an elderly, infirm husband, illustrates the complex and protracted cross-class and cross-race clashes that often characterized the relationships between social workers and clients.[2] Mary Dewson, superintendent of the Massachusetts Industrial School for Girls, urged social workers to heed their clients' hopes, "to set [them] on the road toward realizing [their] dreams or toward realizing some more feasible substitute."[3] Social workers, however, possessed the power to override, undermine, reduce to subtext, or impose "more feasible substitute[s]" for clients' dreams, while many clients remained fiercely devoted to their own ways of living and mothering. The story of Rosa's rocky relationship with her caseworker dramatizes divergent views of proper maternal conduct.

The Case of Rosa

Minneapolis Family Welfare Association (fact sheet, "Case of Rosa"): Problems—William—husband—cataracts, old age, shiftlessness, laziness, uneven employment, and blindness; Rosa—wife—dirt, poor housekeeping, works too much, and neglect of family; Louise—eldest daughter—heart trouble; Edward—eldest son—delinquency; Marion—youngest daughter—not bright.

Probation officer: The whole family is a dirty lazy outfit.

Child Protective worker: Rosa was a very pleasant woman and seemed most interested in her children.

Society for the Blind worker: Rosa is a superior woman well worth working with although she has failed to care properly for her children and her house is not clean.

Family Welfare caseworker: I intend to check up very closely on Rosa.[4]

Rosa's case was first opened in 1905, when she came to the Minneapolis Family Welfare Society (MFWA) looking for work.[5] Although her story, told by an FWA caseworker, was a professionally guided telling, Rosa's conflict with her caseworker over what constituted "adequate" mothering permeates the narrative.[6] Rosa's many resistances to the social worker's judgments about motherhood and her own dreams of working hard enough to win a better life resonate throughout the surviving account.[7]

In 1905, MFWA advised Rosa either to take legal action against her husband, William, because he was "not ambitious," or to seek employment on a farm. Rosa did neither. The next record, from 1914, shows William seeking food, fuel, and employment from MFWA. At this time, the social worker recorded fragments of William's history, including the fact that he had been born into slavery, had never attended school, and had worked as a railroad porter. William had met Rosa on a train shortly after her graduation from high school, when she was on her way to work at Tuskegee Institute. They soon married and moved to Minneapolis.

Learning that Rosa worked all day, the social worker deemed it "peculiar" that William "seemed to know no more about his wife's actions than if he had been a stranger and all he seemed to know was that he was without food and fuel." Food and fuel were given, but the worker made it clear that no additional aid would be forthcoming unless she were able to talk to Rosa directly.[8]

In 1920, a probation officer reported to MFWA that Rosa's family needed a visiting housekeeper. The officer also noted that Rosa's son Edward was serving time at a juvenile institution for housebreaking, that William "loafed around," and that because Rosa was "away so much of the time," she did not devote adequate attention to housekeeping. The MFWA worker embarked on a visit and found, however, that "things were fairly neat and not extraordinarily dirty." William was out of work and recovering from an automobile accident. On the next visit, the worker noted that when she arrived, "William ran and put his jacket on to cover his torn clothes." Once again, the elusive Rosa was not at home. In her case narrative, the worker concluded, "It seemed impossible to make any headway with the family as they seem quite contented to live in their dirt and filth. The man did not seem responsible enough mentally to talk intelligently and the woman seemed quite willing to work and support the family."

No further entries were made in Rosa's record until October 1922, after a teacher informed MFWA staff that Rosa's children would not be allowed to attend school because of the quality of their clothing. After visiting, the caseworker reported that William had "film growing over his eyes and could hardly walk," adding "They have three living children and three who are dead. Said his wife was well educated and insisted upon the children going to school."

On November 12, 1922, Rosa made her debut in the case record. The social worker narrated her first impressions as follows:

> Rosa is a small neat negress. She was very cordial to visitor. She explained that she was not dressed very neatly because she was very tired and resting. She was working very hard. Visitor tried to make her realize that she was working too hard and that she should rest at least a half a day during the week if not a whole day. The visitor impressed upon her the needs of her family that she should take care of them even if she should not earn as much money. The women said they had gotten along well until lately since they needed coal and warm clothing. Last month was rather hard on account of taxes. The woman said she never wanted to accept charity as she could work and support the family. She thought that there was so many

others who needed aid that she hated to accept any. She wished FWA would help her with the court proceedings for her husband's accident. If they could realize money from this source they could get along. She hoped that something could be done about William's eyes. Then he could take care of the housework and keep the children in better condition. She did not think he could work even if he could see because he staggered from old age. She was proud of Louise who was taking an industrial course at the high school. The family attitude was very good. They acted very natural and seemed affectionate towards each other.

At this time, the caseworker took a hopeful and buoyant stance. She obtained clothing for Rosa's children, monitored Edward's school attendance, arranged an eye operation for William, and devoted much time to conversations with Rosa, who voiced daily irritations with her son. Rosa complained about her son's carelessness with money, his refusal to hold a job and obey his aging father, and his school truancy. She told her caseworker that Edward did not "lift his feet when he walk[ed]" and thus wore out his shoes quickly. The caseworker opined that Rosa "realize[s] Edward is neglected because of her necessary work and his father's blindness. She has tried to rear him in a right way but realizes he is a problem and is willing to have force used by outside sources." With prodding from the caseworker, and because she felt that Edward would do better under the eyes of the court, Rosa allowed a complaint of incorrigibility to be issued against her son. These court proceedings offered a hint of what was to come. The judge admonished Rosa for her working ways, telling her that she should spend more time at home, since she was answerable for her son's behavior. Rosa reportedly "resented this and said she had to make a living and couldn't be at home and at work at the same time."

There are no hints in Rosa's case record that she drank, nor were there whispers of sexual immorality, both portentous signifiers that often led to the removal of children from their homes. Caseworkers never tried to sever Rosa from her children, since conditions for the rescue of her family remained "favorable." Presumably, they found evidence of Rosa's genuine concern for her children, although one can also speculate that placing out African American children was not a favored agency policy. Social workers hoped that Edward would be strictly supervised, that William's health would improve so he could contribute to the household, and that Rosa would shorten her work day. Spurred on by propitious circumstances, the caseworker contacted the Society for the Blind on behalf of the family and eventually procured fifteen dollars a month from them.[9] This aid, given to MFWA on the condition that the agency oversee Rosa and her family, opened the door to the zealous supervision of Rosa's home and mothering as well as to a protracted battle to reform Rosa's working ways.

From then until her case was closed in 1928, the MFWA caseworker aspired to get Rosa to spend less time at her waged jobs and more time with her children and husband. She demanded that Rosa give up four work days a week so that "she could take better care of family and keep the house in better shape." The casework thus shifted from congenial talks, a listening ear, and donations of clothes and toys to a persistent concern over Rosa's maternal failure, which stemmed from "too much work."

From this point on, the caseworker harped on the tidiness of the house and the diet and dress of Rosa and her family. A particularly poignant exchange occurred not long after the caseworker had noted in the record that she had seen a notice in the newspaper of the death of Rosa's daughter Louise from tuberculosis. The case record reads,

> [Rosa] agreed that the children needed her at home and also that it was very hard for her to continue working as hard as she was, but that she could see no way out of it. She had indebted herself to the plumbers. She explained that although it might appear to the average person coming into her home that she did not care how she lived, *she really had a dream about how she wanted to live* [emphasis added] and hoped that someday she might obtain it. She was employed doing day-work everyday of the week, except Sunday, and right after work would rush home, get the evening meals, make a fresh fire, put the children to bed, and rush to a dressmaking establishment where she worked every night. She admitted that it was beginning to wear on her and did not know how long she would last. She also agreed that Edward was delinquent on account of the lack of care but she could not see a way out of the situation.

Rosa's caseworker, however, was not moved by Rosa's dream, nor was she impressed with Rosa's resolve to provide for her family. Although she noted the "decline in family conditions" after Louise's death, she insisted upon middle-class norms for cleanliness and motherhood while failing to acknowledge the enormous efforts undertaken by Rosa to provide and care for her family. The worker never gave up her ambition to impose middle-class ideals of domesticity upon Rosa, nor did Rosa's fierce determination to carry on as she saw fit abate. In one subsequent contact, for instance, the caseworker explained to Rosa that "her first duty was with her family and the second duty was to go out to work." Rosa retorted that "she did not see it that way and she did not think the house was in such deplorable situation as she thought the visitor had different ideas as to what a dirty house was."

Volleys between Rosa and her worker over dirt, dress, demeanor, and delinquency persisted for years. On February 10, 1925, for instance, the visitor recounted that Rosa had been "quite indignant throughout the interview."

> [Rosa] talked at length about the difficulties she always had with FWA and was very emphatic in telling visitor she had no intention of cleaning up. She expended all the energy she intended on the house and did not intend to do more. If the house needed scrubbing every day she would let it need scrubbing. She would do it once a week and that was all. Visitor then went on to explain to her that her daughter Marion should not have been sent to school with two sweaters on. She should have had a coat. She said she would send her in whatever she wanted. She would not tell Visitor any of her affairs and became quite indignant and left the office.

Many such volatile encounters reveal Rosa's determination to subvert the caseworker's agenda. On one occasion, the caseworker reported that "Rosa became very angry at the visitor and said she didn't think a little dirt hurt anyone and furthermore, she was not going to do anything more towards keeping the house clean." Later, after missing an appointment with the visitor and being told to explain herself, Rosa declared that "she had so many things on her mind that it slipped by her without doing it. She did not seem to think that it was wrong to break an appointment and said her time was valuable and that she could not just come in at any time." Discord intensified when the visitor suggested the possibility of putting Rosa's aged husband in a home. Rosa explained that "she would never do this, that she thought he was happy where he was, and that he did not mind the dirt as much as the visitor did." At one point the visitor threatened to take away Rosa's check, but it was never withdrawn.

Despite these numerous conflicts of understanding, Rosa did occasionally turn to her social worker for assistance. Indeed, evidence of cordial interactions can be found throughout the record. Rosa spoke of her frustration with the lack of help and support from her family. She believed that she should be commended for supporting her husband despite the fact that she was young and attractive and could easily get another. Further, the caseworker gave gifts to the family, including tickets to edifying entertainments and a radio for William, so he would not get "lonesome." Once, the caseworker consulted an attorney to sue for damages stemming from William's auto accident as Rosa had requested. When Rosa's husband died in 1926, the visitor offered to help with the funeral arrangements. Rosa, crying, asked her to go to a photographic studio to request that they take a picture of her dead husband. The visitor made such arrangements and picked up the photograph, noting that the picture "showed a very pretty casket and flowers. The man had his beard shaved off and *looked neat and clean* [emphasis added]." Still weaving a tale that revolved around deficiencies rather than fortitude, the case worker rarely failed to write about Rosa without stressing the dirt, squalor, frayed and soiled clothing, stale and greasy food, and odors that supposedly characterized Rosa's household.

On March 21, 1928, Rosa's case was closed because of staff layoffs at MFWA. The last recorded contact between Rosa and her visitor reports a chance encounter in the streets of Minneapolis. Seeing Rosa hurrying down the street and rushing to catch up with her, the worker recorded Rosa's final words, that she "was going to work and they were getting along nicely."

Over the years, Rosa's caseworker recorded the tale of a woman who failed to care properly for her family, not the tale of Rosa's resolve. By contrast, Joanna Colcord, the director of MFWA, initiated a project to collect examples of "wise parenthood among the humble folk" known to MFWA. She highlighted the case of a presumably white family of eight on relief due to the illness and blindness of the breadwinner, a situation resembling Rosa's. Here, however, the record was "bright," since the family was bonded by the following sterling characteristics: "strong affection," "fortitude," "unselfish attitudes," "sharing pleasures and successes," "utilization of opportunities," and "hopeful and unified aims." Boasting that the mother got up from a sickbed to clean taxicabs rather than see her daughter be forced to leave Normal School, Colcord clearly felt she was presenting a paragon of wise motherhood. She asserted admiringly that there were no traces of "self-pity, self-seeking, or complaint" here when "pain, cold, and hunger had to be endured," since "one makes the best of these things, fortified by religion and hope." [10] Such a compassionate description of aspirations, dilemmas, strengths, and sacrifices, however, was never extended to Rosa, as she tenaciously pursued her dream of how she wanted to live.

NOTES

The author thanks David Klaassen and Beverly Stadum for their assistance with this article.

1. The shift toward a "scientific" and professionalized social casework introduced new techniques for observation, investigation, diagnosis, and documentation of the poor and aberrant and was accompanied by a mandate to keep voluminous case records. See Karen Tice, *Tales of Wayward Girls and Immoral Women: Social Case Records and the Construction of Professional Knowledge, 1900–1935* (Urbana and Chicago: University of Illinois Press, forthcoming) for further discussion of the evolution of social casework, professional knowledge building, and emergent interpretive and narrative practices.

2. When it came to their relationships with clients, caseworkers followed no party line. Some sought to be "professional friends." The Boston Society for Girls urged social workers to think of themselves as "best friends to their clients" (Annual Report, Boston Society for Girls, 1922, University of Massachusetts at Boston Special Collections). Mary Dewson also used the friend analogy and argued that social workers needed to think of themselves as the "kind of friend that we should want ourselves if we were to go as a stranger among people who lived and thought in unaccustomed ways" ("Probation and Institutional Care of Girls," in *The Child in the City*, ed. Sophonisba Breckinridge (New York: Arno Press, 1911, 1970), 357. Others, however, established detective and policelike relationships based on the hot pursuit of incriminating evidence, narrating a maelstrom of dirty kitchens, unsupervised children, shabby clothes, painted lips, and mysterious men.

3. Dewson, "Probation and Institutional Care of Girls," 357.

4. Quotations come from the case record of Rosa (not her real name), part of the case record collection of the Family Welfare Association of Minneapolis, located at the Social Welfare History Archives, University of Minnesota, Minneapolis.

5. The Minneapolis Associated Charities/FWA was established in 1884. Designed to prevent "injudicious aid," "to encourage thrift, self-dependence, industry, and better modes of life through friendly sympathy and advice," and "to know the condition of every dependent person," it was part of nationwide efforts to correct sentimental and unscientific relief giving that weakened the character structure of the poor (David Klaassen, "The Deserving Poor: Beginnings of Organized Charity in Minneapolis," *Hennepin County History* 47, no. 2 [Spring 1988]: 15–25). In the hands of benevolent "experts," charity was to be reorganized on scientific and business principles by providing centralized documentation and administration of relief cases and utilizing case-by-case investigation and treatment to weed out unworthy applicants. At FWA, the bottom line was to give advice and support, not cash, since as a 1927 report noted, relief was like a

"crutch" to be removed before permanent damage occurred. The agency did, however, maintain an emergency and loan fund. In her study, of the charity cases of the Minneapolis Family Welfare Association, Beverly Stadum found that more than half of all clients received at least one food order and half a ton of coal (*Poor Women and Their Families: Hard Working Charity Cases 1900–1930* [Albany: State University of New York Press, 1992]).

Stadum also argues that agency standards for motherhood and wage work were nebulous and inconsistent. In the 1905 Annual Report, caseworkers were told that "great care must be taken in giving employment to married women" for fear of tragic effects on children and spouses ("Maybe They Will Appreciate What I Have Done and Struggled: Poor Women and Their Families—Charity Cases in Minneapolis," Ph.D. diss., University of Minnesota, 1987, 258). At that same time many FWA workers believed that maternal wage work caused delinquency, illness, and truancy among children and spousal shiftlessness by disrupting "natural" gender obligations and order, yet were wedded to promoting self-sufficiency through wage work.

6. MFWA, like other family welfare agencies, was staffed largely by white unmarried women. Joanna Colcord, director of the Minneapolis Family Welfare Association, acknowledged the "problem" that many social workers were unmarried, but she argued that workers' "vicarious" experience of motherhood was sufficient ("The Fabric of Family Life," *The Family* 5, no. 7 [November 1924]: 172–75). Social casework leader Mary Richmond, however, asserted that the ideal caseworker was married with children. On the other hand, the suitability of white workers for African American clients was questioned, in light of racist notions that cast blacks as the quintessential "other." Mary Russell, secretary of Memphis Associated Charities, for example, argued that since most social workers were white and numerous "complications" blocked white workers from "real" understanding of black clients, it was essential that white-supervised black workers who understood the "handicaps" of their race be enlisted in reform efforts (Russell, "Possibilities of Case Work With Colored Families," *The Family* 2, no. 3 [May 1921]: 61).

During the years from 1917 to 1926, eighty-eight out of a hundred MFWA workers were women. All the directors were men until Joanna Colcord was hired in 1925. A Slavic worker was hired for a short time in 1913. However, the first black worker was not hired until 1918. A second black worker was hired in 1922. In the fall of 1926, Audre McCullough was hired and eventually given the unprecedented responsibility of visiting white families and supervising white workers, at a time when many other family welfare societies refused to hire black caseworkers to work with black clients (*Opportunity, Journal of Negro Life* 11, no. 10 [October 1933]: 294).

7. MFWA case records are located in the Social Welfare History Archives at the University of Minnesota, Minneapolis.

8. White caseworkers often refused to work with black clients or limited the amount of material assistance they received. For example, Mary Russell noted that black women received Mothers' Pensions less frequently than white women (Russell, "Possibilities of Case Work With Colored Families," 59–62). Elizabeth Lasch-Quinn notes that even within the more environmentally oriented settlement house movement, explanations of black dysfunction still led to attributions of black inferiority and segregated reform efforts. See Lasch-Quinn, *Black Neighbors: Race and the Limits of Reform in the American Settlement House Movement, 1890–1945* (Chapel Hill: University of North Carolina Press, 1993). Such neglect spurred many African American women to establish their own uniquely fashioned settlements, clubs, and institutions within the black community.

9. Stadum, *Poor Women,* notes that in 1918 the Minnesota Department of Labor considered forty dollars a month "below minimum subsistence."

10. Joanna Colcord, "Strengths of Family Life," *The Family* 11, no. 7 (November 1930): 211–16.

Chapter 2

The Sterilization of Willie Mallory

Steven Noll

On November 2, 1917, Willie Mallory of Richmond, Virginia, sued Dr. A. S. Priddy, superintendent of the Virginia State Colony for the Feeble-Minded, for five thousand dollars in damages resulting from Priddy's "perform[ing] an operation upon her by removing her genital organs, or sterilizing her, and unsexing her, and destroying her power to bear children." [1] Four months later, the jury found for the defendant, ruling that Priddy's procedure was performed out of medical necessity. The presiding judge, however, "warned Priddy not to sterilize any other patients until the existing law was changed." [2] The uproar over Willie Mallory's sterilization led directly to the Virginia Sterilization Statute passed in March 1924 and upheld by the United States Supreme Court in the famous 1927 Buck v. Bell decision. [3] Mallory's case is significant in and of itself, however, as it opens a window into the life of a woman the state deemed unworthy to bear children.

Many professionals in the retardation field came to view eugenic sterilization as an important weapon in this ongoing battle against the perceived increasing menace of the feebleminded. Sterilization appeared scientific, efficient, nonpunitive, and utilitarian (in that it placed the needs of society over the rights of individuals), and humanitarian (in that it benefited the individuals operated upon). Superintendent Priddy argued in 1925 that sterilization would prove a "blessing" for those persons who underwent the procedure. "They clamor for it [sterilization]," he continued, "because they know it means the enjoyment of life and the peaceful pursuit of happiness on the outside of institution walls." [4]

At the same time, sterilization was part and parcel of a larger strategy of care and control of Virginia's feebleminded population, particularly women of childbearing age. Feebleminded persons seen as community problems were institutionalized at the Virginia Colony. Priddy viewed sterilization as a necessary condition for discharge of those patients deemed capable of returning to society outside the walls of the institution. According to the Colony's 1932 Annual Report, "Practically all of them [patients who had been sterilized and then released] have been returned to their relatives and the State has thus been relieved of the immense financial burden incident to the care of them and the long line of defective descendants that would naturally have followed." [5]

To Priddy, therefore, sterilization of the feebleminded served a three-fold purpose. First, it served a eugenic function by preventing the continuation of hereditary mental defectiveness. Secondly, it provided a means of upholding morality by offering protection for both society and the individual who was sterilized. Priddy's rationale for sterilization combined concerns about the sexual immorality of those he labeled "the high-grade moron women of the anti-social class" and about the protection of "unsterilized, physically attractive young women." [6] Finally, sterilization provided a cost-effective method of handling the increasing numbers of feebleminded individuals institutionalized in the Virginia Colony. Once sterilized, feebleminded Colony patients could be discharged and live in the community without the potentiality of their bearing feebleminded offspring. In a state where expenditures for social welfare were exceedingly low, sterilization promised to insure that institutional rolls would not continue to grow, as patients would be admitted, sterilized, and then released. Virginia governor E. Lee Trinkle recognized this aspect of sterilization when he wrote to the superintendents of the Virginia state hospital system (of which the Virginia Colony was a part) in 1925, "I notice from the paper the Sterilization Law has been declared constitutional by the Supreme Court. . . . I do hope you people will get busy and use the law as fast as it can be used and help us get rid of our overcrowded conditions." [7]

The use of sterilization in the fight against feeblemindedness centered on lower-class women of questionable moral standards. The conflation of prostitution and feeblemindedness insured that concerns of gender and class received primary attention from institutional leaders. According to one leader in the field, lower-class feebleminded women were "poor, unfortunate, fiendish, yet irresponsible enemies of themselves, society, and the State. Humanitarianism demands their protection, care, and training. Society and good citizenship demand their segregation [in institutions] and asexualization."[8] In Virginia, the 1915 Survey on Mental Defectives in that state examined the relationship between prostitution and feeblemindedness and found it to be direct and strong. Survey takers analyzed the records of 120 Richmond prostitutes and reported 86 of the women as feebleminded. The report concluded that "society should segregate them where they will be protected from licentious men and avaricious women."[9] The Commonwealth of Virginia had already acted upon this recommendation by expanding the State Epileptic Colony to include feebleminded female patients. In 1914, Superintendent Priddy categorized these sixty-one new admittants as "creatures" who were "adept in the use of the vilest language and practices, common among women of their class, and their effect on the children patients [*sic*] is demoralizing in the extreme."[10]

Though Virginia initiated a policy of institutionalizing high-level feebleminded women to protect both the women and society, Priddy quickly realized that "it will be a long time before the public can be educated to the point necessary to put in force such a radical measure [segregation of all such defectives], and to assume the financial burden of enforcing it." Sterilization offered the opportunity to provide maximum benefits to the residents of Virginia at a cost far lower than that of lifelong institutionalization for all patients. Priddy recognized that sterilization was not a panacea: "I have never approved of it as a general measure." However, he did see the procedure as a cost-effective means of dealing with feeblemindedness and its assumed heritability. He announced in 1915 that he would "advocate it in the case of young women . . . who are capable of earning their living . . . who in this way could be kept from becoming a burden on the State." This would "certainly," he concluded, "prevent an increase of defectives from such sources."[11]

Though Virginia had no law authorizing sterilization procedures within institutions such as the Virginia Colony, Priddy pushed the state legislature to draft such a statute as early as 1908. He was aided in his legislative crusade by Joseph DeJarnette, superintendent of Western State Hospital in Staunton. While Priddy made the argument that sterilization benefited both the patient involved and society at large, DeJarnette held no such illusions. In his 1920 poem *Mendel's Law*, DeJarnette used mawkish, rhyming verse to get across his message that unrestricted procreation was detrimental to the human race. "Oh, you wise men take up the burden, / And make this your loudest creed," he wrote. "Sterilize the misfits promptly— / All not fit to breed."[12] DeJarnette also used the more conventional prose approach to rally Virginians to his position that sterilization was a major weapon in the fight against hereditary degeneracy. In his retrospective summary of Virginia's sterilization history, he concluded boldly that "no person unable to support himself on account of his inherited mental condition has a right to be born." [13] The 1908 legislature responded to neither the pragmatic requests of Priddy or the apocalyptic bombast of DeJarnette. Though frustrated by the lack of legislative action, Priddy did not let this prevent the initiation of sterilization proceedings on the grounds of the Virginia Colony. Interpreting his institutional mandate as superintendent broadly, Priddy began sterilization procedures in 1916, when he "sterilized twenty young women of the moron type." [14]

These operations, though not officially sanctioned by legal statute, were performed openly at the Colony. Priddy mentioned them in his Annual Reports on the Colony's operations from 1916 through 1920. Utilizing his rationale of protection for and from the feebleminded, Priddy announced that five sterilized female patients had already been discharged from the Colony "under the control of the proper person" and that fifteen more could leave "as soon as homes could be found." The discharge of these young women would "relieve it [the Colony] of the burden of the population of dependents which threatens society and are burdens on the state and public." [15]

Against this backdrop of state-sanctioned sterilization, Willie Mallory's experience seemed atypical only in the public nature of the proceedings. Except for the fact that she was thirty-eight years old when she underwent the procedure, Mallory represented the quintessential candidate for sterilization: she was a poor woman of questionable moral character whose assumedly demonstrable feeblemindedness was hereditary in nature and who had already given birth to at least two children labeled as feebleminded. In 1916, Willie Mallory, her husband, George, and eight of their nine children lived on the margins of society in a poor, integrated section of Richmond's seventh Ward known as Fulton. Located on Richmond's east side, close to the James River and the C & O railroad yards, Fulton represented the increasingly segregated nature of southern urban housing patterns. Only those whites too poor to move remained in close proximity to African American households. The Mallory household was one of these unfortunate white families, as they lived on a block with five black families. The Mallory family rented six rooms in a two-story house for nine dollars per month. This house represented the second domicile, at least, for the Mallorys in the Fulton District; their previous residence on Denny Street (two blocks from their 1916 home) had been destroyed by fire in late 1915.[16]

The destruction of the Mallorys' home and property caused the family to rely on public charity to get back on their feet. In early 1916, Associated Charities of the City of Richmond paid their rent bill for a month, and George went to work as a sawyer for the superintendent of that organization. By September of 1916, the Mallorys appeared to be back on their feet, with George gainfully employed as a sawyer for a firm in Ashland, Virginia, just north of Richmond. Often gone for two or three weeks at a time, George would send money back to the family to help support them. Married twenty-three years in 1916, George and Willie had their share of rough times. Willie had George arrested for drunkenness within a year of their move to Richmond (sometime between 1913 and 1914). Willie admitted that "he was drinking a little and tearing up a few things I had." Yet she continued to live with George, concluding that "I just made a compromise of it."[17] While George worked at the sawmill, Willie remained at home, taking care of the household and the children, until public authorities intervened and tore the Mallory world apart.

The official version of the ensuing events is terse and matter-of-fact. In September 1916, Willie Mallory was arrested in Richmond for running a bawdy house and brothel. In his defense at the sterilization trial, Priddy maintained that Mallory had "for a long time been well-known to the police of Richmond, and the social and charity workers of the State of Virginia, as a deficient, and as a most troublesome and undesirable citizen."[18] Her eight children at home were removed from the custody of her and her husband and turned over to the Children's Home Society of Virginia. A month later, a commission appointed by the judge of the Richmond Hustings Court held that Mallory and her two eldest daughters, Nannie and Jessie, were in actuality feebleminded and ordered them placed in the Virginia Colony near Lynchburg. To top off this public picture of familial feeblemindedness and depravity, George Mallory was arrested for public drunkenness in November 1916. Willie promptly escaped from institutional supervision at the Colony and returned to Richmond. There she was found, picked up by the police, and returned to the Colony. Upon her return, Priddy sterilized both Willie and Jessie, then released them from the institution on July 1, 1917. Nannie remained a patient at the Colony.

These two sterilization procedures and institutional releases seemed no different from the approximately eighty others that Priddy and his staff performed at the Colony in the years just before 1920. However, George and Willie Mallory did not take the removal of their children or the institutionalization of Willie and her daughters without a fight. They quickly filed three civil suits: to retain custody of their children, to have Nannie discharged from the Virginia Colony under a writ of habeas corpus, and most importantly, to force Dr. A. S. Priddy to pay the family five thousand dollars in damages for "sterilizing her, and unsexing her, and destroying her power to bear children." [19] The fact that the Mallory situation was adjudicated through the court system speaks to the unique nature of this case. How did a family of such modest means manage to pursue such legal remedies at a time when public legal aid was nonexistent? How did the Mallorys retain Richard Ivey, a prominent Richmond attorney, to pursue their legal redresses? In a time when Dr. Albert S. Priddy, one of the most powerful bureaucrats in Virginia, authorized eugenic sterilizations at his institution at his whim, how did Willie Mallory have the wherewithal to sue Priddy for sterilizing her and thus "depriv[ing] her of the comfort and association of her family"? [20] Unfortunately, we can only speculate on the answers to these questions. We can conclude, however, that Willie's desire to be reunited with her husband and children proved a major rationale for these extraordinary measures.

These cases provide a glimpse into the patterns of family life within the Mallory household and the conflict between state and family as to Willie Mallory's fitness as a mother. The state maintained that, by virtue of her immorality and feeblemindedness, Willie Mallory was unfit as a mother and should not be allowed either to raise her existing children or bear any more. The assumed hereditary nature of Willie's problems made them seem even more dangerous to Virginia officials. Thus, their decision to also sterilize Jessie Mallory, Willie's seventeen-year-old daughter, seemed entirely consistent with a policy that placed issues of family firmly within a newly developed social welfare bureaucracy.

The Mallorys' hard-fought struggle to reestablish their family after government interference tells a different story, showing the lengths families went to in order to maintain their integrity. The depositions at the three trials, particularly the case regarding the disposition of five of their children then under the supervision of the Children's Home Society of Virginia, present a different picture of the Mallory family than the one painted by Dr. Priddy.

Born in rural Ashland, Virginia, sometime around 1880, Willie Thomas Hall was orphaned at age thirteen and married at fifteen. After marrying George Mallory, Willie and her husband lived in Hanover County for the better part of nineteen years, before moving to urban Richmond around 1913. Eight of Willie's nine living children still resided with her in the house in the Fulton district. Only twenty-one-year-old Bessie, married with three children, had moved out from under her parents' roof by September 1916. The other children ranged in age from sixteen-year-old Jessie to four-year-old James. While husband George was responsible for financial support of the family, Willie raised the children, ran the household, worked odd jobs in Richmond, and took in boarders in her rented house to supplement George's meager, and periodic, income. According to a witness in the trial to return the children from the Children's Home Society, Willie Mallory "took the best care of them [her children]. . . . They were always kept very neat and clean. . . . Anybody that takes care of her children and works out too does very well."[21] While the state and charity officials may have frowned on Willie's wage earning, her friends and neighbors recognized the need for this extra income to provide support for her family. From their depositions at this trial, a picture emerges of Willie Mallory as a hardworking, industrious woman, devoted to her husband and children. By their accounts, Willie kept her children clean, sent them to school regularly, and provided them with a decent home life. On the night of September 23, 1916, however, the world of the Mallory family was changed forever, as questions about Willie's parental fitness tore the home apart.

George Mallory's arrest for drinking and menacing his wife was not the only brush the Mallory family had with legal authorities prior to the September 1916 incident. Sometime in the winter of 1915–16, Willie Mallory was arrested under bizarre circumstances while returning home from trying to obtain work at the British American Tobacco Company. In a telling comment on the patriarchal nature of their marriage, Willie did not take the job after she was offered it, because "my old man said if I went to work he would stop [working], so I would not go."[22] Mallory was walking down Main Street near the Fulton District at about 8:00 p.m. when she entered a building at the request of a man she thought she "knew in the country as Percy Tombs." This man then "closed the front door and would not let [Mallory] out." As she left to go out the back door, she later testified, "a policeman took me and carried me to the station house and I stayed there all night." After being taken to jail in a patrol wagon, the charges against Mallory were dismissed. Mallory maintained that she never knew what had happened to precipitate the incident or what she had been arrested for. Although there is no existing record of this incident, it appears the arrest was for prostitution. What made the affair so troubling to welfare authorities was that Mallory's daughter Jessie accompanied her to the building that night. Only fifteen at the time of the arrest, Jessie spent the night at the Richmond Juvenile Detention Home, since "she was too young to stay at the station house all night."[23] Jessie was returned to the Mallory household the next day, but it seemed clear that another brush with the law would be grounds for removal of the children from the custody of George and Willie. While the circumstances of Willie's arrest remain vague, her questionable conduct in entering the building that night placed public authorities on the alert for another such incident.

That event took place early on the evening of September 23, 1916 ("long before midnight," according to Mallory boarder Mollie Whorley).[24] Willie Mallory was at her home in the Fulton district, while George remained away working at the sawmill in Hanover County. She had returned from a day of working at the Cedar Works factory, where she was making a dollar per day.[25] The younger Mallory children were all asleep in their upstairs rooms, with the exception of young James, whom Willie was carrying around the house with her. The older girls, Jessie, Nannie, and Irene, were downstairs in the front room entertaining two brothers, one of whom would subsequently marry Jessie. A man, unknown to all occupants of the house, called at the door, allegedly inquiring about a room to rent. As Willie brought him upstairs, the man announced that she was under arrest for running a disorderly house. Mrs. Whorley testified that Willie Mallory still "had the baby in her arms" as the arrest was made.[26]

Willie was arrested and placed in the Richmond City Jail. The two male visitors, Alonzo and Wilbur Bowles, along with Irene Mallory, were also arrested and charged with "being disorderly in the house."[27] Two plainclothes policemen entered the house to take the individuals to jail, as the strange visitor seems to have simply vanished. The swift disappearance of this mysterious caller and the quick entrance of the police leads to the conclusion that public officials planned the arrest of Willie Mallory and the removal of her children. The policemen promptly called a patrol wagon, which took the entire Mallory family to spend the night in jail. The next day, seven of the eight Mallory children were removed from jail and placed in the Richmond Juvenile Detention Home. Willie remained in jail for close to a month, without being able to communicate with her children or husband. When asked what this experience was like, Willie answered, "I suffered from the loss of my dear children."[28]

The five youngest Mallory children were placed in the custody of the Children's Home Society of Virginia. No efforts were made to contact George Mallory, who upon returning from Hanover County, found his family gone. Mallory "thought maybe they had gone to some of her [Willie's] folk," but "Mrs. Whorley told me that the police had locked my wife up." Jail officials refused to let Mallory see his wife, and welfare bureaucrats similarly refused to allow him contact with his children. By the end of October 1916, Willie, Jessie, and Nannie Mallory had been adjudged feebleminded and committed to the Virginia Colony for the Feeble-Minded in Madison Heights, near Lynchburg. Before being transported to the institution, Jessie was held at the Richmond Detention Home. While there, she testified, she heard the house matron call the superintendent of the Associated Charities of Richmond. Jessie recalled hearing the matron say, "'Now I have got the little Mallory children at last.'"[29]

Willie, Jessie, and Nannie Mallory were sent to the Virginia Colony in October 1916. The circumstances of their commitment lend credence to the notion that the label of feeblemindedness stretched as far as public officials wished it to. Willie's commitment hearing took place at the Detention Home, in the presence of her children, whom she was seeing for the first time since her arrest. "Two or three people examined my mind," she recalled. They "asked me if I could tell whether salt was in bread or not, and did I know how to tie my shoes." After the doctor concluded that "I can't get her in," a public welfare official intervened. Mallory stated that "she said to them, 'put on there unable to control her nerves and we can get her in for that.'"[30] It seemed nervousness constituted sufficient grounds for Willie's admission to the Lynchburg Colony. Jessie's commitment contained even more official subterfuge. When later asked if she knew that she was being taken to the Colony, Jessie answered in the negative. Only when "some of the girls" told her did she discover that she had been indeed taken to the Colony for the Feeble-Minded. Upon her arrival at the Colony, Jessie was immediately put to work, cleaning rooms and taking care of "one baby," which seemed ironic considering the charges of immorality that led to Jessie's institutionalization.[31] Upon her confinement at the Colony, Willie quickly made plans to flee the institution, part of a resistance strategy that included both legal and extralegal means. "I had a family that was suffering," she recalled, "and I did not want to stay there." She was caught in Lynchburg and returned to the Colony, where she was placed in solitary confinement.[32] In July 1917, nine months after their arrival at the Colony, Willie and Jessie were released, but only after they had been sterilized. They were released, too, under conditions that still did not allow them to return to their families. Willie was required to live with her married daughter Bessie and her husband in Petersburg, while Jessie was bonded out to Mrs. J. W. Murphy of Nelson County, Virginia. Priddy wrote Murphy explaining that Jessie had been bonded to her so that she would no longer "be exposed to the same immoral surroundings which caused the Juvenile Court of that city to commit her to this institution."[33] Within three months, however, Willie and Jessie had returned to the Richmond area, where they were reunited with George and Irene. Priddy alerted local officials to keep "on the lookout for them and if they move into the city [Richmond] at any time she [Willie] will be arrested and brought back."[34]

Priddy recognized the limits of his power, however. By November 1917 he had tracked down the Mallory family and wrote to both Willie and George in terms that reflected many of the presuppositions underlying Virginia's institutionalization and sterilization policies. Using the tone of a proud but stern parent, Priddy lectured Willie, the woman he had just sterilized and allowed to be released from the Virginia Colony. "I am gratified to know that the operation performed on you did so much good," he wrote, "that you are now able to earn an honest living." His attitude then shifted dramatically to that of the progressive moralist. "[You will now] not live such a life of shame as you did before coming to the institution," he concluded.[35]

While Priddy's words to Willie Mallory reflect the ambivalences of concern and condescension, his correspondence with her husband exemplifies the controlling nature of the emerging welfare system. George Mallory wrote a poignant, anger-filled letter to Priddy on November 5, 1917. In barely legible handwriting, Mallory plaintively asked Priddy, "Dr what busniss did you have opreatiding on my wife and daughter with out my consent . . . there is no law for such treatment . . . she is not feeble minded." Priddy responded by justifying the sterilization procedures as medically necessary. "Your wife and Jessie were both operated on," he wrote, "because they asked me to do so and it was done for diseases they had." He then attempted to intimidate Mallory by revealing the extent of his arbitrary powers. "If you dare write me another such communication," Priddy warned menacingly, "I will have you arrested and brought here too. I have the full record of you and your family from the State Board of Charities and Corrections and the Juvenile Court of Richmond."[36] George Mallory was not admitted to the Virginia Colony, but there is no record either of a continued written correspondence between Mallory and Superintendent Priddy.

On January 24, 1918, the Supreme Court of Virginia heard the case of *Ex-parte Mallory* (originally known as *Mallory v. Children's Home Society*), in which George Mallory fought to have his children returned from the custody of the Children's Home Society. According to the court decision, the children were "not charged with any criminal offense ... but only with being dependent and neglected children." They had been removed from the Mallory household to the authority of the Home Society under the orders of a Richmond justice of the peace, "upon complaint and information on oath before him made by one H. F. Sweet that the children aforesaid were 'exposed to vicious and immoral influences.' "[37] The Supreme Court ordered the children removed from the authority of the Children's Home Society and returned to Mallory, on the narrow legal grounds that the order removing the children from the Mallory household was in error, "nor was any evidence introduced by the Society to the effect that the facts are such that from the standpoint of the welfare of the children the legal right of the father to the custody of the children was superseded." The court made no comment on the question of Willie Mallory's fitness as a parent.[38]

Willie Mallory was similarly successful in obtaining the release of Nannie, then sixteen, from the Virginia Colony in June 1918. Institutionalized in October 1916, Nannie Mallory was admitted to the facility upon the order of a Richmond hustings judge after the finding of an appointed "commission" that she was "feeble-minded and ought to be confined in an institution for the feeble-minded." In a ruling similar to the one in the earlier Mallory custody case, the Virginia Supreme Court ruled that appropriate procedures were not followed in the admission procedure for Nannie Mallory and granted the petition for habeas corpus for her release. Again, the Mallory victory was won on narrow legal grounds, and the court passed no judgment on the applicability of the feebleminded label or the validity (as opposed to the legality) of the institutionalization process.[39] To Superintendent Priddy, this kind of legal battle was becoming altogether too familiar, as institutionalized patients initiated habeas corpus petitions to get themselves discharged from the Colony on a regular basis. In his 1919 Annual Report, Priddy lamented that "our admissions procedures need to be tightened and adhered to so inmates can not win their early release on frivolous habeas corpus decisions."[40]

While the suit concerning Nannie Mallory's discharge seemed annoyingly typical to Priddy, the case involving the sterilization of Willie Mallory was unique. Mallory pressed the state for damages, not only for her sterilization procedure, but also for "illegally depriving her of her liberty ... [and] so depriv[ing] her, by said illegal imprisonment, of her daily wages." The trial, heard in the Circuit Court of the City of Richmond, began in late February 1918 and lasted until March 1. Priddy rested his defense on the grounds that he performed the procedure as a medical necessity, sterilizing Willie Mallory because of "the diseased condition of the plaintiff." There is no other mention elsewhere of Willie's medical condition, either by Mallory herself or Priddy, yet the court deferred to Priddy's expertise. Perhaps with the Mallory case still in his mind, Priddy reiterated this rationale for sterilization in his 1919 Annual Report. Several of the "girls of the higher grade who were social outcasts and charges on the public ...," he reported, "came to the institution suffering with physical diseases as a result of their own vice and requiring surgical operations for their relief, the nature of which rendered them sterile."[41] Following the judge's instructions that the jury would have to find for Priddy if they believed his medical necessity defense, the jury returned a verdict in his favor. They announced that their decision was based on the fact that "the defendant, as a practicing physician, was honestly of the opinion that the plaintiff would be materially benefited by a surgical operation."[42] Once again, the case was decided, this time in favor of the Colony however, on narrow, technical grounds, rather than on the broad social issues which marked the sterilization question.

Though Priddy won the Mallory decision and the legality of that particular sterilization procedure was upheld, the days of sterilization without enabling legislation were numbered in Virginia. Enlisting the support of state senator and Colony counsel Aubrey Strode of Lynchburg, an old friend and business associate, Priddy pushed for the passage of a statute that would permit eugenic sterilization within the walls of Virginia's state institutions. Enacted in 1924, the Virginia Sterilization Act was formulated upon both economic and scientific bases. The statute stated that sterilization would aid those "many defective persons who if now discharged or paroled would likely become by the propagation of their kind a menace to society, but who if incapable of procreating might properly and safely be discharged or paroled and become self-supporting with benefits to themselves and society." It also invoked the scientific rationale for sterilization by emphasizing that "human experience has demonstrated that heredity plays an important part in the transmission of insanity, idiocy, epilepsy, and crime."[43]

Priddy believed that sterilization helped both the individual operated upon and society. He viewed the procedure as a means of using meager public funds in the most cost-effective manner. To Priddy, expediency and economics drove the engine of eugenic sterilization as much as ideology. Priddy also saw the sterilization procedure as an opportunity for feebleminded individuals, particularly women, to improve their position in life. In his 1916 Annual Report, Priddy wrote, "Five young women of the higher grade have been sterilized by order of the board, and at their earnest request, have gone out in the world, and are earning their own good living under the care of proper persons, and behaving themselves well."[44] This attitude was more than simply a cover for Priddy's demands for control of the feebleminded, who constituted "an anti-social class and dependent,... many of who were [*sic*] menaces to the morals and health of the public."[45] Priddy viewed eugenic sterilization as good for all concerned, for society and for the individuals who underwent the procedure. Yet, when push came to shove, as when Willie Mallory sued over her sterilization, Priddy chose to highlight the benefits of eugenic sterilization to society, not to the individual. In doing so, he had to show the danger Willie Mallory posed to the citizens of the Commonwealth of Virginia, to show that it was appropriate and legal to sterilize her since she was "incapable of leading a clean and proper life."[46] As much emphasis as sterilization advocates placed on the benefits of the procedure to the persons undergoing it, the rationale eventually always came down to that charged phrase: "incapable of leading a clean and proper life."

What of Willie Mallory and her family? The victims of well-intentioned reformers and a flawed scientific worldview that conflated poverty and feeblemindedness, the Mallory family won some justice and redress through the Virginia court system. The children were returned from the custody of the Children's Home Society, Nannie was released from custody at the Virginia Colony, and Willie was allowed to return to Richmond to be with her family. In spite of these victories, the sterilizations left Willie unable to have any more children and Jessie incapable of bearing any. Jessie was sterilized to prevent the transmission of feeblemindedness to another generation. In this case (to paraphrase the words of Justice Holmes in *Buck v. Bell*), two generations of "imbeciles" proved enough to warrant state intervention. Briefly in the spotlight in their struggle with the state of Virginia, the Mallorys quickly reverted to their previous anonymous status of a poor working family trying simply to survive. After 1917, Richmond city directories no longer show any listing of George and Willie Mallory and their family.

Willie Mallory's attempts to fight the system showed the lengths to which resourceful women would go to keep their families together. Conversely, the efforts of Virginia officials revealed how intrusive they could become in attempting to police family matters if a mother was deemed unfit to raise her children. The case of Willie Mallory was not only a personal matter between one mother and the state. It is an illustration of the tension arising from differing perceptions of good parenting. In a time in which once again the ideals of appropriate parenting have become contested terrain, Willie Mallory's travails are a sobering example of the invidious effects on poor families of those who profess to foster family values.

NOTES

A much earlier version of this paper was presented to the Annual Meeting of the Organization of American Historians, Atlanta, Georgia, April 1994. The author would like to thank Gerald Grob, Molly Ladd-Taylor, William Leuchtenberg, Louise Newman, Michael Radalet, Nicole Rafter, Lauri Umansky, and Leila Zenderland for their comments and suggestions in the writing and revision of this work.

1. Declaration of the Case, *Mallory v. Priddy* File, Richmond City Ended Law Cases, Common Law Cases, 1918, drawer 383, Virginia State Library and Archives, Richmond.

2. *Mallory v. Priddy.* H. Minor Davis, quoted in W. I. Prichard, "History of the Lynchburg Training School and Hospital—Part I," *Mental Health in Virginia* 10, no. 4 (Summer 1960): 46.

3. *Buck v. Bell*, 274 U.S. 203 (1927). See also *Buck v. Bell*, 143 Virginia 310 (1925). For more on the Buck case, see J. David Smith and K. Raymond Nelson, *The Sterilization of Carrie Buck* (Far Hills, N.J.: New Horizon Press, 1989). Superintendent Priddy was the original defendant in the Buck case, but he died during the appeal process. Dr. J. S. Bell, the new superintendent of the Virginia Colony, became the new defendant.

4. Testimony of A. S. Priddy, quoted in "Case Carried to the Virginia Supreme Court of Appeals," in Harry Laughlin, *The Legal Status of Eugenical Sterilization* (Chicago: Municipal Court of Chicago, 1930), 21. The secondary literature on eugenic sterilization is large and increasing. See particularly Philip Reilly, *The Surgical Solution: A History of Involuntary Sterilization in the United States* (Baltimore: Johns Hopkins University Press, 1991); and James Trent, *Inventing the Feeble Mind: A History of Mental Retardation in the United States* (Berkeley: University of California Press, 1994), especially 184–224.

5. *23rd Annual Report of the State Colony for Epileptic and Feeble-Minded*, n.p., 1932, 5.

6. A. S. Priddy, quoted in Cynthia Pegram, "Dr. Priddy Backed Law," *Lynchburg News*, March 27, 1980, C-4.

7. E. Lee Trinkle to hospital superintendents, November 24, 1925, Governor's Correspondence of E. Lee Trinkle, box 24, State Commissioner of Hospitals Folder, Virginia State Archives, Richmond.

8. Superintendent's Report, January 10, 1919, in Minutes of the Executive Committee of the Board of Directors of Caswell Training School, Caswell Center Archives, Kinston, North Carolina.

9. *Mental Defectives in Virginia: A Special Report of the State Board of Charities and Corrections to the General Assembly* (Richmond: Superintendent of Public Printing, 1915), 66. For examples of contemporaneous analyses of the particular problems associated with feebleminded women, see Harry Hardt, "The State Care of Feeble-Minded Women," *Institution Quarterly* 3, no. 1 (1912): 179–86; Olga Bridgman, "Juvenile Delinquency and Feeble-Mindedness, *Institution Quarterly* 5, no. 2 (1914): 164–67; and Paul Mertz, "Mental Deficiency of Prostitutes: A Study of Delinquent Women at an Army Port of Embarkation," *Journal of the American Medical Association* 72, no. 22 (1919): 1597–99. For recent interpretations of the gendered basis of the concept of feeblemindedness, see Peter Tyor, "'Denied the Power to Choose the Good': Sexuality and Mental Defect in American Medical Practice, 1850–1920," *Journal of Social History* 10, no. 4 (1977): 472–89; Barbara Brenzel, *Daughters of the State: A Social Portrait of the First Reform School for Girls in North America, 1856–1905* (Cambridge, Mass.: M.I.T. Press, 1983); Stephen Schlossman and Stephanie Wallach, "The Crime of Precocious Sexuality: Female Juvenile Delinquency in the Progressive Era," *Harvard Educational Review* 48, no. 1 (1978): 65–94; and Mary Odem, *Delinquent Daughters: Protecting and Policing Adolescent Female Sexuality In the United States, 1885–1920* (Chapel Hill: University of North Carolina Press, 1995), especially 95–101.

10. *5th Annual Report of the Virginia Epileptic Colony, 1914*, 12.

11. *6th Annual Report of the Virginia Epileptic Colony, 1915*, 16–17.

12. Joseph DeJarnette, "Mendel's Law," in Paul Lombardo, Eugenic Sterilization in Virginia: Aubrey Strode and the Case of Buck v. Bell (Ph.D. diss.,

University of Virginia, 1982), 114. The poem was originally published in the *1920 Annual Report of Western State Hospital.*

13. Joseph DeJarnette, Sterilization Law of Virginia, undated pamphlet, Virginia State Library, Richmond. 1. See also DeJarnette to John Dickson, October 24, 1947, Additional Papers of Judge Aubrey Strode, file 3014B, Manuscripts Department, Alderman Library, University of Virginia, Charlottesville.

14. *7th Annual Report of the Virginia Epileptic Colony, 1916,* 13. See also DeJarnette, "Sterilization Law," 1.

15. *7th Annual Report of the Virginia Epileptic Colony, 1916,* 10–11. In addition to the women, Priddy also performed sterilizations on four "vicious and dangerous" institutionalized male patients.

16. Housing information is from *Richmond City Directories* (Richmond, Va.: Hill Directory Company) for 1915 (p. 911), 1916 (851), 1917, and 1918. Information on the Fulton district is from the *1915 Richmond City Directory,* 1333, 1489. Information on the Mallory renting arrangements is from testimony of George Mallory and Willie Mallory, *George W. Mallory v. Children's Home Society of Virginia,* Clerk's Office, Supreme Court of Virginia, Richmond, 15, 27.

17. Testimony of Willie Mallory, *George W. Mallory v. Children's Home Society,* 23, 37.

18. Grounds of Defence [*sic*] of A. S. Priddy, February 16, 1918, *Mallory v. Priddy,* 5.

19. Declaration of the Case, *Mallory v. Priddy.*

20. Declaration of the Case, *Mallory v. Priddy.*

21. Testimony of Maria Mills, *Mallory v. Children's Home Society,* 80.

22. *Mallory v. Children's Home Society,* 38.

23. Testimony of Willie Mallory, *Mallory v. Children's Home Society,* 25–26, 37–40.

24. *Mallory v. Children's Home Society,* 60.

25. *Mallory v. Children's Home Society,* 75.

26. *Mallory v. Children's Home Society,* 60.

27. Testimony of Alonzo Bowles, *Mallory v. Children's Home Society,* 64.

28. *Mallory v. Children's Home Society,* 75.

29. Testimony of George Mallory, *Mallory v. Children's Home Society,* 3; testimony of Jessie Mallory Bowles, *Mallory v. Children's Home Society,* 77.

30. *Mallory v. Children's Home Society,* 31–32.

31. *Mallory v. Children's Home Society,* 43, 44.

32. *Mallory v. Children's Home Society,* 34–36.

33. A. S. Priddy to Mrs. J. W. Murphy, October 19, 1917, case file of *Mallory v. Children's Home Society,* Clerk's Office, Supreme Court of Virginia, Richmond.

34. A. S. Priddy to [name obscured], October 11, 1917, case file of *Mallory v. Children's Home Society,* Clerk's Office, Supreme Court of Virginia, Richmond.

35. A. S. Priddy to Willie Mallory, November 26, 1917, *Mallory v. Priddy* File, Richmond City Ended Law Cases.

36. George Mallory to A. S. Priddy, November 5, 1917; A. S. Priddy to George Mallory, November 13, 1917, both in *Mallory v. Priddy* File, Richmond City Ended Law Cases.

37. *Ex Parte Mallory*, 122 Virginia 299.

38. *Ex Parte Mallory*, 122 Virginia 300.

39. *Mallory v. the Virginia Colony for the Feeble-Minded*, 123 Virginia 205–10. See Petition of Willie T. Mallory for Habeas Corpus, in *Mallory v. Priddy* File, Richmond City Ended Law Cases.

40. *5th Annual Report of the Virginia Colony for the Feeble-Minded, 1918*, 13.

41. Grounds of Defence [*sic*], *Mallory v. Priddy* File, Richmond City Ended Law Cases, 3; *6th A. R. of the Virginia Colony for the Feeble-Minded, 1919*, 12–13.

42. Judge's Instructions; Court Declaration of *Mallory v. Priddy*, both in *Mallory v. Priddy* File, Richmond City Ended Law Cases.

43. Virginia Statute, chapter 394, reprinted in Harry Laughlin, *The Legal Status of Eugenical Sterilization*, 10.

44. *3rd Annual Report of the Virginia Colony for the Feeble-Minded, 1916*, 12.

45. *6th Annual Report of the Virginia Colony for the Feeble-Minded, 1919*, 12.

46. Grounds of Defence [*sic*], *Mallory v. Priddy* File, Richmond City Ended Law Cases, 5.

Chapter 3

Hospitalizing Maria Germani

Emily K. Abel

During the early twentieth century, a mother could be declared unfit if she did not comply with medical regimes. Fearsome diseases such as cholera, typhoid fever, and smallpox, which had attained epidemic proportions decades earlier, were virtually eliminated after the turn of the century, and other common killers, including rickets, syphilis, and dysentery, lost much of their menace. The conviction that the credit belonged to medical science gave urgency to the task of spreading its benefits throughout society and increased skepticism about women's traditional healing practices.[1]

In 1918, the New York Charity Organization Society (COS) engaged in an eight-month conflict with an Italian immigrant couple about the care of their twelve-year-old daughter.[2] COS workers viewed the couple's opposition to the girl's hospitalization as a form of child neglect.[3] The case illustrates the burden that the growing faith in medicine could place on immigrant mothers, who lived and worked in unhealthy environments but were blamed when children fell ill.

The COS first visited the Germani household on January 25.[4] The family consisted of a musician, his wife, and their six children. Mr. Germani was considered "a rather better class of Neapolitan man," but he lacked work, and the family could not make ends meet. Attention soon focused on the oldest child, Maria, who was ill. The COS suspected tuberculosis. It is easy to forget the terror that scourge inspired eighty years ago. A chronic disease, tuberculosis inflicted years of disability on its victims; it also produced more fatalities than any other cause.[5] Although the disease affected the entire population during the nineteenth century, after 1900 it was concentrated among poor people, especially immigrants and people of color.[6]

Tuberculosis control was a top priority of the New York City Department of Health and the city's private charities. At a time when many cities had only fledgling health departments, New York boasted a remarkable array of services, offering curative medicine as well as prevention. The Department of Health launched one of the first major health education campaigns and provided free diagnosis and treatment.[7] The COS supported the department's program by encouraging clients to get tuberculosis examinations, follow medical advice, attend tuberculosis clinics, and enter hospitals and sanatoria. Charity workers considered women responsible for both protecting family members from contagion and ensuring that the sick received appropriate medical services.

At first, the Germanis did not object to the COS's plans for their daughter. They agreed to have Maria's sputum tested, and on March 7 a Department of Health physician diagnosed tuberculosis. The COS's next recommendation provoked more resistance. The COS learned that the doctor considered Maria "a hospital case" and believed that "the sooner she was rushed to the hospital, the better." The doctor's desire to place Maria in a hospital rather than a sanatorium suggests that he considered her case very advanced and recovery unlikely. The Department of Health tried to reserve places at its sanatorium in the Catskill Mountains for people with early stages of disease, who could be "restor[ed] to permanent usefulness in the community."[8] The chief medical officer, Hermann M. Biggs, believed, according to his biographer C.-E. A. Winslow, that "[t]here were individuals—whose lives were so worthless to the community that it would be an unpardonable waste of public funds to give them the benefit of sanatorium care."[9] City hospitals segregated "hopeless" sufferers from the rest of society but provided little treatment. The subsequent struggle over Maria's hospitalization partly expressed a conflict about the meaning of her life. To health officials and charity workers, she was primarily a carrier of disease; to her family, however, she was a unique and precious child.

The struggle also reveals the invisibility and powerlessness of immigrant mothers. Mrs. Germani spoke little English, and although the COS may have relied on a child or a neighbor to translate (as it did in similar situations), we can assume that the charity workers and Mrs. Germani had at least some difficulty communicating. Nevertheless, the COS interacted primarily with the mother and directed much of the blame for Maria's condition at her.

According to the report of the charity worker who came to take Maria to the hospital, the girl "cried and absolutely refused to go. The mother was perfectly willing to have her taken and felt it was the best place for her, but because Maria carried on so she felt it would be better to wait until Mr. Germani came home." Given patterns of male domination in many poor and immigrant households, Mrs. Germani may have been reluctant to make a major decision without her husband. But she also may have been adopting the strategy of many other COS clients, verbally agreeing with advice she had no intention of following in order to avoid a direct confrontation. COS clients feared hospital placement. Most had heard horror stories about the poor quality of care in city facilities. Parents also worried about their own loneliness and their children's homesickness. Immigrants with limited English were especially likely to assume that they would be unable to communicate with hospital staff about their children.

On the morning of March 8, Mr. Germani told a charity worker that he had decided not to send Maria to the hospital. Instead, he would take her to the home of his sister, who lived with her husband in an eight-room house on two acres of land in New Jersey. There Maria not only would be isolated from the other children but also would get the fresh air and rich diet believed to have therapeutic value. Mr. Germani also stated that he had taken Maria to a Brooklyn doctor, who had confirmed the diagnosis but consented to the father's plan.

Mr. Germani did not mention his wife's input into those decisions. He may simply have omitted her role, but it is more likely that he viewed himself as solely responsible for determining Maria's care. Significantly, Maria's aunts—Mr. Germani's sisters—appear to have played a large role in the girl's treatment. One assumed the care of Maria in New Jersey. Later, another tried to intervene with the COS on the Germanis' behalf. The aunts also appear to have provided financial help to the Germani household. Mrs. Germani's dependence on her husband's siblings made her especially vulnerable to their judgments of her.

Mr. Germani's decision to send his daughter to New Jersey prompted the COS to report the case to the Society for the Prevention of Cruelty to Children (SPCC), requesting it to find a way to take Maria "by force" to the hospital. Although the COS stressed the importance of persuading clients to accept medical advice, the organization frequently resorted to compulsion. The Department of Health had permitted the forcible detention of tubercular patients since 1901, and the COS did not hesitate to mobilize state power when it failed to obtain voluntary compliance with requests for hospitalization.

The response of the SPCC in Maria's case must have disappointed the COS. On March 29 the SPCC reported that it could take no action simply on the grounds of the girl's transfer to her aunt's home in New Jersey. A COS charity worker who visited the girl in New Jersey confirmed that she was "getting along very well"; she had "gained weight" and had "plenty of fresh milk and eggs and good care." Nevertheless, the COS remained suspicious of the parents, warning them that the SPCC would be alerted if Maria returned to the city.

Maria did return. On July 9, a COS worker visiting the Germanis after the birth of a baby found Maria at home and her health still poor. She looked "pale and worn" and was dressed in "a heavy white sweater." Mrs. Germani insisted that her own doctor considered Maria "fine" and that she wore the sweater only because she had just returned from the park. The report for July 22 read,

> Maria was sitting in a large rocking chair, propped by a big pillow. Her mother said she had just come in from the park (which seemed very doubtful). Maria looks sick and weak and has a very loose cough. She coughs frequently. [The charity worker] asked if Maria might go with her to the doctor's the next time she called, or if the mother would prefer having the doctor call at the house. Mrs. Germani would much prefer the latter and wants an Italian doctor.

This exchange can be interpreted in several ways. Mrs. Germani and the charity worker may, of course, have disagreed about the state of Maria's health. It also is possible that the mother stressed Maria's recovery in order to discourage further COS intervention in her case. Concealment is a common form of resistance to medical surveillance,[10] and COS clients frequently claimed that even gravely ill family members were "fine" or "getting better" or "had recovered." Finally, the COS worker may have emphasized Mrs. Germani's statements because they reinforced the prevailing stereotype that immigrant mothers were ignorant and indifferent to their children's well-being. For her part, Mrs. Germani's insistence that Maria be seen in her own home by an Italian doctor underlines the mother's determination to keep medical decision making under family control.

The COS informed the SPCC of Maria's return, but it again refused to intervene, noting that Maria was going back to New Jersey and that "the mother has promised to cooperate with the SPCC." Although the SPCC, like the COS, defined children's care as the mother's responsibility, Mrs. Germani's promise of cooperation made her an acceptable mother, not such a "bad" one as it might appear.

The COS's own investigation confirmed that Maria received good care in New Jersey. On August 15, a charity worker found her "sitting in the back yard under a grape arbor." The case worker described the aunt as "a nice looking woman with a very kind, good face," who seemed "very fond of Maria and cannot do enough for her." Some New York relatives who were visiting were "nice refined people and all so interested in and concerned about Maria." The house was "out in the country where you can see the fields and woods for miles and miles. It is a very lovely spot for Maria if the air is dry enough." Although Maria refused the special food prepared for her, the relatives promised to work harder at persuasion.

On September 23, the case took a dramatic turn. Maria was found at home by a truant officer and was hospitalized by court order against her family's wishes. Although the COS earlier had urged the Germanis to institutionalize Maria, the family turned to that agency for assistance. According to the charity worker's notes, Mrs. Cappetti, one of Mr. Germani's sisters living in New York,

> called at the office in a great state of excitement. She said that Maria and her mother had been to court this morning and the judge had ordered that Maria be placed in a hospital. She was taken to the Reception Hospital. The family feel very badly about this and fear the child will grieve herself to death because she is separated from her family. Mrs. Cappetti said her sister in [New Jersey] is willing to keep Maria and they feel that the child has been getting the proper care there and has shown improvement. Mrs. Cappetti takes her regularly to see [the doctor in Brooklyn]. Mrs. Cappetti explained that Maria had come into the city to go to see the doctor. . . . The truant officer called and found Maria at home. Mrs. Germani probably was not able to explain fully to the officer that Maria was not living at home and he, seeing her there among so many children, no doubt thought the best place for her would be in a hospital. Mr. Germani is very much worried about it and asked Mrs. Cappetti to call and see if the COS could help get the child discharged from the hospital. Mrs. Cappetti was told that the Society would do what they could in the matter.

The Germani family faulted Maria's mother for the disaster. When the charity worker visited the Germani home the following morning, Mrs. Germani "implied that her husband and his family blamed her for Maria's commitment." Nevertheless, she had been powerless to prevent it. She had assumed that the officer who came to take her to court was from the school and wanted Maria examined. Her language difficulties had even more drastic consequences in court. The case file continued,

> As [Mrs. Germani] cannot speak or understand the English language very well, she did not comprehend all that was going on in the court room. She tried to explain to the Judge that Maria did not live at home and that she was under a doctor's care, but no one seemed to pay any heed to her remarks. When they got into the automobile, she thought they were going to take Maria to the hospital for an examination, but when they arrived there she was told that the child would have to remain.

Maria was transferred to Metropolitan Hospital. Operated by the Department of Public Welfare on the site of the old almshouse on Blackwell's Island, this facility aroused more hostility than any other city hospital. The COS was well aware of its deplorable conditions. In 1911, the COS Committee on the Prevention of Tuberculosis castigated the city for the hospital's "disgraceful" overcrowding. Beds "regularly lined" the halls; many patients were forced to sleep on mattresses on the floor.[11] Two years later, a client who left the hospital "because he could not stand the place" vividly described his experience in a letter to the COS. The bedding he received had been used by other patients without having been washed or even aired.[12]

Not surprisingly, Maria was miserable in the hospital, begged to be discharged, and steadily deteriorated. In early October a charity worker found her "sitting on a rocking chair all bundled up in her sweater with the saddest and most forlorn look on her face." Mrs. Germani tried to protect her daughter, pointing to Maria's special sensitivities, which made a hospital stay especially intolerable. Unlike her siblings, the girl never expressed her feelings directly but "all the time cries inside." Mrs. Germani feared Maria would "grieve herself to death" if compelled to stay. She also expressed concern about her husband, who took many days off from his new job at a bakery and occasionally threatened suicide. In October, when the 1918 flu epidemic struck New York and city officials placed Metropolitan Hospital under quarantine, both parents became frantic with worry.

Charity workers from the COS tried to allay the Germanis' fears by contacting the hospital administrators to obtain information about Maria. In other ways, however, the COS remained impervious to the parents' concerns. Although various relatives beseeched the COS to work for Maria's release, the organization stonewalled. It continually promised to appeal to influential people on Maria's behalf but then used interviews with those same people to explain why Maria should remain in the hospital. As the family grew increasingly irate at the COS for its failure to act, charity workers turned the blame back on the parents, claiming that if they "had done as they promised to do and had not brought Maria home with them all this trouble would have been avoided." A hospital nurse similarly held the parents responsible, arguing that the girl might have recovered had the parents allowed her to enter the hospital sooner.

As the weeks passed, Maria's condition continued to worsen. By the middle of October, she had stopped eating. "I think it is a sin to have a sick child suffer the way she is," wrote one of Maria's cousins on November 8. Maria died in the hospital eight days later, nearly two months after her admission.

By deflecting blame to the parents, the COS absolved itself of responsibility for Maria's death. The agency portrayed the Germanis as ignorant and indifferent, although its own records suggest otherwise. The parents took Maria to the doctor regularly and placed her in the home of a relative who could provide the fresh air and special diet recommended by the Department of Health. The conflict between the parents and the COS centered not on whether Maria should receive medical attention but on what that attention should consist of and, even more, on who should control it. To the COS and the Department of Health, Maria was primarily a source of infection who should be permanently segregated from both other family members and the rest of society. To the parents, however, Maria's life had unique value. They directed their attention toward promoting her recovery, which they believed could occur only within her family.

The parents' focus on the importance of family connection elicited little sympathy. Today, it is fashionable for both government officials and social service workers to adopt the rhetoric of family love and attachment. But in 1918, the Germanis' use of the language of emotion and family intimacy appears to have reinforced their reputation for irrationality and poor parenting.

The case record also reveals the chasm between the responsibility attributed to the mother and her ultimate powerlessness. Mr. Germani appears to have made the major decisions regarding Maria's care, but the welfare agencies held Mrs. Germani accountable for her daughter's health.

At the same time, Mr. Germani and his sisters blamed Mrs. Germani for Maria's detention, despite the mother's inability to prevent it. Because she spoke little English, she could not communicate adequately with the COS or the truant officer. When she tried to explain in court that Maria did not live at home and was under a doctor's care, "no one seemed to pay any heed to her remarks." Her limited English also led her to misconstrue several events leading to Maria's commitment. Unable to protect her daughter, Mrs. Germani appeared to be a bad mother to her husband and his sisters as well as to the COS. In this case, an immigrant woman's invisibility and powerlessness had tragic consequences for her child.

NOTES

1. On the way the growing faith in scientific medicine affected popular concern with issues of access and distribution, see Rosemary Stevens, *American Medicine and the Public Interest* (New Haven: Yale University Press, 1988). Historians now debate the extent to which medical advances contributed to the decline in infectious diseases.

2. The case files of the New York Charity Organization Society are located in the Community Service Society Archives, Rare Book and Manuscript Library, Columbia University, New York. The case discussed in this essay is no. 2072, box 286.

3. On noncompliance with medical advice as a type of child neglect, see Linda Gordon, *Heroes of Their Own Lives: The Politics and History of Family Violence* (New York: Penguin, 1989), 127–30.

4. Pseudonyms are used in this essay.

5. George Rosen, *A History of Public Health*, expanded edition (Baltimore: Johns Hopkins University Press, 1993), 361.

6. Sheila M. Rothman, *Living in the Shadow of Death: Tuberculosis and the Social Experience of Illness in American History* (New York: Basic Books, 1994), 181.

7. See Daniel M. Fox, "Social Policy and City Politics: Tuberculosis Reporting in New York, 1889–1900," *Bulletin of the History of Medicine*, 49 (1975): 169–95; Barron H. Lerner, "New York City's Tuberculosis Control Efforts: The Historical Limitations of the 'War on Consumption,'" *American Journal of Public Health*, 83, no. 5 (May 1993): 758–68; Elizabeth Fee and Evelynn M. Hammonds, "Science, Politics, and the Art of Persuasion: Promoting the New Scientific Medicine in New York City," in *Hives of Sickness: Public Health and Epidemics in New York City*, ed. David Rosner (New Brunswick: Rutgers University Press, 1995), 155–96; Rothman, *Living in the Shadow of Death*.

8. Hermann M. Biggs, *The Administrative Control of Tuberculosis* (New York: New York City Department of Health, 1909), 21.

9. C.-E. A. Winslow, *The Life of Hermann Biggs, M.D., D.Sc., LL.D., Physician and Statesman of the Public Health* (Philadelphia: Lea and Febiger, 1929), 198.

10. See Michael Bloor and James McIntosh, "Surveillance and Concealment: A Comparison of Techniques of Client Resistance in Therapeutic Communities and Health Visiting," in *Readings in Medical Sociology*, ed. Sarah Cunningham-Burley and Neil P. McKeganey (London: Tavistock/Routledge, 1990), 159–81.

11. Committee on the Prevention of Tuberculosis of the Charity Organization Society, *The Need of Hospitals for New York's Consumptives* (New York: Charity Organization Society, 1911), 3.

12. Letter from J. F. to H. M. Johnson, n.d., filed with case no. R966, box 278. COS staff were so impressed with this letter that they sent copies to numerous city officials.

Chapter 4

Taking on a Mother's Job
Day Care in the 1920s and 1930s

Elizabeth Rose

Distrust of mothers was very influential in shaping child care programs in the early twentieth century. Fears of maternal incompetence shaped ideas about the purpose of day care, the types of care that were provided, and the relationships among mothers, teachers, and children that evolved. But concerns about bad mothering did not always have the same result. Mothers of all classes and backgrounds could be "bad" mothers, although their incompetence sprung from different sources. Poorer women who worked for wages might be bad mothers because they left their children alone while they went out to work, while their more affluent counterparts were bad mothers because they paid too much attention to their children, preventing them from developing their independence and individual personalities. Thus nursery schools aimed to help children who risked being smothered by their mothers, while day nurseries offered physical care and discipline to working-class children who seemed to suffer from a deficit of maternal attention.

Class differences between the two gave rise to other differences as well. While day nurseries provided custodial care for the children of poor mothers who "had to work," nursery schools offered an educational, enriching experience for the children of well-educated, affluent families. In day nurseries, child care was offered as a charitable gift to the poor, while in nursery schools, it was sold to parents who had other choices. Day nurseries were seen as a temporary, stop-gap solution to family crisis, while nursery schools were heralded as the wave of the future in progressive education.

Yet the two types of programs had much in common. Both day

nurseries and nursery schools took on "a mother's job" of caring for and training young children, and both sought to transform mothers as well as children in the process. Supporters and staff of both day nurseries and nursery schools believed that the mothers they served were incapable of raising healthy children without expert advice and intervention. They encouraged women to doubt their own mothering skills and to believe that only by relying on the guidance of experts could they hope to do right by their children. The help that both kinds of child care programs offered to mothers thus came mixed with messages of maternal failure. Yet many mothers sought out the help that such programs offered, even finding in their new dependence on professionals a measure of class status and modernity. Using Philadelphia as a case study in a national trend, this article will explore the ways in which fears of maternal incompetence both damaged and empowered mothers as they sought help caring for their children.

Day Nurseries and Working-Class Mothers

At the turn of the twentieth century, working-class and poor mothers throughout Philadelphia went out to work, whether as textile mill hands, waitresses, garment operatives, or domestic servants. For these women, working for wages was the fulfillment, not the abdication, of their responsibility to their children. For instance, one Jewish immigrant woman wrote to a day nursery social worker, "I have to give eat a whole family . . . I want to work and make a living for my children."[1] For these women, motherhood was about providing as well as nurturing. Wage work was an extension of family responsibility, a way to help out one's husband in his task of supporting the family, and a fulfillment of a mother's duty to her children. Although these women worried about their children, they did not think that they were inadequate mothers because they went out to work.

But to the elite women who founded day nurseries in Philadelphia from 1880 to 1920, a mother's decision to work for wages deprived her children of a "normal" childhood and family life. Just as a family without a breadwinner was an "unhallowed thing," a home without a full-time mother was cold and empty, not really a home at all.[2] Children on the streets, like mothers in factories, signified a world turned upside down. While other reformers built playgrounds or established juvenile courts, these elite women sought to make things right by establishing day nurseries to care for the children of working mothers. If mothers had to take on a father's job of breadwinning, the nurseries would take on part of a mother's job by caring for children during the day. By 1920, fifty charitable nurseries had been established to serve native-born white, immigrant, and black children in different working-class neighborhoods of Philadelphia.[3] These charitable nurseries were typically founded, funded, and managed by upper-class women, although a few were established by neighborhood women.[4] Catholic nurseries were often initiated by clergy, although their work was carried out by nuns and supported by women parishioners. The nurseries tried to meet wage-earning mothers' needs by staying open long hours, charging only a minimal fee, and accepting children from infancy through the age of twelve.

For the founders of Philadelphia's day nurseries, working mothers were noble but pitiable figures, inadequate mothers by virtue of their daily absence from the home. It was that inadequacy that made it legitimate for the nurseries to take on a mother's job during the day. Indeed, day nursery managers often described their nurseries as providing surrogate mothers and homes to children who seemed to be motherless and homeless (although the children had both mothers and homes). For instance, the president of the board of the Franklin Day Nursery stated point-blank in her annual report that the children who attend the nursery "have no mothers. They are dead or working ten and twelve hours a day in shops and mills."[5] Wage-earning mothers, in this equation, might as well be dead; their children were effectively orphaned and had to be taken in by the nursery. Similarly, a board member of the Baldwin Day Nursery described the nursery as a "foster mother" to two of the children who attended, despite the fact that the children's own mother lived with and supported them; another explained that the nursery "supplied the parent that was missing" for children who "lacked a mother's care."[6]

Day nursery managers were profoundly ambivalent about mothers' wage work. Strong believers in the idea that men should be breadwinners and women full-time mothers and housekeepers, they never wanted to encourage women to seek paid work. Rather, they sought to shelter the children of those women who had no other choice, those who would otherwise have to place their children in orphanages or leave them with inadequate supervision. So they carefully defined the day nursery as a charity, restricted their services to poor mothers in desperate economic straits, and investigated each case to make sure the mother really "needed" to work for wages. In annual reports and other publicity, day nursery supporters portrayed their clients as desperate but heroic, focusing especially on the struggling widow or deserted wife who could not be condemned for going out to work. Marion Kohn of the Neighborhood Centre Day Nursery wrote in an annual report in 1914, "Too high a tribute cannot be given to the Nursery mother whose every day living means sacrifice and loving devotion to her children, and sometimes, almost super-human effort to keep her family together."[7] Similarly, a poem written in 1948 to celebrate the 25th anniversary of the Strawberry Mansion Day Nursery, which served an immigrant Jewish neighborhood, recalled "the method used in admission":

> D.D.D. was the key to the code
> Desperate, deserted and destitute.
> The louder the wails, the shorter the road,
> That led to this child care institute.[8]

The desire to paint a compelling picture of the desperation of day nursery families sometimes led supporters to exaggerate the proportion of struggling single mothers, to highlight stories of single fathers (who represented only a tiny fraction of families applying for day nursery care), and to deemphasize the large number of women who worked because their husbands earned insufficient wages.

While day nursery managers praised the sacrifices made by wage-earning mothers, they made it clear that they did not mean to encourage such arrangements. Rather, their greatest hope was to "restore the family to normal conditions," with a breadwinning father enabling the mother to be at home with her children. For instance, when day nursery director Marion Kohn was not praising the devotion of day nursery mothers, she was stressing the deviance of their family life, declaring, "I can imagine no life more abnormal than that of the Day Nursery mother and child."[9] She frequently described the goal of the nursery as "the re-establishment of a family to normal conditions," "home rehabilitation," or "building up the home."[10]

The managers' concern about the dangers of taking on a mother's job had been present from the beginning of the day nursery movement, but it intensified during the 1920s as trends in child welfare (especially the support for mothers' pensions) and the emergence of professional social work strengthened the idea that mothers belonged at home with their children, not in the work force trying to support them. For instance, in

1923, a speaker addressing the Philadelphia Association of Day Nurseries "emphasized the fact that there is danger of freeing the mother from maternal responsibilities and not working for the interests of the home."[11] In response to such criticism, many day nurseries tightened up their guidelines for admission and hired social workers to carry out investigations and do casework with day nursery families. A leading social worker articulated her vision when she wrote, "The nursery's obligation is not discharged until to every family under its care has been restored, as nearly as possible, that normal home life on which our modern society was founded."[12]

To ease their fears about the consequences of taking on a mother's job, day nursery staff worked to reshape the children and mothers who came to the nursery. Day nursery managers hoped to use the nursery as a model home to teach mothers efficient, sanitary, and modern techniques of housekeeping and childrearing and to instill in the children a love of cleanliness, order, and nutritious food, good manners, and patriotism. A board member of the Franklin Day Nursery, after detailing the miserable backgrounds from which children came to the nursery, explained, "Here in the Nursery they get their first glimpse of home life as it ought to be for them. . . . How quickly they yield to the influence, you can see, and it is encouraging to notice how earnestly their parents try to live up to the rules of the Nursery and help the work begun there."[13] A survey of the city's day nurseries in 1916 commented, "The nursery is potentially the greatest power for good in the life of an impoverished family since, through its control of the children, it has a greater influence than either the settlement or the school. Among the legitimate functions of the day nursery," after providing food, shelter, and medical care and maintaining the family by providing an alternative to the orphanage, were "to instill in the child habits of order, cleanliness, courtesy and obedience" and "to instruct the mother . . . in proper feeding, bathing and general care of her children."[14] Several years later, a list of the "social values of the nursery" described it as "a place in which to teach 'mothercraft,' through contrast and by suggestion . . . [T]he child itself, if properly dressed, washed, etc., offers a suggestion to the mother."[15]

Social workers and day nursery board members sometimes claimed that this broad-based education in citizenship, discipline, and cleanliness was in fact the larger purpose of their work. A 1928 Neighborhood Centre report explained, "The physical care we furnish in the Nursery for our children is but a small part of our program. Our larger purpose is the

projection of Nursery ideals into the home." Women who were ambivalent about encouraging mothers to work for wages took solace in the
thought that they were improving working-class motherhood and shaping
the values of the next generation. Taking on "a mother's job" was legitimate if its larger goal was to train mothers to do their job better in the
long run.

Instruction in housekeeping and child care at the nurseries was often
linked to Americanization. Giving children daily baths, feeding them
vegetables, and taking them to a doctor regularly were seen as important
ways in which immigrant mothers could become American. Immigrant
children, too, would learn American values by attending a day nursery.
According to the president of the Franklin Day Nursery, the most inspir-
ing aspect of the nursery was not the "warm baths and motherly nurses
for curly-headed babies" but the sound of a hundred clean and well-
dressed children singing "My Country 'Tis of Thee" and pledging allegiance to the flag.[16]

Day nursery workers placed great faith in the idea of children carrying
the lessons of the nursery back into their homes and influencing their
mothers in the direction of hygiene and nutrition. They hoped that after
experiencing life in the nursery, children would insist that their mothers
conform to nursery standards at home. Commenting on the San Cristoforo Day Nursery's sewing school, a board member wrote, "An interesting
part of the instruction given is the training of the elder girls in housework. This is beginning to show in their homes, where they try to teach
their mothers order and cleanliness."[17] (The apparent enormity of the
task is suggested by the verb "try.")

But to get their message across, day nursery workers did not rely only
on children pressuring their mothers at home. Nursery personnel also
tried to teach the mothers directly, "lest the web which is so carefully
woven by day be unraveled each night" by uneducated mothers.[18] Mothers' meetings or clubs were a valuable "teaching ground," combining
social events with "instructive talks" by day nursery workers or local
doctors, nurses, and nutritionists.[19] Neighborhood Centre's house physician organized special health meetings for the nursery mothers there,
recruiting other physicians and dieticians as speakers. "The response of
the mothers," reported the social worker, "has been most gratifying. They
ask many questions of the doctors and discuss the meetings with us on
many other occasions."[20] The presence of doctors and nutritionists was

important, for one of the long-term goals of these mothers' meetings was to train nursery mothers to listen to experts.[21] Topics varied, but the meetings tended to focus on practical tips for childrearing and housekeeping, areas in which day nursery mothers were presumed to need instruction. For instance, the Sunnyside Nursery sponsored "a very successful supper in which we tried to demonstrate a simple and nutritious meal, not hard to prepare."[22]

This training in motherhood was necessary because mothers could not be trusted to sustain their children's health on their own. For instance, the Neighborhood Centre nursery prepared bottles of milk for mothers to take home at night, "thereby assuring the baby of proper food."[23] At the Cathedral Day Nursery, the nuns, fearing vermin, sometimes destroyed the clothes in which the children arrived.[24] The daily medical inspection was a particular point of contention between mothers and nursery workers, for it was a process in which the authority of the nursery staff superseded a mother's judgment about her child's health. Mothers knew that when their child "failed" a morning inspection, their work as mothers had been judged inadequate; they also risked losing a day of work (and possibly a job) if a child was sent home for a condition that she did not judge to be very serious.[25] So when a morning inspection detected lice or other evidence that a mother had not been keeping her child adequately clean, mothers often took offense. In fact, when the San Cristoforo nursery tried to cut their children's hair short to avoid lice, so many Italian mothers were irate that the nursery almost closed down.[26] Similarly, a woman who sent her children to the First Day Nursery in 1919 was very angry when the nursery doctor found nits and bugs in her children's hair. "I am afraid all of our efforts with Mrs. P and her children have come to an end," the nursery's visitor wrote. "She has left us in high temper and withdrawn the children from our care" with a "hateful" note.[27]

Home visits were another way in which day nursery social workers sought to improve their clients' housekeeping and childrearing skills, believing that expert intervention could make these women into good mothers. For instance, a mother who used the Neighborhood Centre nursery in the 1920s was visited by a home economist twice a week; although she "had quite a difficult time convincing [the] woman that her ideas were wrong," the home economist continued to visit, instructing the woman in "how to prepare various nutritious foods for the family" and giving her lessons in managing her children. The mother, who worked with her husband selling goods from a pushcart as well as caring for her six children, had earlier complained about her oldest son's disobedience, saying that "he shortens my days" with his laziness and cursing. The home economist "tried to explain to the woman that the fault lay within her and that she must be more careful and use better disciplinary measures with the children." The social worker held out hope that the children would pressure their mother to improve: she noted that under the guidance of the nursery, the children "have become fastidious about their appearance and also the type of food the mother offers them, and we think that the children are setting a higher standard for the parents." [28]

Some mothers resisted attempts to change their mothering practices, but others welcomed the interest and advice of social workers. Leah Nadel, whose two children attended the nursery at Neighborhood Centre while she sewed buttons at a factory, was sometimes skeptical of the mothering advice she received, but she did her best to comply. For instance, a nurse from the Centre's public health clinic who visited the home in 1928 reported that Leah was "interested in the various vegetables[;] although she said she is quite sure she will never learn to like them she will cook them for the children." On an earlier visit, when a social worker told Mrs. Nadel that it was "unwise" to let her son and daughter sleep together in the same room, she "did not understand our point of view and said that she believed that having the children sleep in the same room would strengthen their moral standards. She promised, however, to make other adjustments." [29]

Other mothers accepted the nursery's emphasis on hygiene and physical care but rejected advice about training and discipline. For instance, a day nursery social worker complained that one woman "keeps her children very clean and is under the impression that she is doing her duty." [30] Others threw their hands up, in effect telling social workers that if they knew so much about how children should be trained, they should go ahead and do it themselves. [31] Still others fought for control of their children, even withdrawing them from a nursery when they felt that the demands of nursery workers threatened their maternal dignity, their children's health, or even their legal rights to their children. [32] Whatever their particular response, all these women learned that supervision by childrearing "experts" invariably accompanied the day nursery's willingness to help them take care of their children.

Nursery Schools and Middle-Class Mothers

Through home visiting, individual counseling, and example, day nurseries sought to instill in the working-class mothers they served the same commitment to cleanliness, nutrition, and expert knowledge that they assumed middle-class mothers possessed. By uplifting poor and immigrant mothers to a middle-class standard of mothering, reformers hoped to bring poor families into the mainstream of American society.[33] This hope, present from the beginning of the day nursery movement, became even more pronounced in the 1920s as professional social workers gained more influence.

But even as day nursery workers were intensifying their efforts to improve their clients' mothering skills, middle-class motherhood itself was coming under new scrutiny. As Kathleen Jones's essay in this volume explains, the 1920s and 1930s saw the development of a "harsh critique of American motherhood," focused particularly on women from relatively comfortable economic backgrounds. Whereas reformers at the turn of the century had assumed that poor mothers were the ones who needed help to become "good" mothers, in the 1920s even affluent, well-educated women who devoted all their time to mothering were being told that they could not rear emotionally healthy children without the guidance of experts. The problem here was not poverty, unstable family structures, or ignorance (the common explanations for "bad" mothering among immigrant and poor families) but failure to moderate the flow of emotion between mother and child. Mothers were guilty of overprotecting their children as well as of rejecting them; nagging, overindulgent, and overanxious mothers could create serious emotional and behavioral problems in their children, leading to maladjustment and juvenile delinquency.[34] As advice to mothers shifted from a focus on physical health, nutrition, and hygiene to matters of mental health and emotional adjustment, the task of motherhood appeared more complex. For instance, the Children's Bureau's popular 1914 booklet *Infant Care* had given detailed instructions for keeping children healthy, clean, and well fed, but by 1928, a new pamphlet asked, *Are You Training Your Child to Be Happy?*[35]

Not only was a mother's job complex, it was also fraught with danger. As historian Nancy Cott has remarked, the only common ground of the new literature on parenting was its "redefinition of the parent-child relation as a *problem*,"[36] and the mother was generally at the root of the problem. All mothers (not just poor or immigrant mothers) were now seen to be ignorant, and untrained mothers were likely to inflict great psychological damage on their children. At a time when science, efficiency, and expertise were seen as offering solutions to social problems, maternal instinct and love did not seem to be enough. Many experts, like behaviorist psychologist John Watson, saw maternal love as a dangerous force, leading to "smothering" a young child's will, destroying the child's independence, and impeding the development of a healthy personality.[37]

One way in which middle-class mothers could improve their mothering skills and ensure their children's healthy development was to send them to one of the new nursery schools that were established during the 1920s. In effect, the nursery school placed both child and mother under the supervision of experts, while providing researchers with an ideal laboratory in which to study child development. Nursery schools promised to help children develop social skills, play in a group, and learn to control both emotions and bodily functions. Influenced by behaviorist psychology, nursery school proponents argued that children needed to be trained as early as possible to exercise self-control and to "adjust" themselves to a social group.[38] The schools were also to be "laboratories for parents"; some schools had mothers take notes on the teachers' techniques and later discuss them with the nursery director, and most required mothers to spend time observing the classroom on a regular basis.[39] In 1929, the director of the nursery school at Vassar College observed, "The nursery school is fundamentally a training school for parents to teach them how to train the child."[40] The nursery school often combined help for mothers with criticism. One nursery school director, Caroline Pratt, stated confidently that there were "no bad children, only bad parents," and confessed that she sometimes believed that children would be better off without their parents altogether.[41]

Supporters of nursery schools frequently argued that the nursery school was a necessary institution for the "modern family." Smiley Blanton, director of the nursery school at Vassar College, declared,

> Just as the luncheon clubs have come in to take the place of the old corner grocery store . . . just as the golf club has come in to take the place of the farm and the demand to get out and exercise, so the nursery school has become an absolute necessity in modern life. It takes the place of the old home, commodious, full of children, with aunts and uncles and grandparents about with whom the child might associate.[42]

In linking the nursery school to the needs of modern life, Blanton also signaled the social class of nursery school families. The nursery school as he described it was intended to serve people who ate in luncheon clubs and frequented golf courses—a very different group of people from those who sent their children to day nurseries. Indeed, nursery schools were typically aimed at well-educated, affluent professional families, often centered around universities; one nursery educator referred to nursery schools as serving "the children of the intellectual classes." [43] Faculty wives at the University of Chicago established the first nursery school in the United States in 1916; it was soon followed by other university-based nursery schools and by private nursery schools, both of which catered largely to children of the middle and upper classes. [44] At the Merrill-Palmer School in Detroit, a prominent training school for child development professionals, students and faculty remembered that the laboratory nursery school was reserved for "the cream of the crop parents, the best," who represented the "wide variety of elements found in what is called the 'great middle class.' " [45] Because nursery schools were intended primarily to benefit the child, not to free the mother, and because they were either self-supporting or subsidized by the university that housed them, they carried none of the stigma attached to the charitable day nurseries.

Middle-class families turned to nursery schools because they had been convinced that mothers alone could no longer perform the complicated task of fostering children's emotional and social development. Nursery schools were necessary, as one chapter of the Child Study Association agreed in 1930, because "very few homes could be normal in this complicated age in which we are living." [46] Whereas earlier commentators had reserved the word "abnormal" for families disrupted by death, desertion, poverty, abuse, and mothers' wage work, comments like this suggested that even educated, middle-class, two-parent families with some resources could not be trusted to bring up their children to be "normal" adults without help. Smiley Blanton of the Vassar Nursery School pointed out that few parents had any formal training in childrearing, and that, furthermore, "the average mother doesn't know how to give the child a bath or what kind of soap to use or how many clothes to put on the child unless she is specifically told by some doctor or unless she reads it out of a book." [47] If mothers needed to rely on the knowledge of experts for such simple matters, Blanton implied, then surely expert knowledge was required for the more complicated, psychologically fraught tasks of child training. An article in the *Women's Home Companion* answered the question, "But is it not better for mothers to train their own little children?" by saying, "No doubt, when they know enough of what experts know about the mental and physical hygiene of little children, are wise and patient, and have plenty of time for patience!"[48] As child development emerged as a specialty, young college women seeking a "feminine" profession came to fill positions in nursery schools. Parents who valued educational credentials, but were anxious about their own ability to guide their children through a changing world, were likely to believe that teachers' academic training in child development gave them skills superior to their own.

The nursery school's promise of producing children who were "well adjusted," who could get along in a group, and who had learned self-control (of emotions as well as of excretion) at an early age was particularly attractive to middle-class parents who worried about how their children would fare in the new business world that was taking shape in the 1920s. If this new world judged people on "personality" and their ability to work well with others, then children who developed these skills early would have an advantage. As Smiley Blanton of the Vassar Nursery School remarked, "Competition is so fierce in modern life that we can hardly afford to overlook any one factor that may make for success." He asserted that children who were timid, anxious, grouchy, ill-tempered, moody, irritable, overaggressive, or oversensitive were just as worrisome as those with crooked feet or curvature of the spine. The nursery school could fix these emotional maladjustments before they turned children into people that "you wouldn't want as sons-in-law, you wouldn't want as secretaries, you wouldn't want to work with them in an office."[49]

Children needed to learn not only to "get along," but also to express their individuality. Researchers studying children's development in the 1920s frequently remarked with surprise at the variation in children's patterns of behavior and learning, and the ideal nursery school tailored its approach to each child's individual temperament and developmental needs. Blanton described the Vassar Nursery School's technique of intensively studying each child through interviewing parents and testing the child's IQ, then arranging situations in the nursery school that would help the child with his or her specific needs. A shy child was urged to play the leading part in certain games and encouraged to fight when other children tried to take toys from her; a child who had had no contact with other children was gradually taught to play in the right way; a child weeping at being separated from his mother was left alone out of respect for his grief.[50] The supervised freedom of the nursery school child was different from the unsupervised freedom that children in understaffed day nurseries might have had, for it was carefully constructed in order to meet a child's individual emotional needs. Indeed, the whole emphasis in the nursery school on nurturing individualism was probably unfamiliar to most day nursery workers, who tended to emphasize discipline and order, treating the children in their care as a group with similar needs for physical care, rest, and recreation.[51] Thus while the nursery school trained middle-class children to develop personalities and habits which would help them succeed in the business world, the day nursery socialized its working-class children to habits of discipline and group identity that would be important for their futures as factory and clerical workers.

Like day nurseries, nursery schools aimed to improve the ways in which women mothered their children and included "parent" education as part of their mission. But while parent education in the day nurseries was largely concerned with hygiene, nutrition, and housekeeping skills, the education offered to nursery school parents focused on child development and psychology, learning how to manage a child's emotions and how to train children to be self-sufficient, independent, and well-adjusted. Although both day nurseries and nursery schools assumed that mothers were incapable of raising their children successfully, the nursery school mother who was actively seeking help from professionals may have seemed more promising than the day nursery mother, who often had to be trained and sometimes even forced to listen to expert advice.[52]

Their mistrust of women's mothering skills led nursery school advocates to develop more positive attitudes toward group care for children. By claiming that it was good for children to be separated from their mothers, they turned earlier arguments about the dangers of taking on a mother's job on their head. Nursery school director Caroline Pratt, for example, saw the nursery schools as the first step in the child's "emancipation from the home."[53] If mothers were domineering, overanxious, unhappy, or too wrapped up in their child, their children would flourish only when they were released from the emotional intensity of the home. Indeed, if mother love was in fact a dangerous force, the best thing mothers could do was to get out of the way. Pratt defined a mother's main job as helping her child become independent, "setting him gradually free among his equals," and saw the nursery schools as the first step in the child's "emancipation from the home."[54] Another nursery educator wrote,

> By four, the child ... trained [by nursery school methods] has acquired spontaneously and unconsciously many of the habits that the isolated child

in the home is still struggling and fighting over. Spinach, for instance, eaten in a group, is rarely either as distasteful or as interesting for dramatic purposes as when a devoted mother and nurse make it and the child the daily center of a thrilling emotional scene.[55]

This need for separation was typically seen as a need of the *child,* although some did note that mothers sometimes needed to be liberated from their children as much as vice versa.[56] In the words of Smiley Blanton,

> No business man, would act as a night watchman in his business all night and work at his business all day, and that is exactly what the average parent has to do with the young child. . . . The result is that the average mother is too tired; she is so tired that she has not that resiliency nor that background which will enable her to do the best for the child when she is with him. The nursery school . . . gives the parent time to get rested, to get a new perspective.[57]

Others mentioned, as an additional selling point, the fact that the nursery school freed the mother to pursue her own interests for at least part of the day. Mothers could thus become "modern" in more ways than one. Paul Klapper wrote that for an "intelligent" mother who had a profession before marriage, the nursery school might be "an avenue of escape from a regimen of housekeeping that is physically exhausting and mentally stupefying."[58] According to this line of thinking, the mother's needs for activity outside the home dovetailed nicely with the child's needs for companionship and play outside the home; it was healthy for both to be separated from each other temporarily. Discussions about combining a professional career with marriage in the 1920s sometimes mentioned nursery schools as a good way to meet both children's and mothers' needs. Because the nursery school was justified primarily as a beneficial experience for children, not as a convenience for mothers, and because families paid for the service, nursery educators seem to have seen mothers' work in somewhat more positive terms than did most social workers concerned with working-class families. Liberating children from the home could also liberate women: one nursery school director, herself a mother, wrote that it was normal for a mother "to have interests which absorb her" and to want to pursue them. She suggested that mothers as well as children would find the hours spent at home "more precious because of the nursery school, more precious because they are less a matter of routine."[59]

But such arguments were unusual; most nursery educators wanted mothers to focus more on their childrearing, not less, and even most career-plus-marriage advocates were wary of encouraging women to combine full-time work with motherhood.[60] Those who did propose that mothers and children would benefit equally from a period of separation found themselves trying to defend mothers from the charge that they were "shirking" their duty to their children by using a nursery school.[61] At any rate, the mother-child separation envisioned by nursery educators was to be very temporary: many nursery schools ran for only a half day and also required mothers to spend time observing and helping in the school.[62] Whatever "outside interests," including paid work, a mother wanted to pursue had to be fitted around this schedule.

Although nursery schools aimed to reinforce women's sense of the complexity of modern motherhood rather than simply to relieve their burdens, they did offer a welcome respite to the mothers who used them. Nursery schools released mothers from constant responsibility for their children, and perhaps more importantly, widened beyond the confines of the family the circle of adults interested in an individual child. As "training schools for parents," they also offered mothers expert guidance at a time when motherhood was a source of great anxiety. Of course, the very guidance and advice they offered often served to exacerbate the anxiety associated with motherhood and increase women's dependence on experts. Ironically, as Kathleen Jones has argued, mothers may have welcomed the experts' diagnosis of their incompetence, for this opened the door to the nursery school, justified their need for respite from full-time motherhood, and also gave them a chance to talk about their most intimate problems.[63]

Neighborhood Centre: A Nursery School for the Working Class?

As the idea of the nursery school gained acceptance, day nursery leaders sought to ally themselves with the nursery school movement by creating nursery schools within or alongside their day nurseries. In the late 1920s, the National Federation of Day Nurseries encouraged its members to expand their work by creating nursery schools in conjunction with, or instead of, day nurseries. The day nurseries that adopted the nursery school plan, however, were pulled back and forth between their educational and their charitable missions, and most did not continue the

nursery school programs for long.[64] Looking at one of the most successful
of these programs in Philadelphia allows us to see the convergence of
different understandings of what constituted a mother's job and of when
it was legitimate for mothers to ask for help.

Neighborhood Centre, Philadelphia's Jewish settlement house, had initially been established by Jewish women of German heritage for the
purpose of Americanizing new Jewish immigrants from eastern Europe.
In addition to offering classes in English, cooking, and citizenship, clubs,
and playgrounds, the settlement established a day nursery in 1885 to serve
poor children whose immigrant parents worked in nearby sweatshops,
laundries, factories, and small stores.[65] The day nursery at Neighborhood
Centre was one of the larger and more professionally run day nurseries in
the city. It was among the first to integrate the services of social workers,
psychologists, nutritionists, and other professionals into the work of the
nursery, so it is not surprising that it would also be among the first to
establish a nursery school. The nursery school was part of the larger day
nursery but served a smaller group of children and employed a trained
teacher who introduced special play equipment and more carefully structured activities. When the nursery school was begun in 1924, it seemed
attractive to both settlement workers and local families. Neighborhood
Centre staff were clearly excited to be part of an educational experiment
linked to the new science of child development, and one which carried
more status than the work of the day nursery. At the same time, the
nursery school appealed to nearby families whose class position was
gradually shifting. As the Jewish immigrants who were Neighborhood
Centre's main clientele achieved a degree of social mobility and sought to
enter the American middle class, they experienced both economic stress
and concerns about their children's development.[66] But the existence of
the nursery school allowed them to find help with child care by high-
lighting their children's educational needs rather than the precariousness
of the family economic status. Many mothers, seeking the status that went
along with middle-class American motherhood, seem to have preferred
to claim that they were unable to properly manage their children than to
admit that they needed to work, for embracing the identity of an incompetent mother was more appealing than claiming poverty.

Like other nursery schools, the Neighborhood Centre school sought to
train children in good habits and to teach parents how to manage their
children at home. Thelma Day, the Nursery School teacher, wrote in 1928,
"When we can be assured that our work has carried over into the homes

of our children so that the child receives the same type of care while he is at home as he has received while he is with us, our work will have real value."[67] Descriptions of two "success stories" in a 1928 report show the central role that parent education played in the mission of the Nursery School. The mother of the first child, Lily, "had been helpless in her efforts to manage [her] because of the child's temper tantrums, night-terrors, her fear of animals and absolute dependency upon her mother." After a "long and arduous" process of work with the family, which "meant constantly directing the mother and other members of the family in their treatment of Lily," the child adjusted to new expectations and replaced her undesirable traits with "a set-up of wholesome habits."[68] In another case of two children with many behavior problems,

> work in the Nursery and in the home ... brought the mother to a better understanding of her children.... Literature on child training has been furnished [the parents] by the Nursery School teacher. The mother is constantly coming here for advice and suggestions. The father, while out of work for a half a day not long ago, spent that time observing in the Nursery School.[69]

In both these cases, it was not only the transformation of the child that the social worker celebrated but the change that had taken place in the parents, especially their willingness to follow expert advice in training their children.

Knowledge of the educational mission of the Nursery School quickly spread among neighborhood families, altering the grounds on which they could legitimately ask for help with their children. Instead of presenting themselves as forced by poverty to go out to work, mothers talked about the more intangible needs of their children. Neighborhood Centre was now seen not only as a place where the children of poor working mothers would be safely taken care of but as a place where parents could turn for help with children who misbehaved, had eating problems, lacked play-mates or adequate play space, or needed more attention when a new baby was born into the family. Clearly, this shift in understanding the purpose of day care widened the range of people who saw themselves as potential clients of a day care agency.[70]

Some working-class women turned to the Neighborhood Centre Nursery School for the same reasons that their more affluent counterparts turned to private nursery schools: they wanted help carrying out the complex duties of modern motherhood and believed that the nursery school would be good for them and their children. For instance, Ethel Roszcuk became terribly jealous when her baby brother was born in 1926, and her mother, a single woman who supported herself sewing coats, was concerned. The Family Society, which supported the mother, wrote to Neighborhood Centre, "We thought it would be a good idea if Ethel could be admitted to the nursery school for a time, at least until she has gotten over to some extent being so tied up with her mother."[71] In a similar case, Faye Levinstein, who was troubled by her daughter Linda's eating habits and at the same time "much occupied" with the care of a new baby, told a visitor from Neighborhood Centre that "we could do her as well as child a great deal of good if we could take her into our nursery school." She explained that Linda almost "drove her crazy" during her pregnancy; the child was so disobedient that Mrs. Levinstein would lose patience and whip her, leaving both mother and child "in a state of exhaustion." Now, she explained, she was trying hard to train the baby to "avoid mistakes she made with Linda." The nurse at Babies Hospital, where Linda had attended a different nursery school, hoped that putting Linda in the nursery school at Neighborhood Centre would not only help Linda become a "normal child" but also enable Mrs Levinstein to give the baby better care. The family doctor concurred; remembering Linda as the child who always upset things when she came to his office, he told the social worker that "if a nursery could take her for a week or two and 'give her a piece of your mind,' it would do both the mother and child a great deal of good."[72]

The anxiety of "modern" motherhood also brought Anna Kelman to the nursery school, hoping for help with three-year-old Herbie's temper tantrums and disobedience. Rather than imitate Herbie's aunt, whom he obeyed because she "has him scared out of his wits," Anna sought a more scientific solution. In the words of the social worker who kept Herbie's records, his mother "has tried everything with Herbie, consulted physicians at Babies Hospital, she has read books, she has spoken to others about their children, trying to find some points of similarity so that perhaps she might learn what others did with their children. . . . Told us she tried to find 'psychological reasons' for Herbie's behavior." Unable to find answers either from doctors or from other mothers, "Mrs. Kelman said that she was on the verge of a collapse from worry because of her ineffectual treatment and because of strained relations between herself and husband. Mr. Kelman cannot understand why Herbie should be behaving as he does and feels that Mrs. Kelman is somehow to blame."

Caught between her inability to control her son and her husband's insistence that she do so, Mrs. Kelman turned to the Nursery School.[73]

Mothers such as these now had a place to go when they needed help with the work of mothering. But accepting the help of the nursery school often meant accepting one's own inadequacy as a mother, and agreeing to change. Some mothers were perplexed by the new demands placed upon them. Lena Kleinfelt, a substitute teacher who started bringing her daughter Pearl to the Nursery School in 1928, worried about her inability to control her child. Kleinfelt was more aware of trends in psychology and childrearing than most nursery mothers and sought a psychological diagnosis to explain her daughter's misbehavior. Social worker Helen Landis noted that Kleinfelt was "very proud of the fact that she has read many books on child training, however, it seems evident that she does not apply this reading in the case of her own child." Concerned with her daughter's thumb sucking and worried that the child was developing an "inferiority complex," she took Pearl to the Child Guidance Clinic. The social worker there recorded that she was "very anxious to know child's IQ, also to find out whether her methods of training child are correct." The psychiatrist at the Child Guidance Clinic decided that the problem was not with the child but with her mother. (As Kathleen Jones notes in her essay, this was a common diagnosis at child guidance clinics during this period.) Dr. Pearson reported that in their first appointment, Kleinfelt said that she did not understand "just what kind of work the clinic did. Was there anything wrong in the way she handled Pearl. She thought the clinic could do something with Pearl and apparently the object was to treat her instead." Although she tried to get some direct suggestions regarding her daughter's behavior, "he did not seem to want to talk about her but only about myself."[74]

Not every mother agreed to transform her mothering style in exchange for child care and professional advice. In some cases, nursery school staff found that training the mother was more difficult than training the child. Beatrice Cook, who was described as being "disturbed over her inability to handle" her son Mitchell, ran into conflict with the nursery school staff when she came to observe one day. Against the wishes of the teacher, she sat down and started to feed Mitchell his lunch, spoonful by spoonful, "commenting all the time how awful the food was and said she could not blame the child for not eating it." When the angry teacher, confronting her, asked what her reasons were for bringing the child to nursery school, she responded, "I would never have brought him had I been able to manage him myself." [75] Although she thought she needed help managing her son, she was unwilling to be guided by the teacher's professional advice.

In another case, we see that the idea that mothers had a right to some relief from caring for their children could be empowering. Mrs. Meltz, whose two sons attended the Nursery School, came into frequent conflict with the Neighborhood Centre social worker, who was frustrated with Meltz's lack of interest in improving her childrearing methods. One day the exasperated social worker asked Meltz "what she thought was being accomplished by keeping Isaac in school. 'I get a little rest,' she said promptly, 'you yourself say that is important.' Triumphantly, she said that." [76] Whether or not mothers decided to cooperate with the teachers, the Nursery School provided a welcome respite from, and help with, children they felt were beyond their control.

Even when women fully accepted the idea that they needed expert guidance, some family members believed that it was a mother's duty to raise her children without relying on outside help, expert or no. For instance, when Anna Kelman brought her Herbie to the Nursery School, she faced opposition from her husband, who said "that it was Mrs. Kelman's duty to raise Herbie." Mr. Kelman blamed his wife for the child's misbehavior and thought she should not rely on others to help her "fix" it. Anna, who feared that the boy's problems were putting a dangerous strain on her marriage, continued to send Herbie to the Nursery School, and her husband eventually became reconciled to the plan, although he refused to talk with the social worker. [77] Another story also suggests the difficulty that many women had negotiating conflicting definitions of a mother's responsibility, even years after the Nursery School had become a familiar part of the neighborhood landscape. When she first came to apply for care for her two-year-old son Joseph in 1941, Eva Weiss explained that she wanted him to attend the Nursery School for both economic and educational reasons: she wanted to work to supplement her husband's salary, and at the same time wanted to provide companionship for Joseph and enable him to learn "how to eat." Her image of the Nursery School as a place where children "have companionship of other children, and a place to play away from traffic" appealed to her, but the social worker noted that she seemed to fear the service as much as she wanted it. When asked how her husband felt about enrolling Joseph in the Nursery School, "she told us that he felt that she should be able to take care of him herself. That she might use such a service, only if she went out to work, but not to be rid of him." She seemed to accept this idea that day care was acceptable for working mothers, but not for any other reason, and once she gave up finding a job, she was consequently plagued with guilt at the idea (constantly reinforced by her in-laws) that she was trying to get rid of her son. The social worker noted, "Her guilt seemed so overpowering about the fourth week Joseph had been in school, we stopped her, and asked . . . whether NS was serving the purpose she wanted it to, and whether she felt that Joseph was getting something out of the experience. She burst into tears, and sobbed out that she was a bad mother." When she got control of herself, she explained that her in-laws had been "expressing their disapproval in strong language," and that she herself was confused about what she was doing. The social worker made a case for the educational value of the Nursery School, trying to convince Mrs. Weiss that part of a modern mother's responsibility was to provide a nursery school experience for her child: "We suggested that she think about it, in terms of education rather than of 'putting him away.' Could she duplicate the Nursery School environment in her own home? . . . She seemed to need help in recognizing the school as such, and not as a place to hide children by the day." But the conflict continued, and after much vacillation she finally decided to withdraw Joseph. She explained that she knew "she should be grateful for the opportunity of this service which is generally available only to the very wealthy," but that she realized the only time she had not felt guilty about it was during a brief period when she was employed. "The rest of the time she has been quite miserable and unhappy because she felt that everyone was critical of her."

Although Eva Weiss's problems clearly originated in a conflict between her family's ideas about total maternal responsibility and a more "modern" assumption that nursery schools were good for children as well as for mothers, the social worker summarized the case by blaming her. "Although Joseph was making progress in the Day Nursery and benefitting from the program," she wrote, "his progress was blocked by his mother's conflict about his separation from her and her need to have him dependent on her."[78] Eva Weiss faced a no-win situation: either she was trying to get rid of responsibility for her son, or she was not willing to give him up. While her family saw her as neglectful, the social worker saw her as smothering. No matter what she did, she could be condemned as a bad mother. In the end, however, her family's condemnation mattered more to her than the diagnosis of nursery school social workers.

By the time the mission of nursery school training and of parent education in general had become well known in the late 1930s, it was rare to find a family applying to Neighborhood Centre who defined their need for day care solely on financial grounds—even if financial reasons were in fact paramount. Every request for day care came to include some special need for the Nursery School, whether because of behavior problems, inadequate play space, or the need for group association. An analysis done by Neighborhood Centre staff in 1932 of forty-six families who applied to the Nursery School shows that the most common reasons for applying were the need for "habit training" (including food, social, emotional, and physical habits) and the need for the companionship of other children. But in most of these cases, these psychological reasons were accompanied by financial pressures making it necessary for the mother either to help her husband in his business or to work at an outside job.

As a nursery school serving a working-class neighborhood, the Neighborhood Centre Nursery School played a complex role in the upward mobility struggles of the families it served. Many of these second-generation immigrant families were on the road toward upward mobility, owning small stores or businesses and sending their children to high school and even college, but they still required a mother's labor (either in the family business or as an additional wage earner) to carry them through. The transition in class status that many of these families were hoping to make is reflected in the words of one child, who was questioned about his plans for the future during a psychological exam in 1937. First he told the examiner that "of course he was going to be a doctor." When she "suggested that this was a difficult profession to enter, he casually stated, 'Well, maybe I'll be a hosiery worker. Just like my father.' "[79] The Nursery School at once gave families like this boy's a "respectable" way to justify seeking day care that would enable mothers to work and at the same time offered them the comfort of knowing that their children were receiving the benefits of nursery school training, which was usually only available to more affluent families.

Indeed, calling on the help of psychologists and trained nursery school teachers may have become a symbol of middle-class American motherhood for these women, like relying on doctors for advice about the physical care of their children rather than turning to "remedies" from the old country or the advice of their own mothers. For many women, expert medical advice on mothering was an essential part of their definition as

American, modern mothers. One Jewish woman who raised her children in Philadelphia during the 1930s remembered, "Just because your mother and your grandmother did it, I didn't think that was the best thing. I was a modern mother and the modern way was to go to a specialist."[80] Ideas about how to discipline children had changed just as much as ideas about how to sustain their health, and modern mothers needed scientific expertise from professionals, not old-fashioned advice. Although the nursery school teacher did not have the cultural authority of the medical doctor, her advice could play a similar role, enabling the nursery school to become an emblem of modern, progressive, American mothering— unlike the day nursery with its taint of charity and poverty. Seeking professional help with the work of mothering, although it involved an admission of failure, could also be a sign of status, a way of distinguishing oneself from one's neighbors. For instance, Sophie Fineman, who helped her husband manage an apartment house near the settlement house, requested nursery school care for her two-year-old son because she did not want him to play with the "colored" children in the neighborhood.[81]

Both mothers and staff seem to have preferred the Nursery School's approach to taking on a mother's job to the more restrictive and less "modern" approach of the day nursery. Ultimately, however, the charitable agency which funded the settlement house was not willing to devote community resources to taking on the job of at-home mothers. The tension between the educational and the welfare purposes of the nursery became more prominent as the families who used Neighborhood Centre became more prosperous. Throughout the late 1930s and early 1940s, the staff and board members were clearly torn between a belief in the educative value of the Nursery School and an awareness of Neighborhood Centre's role as a social welfare agency, not a private school. While Nursery School staff believed in the value of their program and wanted to make it available to everyone, the funding agency's concerns about cost forced the settlement house to limit access to the Nursery School in 1941, and ultimately to eliminate the Nursery School itself, returning to a day nursery program for working mothers.[82] Nursery School parents protested the closing and the thinking behind it: they formed a "Committee to Save the Nursery School," argued with representatives of the funding agency that nursery school service was not a charity and should be available to anyone in the community who needed it (not just to the underprivileged families who were still eligible for the Day Nursery), and discussed running a nursery school themselves on a cooperative basis. At a meeting held by these parents, "The general feeling of the group was unanimous in preferring a N.S. to a Day Nursery if it was possible to have a preference."[83] The parents' efforts to save the Nursery School, however, were not successful. Like Eva Weiss's relatives, private charity officials believed in day care for working mothers, but not for anyone else. Nursery education would be a luxury available only to those who could pay for it.

Like the day nurseries, nursery schools could only justify their work by devaluing the work of mothers in the home and by arguing that mothers were incompetent to meet their children's most important needs without expert guidance. Both day nurseries and nursery schools sought to be "foster mothers" to children whose own mothers did not appear to be able to rear them properly, whether that was because they were out of the home earning wages during the day, because they did not know how to prepare nutritious meals or keep children clean, or because they did not know how to respond to temper tantrums or to signs of psychological maladjustment. While the assumption of maternal incompetence behind both types of programs could clearly damage mothers' faith in themselves and their mothering skills, however, it also made it possible to establish day care programs at a time when hostility toward the idea of maternal employment ran deep. By claiming that all mothers needed help in raising their children, supporters of day nurseries and of nursery schools simultaneously increased women's anxieties about their ability to mother their children, offered them respite from full-time motherhood, and lay the groundwork for broader claims for public support of child care in the future. In the long run, the idea that mothers needed help in rearing emotionally healthy children, that the home was not always the best environment for children, and that group care could be educational and desirable for children would alter the image of day care, legitimizing the idea of women's paid work, changing the grounds on which women could seek help with their children, and widening the circle of women who would consider using it. Thus despite its many damaging effects, the assumption of maternal incompetence that lay behind the development of child care programs in the early twentieth century could end up serving the interests of mothers and children as well as those of experts.

NOTES

I would like to thank Vanessa Davis, Jack Dougherty, Joel Harrington, Annette Igra, and the participants in the 1996 Berkshire Conference session at which an earlier version of this paper was delivered, for their questions and comments.

1. Neighborhood Centre (hereafter NC), Case 20, Neighborhood Centre Collection, Philadelphia Jewish Archives Center, Philadelphia. All names in case records have been changed to protect client confidentiality.

2. Social worker Mary Richmond, quoted in Martha May, "'Home Life': Progressive Social Reformers' Prescriptions for Social Stability" (Ph.D. diss., SUNY-Binghamton, 1984), 149.

3. The First Day Nursery was founded in 1863, but day nurseries did not become widespread in Philadelphia until the 1890s; the Philadelphia Association of Day Nurseries (hereafter PADN) was founded in 1898. See Elizabeth Rose, *A Mother's Job: The History of Day Care, 1890–1960* (New York: Oxford University Press, forthcoming) for more information on Philadelphia. In 1892 there were at least ninety nurseries across the country, and by 1912 there were five hundred. Anne Durst, "Day Nurseries and Wage-Earning Mothers in the United States, 1890–1930" (Ph.D. diss., University of Wisconsin, 1989), 134. See also Sonya Michel, "The Limits of Maternalism: Policies toward American Wage-Earning Mothers during the Progressive Era," in *Mothers of a New World: Maternalist Politics and the Origins of Welfare States,* ed. Seth Koven and Sonya Michel (New York: Routledge, 1993), 281.

4. The elite status of most day nursery managers is suggested by the fact that 70 percent of the officers of the PADN were listed in the exclusive *Social Register* or the *Blue Book* for Philadelphia.

5. Marian Newhall Horwitz, *Annual Report of the Franklin Day Nursery,* 1915, Urban Archives, Temple University Library, Philadelphia.

6. *Annual Report of the Baldwin Day Nursery,* 1917 and 1914, Lighthouse Collection, Historical Society of Pennsylvania, Philadelphia. Similar sentiments were expressed in other nurseries' annual reports, which also stressed the day nursery's importance as a surrogate home for children.

7. NC, Annual Report of Day Nursery, 1914. Although according to Kohn's own figures, no more than 25 percent of families applying for nursery care were headed by deserted women, she claimed in one report that 75 percent of nursery children came from homes which the father had deserted. NC, Annual Report of Day Nursery, 1914. Single fathers represented a tiny fraction of the families applying for day nursery care (averaging 1.8 percent at five nurseries) but were appealing figures to day nursery managers. Thus the Baldwin nursery's annual report in 1900 referred not only to "the widow and deserted mother" but also to the "much-perplexed and overwrought widower" as needing the nursery's help. The report did not include in this brief description of the nursery's clientele the

much more frequent cases of women who worked because their husbands earned insufficient wages. *Annual Report of the Baldwin Day Nursery,* 1900.

8. "Our History," reprinted in brochure for dedication of new building, March, 1956, Strawberry Mansion Day Nursery Collection, Philadelphia Jewish Archives Center, Philadelphia.

9. Neighborhood Centre Day Nursery (hereafter NCDN), Annual Report of Nursery and Shelter, 1914, 3; this phrase is also found in a 1919 report on child care.

10. NCDN, Annual Report of Nursery and Shelter, 1915, 6.

11. PADN, Minutes, March 21, 1923, Urban Archives. The "interests of the home" were clearly identified with the mother's presence there, not with the benefits her paid employment might bring to the home and the family.

12. Helen Glenn Tyson, *The Day Nursery in Its Community Relations* (Philadelphia, 1919), 35. From 1908 to 1931, nineteen out of the twenty-nine day nurseries that joined the Philadelphia Association of Day Nurseries reported hiring social workers; most of these were hired after 1920.

13. Alice Griswold, *Annual Report of the Franklin Day Nursery,* 1917.

14. A 1926 report of the Franklin Day Nursery commended the children's response to the patient training in obedience, honesty and cleanliness which is as important a part in Nursery work as the nourishing diet and rest. Child Federation, *A Study of the Day Nurseries of Philadelphia* (Philadelphia: Child Federation, 1916), 21.

15. Address to the PADN by Dr. Matilda Hunt of the Association of Maternity Welfare Centers for Great Britain, February 18, 1921.

16. *Annual Report of Franklin Day Nursery,* 1915.

17. *Annual Report of the San Cristoforo Day Nursery,* 1909, 6. Urban Archives.

18. NCDN, PADN *Joint Annual Report,* 1925.

19. The phrase "teaching ground" is from a report of the Willing Day Nursery in *Twenty-One Day Nurseries* (PADN Joint Annual Report, 1928), 51. Many nurseries also gave the mothers material so they could spend meetings making household items for their own use or costumes for the children's celebrations at the nurseries. Although many of the mothers' clubs were theoretically governed by the mothers themselves, their agendas seem to have been set in advance by nursery social workers who wanted the opportunity to instruct the mothers.

20. NCDN, Report of Family Worker, December 1927.

21. Julia Grant, in her study of mothers' clubs, suggests that in clubs organized for less privileged women, mothers "had to be trained to listen to experts." Mary Julia Grant, "Modernizing Motherhood: Child Study Clubs and the Parent Education Movement, 1915–1940" (Ph.D. diss., Boston University, 1992), 165.

22. Sunnyside Day Nursery, PADN *Joint Annual Report,* 1926. Topics discussed at the mothers' meetings held by the Neighborhood Centre house physician over the years included infant mortality, first aid to the injured, "The Province of the

Home," "Women in the World of Industry," children's behavior problems, and selecting toys for children.

23. NCDN, Annual Report, 1916.

24. Sister Frances Findlay to Sister Visitation, n.d., 5, Cathedral Day Nursery Collection, Archives of the Daughters of Charity of St. Vincent de Paul, Northeastern Province, Albany, New York.

25. See Ellen Ross, *Love and Toil: Motherhood in Outcast London, 1870–1918* (New York: Oxford University Press, 1993), 209–15, for a discussion of mothers' feelings about school medical inspections and for the argument that working-class mothers did not take seriously medical conditions that they did not consider to be possibly life-threatening.

26. PADN, Minutes, April 22, 1909.

27. First Day Nursery Visitor's Report, July 1919. First Family Day Care Association Collection, Urban Archives.

28. The Jewish Welfare Society, which had sent the home economist at the day nursery's request, wrote that the her visits were "helping Mrs. Grossman to become a home-maker." NC Case 837.

29. NC Case 751.

30. The social worker clearly felt that keeping the children clean was not enough. She had repeatedly visited the mother "for the purpose of instructing Mrs. Silver in how to obtain obedience from Pauline and Albert," and Mrs. Silver had repeatedly ignored the worker's suggestions by shouting at the children, threatening to put them in an orphanage, and giving them money to go to the movies. When Mrs. Silver came to talk to the worker at the office, knowing she was in for another round of criticism, she went on the offensive. The social worker reported, "She was very excited and said 'Youse have my children all day so why can't you train them? I am too nervous and they don't mind me.' She went on in this train for almost a half hour. She spoke at the top of her voice." The worker, who may indeed have been ready to give up on Mrs. Silver at this point, reminded her "that the children belong to her and that it is her duty to train them." NC Case 740.

31. For example, NC Case 998.

32. For instance, Rose Schwartz withdrew her daughter from the Neighborhood Centre when Marion Kohn, believing that Mrs. Schwartz's sexual behavior would cause the child to be "lost to Society," made a legal appeal to have the child taken away from her. NC Case 9. Likewise, a mother applying to the First Day Nursery withdrew her application rather than comply with the nursery's requirement that she vaccinate her baby. First Day Nursery Visitor's Report, July 1919.

33. They shared this hope with other "maternalist" reformers who devoted themselves to working for mothers' pensions, Americanization, public health clinics, and infant health campaigns. See Gwendolyn Mink, *Wages of Motherhood:*

Inequality in the Welfare State, 1917–1942 (Ithaca: Cornell University Press, 1995) for an argument about the racial dimensions of maternalist reform.

34. Kathleen Jones, " 'Mother Made Me Do It': Mother-Blaming and the Women of Child Guidance," in this volume.

35. *Infant Care* was first issued in 1914, and a version is still in print. Sociologist Julia Wrigley, in her analysis of over more than a thousand magazine articles about children, notes a rapid increase from the 1910s to the 1920s in the number of articles focusing on children's social and emotional development. Wrigley, "Do Young Children Need Intellectual Stimulation? Experts' Advice to Parents, 1900–1985," *History of Education Quarterly* 29, no. 1 (Spring 1989): 47.

36. Nancy Cott, *The Grounding of Modern Feminism* (New Haven: Yale University Press, 1987), 169. Emphasis in original.

37. John Watson, *Psychological Care of Infant and Child* (New York: W. W. Norton, 1928), 84–85.

38. Steven Schlossman, "Before Home Start: Notes toward a History of Parent Education in America, 1897–1929," *Harvard Educational Review* 46 (August 1976): 461.

39. Julia Wrigley, "Different Care for Different Kids: Social Class and Child Care Policy," *Educational Policy* 3 (December 1989): 427. The phrase "laboratory for parents" comes from Mary McElravy and Jean Van Note, "Laboratories for Parents," *Parents' Magazine* 19 (December 1944): 26.

40. Dr. Smiley Blanton, "Functions of the Nursery School," *Proceedings of the Conference of the National Federation of Day Nurseries*, April 1929, 17.

41. Quoted in Barbara Beatty, *Preschool Education in America: The Culture of Young Children from the Colonial Era to the Present* (New Haven: Yale University Press, 1995), 138–39.

42. Blanton, "Functions of the Nursery School," 16.

43. Remarks of Dr. Patty Hill, *Proceedings of the Conference of the NFDN*, 1929, 28.

44. Although the British nursery school run by Margaret McMillan, which had been the inspiration for some of these early schools, was seen largely as a health and welfare measure for poor children in a London slum, in the United States the nursery school was associated with relatively privileged families. By 1931, seventy-four American colleges and universities sponsored nursery schools. Lawrence Cremin, *American Education: The Metropolitan Experience, 1876–1980* (New York: Harper & Row, 1988), 302; Women's Bureau Bulletin 246, *Employed Mothers and Child Care* (Washington, D.C.: Government Printing Office, 1953), 13; Emily Cahan, *Past Caring: A History of U.S. Preschool Care and Education for the Poor, 1920–1965* (New York: National Center for Children in Poverty, Columbia University, 1989), 32. In Philadelphia, laboratory nursery schools were established at Temple University, the University of Pennsylvania, and at Drexel Institute of Technology; by 1951, many of the city's most exclusive private schools included

nursery school classes, and there were a number of independent private nursery schools as well. Clark Moustakas and Minnie Berson, *A Directory of Nursery Schools and Child Care Centers in the United States* (Detroit: Merrill-Palmer School, 1951) shows twenty-four private schools in the city limits, one cooperative nursery school, one public nursery school, and four laboratory nursery schools.

45. Immigrant and other working-class parents came into contact with Merrill-Palmer students through public health programs and nutrition classes but were not invited to use the nursery school. Kyle Ciani, "'Great, Wonderful Years': Professional Training at the Merrill-Palmer School, 1920–1940," presented at the Tenth Berkshire Conference on the History of Women, Chapel Hill, North Carolina, 1996. The first quote is from Florence Willson Duhn, a student at Merrill-Palmer in the late 1920s; the second is from the school's annual report in 1940. Ciani argues that the desire of child development researchers to study "normal" children (and together with the researchers' class- and race-specific definition of "normalcy") reinforced the tendency of university-based nursery schools to serve native-born white, middle-class and professional families. Hamilton Cravens makes a similar point about the Iowa Child Welfare Research Station in *Before Head Start: The Iowa Station and America's Children* (Chapel Hill: University of North Carolina Press, 1993).

46. Grant, "Modernizing Motherhood," 222.

47. *Proceedings of the Conference of the NFDN,* 1929, 16–17.

48. Ethel Howes, "The Nursery School," *Woman's Home Companion* 50 (December 1923), cited in Wrigley, "Different Care for Different Kids," 427.

49. Blanton, "Functions of the Nursery School," 23.

50. Blanton, "Functions of the Nursery School," 16–20.

51. This tendency to treat day nursery children as an undifferentiated group must have been shaped by the fact that day nurseries typically had many more children per staff member than did nursery schools. The size of groups and the ratio of staff to children varied enormously, but a model nursery school, such as the one conducted by Harriet Johnson in New York, had two teachers on duty for a group of eight children (with a third teacher whose time was devoted to record keeping), while the typical day nursery belonging to the Philadelphia Association of Day Nurseries had about three adults to minister to a group of fifty children. Harriet Johnson, *Children in the Nursery School* (New York: John Day Company, 1928), xviii; Rose, *A Mother's Job,* chap. 2. The contrast between children's experiences in good nursery schools and in day nurseries is echoed today in ethnographer Sally Lubeck's contrast between a middle-class preschool and a Head Start program. Children in the preschool that Lubeck observed were encouraged to make individual decisions about how to spend their time and were urged to act on their environment, whether by painting at the easel or playing with sand. Children in the Head Start program, however, were treated as a group, taught to take responsibility for each other, and spent as much time in group

activity as the preschool did in individual play. Sally Lubeck, *Sandbox Society: Early Education in Black and White America, A Comparative Ethnography* (Philadelphia: Falmer Press, 1985).

52. This privileging of middle-class parents as more promising targets of professional attention is clear at the Merrill-Palmer School, where students did some outreach work with working-class families, but faculty reserved their real attention for the "cream of the crop" parents in the nursery school and in local child study groups. Ciani, "'Great, Wonderful Years.'"

53. Beatty, *Preschool Education in America*, 139.

54. Quoted in Beatty, *Preschool Education in America*, 139.

55. *Day Nursery Bulletin*, November 1927.

56. Beatty, *Preschool Education in America*, 141.

57. Blanton, "Functions of the Nursery School," 22.

58. Preface to Josephine Foster and Marion Mattson, *Nursery School Procedure* (New York: Appleton, 1929), ix.

59. Harriet Johnson, *Children in the Nursery School* (New York: John Day, 1928), 97–98.

60. Cott, *Grounding of Modern Feminism*, 197; Lois Scharf, *To Work and To Wed: Female Employment, Feminism, and the Great Depression* (Westport, Conn.: Greenwood, 1980), 32.

61. This phrase was used by Paul Klapper in the preface to Foster and Mattson, *Nursery School Procedure*, ix; Harriet Johnson wrote, somewhat defensively, "we are not proposing to substitute the nursery school for the home." Johnson, *Children in the Nursery School*, 98. Abigail Eliot, founder of the Ruggles Street Nursery School, told an interviewer that many social workers were hostile to the nursery school idea, fearing that it would "undercut family life." James Hymes, Jr., *Early Childhood Education Living History Interviews, Book 1: Beginnings* (Carmel, Calif.: Hacienda, 1978), 20. By defending mothers who used nursery schools, of course, nursery educators were also defending their own belief in the value of the nursery school experience.

62. Mothers whose children attended cooperative nursery schools often found that their involvement in these schools amounted to a full-time job in itself. Beatty, *Preschool Education in America*, 166.

63. See Kathleen Jones, "'As the Twig Is Bent': American Psychiatry and the Troublesome Child, 1890–1940" (Ph.D. diss., Rutgers University, 1988) and her essay in this volume.

64. Several day nurseries in Philadelphia started nursery schools as part of their program in the mid-1920s. These included San Cristoforo, Willing, Joy, and Sunnyside Day Nurseries; the nursery school at Sunnyside was used for observation by students at Temple University until Temple established its own nursery school in 1929. Temple University College of Education, Annual Reports, 1927 and 1929, Templeana Collection, Temple University Library, Philadelphia.

65. One of its founders wrote in 1910 that the organization's mission was "to make of the children good American citizens, to imbue them with the best American ideals." Another said proudly, "We have helped to rear a generation of American citizens imbued with a serious purpose and realizing the responsibilities of citizenship." *History of the Young Women's Union of Philadelphia, 1885–1910* (Philadelphia: Young Women's Union, 1910), 3, 15. Neighborhood Centre Collection, Philadelphia Jewish Archives Center.

66. Although the majority of Neighborhood Centre clients continued to be factory workers or skilled laborers, there was a definite increase after 1925 in the proportion of parents who owned small family businesses or worked at sales and clerical jobs, as well as of those who owned their homes or prolonged their children's education.

67. NC Nursery Report, October 1928.

68. NC Nursery Report, December 1928.

69. NC Nursery Report, December 1928.

70. Indeed, in one case, a Neighborhood Centre board member applied to place her grandson in the Nursery School during the summer while the university-affiliated nursery school he usually attended was closed. Before the creation of the Nursery School, it would have been unthinkable for a board member to consider enrolling a member of her family in the Day Nursery. NC Case 1118.

71. NC Case 1033. The father had deserted the family, and the new baby was the result of a relationship with another man who had promised to help the mother out financially.

72. NC Case 1137.

73. NC Case 1152.

74. NC Case 1064. For more on the treatment of mothers in child guidance clinics, see Jones, "'As the Twig Is Bent,'" and Margo Horn, "The Moral Message of Child Guidance, 1925–1945," *Journal of Social History* 18 (1984): 25–36.

75. NC Case 1187.

76. NC Case 1239.

77. NC Case 1152.

78. NC Case 1325.

79. NC Case 1132.

80. Jacquelyn Litt, "Mothering, Medicalization, and Jewish Identity, 1928–1940," *Gender and Society* 10, no. 2 (April 1996): 188 and passim.

81. NC Case 1249. Similarly, Evelyn Platsky, who requested care for her Samuel because she was needed to work at the family store, later explained that all her difficulties with him were related to the bad influences of the neighborhood, from which she hoped to segregate him by sending him to the Nursery School. And a third mother explained that her child needed the freedom to run around in the Nursery School, for he could not play in his neighborhood: "He is not allowed out because they live in a very poor neighborhood where the children are

left on the street unkempt and ill while parents are working or in taprooms." NC Cases 1427 and 1193. Jacquelyn Litt describes how some of the women she interviewed distanced themselves from women (often non-Jews) who did not rely as much on doctors and modern medicine. For instance, "this one neighbor who lived next door to me was not like I was. I mean, she didn't believe." Litt, "Mothering, Medicalization, and Jewish Identity," 194.

    82. NC Nursery School Annual Reports, 1939, 1940, and 1941.

    83. NC Nursery School Annual Report 1942.

Chapter 5

"Mother Made Me Do It"
Mother-Blaming and the Women of Child Guidance

Kathleen W. Jones

In January 1935 a junior high school teacher, frustrated by her inability to motivate eleven-year-old Richard Bush, urged Richard's mother to consult the staff of Boston's preeminent child guidance clinic, the Judge Baker Guidance Center.[1] Amelia Bush agreed. Richard was lazy; he did not apply himself in school, at least not to the degree his IQ tests suggested possible. Apparently well versed in the modern child sciences, Richard's teacher suspected undetected emotional troubles and recommended the best diagnostic and treatment program for juveniles that Boston had to offer.[2] Since 1917, the Judge Baker clinic, directed by child guidance pioneers William Healy and Augusta Bronner, had provided Boston with "state of the art" psychological studies and therapy for children from all walks of life. With support from the Commonwealth Fund (one of several private philanthropies financing child health and welfare programs in the early twentieth century) the child guidance movement spread nationwide in the 1920s. When Richard Bush was first tested at the Judge Baker, child guidance was a flourishing service industry, sustained by more than two hundred separate specialized clinics, as well as the requisite professional journals and an active professional organization, the American Orthopsychiatric Association.[3]

In 1935, about half the cases seen at the Boston clinic arrived via juvenile court referrals or by way of local welfare agencies, child-saving operations that sought help in placing dependent and delinquent youths in suitable homes or institutions.[4] The search for solutions to the juvenile delinquency problem had provided the impetus for the child guidance movement after World War I, and work with social workers and probation officers constituted an important part of the clinic's mission. An equally large proportion of the cases resembled that of Richard Bush. They were children whose troublesome behavior came to the attention of school officials or youths whose actions so deeply annoyed parents that outside intervention seemed the only solution. While referrals from public institutions most often represented the children of Boston's working classes, self-referred clients such as Amelia Bush more frequently came from families with some degree of financial comfort. The misbehavior that brought self-referred parents to the Judge Baker might be, as in the Bush case, school-related; truancy, disruptive classroom behavior, or failure to perform were common teacher complaints. General adolescent unruliness, defiant behavior, and instances of sexual impropriety were also patterns of behavior that brought children and adolescents to the Judge Baker Guidance Center. Though not a delinquent, Richard was a typical troublesome child, and the issues raised in his case were representative of the Judge Baker case load during the 1930s.

A disproportionately small number of cases came from African American families, while the ethnic mix of cases paralleled that of the Boston population. In this essay, when I speak of the mothers at the clinic, I refer primarily to those who were white, sometimes ethnically identified, and from families who could not be classed as "dependent" on social welfare. Amelia Bush, therefore, typified mothers who made requests for Judge Baker services.

Typical also was the "interpretation" of Richard's problems arrived at by the child guidance team of psychiatrists, psychologists, and social workers, who tested and interviewed each child and collected additional information from parents and other concerned agencies before developing a diagnosis and plan of action. The clinic's experts quickly located the source of Richard's laziness in the unresolved emotional problems of his mother. Richard's case thus came to exemplify a pattern of parent-blaming that dominated early child guidance work, a pattern that subordinated other factors to the critique of motherhood.

Both in its multiprofessional structure (the "team" of experts) and its theoretical orientation, the child guidance movement had been committed from its inception to an eclectic interpretation of causation. Mental incapacity, emotional disturbances, environmental influences, or physical disabilities were given equal weight as contributing factors in the development of troublesome behavior. By the time Richard and his mother made their way to the Judge Baker clinic, however, the staff was working within a new paradigm. Although officially embracing child guidance eclecticism, the clinic experts now assumed that parental attitudes best accounted for a child's misbehavior. In more than 60 percent of the new cases opened at the Judge Baker clinic during 1935 practitioners located the source of the problems in faulty family relationships.

Child guidance professionals from all fields spoke of flawed parental attitudes, yet even as they used the generic term, these professionals took aim at one parent in particular. During these decades clinic practitioners participated in the development of a harsh critique of American motherhood, which emerged in the 1930s as the essence of child guidance and child psychiatry. Mother-blaming dominated explanations of childhood neuroses and psychoses at mid-century, and continues yet to influence interpretations of juvenile behavior. Wartime worry about latchkey children and ego-deficient servicemen, and postwar concerns about maternal deprivation and the schizophrenogenic mother had their roots, in the United States, in the diagnoses of the child guidance clinics of the 1920s and 1930s. A clustering of research and theoretical explanations—studies often based on clinic case records—surfaced during those two decades, admitting to child guidance vocabulary new terms, including maternal overprotection, overdirection, maternal rejection, dominance, and affect hunger. Drawn from the conceptual framework of psychoanalysis, the new vocabulary expressed the unique concern of child guidance professionals with the emotional environment created by mothers.[5]

How did motherhood so quickly and so easily become the target of child guidance professionals, and in what ways did this critique of motherhood mediate the relationship between mothers and experts? To understand why child guidance framed juvenile misbehavior as a consequence of pathological motherhood the place to begin is in the clinic, observing the interactions of the professionals with clients like Amelia Bush and her son. I will argue that the critique of motherhood benefited both child guidance experts and their clients; mother-blaming spoke to the needs of two groups of women, the mothers and the female social workers who treated them.[6]

The Judge Baker staff followed normal procedures during the first appointments with Richard and his mother. A staff psychologist examined the boy, using a variety of tests for intelligence and aptitude, and agreed that Richard was a markedly intelligent youngster. Other, less readily apparent sources for Richard's poor grades had to be sought. The physician/psychiatrist's medical examination at first suggested the possibility of an endocrine deficiency, but further probing pointed the psychiatrist to less biological reasons for Richard's sluggish behavior. After the physical, the boy told his "own story" to the doctor—a procedure developed by Judge Baker director William Healy during his initial work with juvenile delinquents twenty years earlier. A conversation with Richard told Dr. Finley, the staff psychiatrist, that the boy was normally fond of his mother, and the doctor picked up no evidence of rivalry with his brothers for her attention. To the psychiatrist, Richard seemed like a normal, gregarious youth, although he did display a "puzzled wonder" about his parents' divorce.[7]

The multicausal approach to behavioral problems developed by William Healy during the Progressive Era, incriminated everything from intellectual ability to impoverished home life, caffeine, "mental mechanisms" (Healy's term for psychoanalytic constructs such as sublimation), or parental mismanagement. Physical complaints were certainly credible explanations of misbehavior, and doctors at the Judge Baker considered the condition of tonsils, eyes, and glands in their search for motivation. By the mid-1930s, endocrinology was quite popular in some psychiatric circles, and in recommending glandular studies as one aspect of Richard's therapy, psychiatrist Finley was taking the basic eclectic approach to problem behavior.[8]

Sibling rivalry, however, was a new concern and a new diagnostic concept in the 1930s, symptomatic of a new emphasis in child guidance on perverted family relations as a source of troublesome juvenile behavior. Many professional childrearing experts were beginning to recognize the serious hindrance to healthy personality development caused by the jealousy and competition between brothers and sisters for the affection of parents and especially of mothers. When Finley found no evidence of rivalry in Richard's story, the staff turned to other avenues of investigation—beginning with (and ending at) Richard's mother.[9]

While Richard was speaking with the staff psychiatrist, Amelia Bush talked to one of the clinic's social workers. This division of labor was firmly established in child guidance procedure in the 1930s: psychiatrists and psychologists met with and tested the children, and social workers concentrated on building a "social history" of the problem by talking to other family members, and principally to mothers. Psychiatric social workers at the Judge Baker were all women, many of whom were trainees from local college social work programs. The one who talked to Richard's mother was a student practitioner, probably from Simmons College, although the Smith College social work program also sent students for a school year of internship at the Judge Baker Guidance Center. Her report, as were the records kept by most of the social workers, was exceptionally thorough.[10]

The story Amelia Bush told her social worker immediately set off alarms. Amelia reconstructed the tale of her marital breakup and revealed that her marriage at a young age had thwarted plans to attend college. She also explained that, although she and her sons were able to live in relative comfort in a nice residential area, she was currently attending secretarial classes and planning to find work, now that her youngest child was nine. The divorce, the unhappiness with her present life as full-time mother, coupled with Amelia's comparison of Richard's personality and appearance to that of her own father led the social worker to see here a woman who could use some help adjusting to her own situation, regardless of the trouble Richard was experiencing at school. With this information the clinic staff swiftly altered the direction of the inquiry from a question of school performance to a problem of the boy's emotional insecurity and the mother's personality maladjustment and concluded that a causal connection existed between Richard's lack of application and the dissatisfaction of his mother. In conference, the three staff members formulated several recommendations for Richard and his mother based on this finding: the endocrine study, a grade advancement to supply more educational challenge, and, most important, regular visits to the clinic for psychotherapy for both mother and son. At a follow-up appointment the student social worker presented these suggestions to Amelia Bush and anticipated the scheduling of future sessions with this client.

Up to this point in the case file the relationship between the Bushes and the clinic reflected the experiences of the hundreds of families who turned to the Judge Baker for childrearing assistance. The clinic reformulated the annoying childhood behavior in the language of family dynamics, muted its critique of motherhood in conversation with the clients, and made an offer of individualized therapy for both parent and child. In the mid-1930s, when Amelia Bush contacted the Judge Baker Guidance Center, clinic sessions for mothers as well as children had become an accepted part of therapeutic practice. Treatment suggestions in the Bush case followed standard clinic procedure.

Amelia Bush, however, was not a standard, compliant patient. Although she had answered the social worker's questions, Amelia made known her misgivings about psychiatric evaluations and expressed her belief that Richard simply would outgrow his unwillingness to work in school. She neither questioned her competency as a mother nor believed psychiatry should uncover hidden feelings, and she rejected the clinic's recommendations for "family guidance" (the term used in child guidance circles to designate the work they believed necessary with parents). She had come to the clinic, as did many other parents, looking for specific advice to alleviate a problem she felt she fully understood. Rather than a recasting of the issues, Amelia wanted to pacify school authorities and expected from the psychiatric professionals a plan that meshed with her interpretation of Richard's behavior, and with her maternal self-perception. She agreed to the grade change, rejected the endocrine study as just a "fad," pressed the doctor for concrete reasons to continue Richard's interviews, and reluctantly agreed to only one more session for herself. The student social worker called on the psychiatrist to press the clinic's view. According to the social worker's detailed record of the conversation, Dr. Finley, exasperated by this mother's skepticism, told Amelia "quite frankly" that "really *she* was the basis of the whole problem" (emphasis added). If Amelia "could work out her problem and past difficulties and see the relationship that they had with [Richard's] present difficulties, it might not even really be necessary to have [Richard] come in."

As the Bush file indicated, by the mid-1930s the crux of child guidance, the theoretical framework that supported the whole structure, was a stinging critique of mothers. Mothers, as Dr. Finley so bluntly put it to Amelia Bush, had become "the basis of the whole problem." From the files of new cases seen at the clinic in 1935, I chose to narrate this one simply because Amelia Bush's recalcitrance forced such explicit statements of ideology from the psychiatrist and social worker. Clients more compliant than Bush appear only to have been less forcefully advised of their culpability. Culpability, however, was a given, and, as in the interview with Amelia Bush, mothers were clearly prompted by questions that elicited evidence of flawed or faulty family relations and personality maladjustments. It was so obvious to the clinic staff that Amelia caused her son's lack of progress in school, that once this mother rejected a therapeutic relationship with the clinic, no further action was taken on the supplementary recommendations. In 1935, the staff of the Judge Baker clinic agreed with child guidance experts throughout the United States that some forms of mothering were potentially dangerous to the well-being and future happiness of the children. Amelia Bush would not (indeed, could not) be helped with her son's laziness if she rejected this basic postulate.

Child guidance professionals were convinced that they saw the results of poor mothering "with monotonous regularity." "Selfish, demanding, undisciplined" youngsters formed a significant part of the clinic's caseload.[11] Support for the critique of motherhood came from every child guidance discipline. The behaviorist John B. Watson dedicated his book *Psychological Care of the Infant and Child* (1928) to the first mother capable of bringing up a happy son or daughter, but then proceeded to question the likelihood of such an event. Mothers, Watson believed, treated their offspring with too much affection and stifled their independence. Sociologist Ernest Groves called motherhood quite simply "pathological." Child guidance researcher Mary Sayles, who analyzed two hundred cases from several child guidance clinics, concluded that even "normal" parental love could cause a child to behave badly. How much worse then was "exaggerated parental love"? Among the work of psychoanalysts, J. M. Flugel's *The Psychoanalytic Study of the Family* (1921) was regularly cited as a source; Flugel observed that a "nagging or over anxious mother" would frequently produce a "rebellious son or daughter . . . [who] may even become unfit for taking their place in any scheme of harmonious social life." Such comments were ubiquitous in the professional literature of child guidance, and the popular press concurred. Mothers were to blame for the emotional and behavioral problems modern children presented to adult authorities.[12]

Researchers and clinicians alike in the 1920s and 1930s focused primarily on the effects of "maternal overprotection," which signified a woman's intense involvement with the demands of mothering, often to the exclusion of other important emotional relationships. This involvement might be communicated either as domineering, intrusive behavior or as overindulgent, structureless childrearing which gave in to every childish whim. According to New York City child psychiatrist David Levy, who first identified "maternal overprotection" in 1929, the picture was "well portrayed by a mother who holds her child tightly with one hand and makes the gesture of pushing away the rest of the world with the other."[13] Ernest and Gladys Groves, in more graphic commentary, described her simply as the "octopus-mother," who was "unwilling to hand her child over to other people, save to be admired as her creation."[14] In either case, the result of faulty mothering was an unhappy, maladjusted child who had not developed proper ego strength, was not normally emancipated from the family, suffered feelings of inferiority, compensated for that inferiority through acts of rebellion, and ended up at the child guidance clinic.

Richard's lackadaisical attitude and Amelia's talk of thwarted ambitions were symptoms of maternal overprotection, although the Judge Baker staff did not use these specific words in their records of the Bush case. Other cases from the Judge Baker files showed the range of maternal behavior clinicians deemed emotionally destructive. There were infantilizing mothers, one of whom was discovered by the staff holding the hand of her ten-year-old son as though he were no older than five; or watchful mothers given to intervene when children faced risky situations, such as the woman who denied her son a bike because they lived near a street trafficked by automobiles.[15] Some mothers simply "mothered" too conscientiously, dressing and feeding children beyond the age of infancy, cajoling and nagging school-age youths about being on time and doing homework. Maternal overprotection was a useful catchall to describe patterns of "too much" involvement in the emotional tasks of mothering, behavior that appeared to the child guidance staff to prevent children from developing strongly independent personalities.

Although discussions of overprotection were pervasive, child guidance professionals also identified other types of troublesome mothers in the 1920s and 1930s, women who generated problems for both their children and the clinic and contributed to the growing consensus surrounding maternal pathology. There was the type of mother who, the clinicians believed, simply wanted the latest diagnosis to share with her bridge club. For her, child guidance was just the latest fashion and not a serious attempt to confront troublesome juvenile behavior.[16] Mothers like Amelia Bush openly resisted the clinic's authority, while others passively rejected the clinic's help by skipping appointments. To us these actions might seem more bothersome than "pathological;" to child guiders the behavior spelled trouble and added further justification for the critique of motherhood.

More important for the developing consensus of pathology was the rejecting mother—difficult to define, wrote one observer of thirty-three cases, because maternal rejection "is a matter of degree."[17] All mothers might "reject" a child's demands at some point in childrearing, just as all mothers might occasionally "overprotect," without showing signs of morbidity. But the rejection the child guidance community worried about was more profound. Levy described its effects on the child as the creation of "affect hunger [meaning] an emotional hunger for maternal love and those other feelings of protection and care implied in the mother-child relationship," and he compared it to a "state of starvation."[18]

In the child, symptoms of rejection or affect hunger were similar to those of overprotection: too much aggression, or too little initiative. The similarities made precise diagnosis a tricky task and in the clinic setting, the subtleties of theory often eluded practitioners. At the Judge Baker, if a mother did not exhibit "overt rejection," her behavior was regarded as simple "overprotection" or "overdirection" and treated as such. In the mid-1930s clinicians used maternal overprotection as a diagnosis far more frequently than maternal rejection.[19] Levy, on the other hand, worried that cases of maternal overprotection were really masking rejection, that rejecting mothers compensated for guilt feelings by being overly solicitous (Amelia Bush might have fit this description). Making the distinction was significant for treatment, however, since practice seemed to prove that it was far more difficult to alter the behavior of rejecting than of overprotective mothers.[20] Whether diagnosing rejection or overprotection, child guidance professionals in the 1930s held American mothers accountable for the failure of their offspring to measure up against a standard for youthful independence, civility, and emotional maturity.

When investigating the emotional content of family relationships as a cause of troublesome juvenile behavior, child guidance professionals did not completely exclude fathers from the equation. But the authoritarian dad and the ineffectual male—the two masculine traits recognized as sources of childhood emotional problems—were quite often traced back to the errant mother.[21] Domineering wives, for example, created spineless husbands who stayed away from their children to avoid confrontations and thus deprived children of necessary guidance. In general, the criticisms of fathers lacked the refinement, the depth of support, and the sheer gusto child guidance experts gave to the critique of motherhood. Certainly clinicians saw mothers far more frequently than they did fathers; mother was the parent most likely to take a troublesome child to the clinic in the first place. But the explanation for this critique involves more than simple familiarity, or familiarity breeding contempt.

To be sure, this clinical critique was part of a broad devaluation of motherhood in the mid-twentieth century.[22] One argument frequently advanced to explain this devaluation attributes the behavior of the child guidance specialists to persistent male professional misogyny. Barbara Ehrenreich and Deirdre English, for example, present a model of medico-psychological experts who were determined to shore up patriarchal authority in the home, determined to bring maternal affection under the control of one "who would make it *his* specialty to tell the mothers what to do" (emphasis in the original).[23] Such an interpretation rests on two assumptions, the first of which is the presumed masculine gender of the professionals. Experts, in this argument, deliberately victimized mothers, because motherhood was a threat to the authority of male professionals, and because contemporary motherhood debased the power of men in the home. A finding of maternal pathology was, presumably, the first step toward reestablishing a "normal" gender hierarchy within the family. Secondly, such an argument assumes that there was no organized female opposition to the critique of "medico-psychological experts." With feminism seemingly in disarray after the passage of the suffrage amendment, organized womanhood offered no counters to the experts' accusations of maternal incompetency. Advice handed down was advice received, uncritically accepted, and debilitating for the average mother.[24]

Defense of motherhood might have been expected from the community of women reformers who built up a professional expertise around issues of maternal and child welfare. As several historians have argued, however, the professionalization of the women's reform movement seems to have been accomplished precisely through devaluation of the skills of individual mothers. Female experts defined poor mothers as incompetent child care managers and directed their expertise toward establishing the institutional structures necessary to provide these women with professional guidance. Although concerned primarily about the ineptitude of working-class mothers, these female experts also contributed to a pervasive critique of motherhood. Their contribution suggests that it was not the gender of the professional but professionalism itself that accounted for the disempowerment of mothers; skilled professional women, as well as men, earned legitimacy through devaluing the mothering skills of nonprofessional women.[25] Thus more recent women's history scholarship does little to challenge the pervasive explanation which finds professional self-aggrandizement at the root of attempts to discredit motherhood.

There is another, less politically charged though nonetheless gendered, explanation for the popularity of diagnoses of maternal pathology. This theory was popular *in the clinics,* where most child guidance professionals, male and female, worked and where the presumably pathological mothers of all classes sought help. It is at this local level that we must seek the reasons for the pathological-mother diagnosis. The answer lies in its functionality. Maternal pathology was a useful designation for the psychiatrists and social workers. In designing and applying labels of protection and rejection, representatives of the two professions differentiated the boundaries of their clinical responsibilities. The professionals, however, were not the only beneficiaries of the critique of motherhood. Morbid motherhood was a useful diagnosis, too, for the families investigated by the child guidance professionals.

A clear weakness in previous efforts to explore the meaning of the critique of motherhood is the absence of the voices of its "victims." Did the women diagnosed as pathological mothers simply absorb without question the harsh name-calling of the professionals? Or would their side of the story cast the critique of motherhood in a somewhat different light? The tales in the Judge Baker records suggest the need for another look at the professionals' conspiracy to usurp parenting authority.[26]

In the first place, some mothers, like Amelia Bush, simply refused to be engaged by the clinic's analysis and recommendations. If there was no organized feminist opposition to the critique of motherhood, there were certainly individual women who objected quite strenuously to the staff's diagnosis of their culpability. "I'm not on trial here," one told her social worker, "I'm not the problem." In response, the clinic staff concluded that the mother's rejecting personality was just "not modifiable" and closed the file without further action. This mother's behavior did not suggest intense anxiety about maternal fallibility, despite the troublesome behavior of her child. It might have been related to cost, especially during the Depression years, or, as was noted in some records, to a father who intervened and discouraged contact with the clinic. More likely, failure to continue with the clinic's treatment program represented at least in part a grass-roots unwillingness to concede the diagnosis, even by mothers whose children were annoying enough to lead them to child guidance services. Parent wishes and clinic diagnoses frequently did not mesh, and the dissonance created the disappearing patient.[27]

While some rejected the clinic's "interpretation" and disappeared quickly from the records, another set of mothers became clinic regulars, kept scheduled visits, and formed tight therapeutic relationships with members of the clinic's staff. But here too the stories in the files suggest that continued contact with the clinic may have had little to do with acceptance of a diagnosis of maternal incompetence. They show, instead, a desire to manipulate the therapeutic interviews with social workers. By assigning the labels of pathological motherhood, the clinic provided some women with an opportunity to sort out questions about husbands and marriage, issues they distinguished from ones that concerned the welfare of their children.

The social and economic context in which many of these women lived helps to explain the personal dilemmas they faced and the manner in which they secured support from the clinic. Above all, they represented Boston's middle classes. Those who voluntarily sought the clinic's help generally had the financial resources to pay for the services of child guidance practitioners, and quite likely the leisure time to avail themselves of the clinic's offer of therapy.[28]

They were also women coping with unfamiliar childrearing pressures. Already in the 1920s middle-class families had begun to worry about some new and rather troubling behavior in their offspring. Nationwide, otherwise "normal" adolescents pushed parents to the limit over use of the family car, unchaperoned dating, and new forms of entertainment and attendance at movies. Families at the clinic reported similar conflicts. Parental strictures from the generation before seemed woefully out of date to "modern" mothers, who turned for advice to everyone from the local minister to the syndicated column in the local paper. For mothers, parenting a modern child *was* stressful; a protective stance easily might have been read as a quite logical desire to reassert control over socialization in an age of uncertain cultural values. At the very least their childrearing concerns were legitimate and grounded in social reality, no matter what emotional attitudes might underlie their requests for help.[29]

Furthermore, these were women whose lifestyle suggested that they rarely questioned normative middle-class gender roles. The two-parent household with a male breadwinner and a stay-at-home mother was still the basic framework of the family for these women. Yet their expectations of family life had begun to change, to include a greater degree of intimacy between husbands and wives. According to the popular press, middle-class marriages were to be "companionate" or "democratic," meaning that women expected to spend more time with their spouses and expected spouses to devote their leisure time to the family. While feeling pressed to meet these new standards of domestic felicity, middle-class women also found that their traditional role—the care of home and family—had lost its allure. Modern motherhood lacked the excitement of the working girl's independence and easy sexuality. Middle-class mothers in the files of the Judge Baker clinic were caught in the trap of modernity. Self-fulfillment conflicted with the traditional satisfaction in maternal self-sacrifice; companionate marriages upped the ante for personal gratification.

For some of these women the diagnoses of rejection and overprotection made possible the voicing of complaints and the negotiating of personal accommodations. The Judge Baker clinic offered its pathological mothers several treatment options, ranging from advice and encouragement to intense psychotherapy. Each of the options assured the women of frequent contact with a social worker. Their troublesome children drew them to the clinic, but once enmeshed in the clinic's procedures, the maternal pathology label enabled them to articulate the broader dimensions of dissonance in their lives.[30]

Superficial advice—practical suggestions and reassurance—was offered most often. Social workers simply gave out tips designed to make children more independent, such as the advice to the mother of a lazy and thus frequently tardy fourteen-year-old: she was told to purchase an alarm clock and return "all waking responsibilities" to her son.[31] Even when direct advice seemed to the clinic the best solution to the child's problem, mothers might channel the prescription to their own ends. A woman rejected as a candidate for intensive therapy was nonetheless allowed to set appointments according to her "feeling of need." In this instance, need dictated twenty-six additional visits, interviews she used to report on her situation and garner emotional support.[32]

"Insight therapy," pioneered by David Levy in his work with overprotective mothers, was a more intense approach than advice giving, one designed to elicit the mother's understanding and acknowledgment of a connection between her child's behavior and her own attitudes.[33] From the case records at the Judge Baker it is difficult to determine exactly how the practicing social workers distinguished "insight" therapy from advice giving. But one example suggests that a perception of the possibility for change was a determining factor. The stepmother of a sulky, disobedient eleven-year-old with violent temper tantrums was at first "encouraged" "to express her own unhappiness and dissatisfactions," and in doing so to recognize the relationship between her emotions and her treatment of the boy. But the staff declined to pursue these issues, because "it might be better not to stir up conflict which can in no way be improved under the present situation. . . . As long as her attitude does not seriously interfere with the boy's mental development, it would be wiser to leave her more or less alone."[34] Insight therapy represented a halfway point between programs to simply modify behavior and plans designed to generate self-awareness. In this case, however, the stepmother was not looking for self-awareness. Instead she vented her anger at a husband who preferred bridge and golf to helping her with the children. From her perspective, the clinic increased her husband's awareness and his attentiveness, even if the boy's behavior remained virtually unchanged.

Far more intensive, and reserved for only a small portion of child guidance clients was "attitude therapy," a technique in which client and social worker agreed to use the regular appointments for "free elaboration of [the mother's] feelings." Successful completion required two or three sessions a week, over a two-year period, and David Levy, who named the procedure, preferred to save attitude therapy for use in "cases where treatment of the child failed because of problems in the mother."[35] Although this specific label was not available in 1935, the staff of the Judge Baker clinic sometimes debated the appropriateness of a case for intensive psychotherapy. It was, however, a procedure only infrequently attempted. Professionals at the Judge Baker apparently believed they were designing treatment programs to expose a mother's contribution to her child's problems rather than recognize her (separate) emotional needs. As in insight therapy, the clinic identified the problem in terms of the child's needs; it was the mothers who reconfigured the therapeutic relationship.

Some mothers found that their experience at the clinic did allow them to devise new standards of parental authority and that it provided some respite from the trials of parenting the modern child. Few matched the gratitude of a Kingston mother who sent the staff an invitation to her son's wedding and an announcement of the birth of a grandchild, and, during an impromptu visit to the clinic in 1944, mentioned plans to change her will and leave a bequest to the Judge Baker Guidance Center. More common was the woman who referred to the clinic as her "safety valve."[36] Follow-up reports collected in 1940 and 1941 do tend to suggest that the youngsters and their parents usually survived adolescence satisfactorily.

Quite a few mothers, however, also found the clinic helpful with more than just the trials of parenting. They manipulated the structure of treatment—the regularly scheduled conversations with a social worker—to focus attention on the anxieties of modern marriage and family life. And the manipulation was tacitly agreed to by their female social workers.

"It has been obvious from the very beginning," observed Katherine Moore, a social worker at New York's Institute for Child Guidance in 1933.

"[M]others tended to use the interviews consciously or unconsciously for their own purposes aside from help with the child."[37] At the Judge Baker, husbands and sex made up the bulk of the complaints. Comments on men who failed to share responsibilities and provide companionship for their mates were matched by expressions of dislike for sexual intercourse. Sex was something many of these women endured rather than enjoyed, at a time when messages from movies, advertisements, and marriage manuals promised only pleasure in the marriage bed. In January 1935, the mother of a high school junior observed to her Judge Baker social worker that she had been talking very little about her son in recent interviews and much more about herself and her marriage. Reassured by the worker, this mother continued to describe her husband's immaturity and lack of ambition, her thoughts of a legal separation, and her rejection of his sexual attentions. "M[other] says she feels better after talking about things that are bothering her," the social worker wrote for the record. She felt she could not "do this with friends," but talk with the social worker was "different."[38]

Some clients thus saw their patient status as an opportunity to examine their lives as women, not just their performance as mothers. Although the interviews may have confirmed for child guidance experts the general incompetency of American motherhood, mothers understood the process quite differently. This is not to suggest that Judge Baker clients were in fact "maladjusted," but they were, some of them at least, certainly unhappy in family settings that restricted outside activities, demanded a difficult-to-attain companionship between husband and wife, or created a perhaps unrealistic measure for sexual satisfaction. For these mothers the clinic's critique of motherhood offered a chance to talk about their concerns and voice their misgivings in a conservative fashion that would rarely threaten the family status quo.

The clinic staff offered women no innovative solutions to the problems they faced: children continued to be the focus of the therapy and continued to dominate the team's overall perspective on motherhood. Neither suggestions for medical studies in cases of sexual dysfunction nor recommendations for psychotherapy beyond that provided by the clinic can be found in the case records. Although work outside the home might have served to lessen the emotional bonds between mother and child, social workers did not champion careerism. Child guidance experts, even in the 1930s, continued to wonder why mothers would voluntarily choose paid labor over domesticity. Nor did the staff urge divorce in cases of clearly

mismatched husbands and wives (although social workers did not intervene in the few instances when women chose this path). Instead, the
professional literature recommended a strengthening of the husband-wife
bond as a cure for an overly intense mother-child relationship, and the
Judge Baker social workers followed that line. In most instances the clinic
staff provided a sympathetic ear and advised mothers to strive for some
form of accommodation. But it would be unrealistic to say that these
women wanted more from the clinic. The minimal benefits enabled some
of them to use the misbehavior of their children to take stock of their
personal situations and to discover private, individual adjustments to
widely shared problems.

The new status of the mother in child guidance practice—as etiologi-
cal factor in juvenile misbehavior and as patient—was also instrumental
in resolving the discontents of another group of women. Psychiatric social
workers, a group largely female in the 1920s and 1930s, shaped a separate
professional identity in the child guidance clinics out of their association
with the middle-class, self-referred pathological mothers. Social workers
had been part of the child guidance team from the first, serving as
gatherers of information about the child's social environment and as the
clinic's liaison with the child's family or the referral agency. To their
dismay, women in this profession often found themselves functioning as
mere "errand girls" for the psychiatrist-directors, their skill at gathering
"social histories" insufficiently valued as child guidance became more and
more enmeshed in the emotional factors causing juvenile misconduct.[39]
During the 1920s social work leaders began to magnify the therapeutic
importance of their interviewing techniques. They incorporated the
teachings of psychoanalysis into social work training, and along with the
child psychiatrists, narrowed the definition of "environment" to the primary familial relationships. The changes had taken place mainly in eastern clinics, where observers in the 1930s found the new techniques and
theories of the psychiatric social worker in some ways indistinguishable
from those of the psychiatrist. As measures of specialization became
blurry, professional boundary discussions began to appear at professional
meetings and in print, discussions sometimes described as acrimonious.
The new-style social worker thus threatened to disrupt the interprofessional harmony of the child guidance team.[40]

The critique of motherhood helped to establish the grounds for continued cooperation at the Judge Baker and other child guidance clinics. The
two competing groups of professionals preserved occupational distinc-

tions by identifying separate therapeutic spheres of interest. Psychiatrists continued to work with the mind of the child, while social workers handled the attitudes of the mothers. A social work-sponsored study of cases at the Judge Baker clinic in 1932–33 showed that mothers who were child guidance patients saw psychiatrists only infrequently, and that many of the children of these mothers received no psychiatric therapy. The new-style social workers had acquired much greater responsibility at the clinic, much greater professional prestige, and a sharper focus for specialization as a result of the pathological mother.[41]

In sum, labeling the mothers as pathological promised immediate benefits for two groups of women at the Judge Baker clinic. Both middle-class, self-referred mothers and social workers found in the new procedures temporary means to resolve issues of powerlessness, in relationships with husbands and children, or in alliance with the psychiatric professionals. These benefits help explain the persistence of the diagnosis, but the critique of motherhood remained just that: a damning indictment of maternal emotions. Neither group of women emerged empowered by it in the long run.

The qualified independence in clinic procedure did not resolve all issues of professional identity for the psychiatric social workers, for the position of psychiatrist in this new team effort in family guidance remained the favored one. As the diagnosis of pathological motherhood became more entrenched, social workers took on a greater share of the clinic's workload. Yet while social workers carried out the "insight" or "attitude" therapy, staff psychiatrists maintained careful direction of the treatment. David Levy was quite specific about the professional hierarchy: "The social worker must be trained, as she is, to recognize the limitations in her therapy and to have free recourse to the psychiatrist. As an independent method out of contact with a clinical group [attitude therapy] may be used indiscriminately and destructively."[42] Social workers may have established their specific expertise, but this did not generate professional autonomy. Moreover, the construction of attitude therapy, for use "where treatment of the child failed because of problems in the mother," limited the psychiatrists' responsibility for the continued misbehavior of their juvenile clients.[43] Social work could be held accountable if a child's behavior remained unchanged, since mothers caused the emotional turmoil and social workers were their therapists. "Case closed" because of an "uncooperative mother," leaving a "poor prognosis" for the child, was a familiar refrain in the clinic's records. Child psychiatrists had won the authority to define the causes of the emotional and behavioral problems of youngsters, yet they had shed the responsibility for producing solutions. In the child guidance industry social workers became the work force, while psychiatrists were management.

For mothers, however, the consequences of the critique of motherhood are harder to measure and the lines of authority were less clearly established in the relationship between experts and clients than between professions. The case files show that accommodation, rather than autonomy, independence, or self-awareness, was quite likely the principal accomplishment of child guidance therapy. The clinic's services enabled some women to adjust to dysfunctional family situations, or at least to survive the parenting phase; they showed their gratitude and respect for the clinic's services by recommending it to friends and relatives. Former, and presumably satisfied, patients helped to build the clinic's reputation in the Boston community. More important, the complicity of these mothers helped to solidify child guidance adherence to parent-blaming. Building on the research of the 1930s, child psychiatrists in the post-war period continued to popularize and implement the critique of motherhood until two chroniclers of psychiatric history would write in 1966, "The mother-child relationship is so important for ensuing pathology that it has probably received more attention than any other aspect of child psychiatry." [44]

Just how completely, however, did this critique succeed in undermining the resiliency of the mother of the "everyday child"? [45] To what extent did women absorb and replay this power dynamic that blamed "bad" mothers for producing children with emotional and behavioral flaws and equated a competent mother with one who sought out professional guidance? By the 1940s a few professionals expressed concern about the effects of the critique on individual mothers. Leo Kanner, whose work situated the etiology of autism in the critique of motherhood, also published *In Defense of Mothers* (1941) to shore up maternal "common sense," weakened, he believed, by the fanaticism of the "more zealous psychologists." [46] Yet Kanner's book, like Dr. Spock's similarly focused *Baby and Child Care* (1946), also stressed the important role medical and psychiatric experts should play in childrearing. Both books might well be read as indicators of professional insecurity. They were efforts to reassure professional experts of their authority in the home as well as attempts to confront the presumed fears of the average mother.

In addition, the case records at the Judge Baker clinic would seem to modify at least partially the conviction that professional attitudes and advice generated less confident mothers. In fact, the critique of motherhood seemed virtually powerless against some intrepid spirits, like Amelia Bush, who persisted in trusting their abilities as mothers. These women came to the clinic in search of specific solutions to behavioral problems, and when the child guidance team began to reinterpret the question so as to reshape not just the child but the parent too, they left. The disappearance of clients from the records—the unfinished cases, the unanswered letters, the broken appointments—suggests that the critique of motherhood had not seeped very far into maternal consciousness. The authority of child guidance and psychiatric professionals was limited, even among that class of Boston women specifically targeted by the Judge Baker staff. The stories of the "bad" mothers who stuck with the clinic, returning for appointments and meeting the staff's expectations of the compliant patient, also raise questions about the degree to which women identified with the child guidance representation of motherhood. The diagnosis of overprotection or rejection generated an opportunity for therapy; how these mothers used that opportunity was often at odds with the staff's understanding of the needs of the children.

This essay does not begin to address the public policy implications of the child guidance perspective on pathological mothering; were we to examine the uses of these images in labor, education, or welfare policies the implications of the critique of motherhood would appear less benign. Instead I have used the case records to explore the private consequences of the child guidance critique of motherhood. The relationship between cultural representations of motherhood and the personal experience of mothering clearly deserves further investigation, but the behavior of the Judge Baker mothers cautions against making a simple assumption of correlation.

NOTES

1. Judge Baker Guidance Center, Case Files, Francis A. Countway Library of Medicine, Boston, Mass., case file 9201. All references to case material used in the research for this paper refer to the Judge Baker collection. The reference numbers used here are the numbers noted on the original files. All names are fictitious to protect patient confidentiality, but I have tried to remain faithful to the stories as told by the parents and children and recorded by the clinic's staff. Patient files consist primarily of the reports of psychological and medical examinations; the accounts of the psychiatrist's interviews with the child; notes from social workers

recounting conversations with parents, relatives, and concerned social agencies; plus case conference notes, periodic updates on the status of the case and in most instances, follow-up material collected in 1940–41. In addition, the files contain letters to and from the clinic, court or agency reports, and miscellaneous material—Christmas cards, photographs, and so on—indicative of the quality of the relationship between clients and the clinic's staff. They are an immensely rich resource for study of the origins of modern psychiatric expertise. This essay is based on a reading of 345 records, all representing new cases opened during 1935.

2. "Child sciences" is Hamilton Cravens's term for psychology, psychiatry, pediatrics, and education—the fields of study that, in the first half of the twentieth century, professionalized the child-saving reforms of the Progressive Era. See Cravens, "Child-saving in the Age of Professionalism, 1915–1930," in *American Childhood: A Research Guide and Historical Handbook,* ed. Joseph M. Hawes and N. Ray Hiner (Westport, Conn.: Greenwood Press, 1985), 415–88.

3. The background for this essay appears in my book *Taming the Troublesome Child: American Families, Child Guidance and the Limits of Psychiatric Authority* (Harvard University Press, forthcoming). See also two recent studies which explored the history of the child guidance movement, setting it in the context of early twentieth-century philanthropy: Theresa Richardson, *The Century of the Child: The Mental Hygiene Movement and Social Policy in the United States and Canada* (Albany: State University Press of New York, 1989); and Margo Horn, *Before It's Too Late: The Child Guidance Movement in the United States, 1922–1945* (Philadelphia: Temple University Press, 1989).

4. "Child-saving" is a term coined by Anthony Platt and used pejoratively to describe the interventionist efforts of turn-of-the-century reformers to control the lives of lower-class families, and in particular, to instill middle-class values in their children. See *The Child Savers: The Invention of Delinquency,* 2d ed., enl. (Chicago: University of Chicago Press, 1977). I use the term in a neutral spirit, as descriptive of what the reformers thought they were doing, irrespective of their actual motivations or consequences.

5. Philip Wylie's *Generation of Vipers* (New York: Rinehart, 1942) grotesquely exaggerated and popularized these ideas. On mother-blaming after World War II, see Elizabeth M. R. Lomax, Jerome Kagan, and Barbara G. Rosenkrantz, *Science and Patterns of Child Care* (San Francisco: W. H. Freeman, 1978). Also useful is Denise Riley's study of post–World War II Britain, *War in the Nursery: Theories of the Child and Mother* (London: Virago Press, 1983). Paula J. Caplan's studies suggest how little has changed. See her essay "Mother-Blaming" in this volume; Paula J. Caplan and Ian Hall-McCorquodale, "Mother-Blaming in Major Clinical Journals," *American Journal of Orthopsychiatry* 55 (1985): 345–53; and Caplan's more popular study, *Don't Blame Mother: Mending the Mother-Daughter Relationship* (New York: Harper and Row, 1989).

6. This essay owes a great deal to the questions raised by Meryle Mahrer

Kaplan in *Mothers' Images of Motherhood* (New York: Routledge, 1992). See also Maxine Margolis, *Mothers and Such: Views of American Women and Why They Changed* (Berkeley: University of California Press, 1984); and Susan Contratto, "Mother: Social Sculptor and Trustee of the Faith," in *In the Shadow of the Past: Psychology Portrays the Sexes; a Social and Intellectual History,* ed. Miriam Lewin (New York: Columbia University Press, 1984), 226–55.

7. The four-part, three-professional diagnostic procedure distinguished child guidance work from other arenas for psychiatric treatment of children. In 1940 a Commonwealth Fund study reported the existence of over six hundred child-focused psychiatric clinics; the label "child guidance" was reserved for those utilizing psychology, psychiatry, and social work professionals. See Helen Leland Witmer, *Psychiatric Clinics for Children* (New York: Commonwealth Fund, 1940). The tripartite professional structure emerged from William Healy's work with Chicago delinquents and it was recreated in the Commonwealth Fund's "demonstrations." A useful contemporary description of the "team" can be found in George S. Stevenson and Geddes Smith, *Child Guidance Clinics: A Quarter Century of Development* (New York: Commonwealth Fund, 1934).

William Healy spoke of his conversations with delinquents as listening to the child's "own story." By the second decade of the century listening to patients certainly was not novel in psychiatric circles. Healy, however, with one foot in medicine and the other in the domain of the child-savers, privileged the child's voice to a much greater degree than most in the child welfare field. Juvenile Court judge Ben Lindsey utilized a similar style in his Denver courtroom, eliciting the trust of the boys brought before him through friendly conversation and a willingness to listen. Healy's account of the significance of his contribution is in William Healy and Augusta F. Bronner, "The Child Guidance Clinic: Birth and Growth of an Idea," in *Orthopsychiatry, 1923–1948: Retrospect and Prospect,* ed., Lawson Lowrey and Victoria Sloane (New York: American Orthopsychiatric Association, 1948), 3–49. James Bennett, *Oral History and Delinquency: The Rhetoric of Criminology* (Chicago: University of Chicago Press, 1981), 111–22, discusses Healy's concept of the child's "own story" in the context of other oral history takers in social work and criminology.

8. William Healy outlined this eclectic approach to interpretations in child guidance in *The Individual Delinquent* (Boston: Little, Brown, 1915), his path-breaking study based on work at the Juvenile Psychopathic Institute in Chicago. It owed much to the ideas of Adolf Meyer, the most influential early twentieth-century American psychiatrist, whose theories of "psychobiology" stressed the interaction of psychological and biological factors in mental illness and personality problems.

9. Alfred Adler, physician and disciple of Sigmund Freud, promulgated a theory of hostile, jealous sibling relationships in the early 1920s. American psychiatrist David Levy coined the term "sibling rivalry." Drawing his inspiration

primarily from Freud and Adler (Levy was among the first to attempt scientific trials of Freud's theories), Levy developed a series of directed play experiments to study "motivation in social relationships," primarily family relationships. Children were induced to play with an "amputation doll"—a mother figure—and her celluloid baby, and encouraged to act out hostility by tearing the dolls apart limb by limb. Levy's experiments were published collectively as *Studies in Sibling Rivalry* (New York: American Orthopsychiatric Association, 1937). Peter N. Stearns discusses the history of sibling rivalry in *Jealousy; The Evolution of an Emotion in American History* (New York: New York University Press, 1989), 88–100.

10. Roy Lubove's *The Professional Altruist: The Emergence of Social Work as a Career* (Cambridge: Harvard University Press, 1965) is still one of the best introductions to the history of social work. Elizabeth Lunbeck, in *The Psychiatric Persuasion: Knowledge, Gender, and Power in Modern America* (Princeton: Princeton University Press, 1994), uses a gender analysis to explore the relationship between psychiatrists and social workers in a psychopathic hospital.

11. The quotes came from David Levy's study *Maternal Overprotection* (New York: Columbia University Press, 1943), 160. Levy's book represented a compilation of his research begun in the late 1920s and it served to codify a diagnostic category used widely by child guidance professionals throughout the 1930s.

12. John B. Watson, *Psychological Care of Infant and Child* (New York: W. W. Norton and Company, 1928); his chapter is entitled "The Dangers of Too Much Mother Love." The theme pervades the work of Ernest R. Groves and Gladys H. Groves; see particularly *Parents and Children* (Philadelphia: J. B. Lippincott, 1928), 116. Mary Buell Sayles, *The Problem Child at Home* (New York: Commonwealth Fund, 1932), 25–32. Sayles called the phenomenon "exaggerated solicitude" (116). See also Douglas Thom, *The Everyday Problems of the Everyday Child* (New York: D. Appleton, 1928), 36–37. J. M. Flugel, *The Psycho-Analytic Study of the Family* (London: Hogarth Press and the Institute of Psycho-Analysis, 1960, reprint 1921), 46. In this same passage Flugel also condemned authoritarian fathers. While fathers did come in for some criticism, American child guidance experts made motherhood their special preserve. A good summary of the impact of psychoanalytic ideas of family dynamics in theories of juvenile behavior is Percival Symonds, *The Psychology of Parent-Child Relationships* (New York: D. Appleton-Century Company, 1939). Symonds credited Flugel's influence on American thinking about family relationships (5), and researchers tended to reference Flugel's book more frequently than any of Freud's own writings.

13. Levy, *Maternal Overprotection*, 36–38. David Levy and a bevy of student social workers at the Institute for Child Guidance in New York City developed the criteria for diagnoses of maternal overprotection. According to their work, such a diagnosis could be based on any one of four qualities of mothering: (1) excessive contact ("the mother is always there"), (2) infantilization ("she still

treats him like a baby"), (3) prevention of social maturity ("she won't let him grow up"), and (4) inadequate or inappropriate maternal control (behavior that was either domineering or overindulgent).

14. Ernest R. Groves and Gladys Hoaglund Groves, *Wholesome Parenthood* (Boston: Houghton Mifflin Company, 1929), 244.

15. Judge Baker Guidance Center, case files 9220, 8122.

16. Such a mother is described by Leo Kanner, *Child Psychiatry* (Springfield, Ill.: Charles C. Thomas, 1935), 20.

17. H. W. Newell, "The Psycho-dynamics of Maternal Rejection," *American Journal of Orthopsychiatry* 4 (1934): 387–401.

18. David Levy, "Primary Affect Hunger," *American Journal of Psychiatry* 94 (1937): 643–52.

19. Only a few cases of maternal rejection were recorded in my sample from 1935. See the Judge Baker Guidance Center, case files 9212; and 9274, overt rejection of a "fat, unlovable" female adolescent. Maternal rejection as a clinical concept was more fully developed after World War II, when psychiatrists worked with children orphaned during the war and reared in institutions, discovered symptoms of "maternal deprivation," and extended these specific findings to the average family.

20. For his study Levy claimed to have selected only "pure" cases of overprotection, in which the child was a "wanted" child. In the case of an unwanted child, he argued, overprotective behavior masked maternal rejection. *Maternal Overprotection*, 18.

21. Ibid., 150–55. On representations of fatherhood during these years, see Robert L. Griswold, *Fatherhood in America: A History* (New York: Basic, 1993), 88–118.

22. Ann Douglas discusses this devaluation in *Terrible Honesty: Mongrel Manhattan in the 1920s* (New York: Noonday, 1995).

23. Barbara Ehrenreich and Deirdre English, *For Her Own Good; 150 Years of the Experts' Advice to Women* (Garden City, N.Y.: Anchor/Doubleday, 1979), 196. Christopher Lasch, in *Haven in a Heartless World: The Family Besieged* (New York: Basic Books, 1977), made a similar argument, laying blame for the demise of the family at the feet of intrusive professional experts.

24. For the power and influence of a separate female political culture in the early twentieth century, a power that was justified in part by the domestic imagery of Victorian motherhood, see Paula Baker, *The Moral Frameworks of Public Life: Gender, Politics and the State in Rural New York, 1870–1930* (New York: Oxford University Press, 1991); Robyn Muncy, *Creating a Female Dominion in American Reform, 1890–1935* (New York: Oxford University Press, 1991); and Linda Gordon, *Pitied But Not Entitled: Single Mothers and the History of Welfare, 1890–1935* (New York: Free Press, 1994). Settlement house workers and suffragists alike proclaimed that the problems of city and state were only those of the home writ

large and observed how badly these institutions "needed their mother." The quote is from Rheta Childe Dorr, *What Eight Million Women Want* (Boston: Small, Maynard, 1910), 327.

Feminist unity, built around the drive for suffrage, splintered in the 1920s after the passage of the Nineteenth Amendment. Although feelings of female political independence and power were at first widespread and the flapper arose as the symbol of the new sexual freedom of young women, organized feminism appeared to disintegrate. On feminism in the 1920s, see Nancy F. Cott, *The Grounding of Modern Feminism* (New Haven: Yale University Press, 1987). Julie Weiss, "Womanhood and Psychoanalysis: A Study of Mutual Construction in Popular Culture, 1920–1963" (Ph.D. diss., Brown University, 1990), contends that the absence of a feminist movement permitted the psychoanalytic restructuring of female roles in the 1930s and 1940s, and motherhood was one facet of the restructuring. With no feminist movement to refute the critique of motherhood, individual mothers were left to fend for themselves (unsuccessfully) against the growing obsession with maternal pathology.

Exactly how a feminist movement might have countered the critique of motherhood is unclear. Feminist analysis of motherhood during the most recent women's movement of the 1970s seems to have had only a nominal impact. A content analysis of articles in contemporary child psychiatry journals shows continued widespread mother-blaming. It seems unlikely, therefore, that the absence of a feminist movement can explain the growth of the maternal pathology diagnosis in earlier decades. See Caplan and Hall-McCorquodale, "Mother-blaming in Major Clinical Journals."

25. Both Muncy, *Creating a Female Dominion in American Reform*, and Molly Ladd-Taylor, *Mother-Work: Women, Child Welfare, and the State, 1890–1930* (Urbana: University of Illinois Press, 1994), make this argument.

26. Linda Gordon, in *Heroes of Their Own Lives: The Politics and History of Family Violence: Boston, 1880–1960* (New York: Penguin Books, 1988), demonstrates that clients used welfare agencies for their own purposes, as does Michael B. Katz in *In the Shadow of the Poorhouse: A Social History of Welfare in America* (New York: Basic Books, 1986).

27. Judge Baker Guidance Center, case file 9274. Examples of paternal negativity can be found in files 9241, 9269, and 9288.

28. The quote is from a description of Levy's work with mothers at the Institute for Child Guidance in New York City. See Lawson Lowrey and Geddes Smith, *The Institute for Child Guidance; 1927–1933* (New York: Commonwealth Fund, 1933), 44.

29. Robert S. Lynd and Helen Merrell Lynd, in *Middletown: A Study in American Culture* (New York: Harcourt, Brace and Company, 1929), and *Middletown in Transition: A Study in Cultural Conflicts* (New York: Harcourt, Brace and World, 1937), explored these generational tensions. On the challenge of youth

culture in the 1920s, see especially Paula Fass, *The Damned and the Beautiful: American Youth in the 1920s* (New York: Oxford University Press, 1977).

Similar dynamics were at work in working-class families. William I. Thomas described some of the dissonance in *The Unadjusted Girl, with Cases and Standpoint for Behavior Analysis* (Boston: Little, Brown, 1923). See Kathy Peiss, *Cheap Amusements: Working Women and Leisure in Turn-of-the-Century New York* (Philadelphia: Temple University Press, 1986); and Mary E. Odem, *Delinquent Daughters: Protecting and Policing Adolescent Female Sexuality in the United States, 1885–1920* (Chapel Hill: University of North Carolina Press, 1995).

30. This discussion of treatment protocols at the Judge Baker Guidance Clinic follows headings devised by David Levy, which included (1) direct advice and suggestion, (2) education (interpreting to parents the child's motives and reactions), (3) insight therapy (efforts to help mothers gain emotional insight into family relationships and their own particular maladjustments), and (4) attitude therapy (a more specialized form of intensive therapy with mothers). See Constance Rathbun, "An Evaluation of Factors Determining Outcome of Treatment in a Child Guidance Clinic" (M.S. thesis, Smith College School for Social Work, 1938), 42. Rathbun's study was a survey of eleven earlier theses discussing treatment regimes at Judge Baker as revealed in case records. Esther Heath, *The Approach to the Parent* (New York: Commonwealth Fund, 1933), also describes varieties of therapy available to social workers. See Margo Horn, "The Moral Message of Child Guidance, 1925–1945," *Journal of Social History* 18 (1984): 25–36, for another discussion of social workers and clients. Horn suggests that social work in the Philadelphia child guidance clinic was nondirective and nonjudgmental, and "showed a fundamental respect for the family's values and preferences."

31. Judge Baker Guidance Center, case file 9187.

32. Judge Baker Guidance Center, case file 9173. Advice could be coupled with more formal instruction for mothers. The Judge Baker clinic sponsored a series of lectures on childrearing topics, and notations in case files indicate that the clinic was holding a mothers' discussion group outside of the regularly scheduled therapeutic visits. Whatever the clinic's intentions, sharing and mutual support must have been one of the benefits of participation.

33. David Levy, "Attitude Therapy," *American Journal of Orthopsychiatry* 7 (1937): 111. Marion Kenworthy and Porter Lee, *Mental Hygiene and Social Work* (New York: Commonwealth Fund, 1929), 106–9 also discussed the need for "insight." (Kenworthy and Lee, like Levy, were associated with the Institute for Child Guidance in New York City.)

34. Judge Baker Guidance Center, case file 9212.

35. Levy, "Attitude Therapy," 103. See also Stevenson and Smith, *Child Guidance Clinics*, 92–93; and Kenworthy and Lee, *Mental Hygiene and Social Work*, 123–39. Judge Baker Guidance Center, case file 9271 shows the staff's reluctance to label the treatment as attitude therapy.

36. Judge Baker Guidance Center, case file 9204 (will); and 9202 (safety valve).

37. Katherine Moore, "A Specialized Method in the Treatment of Parents in a Child Guidance Clinic," paper read at the annual meeting of the American Psychiatric Association, Boston, June 1, 1933, quoted in Stevenson and Smith, *Child Guidance Clinics,* 92.

38. Judge Baker Guidance Center, case file 9271.

39. The phrase was used by Lois Meredith French in "Some Trends in Social Treatment" (1936), published in *Psychiatric Social Work* (New York: Commonwealth Fund, 1940), 203.

40. Ralph P. Truitt, "Relation of Social Work to Psychiatry," *American Journal of Psychiatry* 82 (1925): 104, called for the "alliance of forces" so that psychiatrists would not lose control of the clinic process. For a discussion of interprofessional rivalry among mental health professions, see Gerald N. Grob, *Mental Illness and American Society, 1875–1940* (Princeton: Princeton University Press, 1983), 234–65.

41. Helen Witmer, citing her survey from 1932, noted that at the Institute for Child Guidance in that year two-thirds of the "full-study" cases were handled exclusively by social workers, and in only 3 percent of the cases did a psychiatrist see a parent more than five times. Many children received no psychiatric treatment. Witmer, *Psychiatric Clinics for Children,* 345. Witmer cited an unpublished thesis by Margaret Quick from the Smith College School of Social Work, 1935, to show that a similar division of responsibilities occurred at the Judge Baker Guidance Center in 1932–33 (246). On the division of responsibilities, see the three papers presented as "Symposium: The Treatment of Behavior and Personality Problems in Children," *American Journal of Orthopsychiatry* 1 (1930): 3–60.

42. Levy, "Attitude Therapy," 106.

43. Ibid., 103.

44. Franz G. Alexander and Sheldon T. Selesnick, *The History of Psychiatry: An Evaluation of Psychiatric Thought and Practice from Prehistoric Times to the Present* (New York: Harper and Row, 1966), 383.

45. On the guilt and anxiety induced by the emotional needs analysis and by the psychoanalytic features of childrearing advice, see Nancy Pottishman Weiss, "Mother, the Invention of Necessity: Dr. Spock's *Baby and Child Care,*" *American Quarterly* 29 (1977): 519–46; and Michael Zuckerman, "Dr. Spock: The Confidence Man," in *The Family in History,* ed. Charles E. Rosenberg (Philadelphia: University of Pennsylvania Press, 1975), 179–203. "Everyday child" was from the title of Douglas Thom's popular book of childrearing advice, *The Everyday Problems of the Everyday Child.*

46. Leo Kanner, *In Defense of Mothers; How to Bring Up Children in Spite of the More Zealous Psychologists* (Springfield, Ill.: Charles C. Thomas, 1941), 14. In "Autistic Disturbances of Affective Contact," *The Nervous Child* 2 (1943): 217–50, Kanner attributed that disease to childrearing by a cold, rejecting mother.

Part II

The Middle Years

Chapter 6

Mother-Blaming

Paula J. Caplan

If you really want to know why this child is a mess, just
look at its mother!
— frequent, informal assessment by both real and
armchair psychologists

MOTHER-IN-LAW IN TRUNK
— seen on hundreds of car bumper-stickers

Start with this fact: in our society it is acceptable to blame Mom. Then
add the Perfect Mother and Bad Mother images, which lead us to blame
Mom for not being perfect when she doesn't live up to our idealized
image and, when she does something not so terrific, to blame her for
being horrible rather than only human. This set of practices plagues
mother-daughter relationships.

Most women are stuck in the mother-blaming mold. Journalist Zenith
Henkin Gross studied 121 women who described in depth their view of
their own mothers' mothering performance; only eight women — slightly
more than six percent — saw their mothers as admirable models to be
emulated.[1] This percentage is shockingly low in view of the intense social
pressure placed on girls to be "little mothers": their most salient model is
not regarded as a worthy one.

Mother-blaming is like air pollution. I live in a large city with moderate
pollution I rarely notice — until I get out into the fresh country air, when
I suddenly recall how good it feels to breathe really well. My students and
patients swear that getting away from mother-blaming helps them breathe
more freely.

The essential foundation for improving our mother-daughter relation-ships is a thorough understanding of mother-blaming, for only when we see how easy blaming mother is will we have a chance of doing otherwise. Only when we see the pollution can we clear the air.

We need to explore the fabric of our prejudices with care. We daughters can't expect to forget the irritating or infuriating things our mothers do and just focus on the wonderful ones. But we need to realize that our culture encourages us to focus *only* on our *mothers' faults* and to let their good points slip our minds. Blaming our mothers is so easy that we rarely stop to consider whether anyone else might be to blame, or even that no one is to blame. For us mothers, understanding how mother-blaming operates can lighten our load. After all, untapped energy is bound up not only in the daughter's mother-blaming but also in the mother's self-blame and self-hate.

The less a group is valued and respected, the easier it is to target its members as scapegoats. The undervaluing of mothers is revealed not just through anecdotes but also by hard facts. According to the U.S. Depart-ment of Labor, the skill level needed to be a homemaker, childcare attendant, or nursery school teacher is rated at 878 on a scale of 1 to 887, where 1 is the highest skill level! On this scale, the rating for a dog trainer is 228.[2] Apparently, the skill raters have never tried taking care of children! (With daycare now receiving more attention than in our mothers' child-rearing days, these ratings ought to increase.)

This undervaluing is largely a product of our times. Before the techno-logical revolution mothers did most of their work at home. Their children could see them "in the garden, in the yard, tending chickens, cleaning, laundering, cooking, preparing food, mending, sewing, hauling water and firewood—all obviously hard work," explains sociologist Jessie Bernard.[3] Now, however, mothers spend much of their time and energy trying to meet their children's emotional, psychological, and learning needs; they have nothing concrete, visible, and immediate to show for it—no woven shawls, no fresh eggs. Mothers now are often thought to spend most of their time doing nothing, or nothing of consequence.

How easily did our mothers' work become invisible! How easily did our mothers face the accusations of husbands who assumed women had nothing to do all day! "Why isn't dinner on the table? Why isn't the house in order? Why aren't the kids in bed?" Men wanted their needs met and discounted the fact that mothers were chauffeuring the children to and from school and activities, taking them to doctors' appointments, entertaining them and their friends, refereeing siblings' and neighbor children's conflicts, empathizing with the children about their minor and major life tragedies, and trying to give and receive a little support from other women who were also trying to be terrific mothers and terrified they weren't.

For women raising children today, the undervaluing of our mothering work has become more complex. Those of us with paid employment *may* feel valued in our work environments but often wind up feeling unappreciated for the enormous weight of our double load.[4] Mothering tasks, after all, are still believed to require little or no skill or effort. And hand in hand with mother-blaming goes a taboo against father-blaming.

My friend Mary is a busy psychologist, and her husband Steve is a surgeon. When Mary tired of making all of the travel plans for family vacations, she informed Steve that, for the next December holiday, she would leave all plans for their annual family ski trip to him. He made no plans. When she told him how disappointed she was, their six-year-old son said angrily, "*Don't* get mad at Daddy. He is a surgeon and he works very hard. He's so busy and important that he has to have a nurse *and* an assistant. He doesn't have *time* to make travel plans." And another son added, "That's right. And Daddy's so important that he even has a dictaphone. *You* don't have a dictaphone!" Many people hear such stories and just laugh, not recognizing how much the devaluation and blame can hurt.

Mother-work is not only undervalued but often unnoticed. Even an assembly-line worker in a boring factory receives a regular paycheck, which carries with it the message, "Someone values the work that you do." In contrast, not only are mothers not paid but also most of their boring or difficult work is unnoticed or made light of. What mother has had her children or husband say, "That was a great week's worth of dusting you did! Thanks!"?

You may feel that *your* mother doesn't go unnoticed. In fact, many women tell me that their mothers are "very strong women," as though that means that they are appreciated. That may be true in some cases, but if you think of your mother as strong, be careful: that image is often another way to brand mothers negatively—"Oh, don't worry about my mother. She comes on like a Mack truck!" When we unthinkingly describe mother as strong, we often focus on her power to make us put our dirty clothes in the hamper or make us feel guilty; we don't recognize that she has no power outside the home. Quite possibly, she receives no respect or appreciation even in the home, only mockery and fear.

People whose eyes tear up when they talk about "motherhood" or when they talk *about* their own mothers often treat their mothers with disdain when they are face-to-face. Paradoxically, motherhood *in principle* and *in general* is described in glowing, all-important terms—so that mothers feel ashamed to complain about their low status *in fact* and *individually*.[5]

During the 1950s, an era now infamous for the popularity of the image of happy-little-wife-at-home, author Philip Wylie pulled together every demeaning image of mothers and gave them ugly, vicious form. In his *Generation of Vipers,* his loathing of mothers vibrates with intensity, and although this book is painful to read, we need to know that it was popular when mothers were raising the children who are now in their thirties and forties:

> Megaloid momworship has got completely out of hand. Our land, subjectively mapped, would have more silver cords and apron strings crisscrossing it than railroads and telephone wires. Mom is everywhere and everything and damned near everybody, and from her depends all the rest of the U.S. Disguised as good old mom, dear old mom, sweet old mom, your loving mom, and so on. . . .
>
> . . . Nobody among [American sages]—no great man or brave—from the first day of the first congressional meeting to the present ever stood in our halls of state and pronounced the one indubitably most-needed American verity: "Gentlemen, mom is a jerk."
>
> . . . [Mom used to be so busy with childraising and housework] that she was rarely a problem to her family or to her equally busy friends, and never one to herself. Usually, until very recently, mom folded up and died of hard work somewhere in the middle of her life.
>
> . . . Nowadays, with nothing to do, and all the tens of thousands of men . . . to maintain her, every clattering prickamette in the republic survives for an incredible number of years, to stamp and jibber in the midst of man, a noisy neuter by natural default or a scientific gelding sustained by science, all tongue and teat and razzmatazz.[6]

Wylie's words continue to be widely quoted, used as justification for mother-trashing, used to make men feel ashamed of loving their mothers and of refusing to revile them, used to make women feel that mother love is sick, since who in their right mind could love the kind of creature Wylie so vividly described? Even people who never read Wylie's actual work are familiar with the essential features of his mother images.

Wylie coined the term *momism,* which became widely used to refer scathingly and fearfully to mothers' allegedly excessive domination, reflecting Wylie's own attitude toward mothers.[7] To this day, mother-blaming perpetuates "momism" in a different sense, one that parallels other "isms": sexism, racism, ageism, classism. Perhaps it is time to use the word *momism* to label mother-blame and mother-hate explicitly and succinctly as a form of prejudice as virulent as the other "isms" are acknowledged to be.

In subsequent years, mother-hating books like *How to Be a Jewish Mother* and *Portnoy's Complaint* appeared.[8] How well I remember reading *Portnoy's Complaint* and then, when discussing it with friends, realizing that I was supposed to say I thought it was funny and rang true, although clearly a *little bit* exaggerated (most mothers don't actually wield a large *knife* over their children's heads to make them eat!). Anyone who said that the author of *Portnoy* had cruelly defamed mothers, and Jewish mothers in particular, was accused of having no sense of humor, of not being a good sport. Thankfully, by the late 1960s and early 1970s, expressing anti-Black sentiments publicly was becoming *déclassé* (although racism itself persisted and persists, of course); but it remained acceptable to say venomous things about Blacks as long as they were Black *mothers* or about Jewish mothers, Italian mothers, Catholic mothers, funny old grannies, or mothers-in-law. So racist statements about Blacks or other people of color were on their way out, as were anti-Semitic comments, but only when they were about groups (sex unspecified) or about males. This pattern continues today. Jokes about mothers and mothers-in-law, as noted earlier, are far more common than jokes about fathers and fathers-in-law. And it is a terrible thing to be a mother and know that you are expected to find them funny, that you are not supposed to be deeply hurt by them, that to be hurt is to be overly sensitive—or ridiculous.

Once we're aware that mother-blaming comes easily and that it distorts our view, we can begin to catch ourselves doing it. A friend who knew that I was writing this book explained,

> I couldn't sleep last night. I kept thinking about my 85-year-old mother. She's in a nursing home, and she's very ill and may not live much longer. Every time my sister and I talk on the telephone, we moan and groan, saying, "Do you know what she said to me today!? She asked me why I'd had my hair cut so short! Do you believe it? Why doesn't she leave us alone?!"
>
> I kept thinking about the things she says to me that make me crazy, and

about the things I wanted her to do that she'd never done. Then, I thought about your book, and I sat up in bed and asked myself why I always focus on the ways she has failed or upset me. Why do I never think about the good things she's done for me? And I started remembering how, after my husband and I split up, she came and stayed with the children and me and helped to take care of us. I thought of all the things she had done over the years to make my life easier or to make me laugh.

This woman has begun to see the mother-blaming mold in which her experience has been shaped, and she understands that this threw her mother's love and humor into shadow while turning the spotlight on her mother's weak points. Whether or not she suspects it, she may be using mother-blame to avoid her fear of her mother's impending death.

Mother-Blaming All Around

If you are a daughter, don't think that it's only you—or other daughters—whose view of mothers is distorted. Mother-blaming is interwoven throughout our daily lives. At every level of conversation and discussion, in every conceivable arena, mothers are ignored, demeaned, and scapegoated—in jokes (often unfunny), on bumper stickers, on television and at the movies, in works by popular authors, in our own families, in the research literature, in the courts, and in psychotherapists' offices.

Our everyday language reflects this pattern: try to think of terms that are as demeaning to fathers as everyday terms like "son of a bitch." Even for expressions that are not profane, such as "mama's boy," the parallel "daddy's girl" is not really equivalent. "Mama's boy" calls up images of a smothering, overprotective mother whose "boy" seems psychologically sick, or at least unmanly and ridiculous, through his association with her. A "daddy's girl," on the other hand, is the lucky, feminine daughter who has been singled out by the high-status parent. At worst, she might be thought of as overly reliant on her "feminine wiles." [9]

Mockery of mothers is a staple of feature films. In the popular movie *Dirty Dancing*, hilarious laughter greets the stand-up comic who says, "I finally met a girl exactly like my mother—dresses like her, acts like her. So I brought her home . . . my father doesn't like her."

Toronto social worker Ruth Goodman told me the following story: At the Toronto Festival of Festivals a filmmaker was asked why his film included so much violence. He replied, "If you knew my mother, you'd understand." The audience snickered. This glib response allowed him to disown responsibility for his actions by switching the focus to his mother. Ironically, the only sins of the mother in the movie were that she had corny wallpaper and liked Muzak, whereas the father was a very disturbing person.

When my book *The Myth of Women's Masochism* was published in 1985, I did a great deal of speaking in the United States and Canada.[10] I had carefully avoided mother-blaming, but many readers managed to work it in anyway; strikingly often, one or more women approached me after my lecture and said something like this: "I read your book and really understood what you said, and now I agree with you that women are not masochists, they do not like to suffer. Except one: my mother." Apparently, untold numbers of otherwise thoughtful women believe that *their* mother is the world's only living masochist, the worst of the sickos.

The most poignant instances of mother-blaming within the family are those in which the mother blames herself for whatever goes wrong. Mothers of misbehaving kids blame themselves for "not setting enough limits" if they are slightly less rigid disciplinarians than average, and if they are slightly more rigid, they blame themselves for "coming down too hard" on the child. Mothers whose children get many colds are far more likely to berate themselves for failing to dress them warmly enough (even when they haven't failed to do so) than to blame the pediatrician for not suggesting that the coughs and runny noses could be caused by food allergies or that colds are hard to prevent when kids spend all day in groups. Hearing ourselves and other mothers blamed from all sides, we naturally learn to do it ourselves.

I am still surprised when I hear successful, well-educated women putting themselves down as mothers, even when they might not be totally responsible for all of their children's suffering. One very successful woman was a frequent face on the lecture circuit. Upon learning that one of her daughters was bulimic, she stopped her media tour and rushed home to nurse her daughter back to health—which she succeeded in doing! But she concluded that she was to blame for her daughter's bulimia; she believed that she had neglected her daughter's emotional needs for years, because she had been preoccupied with her own career and had hungrily fed on her daughter's admiration for her work.

Although the typical *father* is preoccupied with his work and wants his children's respect and approval, such fathers are not blamed for their children's problems. Furthermore, the lecturer was divorced from her daughter's father, so what preceded or followed the divorce, perhaps even something in the father's treatment of the daughter, just *might* have contributed to the bulimia. So might a host of other factors. *But the mother never mentioned any of this in her lecture.*

Hearing this successful woman publicly offer up her "guilt" as proof of mothers' failures and their culpability was tragic—and frightening. Not only was she doing an injustice to herself, but also she was reinforcing the blaming of other mothers and their self-blame.

Even when we're not faulting ourselves, other family members often do it for us. Essayist Nancy Mairs said that when her sixteen-year-old daughter Anne went to Central America as a volunteer worker, Mairs's parents-in-law chided her for allowing Anne to go:

> [George's parents] never mentioned the matter to him. I was at first hurt, angry, feeling picked on; later I came to understand that I was the natural target of their misgivings. George couldn't be counted on to know what girls should or shouldn't do, or to communicate his knowledge if he did. But I could. I was Anne's mother.[11]

Mother-blaming among laypeople is well nourished by the words of mental health researchers and practitioners, whom our culture considers to be experts on human behavior. *Because* we consider them experts, we often forget that their theories and their research are influenced by the same tendency to scapegoat mothers that pervades the whole society.

Mother-Blaming Among the Experts

If Researchers Say It, It Must Be True

My student Ian Hall-McCorquodale and I read 125 articles published in nine different major mental health journals in 1970, 1976, and 1982. Some articles were single case studies, and some were reports of research on large numbers of people with emotional problems. We categorized each article according to sixty-three different types of mother-blaming. These ranged from "number of words used to describe mother" and "number of words used to describe father" to the repetition of earlier mother-blaming claims without questioning whether they apply in the current case. We found that, regardless of the author's sex or occupation as psychoanalyst, psychiatrist, psychologist, or social worker, mental health professionals were overwhelmingly indulging in mother-blaming.

In the 125 articles, mothers were blamed for seventy-two different kinds of problems in their offspring, ranging from bed-wetting to schizophrenia, from inability to deal with color blindness to aggressive behavior, from learning problems to "homicidal transsexualism."

Two articles reporting our findings were published in 1985, and the responses were gratifying.[12] In a typical letter, one woman wrote, "My husband and I are both practicing psychiatrists, and I have been trying to convince him for years that mothers get blamed for everything. Now I have documented proof!" Her letter illustrated an important point: most therapists, like this woman's husband, are not even aware of how much mother-blaming they and others do. The rare negative responses we received were all from people who were worried that reducing mother-blame meant increasing father-blame, though we never advocated the latter. The alarm about the *possibility* that father-blaming *might* increase *somewhat* starkly contrasted with most therapists' comfort with mother-blaming.

The biases in research and theory are not new. They predate the time when our mothers were raising us. One sixty-five-year-old mother of three told me that she remembers learning in a university course that the severe emotional disorder called infantile autism was caused by cold mothers who rejected their infants (which was later found to be untrue). She says: "Every time I felt a little tired or distracted when I picked up one of my babies, I was sure I was going to drive her into an autistic state!"

One parallel contemporary example is making it mothers' responsibility to provide the technical help for their children who have learning disabilities. I spent years working with such children and writing about their problems.[13] Even though *by definition* learning difficulties are not caused by motivational problems or lack of exposure to learning, I often heard mothers held totally responsible for dealing with their children's disabilities. As one mother told me,

> I read all the books about how to teach your child to read, and I *tried* to use them to teach Jessica. But we just haven't gotten anywhere. At the end of every tutoring session, she and I both feel like failures. The teacher says I should keep working with Jessica, but I don't know what else to do.

As sociologists Dorothy Smith and Alison Griffith have found in their research, school systems depend heavily on mothers to help them accomplish the work they are supposed to do. This is true not only for children who have problems but right down to the expectation that kindergarten and first-grade students will come to school already knowing their ABCs because their mothers have taught them.[14]

One of the most sobering examples of mother-blaming interpretations of research is in the area of child abuse. Conducting good research about child abuse is difficult, because abuse tends to be hidden, especially among wealthier, better-educated people. For this reason, research on the question "*Who* abuses children?" has given us a skewed picture of the truth. Many so-called authorities on child abuse claim that mothers are more likely than fathers to abuse their children. This comes as a surprise to people who think of mothers in idealized terms as the "Angel in the House." But it fits the darker cultural stereotype about mothers: that they are "Wicked Witches," unable or unwilling to control their unlimited rages.

Researchers who make these claims rarely ask how much time each parent spends with the children. In general, mothers spend far more time than fathers with children, and many of the fathers in studies of abuse have left their families or are rarely home. So for each hour spent with the children, the mothers actually abuse them far *less* than fathers do. But many "experts" continue to believe that mothers are more likely than fathers to commit child abuse—and this belief is a serious distortion.[15]

This distortion affects every mother, because nearly everyone who has taken care of children has sometimes felt so frustrated, exhausted, and helpless that they have used some physical punishment or abused our children outright (then felt horribly guilty for doing so). Although child abuse is wrong and damaging to children, my own work in this area has shown that the misinterpretation of research findings takes the focus off important issues that contribute to the abuse, like mothers' lack of support, their sometimes desperate circumstances, and so on. It feeds the fear that mothers are indeed dangerous, especially compared to fathers, and it can create a self-fulfilling prophecy: when a woman truly believes that she is a horrible mother, her self-esteem plunges and her sense of isolation grows, increasing the likelihood that she *will* be abusive.

Some researchers, who say that child welfare workers should use their findings to identify abusive parents, also focus on mothers. A recent press release from a major university conveyed the impression that only mothers abuse their children. Although the release was headlined, "Study of

Family Interaction Leads to New Understanding of Abusive *Parents*" (my italics), the entire section reporting the study's results describes only mothers. According to the release, researchers produced a profile of abusive "parents," but in fact they studied only mothers—one hundred of them! Then, reporting their results, they described various kinds of abusive mothers—harsh/intrusive, covert/hostile, and emotionally detached ones:

> "Harsh intrusive" mothers are excessively harsh and constantly badger their child to behave. . . .
> A "covert/hostile" mother shows no positive feelings towards her child. She makes blatant attacks on the child's self-worth and denies him affection or attention. . . .
> An "emotionally detached" mother has very little involvement with her child. She appears depressed and uninterested in the child's activities.[16]

Thus, the blame is placed on the mental illness or just plain nastiness of individual mothers, as though fathers are never abusive, as though more complex family and social factors play no role in leading to abuse.

Often, a researcher's mother-blaming work is used by someone else as a source of information, with the second party unquestioningly taking on the researcher's mother-blaming attitude. In a pamphlet published by a highly respected nurses' association, case workers were told that child sexual abuse is characterized by the following: the mother is aware of the abuse, may see it as a relief for herself, organizes time for her husband and daughter to be alone, may have refused to sleep with her husband, and will not risk exposing the abuse.[17]

This list is unforgivable, in view of what is really known about father-daughter incest. As Dr. Kathleen Coulbourn Faller of the University of Michigan School of Social Work has shown in her paper based on more than three hundred cases of sexual abuse, the mother usually does *not* know that it is happening. When she does know, she usually brings it into the open and takes steps to ensure that it stops; when she doesn't report it, she is often afraid of her husband's threats to harm her and their daughter further if she tells or because she has been taught that a good woman's first task is to keep the family together (and perhaps even to obey her husband, no matter what). And, of course, the discovery of abuse often *does* destroy the two-parent family.[18]

Some daughters who try to inform their mothers about the abuse do so in such vague or unclear ways—because they feel afraid or guilty—

that mother doesn't understand; and since sexual abuse is unthinkable for most people, often the mother genuinely never realizes what her daughter is trying to tell her. (This may be all the more true if the abuser is the mother's *own father*.) As one highly educated, loving mother said, "Before I found out that my ex-husband was abusing my daughter, if you had asked me, I would have said, 'He's selfish and ruthless and sneaky—but sexual abuse? *That* he would *never* do.' "

In the nurses' association pamphlet, the "indicators" were unduly focused on mothers. They did not include, for example, the well-documented sneakiness of the fathers who perpetrate incest. In general, these men are like alcoholics in the lengths to which they will go to deny and conceal the incest.[19] And, of course, a mother who does *not* "organize time" for father and daughter to be alone risks being called possessive and smothering.

Even in extreme cases of mother-blaming for abuse, however, there is hope.

> One incest survivor, a woman in her twenties, disclosed at her survivors' group meeting that an adult male neighbor sexually abused her when she was a very young child. She said that when she told her mother about it at the time, her mother had never said a word, never reacted at all. She had always felt that her mother had betrayed her and failed to support her because of this. Her group leader urged her to talk to her mother about it, and the woman gathered up her courage and did so. Her mother's response was, "When you told me I was so afraid that I would say or do the wrong thing, something that would be bad for you, that I tried not to react at all. So I went to the psychiatrist to ask *him* what I should do, and he said that for your sake, the best thing I could do would be never to mention it again."[20]

Naturally, the daughter had spent years blaming her mother; it's what we all are taught to do.

Mother-Blaming among Therapists

Psychotherapists had begun acquiring an aura of authority by the time our mothers were raising us, and that aura very much persists right now. In popular books and articles and on television and radio talk shows, mental health professionals communicate to the public at large the mother-blaming messages they learn in their training. Psychotherapists had even more influence in our mothers' childraising days, because in the 1930s, 1940s, and 1950s the public tended even more than now to defer to psychiatrists.

Some fair and sensitive psychotherapists have been enormously supportive and helpful to distraught mothers and daughters. But all too many—knowingly or unwittingly—have intensively promoted mother-blaming in their capacity as therapists, both in our mothers' childrearing years and in our own adult years, and this has often been even more devastating to mothers than mother-blaming research. A psychotherapy patient reveals her most intimate feelings and her most shameful secrets to her therapist. Her therapist learns things about her that no one else has ever known. She goes to the therapist seeking help both to feel better and to learn more of the truth about herself and her life. This gives the therapist enormous power over her. Because the training for most therapists involves so much mother-blame and woman-blame, only the unusual ones help the patient to go beyond mother-blame and self-blame. Traditional therapists tend to believe sincerely that mother-blaming fits reality, and they regard themselves as helping their patients to accept this reality. Thus, women are primed to accept the therapist's descriptions of them and their mothers—or themselves *as* mothers—as manipulative, overprotective, intrusive, cold, rejecting, and so on. Let us look at some examples of therapists' demeaning descriptions of mothers.

Since the 1960s, therapists' attitudes toward mothers have been widely influenced by Margaret Mahler's work on the importance of the child's psychological "separation and individuation" from its mother. (Although Mahler did important work on profoundly disturbed children, her writings have been widely applied in mother-blaming ways.) Mahler advised therapists to watch carefully when a mother entered the room used for observing the family's dynamics. They were to take note of whether she carried the child "like a part of herself"—which would then brand the mother as being unable to separate from the child—or "like an inanimate object"—which would label her as the cold-and-rejecting type.[21] Imagine being a mother observed by a therapist who used such a pigeonholing scheme, in which each pigeonhole is a different form of bad mothering! Even more painful to imagine are the kinds of messages such a therapist would convey to the mother about her relationship with her child.

The names of Mahler and some of her like-minded colleagues never became known to most laypeople, but many theories that share the same mother-blaming foundation have become familiar as presumed truths. In one currently fashionable type of psychotherapy, the wives of alcoholics, drug addicts, compulsive gamblers and womanizers are said to make life hard for their children, because they support their husbands' addictions and compulsions. Proponents of these theories use the term "codependent" to describe the wife/mother, and they say she "needs" or "likes" her husband's problems to continue: "She loves playing the holier-than-thou game with him" or "She gets her jollies from seeing how abject and disgusting he is when he is drunk."

In fact, however, if you ask these women how they would feel if you could magically take away their husbands' problem behaviors, they sigh with relief at the thought. Men who try to stop their addictive behavior find it physically and/or psychologically difficult, and all too many take out their frustrations on their families, including subjecting their wives and their children to severe beatings or verbal abuse. When the wives bemoan this worsened behavior, many therapists say, "Aha! She doesn't *want* him to stop drinking!" They ignore the fact that the wives wish the men would stop both the drinking *and* the abuse.

Other recovering men are humiliated to face the wives who knew them when they were drunks, so they want to leave them. No wonder some women are frightened by the prospect of their husbands' recovery—but this is a far cry from wanting the compulsion to continue. The irony is that mothers who *leave* such husbands are blamed for breaking up the family and depriving the children of their father, but women who *stay* are given the demeaning, pathologizing term "codependent" and are accused of "loving too much" and failing to save the children from their father's addictive behavior.[22]

You don't have to be a mental health professional to absorb the cultural propensity for blaming mother for father's alcoholism. Television star Suzanne Somers has described the anger that she and her siblings felt toward their mother because of their father's drinking. Sensing the danger in confronting their abusive, alcoholic father but trying to find a way out, they directed their disappointment and rage toward Mom. The happy ending to Somers's story is that their father is sober, and she and her siblings appreciate their mother's strength and love, which enabled them to overcome the bad times.[23]

As I have mentioned, when the patient is not the mother's husband but rather her child, mother-blaming knows no bounds. A friend described for me her experience in 1987 as the target of psychiatrists' mother-blaming, in a situation in which she already felt helpless and frightened because her child was sick. The mother, whom I'll call Caroline, took care of her ten-year-old daughter, Laurel, who had what seemed to be a stomach virus, including nausea and vomiting. For weeks after the vomiting stopped, Laurel was extremely tired and listless, and she said she could not eat anything without feeling nauseated. Caroline used every gentle technique she could think of to induce her to eat a little, but the listlessness and nausea persisted. The family doctor ordered numerous, expensive medical tests, which revealed no physical problem; so the doctor sent Caroline and Laurel to the state university's hospital, a three-hour drive away.

The university's regular medical staff found no physical cause for Laurel's problems and transferred her to the psychiatric ward. The psychiatric staff instructed Caroline to leave Laurel there for three weeks and have no contact with her during that time. When Laurel wept from loneliness, the psychiatrists concluded that her problem was that "her relationship with her mother is too close, symbiotic." At the end of the three weeks, they shipped her home, still physically ill and depressed. Both Caroline and Laurel were now psychiatrically labeled, and Caroline felt guilty and ashamed. Months later, on the advice of a friend, Caroline gave Laurel a little of a commercially available medication that soothes the digestive tract. Laurel's nausea vanished, she began to eat normally, and as she became well nourished, her depression disappeared.

Of course, there are many, many variations on this limited set of examples. For instance, in my own investigation of mother-blaming, I found an article in which the authors' stated purpose was to study whether children of male prisoners-of-war suffered because of their fathers' experiences.[24] They described these fathers as filled with various feelings of distress and emotionally distant from their families. The authors found that these children indeed had a high incidence of emotional problems; however, they said that the fault was their mothers'! They presented their reasoning clearly: the women were upset at seeing their husbands' anguish, and this interfered with their ability to mother their children properly! These children are now fully grown, but mother-blaming in similar situations hasn't abated, as Aphrodite Matsakis documents in her new book about Vietnam veterans' wives, who are blamed for the ill effects their husbands' psychiatric symptoms have on their families.[25]

Therapists often make explicit, crude attempts to alienate daughters from their mothers. Fraydele Oysher, mother of comedian and mimic Marilyn Michaels, told an interviewer that Marilyn doesn't call her mother very often: "It began," says Ms. Oysher, "when she started seeing a psychiatrist. She said her psychiatrist told her she had to be her own person. So now she's the psychiatrist's person." [26] Fraydele Oysher clearly has a kind of insight that is rarely displayed by the so-called "professionals." She saw not only the psychiatrist's dangerous tampering with Marilyn's feelings about her mother but also the insidious way in which he simply shifted her from dependence on (or quite possibly her warm involvement with) her mother to dependence on him.

Usually, women who are able to go beyond mother-blaming do so on their own or with the help of other people, not their therapists. A forty-year-old professional woman told me that her therapist had helped her to get angry at her mother but not to go beyond that:

> My mother was intimidated by my father, and she did use me to stand up to him, from the time I was four years old. She and I both knew that I had the guts to say things to him that she didn't dare say. And it wasn't fair to put me in that position. My therapist helped me feel my anger about that, but then he just left me there, furious at my mother for being so manipulative.

What changed this woman's view was her own later experience, not her work with her therapist:

> Only after I became a mother myself did I put her "manipulations" in perspective. First of all, I realized that, yes, she had been somewhat manipulative, but *mostly* she had been a terrific mother. And all my therapist wanted me to do was talk about the bad side of her. Having my own children and seeing how hard it was to work toward that impossible image of the perfect mother made me appreciate how much she had done for me. Instead of just being stuck thinking of her as getting me to stand up to Dad, other memories started to come back to me: the time she volunteered to drive two hours to pick up the Girl Scout cookies for four hundred Scouts to sell—and then at 2:30 in the morning, as we continued stacking them all through the house, said, "Well, the night is young! And we've only got the mint ones left to do!" She had a wonderful sense of humor and was totally supportive of me and of everything I did. And in the course of my therapy that had slipped my mind.

When we consider such numerous and varied examples of mother-blaming by therapists, that such things can really happen may seem surprising. We must understand that they do occur and to have some idea about why they do.

NOTES

This chapter is reprinted from Paula J. Caplan, *Don't Blame Mother: Mending the Mother-Daughter Relationship* (New York: Harper and Row, 1989).

1. Zenith Henkin Gross, *And You Thought It Was All Over!* (New York: St. Martin's Press, 1985).

2. Ann Crittenden Scott, "The Value of Housework—for Love or Money," *Ms.* 1 (July 1972): 56–59. Note that these were the ratings in 1970, when the women's movement was in the air; our mothers were raising us before that time, so the esteem in which *they* were held would appear to have been very low.

3. Jessie Bernard, *The Future of Motherhood* (New York: Dial Press, 1974), x.

4. Esther Greenglass, "A Social-Psychological View of Marriage for Women," *International Journal of Women's Studies* 8 (1985): 24–31.

5. Jennifer Chambers, personal communication, January 20, 1988.

6. Philip Wylie, *Generation of Vipers* (New York: Rinehart and Co., 1946), 185–86.

7. The definition of "momism" as referring to mothers' "excessive domination" of their families comes from *New Webster's Dictionary of the English Language,* Deluxe Encyclopedic Edition, 1981.

8. Dan Greenburg, *How to Be a Jewish Mother* (Los Angeles: Price Stern Sloan, 1965); Philip Roth, *Portnoy's Complaint* (New York: Random House, 1969).

9. For excellent readings on these issues, see Ethel Strainchamps, "Our Sexist Language," in Vivian Gornick and Barbara K. Moran, eds., *Women in Sexist Society* (New York: Basic Books, 1971), 347–61; Letty Cottin Pogrebin, *Growing Up Free: Raising Your Kids in the 80s* (New York: McGraw-Hill, 1980); Casey Miller and Kate Swift, *Words and Women* (Garden City, N.Y.: Anchor Books, 1977); Dale Spender, *Man Made Language* (New York: Routledge/Chapman Hall, 1985).

10. Paula Caplan, *The Myth of Women's Masochism* (New York: E. P. Dutton, 1985, and New York: Signet, 1987 [paperback edition with additional chapter, "Afterword: A Warning"]).

11. Nancy Mairs, *Plaintext: Deciphering a Woman's Life* (New York: Harper and Row, 1987), 72.

12. Paula Caplan and Ian Hall-McCorquodale, "Mother-Blaming in Major Clinical Journals," *American Journal of Orthopsychiatry* 55 (1985): 345–53; and Paula Caplan and Ian Hall-McCorquodale, "The Scapegoating of Mothers," *American Journal of Orthopsychiatry* 55 (1985): 610–13.

13. Marcel Kinsbourne and Paula J. Caplan, *Children's Learning and Attention Problems* (Boston: Little, Brown, 1979).

14. Alison I. Griffith and Dorothy E. Smith, "Contributing Cultural Knowledge: Mothering as Discourse," in J. Gaskell and A. McLaren, eds., *Women and Education* (Calgary: Detselig Press, 1987), 87–103; Alison I. Griffith and Dorothy E. Smith, "Coordinating the Uncoordinated: How Mothers Manage the School Day," *Perspectives on Social Problems*, vol. 2 (Greenwich, Conn.: JAI Press, 1990), 25–43; Dorothy E. Smith, "Women's Work as Mothers: A New Look at the Relations of Family, Class and School Achievement," in Gale Miller and James Holstein, eds., *Perspectives on Social Problems*, vol. 1 (Greenwich, Conn.: JAI Press), 109–25.

15. Joseph Pleck, "Employment and Fatherhood: Issues and Innovative Policies," in Michael E. Lamb, ed., *The Father's Role: Applied Perspectives* (New York: John Wiley, 1986), 385–412; Paula J. Caplan, Jessie Watters, Georgina White, Ruth Parry, and Robert Bates, "Toronto Multi-Agency Child Abuse Research Project: The Abused and the Abuser," *Child Abuse and Neglect: The International Journal* 8 (1984): 343–51.

16. "Study of Family Interaction Leads to New Understanding of Abusive Parents" (Press release, University of Toronto Research Highlights, Simcoe Hall, University of Toronto, Public and Community Relations, October 1987), 1.

17. Helen Thomas, *Child Abuse, Neglect, and Deprivation: A Handbook for Ontario Nurses* (Toronto: Registered Nurses Association of Ontario, 1983), 21.

18. Kathleen Coulbourn Faller, "Decision-Making in Cases of Intrafamilial Child Sexual Abuse," *American Journal of Orthopsychiatry* 58 (1988): 121–28.

19. Carolyn Cole, personal communication, May 1986.

20. Carolyn Cole, personal communication, September 25, 1987.

21. Margaret S. Mahler, Fred Pine, and Anni Bergman, *The Psychological Birth of the Human Infant: Symbiosis and Individuation* (New York: Basic Books, 1975).

22. Caplan et al., "Toronto Multi-Agency Abuse."

23. Suzanne Somers, on *Donahue* (television show on alcoholism), February 2, 1988.

24. J. Sigal, "Effects of Paternal Exposure to Prolonged Stress on the Mental Health of the Spouse and Children," *Canadian Psychiatric Association Journal* 21 (1976): 169–72.

25. Aphrodite Matsakis, *Viet Nam Wife: The Other Forgotten Warrior* (Kensington, Md.: Woodbine Press, 1988).

26. Fred A. Bernstein, *The Jewish Mothers' Hall of Fame* (Garden City, N.Y.: Doubleday and Co., 1986), 112.

Chapter 7

Antiracism and Maternal Failure
in the 1940s and 1950s

Ruth Feldstein

At the outset of the film *Home of the Brave,* a dramatic voice-over introduces the story of "one American." *Home,* released in 1949, chronicles the wartime relationships between this "one American"—a wounded black private, Pete Moss—and his fellow white soldiers, all of whom have been on a dangerous mission together. Over the course of the film, a white psychiatrist cures Moss of various ailments. Moss not only recovers from hysterical paralysis and amnesia; he also learns to forge positive interracial relationships with white men. By the end, the black soldier overcomes his "disease" of "sensitivity." Moreover, he understands that racist white men "make cracks" about him because "down deep underneath, they feel insecure and unhappy too." As Moss notes with a sense of wonder and conviction, "Everybody's different. But so what? Because underneath, we're all guys." [1]

Home of the Brave was part of diverse and widespread efforts among antiracists in the 1940s and 50s to expose the psychic toll that racism exacted: both on African American "victims" of prejudice and on white Americans "suffering from" prejudice. This dual focus helped to redefine racism as undemocratic and un-American. In particular, focusing on how prejudice hurt whites helped to make race relations a national problem, and issues of race more central to liberal discourse generally. [2]

Ideas about gender, and about motherhood specifically, played a significant role in this form of racial liberalism, which gained credibility in the 1940s and 50s. Indeed, images of women as bad mothers were important to the process through which "racism as un-American" became a dominant paradigm. The gendered dimensions of racial liberalism become apparent in two ways. First, psychosocial analyses blamed certain kinds of mothers for creating racial prejudice in whites on the one hand and for perpetuating ostensible pathology in blacks on the other. Second, this discourse viewed racial hatred as weakening American masculinity specifically. Race relations literature was preoccupied with white and black *sons* whose mothers failed them psychologically, and who, as a result, lacked the codes of masculinity necessary for healthy and productive citizenship.[3] In other words, the multiple problems of prejudice that white and black mothers helped to create undermined the ideal male citizen — the citizen who, like the protagonist of *Home of the Brave*, could say with confidence that "we're all guys."

Philip Wylie gave birth to the term, or more accurately, to the "condition" of "momism" in *Generation of Vipers*, first published in 1942. "Moms," he explained, were all-powerful "middle-aged puffin[s]" and "parasites" who destroyed their "captive sons." He also charged (implicitly) white "moms" with being like Hitler, controlling the American economy, and causing the war. Several years later, Marynia Farnham and Ferdinand Lundberg argued in *Modern Woman: The Lost Sex* that neurotic (white) mothers were responsible for a "slaughter of the innocents" and were "the principal transmitting media of the disordered emotions that . . . are reflected in the statistics of social disorder."[4]

The excesses in these much-quoted diatribes make it tempting to explain "momism" as simply a conservative and misogynist impulse. Scholars have successfully analyzed pervasive mother-blaming in the context of a post–World War II backlash against women workers, a culture of conformity and political apathy, Cold War witch-hunts and fears of the enemy within, and the decline organized feminism. They have explored images of maternal rejection and maternal overprotection in popular and political culture.[5]

Mother-blaming, however, was not beyond the pale of liberal intellectual discourse.[6] Moreover, the charge of "momism" was not restricted to middle-class white women who needed to be "contained" in the suburban domestic sphere. Images of black mothers as "matriarchs" who hurt their offspring proliferated in the same period that those of white "moms" did. In 1939, sociologist E. Franklin Frazier made the concept of a black "matriarchy" — dominant and overnurturing black mothers — central to his authoritative antiracist analysis *The Negro Family in the United States*. In the decades that followed, the assumption that certain kinds of "bad" black mothers interfered with racial progress became solidly entrenched in progressive literature.[7]

To understand mother-blaming, one must consider depictions of white and black motherhood alongside and in relation to each other. Doing so demonstrates that it is tempting, but ultimately insufficient, to dismiss Wylie as an extremist "crackpot" or to isolate Farnham and Lundberg on the "conservative margin" of intellectual and cultural life.[8]

Psychology, Families, and the Fight against Racism

In the early part of the twentieth century, cultural anthropologist Franz Boas, sociologists Robert E. Park and Ernest W. Burgess, and linguist and anthropologist Edward Sapir had influenced and trained a generation of social scientists in approaches that were cultural, relativist, and psychological. They emphasized the need to go beyond quantitative data, and instead, to consider how individual personalities and behaviors developed within larger networks of relationships.[9] Working within these parameters, social psychologist John Dollard and a team of researchers at Yale University developed in 1939 an extremely influential paradigm: that *"aggression is always a consequence of frustration."*[10] Frustration, a range of intellectuals argued in the coming years, had insidious consequences. It turned into aggression and contributed to crime, juvenile delinquency, and a host of other social ills. Analyzing personal sources of frustration became a precondition for understanding aggressive behavior that was "distinctively democratic, fascist, or communist."[11]

International events in the 1930s and 40s made race more central to these discussions of frustration and aggression.[12] As German armies spread through Europe, Americans increasingly concluded that unhealthy aggression was an emotional disorder that was *politically* dangerous. During the war, the dangers of excessive racial and ethnic hatred emerged starkly. When atrocities inflicted in the name of "racial purity" became apparent, intellectuals and others asked how individuals had ever developed these violent hatreds, and how willingly cruel, excessively aggressive, and authoritarian personalities came into being.[13]

Further, fighting a war against National Socialism compelled many to consider American racism as a point of comparison. The war made many people wonder, with fear, if what happened "over there" could ever happen "here." Americans sought assurance that democracy in the United

States was secure, and one source of such assurance was to reject and combat racism. Thus, fascism, the holocaust, and the "new" enemy in the postwar period—communism in the Soviet Union—gave added political weight to concerns about aggression.

At the same time, the scientific racism that National Socialism specifically enacted profoundly discredited biologically based theories of personality development and racial difference.[14] This delegitimation of biologically based theories of race at precisely the moment when issues of race assumed such urgency created an opening of sorts. It was in this space that interdisciplinary psychosocial research came to dominate studies of prejudice.

Psychology was a rational science grounded in empirical data. But it was also a science concerned with the unconscious and with irrational emotions and was thus useful to a range of experts. Psychoanalytic categories, for example, provided a way for sociologists, anthropologists, political scientists and others to link analyses of individuals and their emotions with analyses of society and states; to examine both the discriminators and the discriminated against; and to envision a society freed from the dangers of excessive hatred, violence, and aggression. This "ice-cold scientific research," wrote one psychiatrist, could determine why "a certain kind of person *needs to hate.*"[15]

Émigré intellectuals, many of them affiliated with the Institute of Social Research in Germany and then New York, also contributed to an increased focus on aggression and prejudice. T. W. Adorno, as well as Erich Fromm, Wilhelm Reich, and others, analyzed anti-Semitism, authoritarianism, and prejudice in both Europe and the United States by integrating psychology, critical theory, and Marxist-oriented analyses. Their work, particularly *The Authoritarian Personality,* in which Frankfurt School theorists and American social scientists collaborated, had a direct and indirect influence on those concerned with prejudice within American borders specifically.[16] So too did Swedish economist Gunnar Myrdal's landmark study *An American Dilemma* (1944). Concerns about prejudiced and aggressive whites are evident in these works, as well as in the collection of essays *Killers of the Dream* (1949) by southern liberal Lillian Smith and the synthetic study *The Nature of Prejudice* (1954) by social psychologist Gordon Allport. Scholars used similar psychosocial approaches to analyze the effects of prejudice on blacks. Among such scholars were sociologist and former New Dealer Charles Johnson, in his study of rural black youth in the South, *Growing Up in the Black Belt*

(1940); sociologists Horace Cayton and St. Clair Drake, in their community study of urban Chicago, *Black Metropolis* (1945); as well as anthropologist/psychoanalyst Abram Kardiner and analyst Lionel Ovesey in their psychoanalytic case studies of blacks in Harlem, *The Mark of Oppression* (1951).[17]

Shared concerns united these discussions of prejudice, which otherwise varied widely in scope, region, and method. For one, in using psychology as a theory that explained both personality formation and political life, scholars seeking to combat prejudice viewed the family as the point of intersection between the private individual and the social citizen. The family, white or black, was a microcosm of society. Further, a virtual consensus emerged that childhood experiences were important in understanding the sources of prejudice in whites and the effects of prejudice on blacks. Prejudiced whites, experts suggested, displaced frustrations that had been with them since childhood. At the same time, blacks subjected to prejudice internalized frustrations that had been with them since childhood. Finally, this body of work reflected a liberal belief in progress.[18]

It is worth emphasizing that this focus on psychology and family dynamics was progressive. It was a paradigm that replaced biological theories of race with psychological theories of racism.[19] At the same time, this progressive impulse directly and indirectly implicated white and black women: both in the dangerous production of racism and in its dangerous effects.

The Origins of Racism and White Maternal Failure

Efforts to grapple with the qualities that constituted healthy democratic citizenship lay at the heart of psychosocial explorations of racial prejudice in whites. Violently prejudiced Americans, experts argued, could not control their aggression and had damaged personalities. Because their disease of racism contradicted tenets of democracy, they were unfit citizens. "What can be done—in homes and schools and churches—to fight a danger which, in its way, may be as threatening as the atomic bomb?" asked an article about "race hate" published in both *Cosmopolitan* and *Negro Digest*.[20] Thus, excessive hatred was a psychological disease afflicting whites specifically. For example, Gunnar Myrdal's *An American Dilemma* was a social history that offered tremendous detail about African Americans. But the "American" of the title—the one faced with the "dilemma"—was a white man. His "dilemma," moreover, was fundamentally psychological. The "ever-raging conflict" in whites between the liberal "American creed" and "group prejudice" was at the crux of this text. It was white America that was *free to choose whether the Negro shall remain her liability or become her opportunity.*[21] This "most influential study of American race relations from its publication in 1944 to the end of the 60s" helped to transform the "Negro problem" into a "white problem" by considering the interrelated moral, psychological, and political effects of racism in whites.[22]

This work implicitly assumed that if racial prejudice was a psychological disease, which developed most often as a result of childhood experiences, then it could also be avoided. Indeed, both the popularity and underlying optimism of this discourse grew out of a focus on whiteness and a belief in change. Myrdal asserted that progress was possible despite centuries of discrimination, because white Americans could not indefinitely tolerate the discrepancies between prejudice and the liberal American creed. "People want to be rational," he asserted, and whites could not live with the feelings of guilt these discrepancies evoked. Moreover it was "significant," according to Myrdal, that "today even the white man who defends discrimination frequently . . . says that it is 'irrational.' "[23]

Mothers played a particularly crucial role in the childhood experiences through which frustrations, and ultimately prejudice, either developed or receded. In *The Authoritarian Personality*, for example, Adorno and collaborators used the "F-scale" (with *F* signifying "fascist") to link types of *personalities* likely to submit to an authoritarian leader to types of *families* and types of family dynamics more specifically. In this "major social psychology contribution of the 1950s," émigré theorists and American social psychologists argued that mothers of prejudiced children were either excessively "sacrificing, kind, submissive," or "domineering, dictatorial, and self-centered."[24] Psychologist Gordon Allport agreed. "Mothers of prejudiced children, *far more often* than the mothers of unprejudiced children," were strict disciplinarians, he explained. They tended to punish children for masturbating and responded with anger and rejection to temper tantrums.[25] These were just some of the maternal behaviors that affected the future political behavior of citizens. The children of such mothers grew up frustrated, and then channeled their frustrations onto minorities.

In these ways and others, maternal failure helped to create the negative childhood experiences through which a generalized sense of frustration and consequent prejudice developed. Several themes recur in this literature. First, even when the mother was not herself racist, she played a central role in the development of racism in her children, particularly in her sons (and I will follow up further on that idea in a moment). The woman's position as "mother" preempted her (mostly elided) position as a political subject.

Second, there was no one kind of behavior that mothers could avoid in order to have prejudice-free offspring. Mothers who generated frustration, later manifest as prejudice, were *both* "henpeckingly dominant" *and* overly "sacrificing." They were alternatively (and/or simultaneously) rejecting and overprotective.[26] The range of "bad" mothers who populated antiracist literature was quite similar, then, to that associated with conservative "momism." The rare "good" mothers in this literature struck that necessary balance between maternal rejection and overprotection: they were "sociable, lovable," and "understanding," yet, they had interests beyond the home and were not consumed by childrearing.[27] In championing such a mother, *The Authoritarian Personality* echoed the bible of permissive childrearing, Benjamin Spock's *Baby and Child Care,* and its call for families "centered about a mother whose primary function is to give love rather than to dominate, and who is not too weak or too submissive."[28] Mother-blaming filtered, then, from general and seemingly race-neutral discussions of the mother-child relationship into progressive discussions of race relations, prejudice, and authoritarianism.

Third, even the relationship between paternal authority and prejudice implicated mothers. *The Authoritarian Personality* repeatedly emphasized that too "distant" or too "severe" a father made sons more inclined toward prejudice and authoritarianism. One son, the researchers argued, longed to "assert his strength against those who are weaker" precisely because his own father was so harsh. But the assumption that mothers were ultimately responsible for childrearing was so pervasive that discussions of patriarchal authority always implied that mothers had not done their job; women frequently contributed to excessive paternal domination or paternal neglect. One boy susceptible to authoritarianism, wrote Adorno, "longs for strong authority" because his cloying mother made it impossible for his father to assert himself.[29] Masculinity and patriarchal authority—whether in dangerous decline or in frightening ascendance— were inseparable from distortions of maternal authority that helped to bring about this decline or ascendance.

As these examples suggest, studies of racism's sources made women causal agents. What women caused, however, was prejudiced men with damaged *masculinity*. Prejudice, in other words, was in part a problem of gender. In case study after case study, the prejudiced male whom experts discussed in detail had failed to resolve his Oedipal issues. By not separating from his own mother, he remained overly identified with femininity. In many cases, this fixation on femininity caused a "'sissy complex' " in effeminate boys. Later in life their dependence and repressed aggression became violent prejudice. A fixation on femininity led boys to overcompensate; *unsuccessful* attempts to identify with masculinity were evident in an "overaggressiveness toward the outer world" and toward "socially sanctioned scapegoats" in particular.[30] Again and again, it was "mother domination" that made it difficult for white boys to forge a healthy masculine identity. Boys whose mothers had dominated them, explained Gordon Allport, confused "sheer aggression with masculinity" and could not forge a healthy heterosexual masculine identity as a result.[31] (And this discourse explicitly and implicitly invoked fears of homosexuality).[32] Racism in white men emerged as a result of feelings of sexual inadequacy and "impotence" (a word that abounds in this discourse) and unresolved Oedipal conflicts — all of which white mothers helped to create.

These intersections between motherhood, masculine aggression, and prejudice crystallized in Lillian Smith's analysis of the "sex-race-religion-economics tangle" in *Killers of the Dream*.[33] Lillian Smith was a white southern woman, an essayist and novelist, and, in a period of entrenched segregation, an ardent integrationist. Psychology consistently enabled her to analyze whites and condemn segregation explicitly. In 1944, in a short essay in the *New Republic* titled "Addressed to White Liberals," she asserted that "we have looked at the 'Negro problem' long enough," and that the "white man himself is one of the world's most urgent problems today." Smith supported integration and an end to a racial caste system that, she argued, caused both white and black children to grow up with "distorted, twisted personalities."[34]

In *Killers of the Dream* Smith elaborated on these themes. "The mother who taught me what I know of tenderness and love and compassion taught me also the bleak ritual of keeping Negroes in their 'place,' " she declared. According to Smith, racism in southern white men developed from the experiences that they had with white and black women as boys. White mothers taught their children that both African Americans and their own sexual feelings had to be "segregated." White mothers, she explained, were themselves repressed by a "patriarchal-puritanic system which psychically castrated them," and in turn, were themselves repressive and "psychically castrated" their offspring. They "armored their children against their fantasies" and sexual desires, and inoculated them with a "hypodermic needle" that was "tainted" with racial hatred. In other words, withholding white mothers interwove sexual desire and blackness, and cast both as dangerous. "Our mother's voice" taught five-year-olds that "masturbation is wrong and segregation is right, and each had become a dread taboo that must never be broken." By contrast, black women who were "mammies" to young white boys, said Smith, were unrepressed. They were excessively nurturing, and physically and emotionally overavailable to their young charges.[35]

Smith concluded that as adults, white men had conflicting sets of desires based on their encounters with white and black mothers. They desired black women, emotionally and sexually. But they feared and hated the objects of their desire because their mothers had reinforced associations between blackness, sex, and sin. White men also ostensibly placed white women on a pedestal and distanced themselves from these desexualized figures who were akin to their own mothers. As a result of these conflicting needs, white men sought to maintain power over African Americans, who had been cast since childhood as feared and hated "objects," even as these same men sought out sexual relationships with black women. Finally, white men projected their own "sins" and desires onto "the Negro male," and then used images of black men as sexual predators to maintain the racial caste system. In this way, they channeled their childhood frustrations *and* preserved their power in the racial caste system. White women were left isolated and resentful, emotionally and sexually frustrated. They were primed to repeat the cycle and inculcate prejudice in the next generation.[36]

In many respects, Smith's analysis duplicated disturbing images of "moms" and "matriarchs." Like Wylie in *Generation of Vipers* she positioned white women in terms of frigidity and repression. Like E. Franklin Frazier in *The Negro Family,* she positioned black women in terms of sexuality and physicality. And Smith depicted all mothers, black and white, as potentially infectious, damaging, and alternatively overprotective and rejecting. The very same criteria for evaluating—and indicting—mothers emerged in Smith's antiracist discourse: mothers were either too emotionally giving or too emotionally restrained, too preoccupied with or too removed from their children's needs, and plagued by sexual frustration. In *Killers of the Dream* as in Farnham and Lundberg's *Modern Woman: The Lost Sex,* feminists, "rejecting their womanly qualities ... cropping their hair short, walking in heavy awkward strides," and reflecting a "kind of fibroid growth of sick cells," were particularly disordered and disordering.[37] Even as Smith wondered if "sometimes we blame Mom too much for all that is wrong with her sons and daughters" and analyzed the cultural context for feelings of female inferiority, she concluded that mothers "did a thorough job ... of leaving in their children an unquenchable need to feel superior to others."[38]

At the same time, the psychosocial frameworks and the focus on prejudiced whites underscored what was most progressive *and* what was most reactionary in Smith's work. Her analysis of racism's origins depended on her psychological analysis of childhood. As a result, her gendered logic—what one might even call misogyny in some instances— was a necessary component of her unwavering resistance to segregation.[39] Smith and others positioned psychology on the border between private and political life. It was a means of creating a greater sense of urgency about American race relations and of framing racism as a "white problem" rather than a marginal question that "merely" affected blacks. Thus, she invoked images of maternal pathology, but these were an essential element of the courageous stand that she took against segregation, and were essential, too, to the ways she located race as central to liberalism.

These contradictions cannot necessarily be resolved, and that is, perhaps, precisely the point. Smith's work is emblematic: of intersections between reactionary misogyny and racial progressivism that proliferated in the 1940s and 50s. The psychological frameworks that underscored antiracism in this period required a logic that assumed mothers were central to the production of interrelated social, psychological, and political problems.

This discourse affirmed a vision of an ideal citizen cured of the disease of prejudice and free from the effects of femininity. This ideal citizen was an autonomous male and sufficiently—though not excessively— aggressive. As a result of his upbringing, he was rational though emotional. He was independent, yet able to cooperate with his family and with other men, black and white. He understood, as the protagonist in *Home of the Brave* did, that what matters is "we're all guys." This same standard of citizenship was a model for black men and surfaced in literature that focused on the psychological effects of racism on African

Americans. It too developed through a gendered logic that required images of maternal pathology.

The Effects of Racism and Black Maternal Failure

Fewer scholars studied the effects of prejudice on blacks as compared to those who analyzed its origins in whites. This was due, in part, to the ways that World War II generated anxiety about authoritarianism and prejudice in white Americans and illustrates the degree to which the pivotal "American dilemma" became essentially a white problem.[40] But those who were interested in the impact prejudice had also used psychology to understand how healthy American identities developed, and to chart the variables that interfered with this development in blacks. Prejudice, explained a range of sociologists, anthropologists, and others who did community studies, psychoanalytic profiles, and sweeping overviews, not only undermined African Americans economically and politically; it also weakened them emotionally and psychologically. Moreover, the feelings of inferiority and self-hatred that prejudice generated—the "mark of oppression," in the words of Abram Kardiner and Lionel Ovesey—originated in childhood and persisted into adulthood.

Liberal scholars directly and indirectly prescribed for black men codes of masculinity associated with white middle-class men. These presumed that healthy self-esteem facilitated moderate aggression in the public sphere and orderly, yet meaningful, emotional satisfaction in the private sphere. In *The Mark of Oppression,* Kardiner and Ovesey used the white family as their "constant control group." Indeed, the two asserted early on (and without qualms) that "our constant control is the American white man. We require no other control."[41]

Experts on the effects of prejudice pinpointed a vicious cycle. Discrimination generated feelings of inferiority and frustration that subjects often internalized. But these feelings made it more difficult to resist discrimination. More specifically, internalized frustration interfered with the development of healthy and strong black American men who could participate successfully in American society. Frustration, then, was both an effect *and a cause* of further inferiority. In this context, racial progress and psychic health required each other; both, moreover, required psychologically adjusted black men who were appropriately, yet not excessively, aggressive.

Authorities concluded that black men all too frequently failed to attain this "control," this ideal proportion of restrained, yet energizing, aggression. Many were not sufficiently aggressive. They were weak and inclined toward "submissiveness" in their private and public lives; preferred "empty dreams of escape" to hard work; and sought "to escape their troubles and status through chronic drunkenness." [42] Many others could not control their excessive aggression. In *Growing Up in the Black Belt,* Charles Johnson explained that some—often unemployed—black men sought "self-assurance in free sexual activity, in a reputation for physical prowess or for being a bad man, and in other forms of anti-social behavior." [43]

Underaggressive black men given to submission and overaggressive ones given to sexual and other excesses were similar in one crucial respect to prejudiced white men: all three groups failed to meet standards of healthy masculinity. Whether black men "gambled and drank and didn't provide for the family" or were impotent and unable to assert themselves, their masculinity itself (or their "patriarchal" roles and "magical powers" as providers, as Kardiner and Ovesey put it) was on the line. [44]

But experts influenced by psychology in the 40s and 50s were not content merely to describe or document this state of affairs. How, asked Kardiner and Ovesey in *The Mark of Oppression,* did weak, violent, and unemployed men "get this way?" The "trouble," they answered, "lies in the original relationship with his mother." [45] The mark of oppression that incapacitated so many black men developed as a result of institutionalized racial exclusions *combined with* family dynamics. Despite and alongside an attention to economic, social, and political barriers that blacks faced, experts on black families and communities located the sources for the problems black men experienced in the home—where, they argued, black mothers played an important role in the low self-esteem that perpetuated racial inferiority.

Certainly, the notion that black mothers could damage black families, and black men in particular, was not new. With an emphasis on "disorganized" families in which women were economically dominant, this discourse reflected a continuity of thought among white and black intellectuals about what was wrong with black family life. "Since she pays the piper, she usually feels justified in calling the tune," wrote St. Clair Drake and Horace Cayton in their study of Chicago, *Black Metropolis.* [46] Increasingly entrenched assumptions about "matriarchal" black women provided the building blocks for what by the 1960s became a widely shared national consensus regarding "black pathology," (and by 1996 enabled a Democratic president to dismantle the New Deal and sign punitive "welfare reform" legislation).[47]

Yet ideas about "matriarchs" assumed particular currency and meaning in the 1940s and 50s. In this period, liberal scholars melded preexisting ideas about black women's economic domination with the psychological terms and images that were circulating in so many arenas, including Philip Wylie's vitriolic attacks on "moms." In one case study, Abram Kardiner and Lionel Ovesey explained that the mother of "B.B." had "devoted all of her time" to her son and "was the real 'boss' of the household"; as a result, they concluded, the adult B.B. retained an infantile neediness and a "struggle for the maternal breast."[48] Here and elsewhere, a centuries-old tradition of black women as quintessential maternal figures intersected with contemporary theories about maternal rejection and maternal overprotection. As Drake and Cayton put it in *Black Metropolis,* mothers alternated between a destructive "defensive hardness" and an equally unhealthy "lavish tenderness" toward partners and offspring.[49] Still other women failed as mothers because, like Wylie's "moms," they were too concerned with the "primacy of pleasure" and "hedonistic" superficial goals.[50] And, like Farnham and Lundberg's "lost sex," black women were inclined toward "sex irregularity": both "frigidity" and promiscuity were frequent problems that black mothers exhibited, according to experts.[51]

In sum, all too many black women failed to mother successfully and thus failed to raise sons equipped to resist racial prejudice. Mothers helped to determine whether black men internalized or displaced their feelings of frustration; they determined whether compensatory behavior in adult black men included "apathy" or "living for the moment." As prominent ego psychologist Erik Erikson explained, maternal behavior yielded three possible "types" of black identities. These were "mammy's oral-sensual 'honey child,'" the "evil . . . dirty, anal-sadistic, phallic-rapist 'nigger,'" and the "clean, anal-compulsive, restrained . . . but always sad 'white man's Negro.'"[52]

Progressive analyses of racism's effects that focused on the private sphere of the home—and on mothers—served several functions. By arguing that undesirable qualities long regarded as innate (such as "laziness" or "shiftlessness" in black men, for example) developed through interactions between the individual and the family of which he was a part, liberal scholars suggested that racial progress was possible. If certain family dynamics could counter the underlying feelings that created this behavior, then the negative behavior could be overcome.

In fact, one important goal of this progressive literature was to dismantle racial stereotypes of black men and to show that they too could achieve respectable levels of masculinity and citizenship. Scholars described families organized around patriarchal gender relations as "proof" that economic, racial, and psychosocial health were possible. As Johnson explained it in *Growing Up in the Black Belt,* "upper- and middle-class [black] families usually follow what might be called a patriarchal setup like that of white families."[53] Similarly, in *Black Metropolis,* Drake and Cayton pointed to middle- and upper-class black men who had an "ordered and disciplined family life." These men saw "individual competition" as a "*racial* duty as well as a personal gain," commented the authors, reinforcing the sense that appropriate aggression in black men was simultaneously of personal, racial, and civic value.[54]

Further, this literature challenged racist myths about black men through representations of black women. In *The Mark of Oppression,* for example, Kardiner and Ovesey argued that black men were *not* the overly aggressive sexual predators that whites imagined: "The most surprising fact about the sex life of the Negro—of all classes—[and here they referred to men only] lies in its marked deviation from the white stereotypes. . . . The Negro is hardly the abandoned sexual hedonist he is supposed to be." Yet, how did they explain this surprising "deviation"? They argued that black men raised in a "female dominated household" had feelings of "frustrated dependency and hostility." These unhealthy relationships with mothers recurred with other women and interfered with healthy heterosexuality.[55] In order to counter racial stereotypes of black men, the authors needed to emphasize psychic distress and female dominance—thereby reinforcing stereotypes of black women as "matriarchs."

Thus, black women who were "bad" mothers "carried connotations of other crises," as Hazel Carby has explained in her analysis of black women migrants. These were the *overlapping* crises of black masculinity and race relations. Images of maternal failure both expressed and resolved these crises. It is important to note that if maternal behavior threatened black masculinity, demonizing black women as mothers also facilitated an affirmation of black masculinity.[56] By explaining deficiencies in black masculinity and in race relations with psychological frameworks that drew attention to maternal failure, scholars reaffirmed black men's potential.

Mother-blaming demystified the effects of racial self-hatred and suggested that it was possible—and necessary—for the individual to change and develop differently.[57]

Rethinking Race and Class in Images of Maternal Failure

Images of bad mothers developed in very different kinds of texts and debates in the 1940s and 50s. As has become clear, however, there was considerable overlap between mothers of prejudiced white men and mothers of black men crippled by prejudice. And these "moms" and "matriarchs" were in turn similar to those in more vitriolic "momism" literature. All forms of maternal pathology caused the same basic problem: sons who were either insufficiently aggressive, inhibited, and sexually passive and repressed; or sons who were too aggressive, insufficiently cooperative, and violent. Adult men confirmed the damage that these mothers inflicted and made it clear that emotional conditions were at the root of social and political problems. Mothers jeopardized the very codes of masculinity and citizenship that liberals deemed essential to American strength and interracial health in this period. Bad mothers, then, were bad precisely because they produced damaged citizens.

In certain instances, "bad" mothers crossed lines of class as well as race. Black "matriarchs" were not always poor and single, as is often assumed. Rather, according to experts, middle-class black mothers also exhibited destructive and "matriarchal" behavior. "A.T.," for example, was a middle-class woman who "married mainly for economic reasons," for whom sex was "ridden with fear and disgust," and who applied unrealistic "perfectionist standards" to her son. Charles Johnson scorned the widow who used her husband's insurance policy to build and furnish an elaborate house. Her constant striving for status symbols made her oblivious to the fact that her daughters were "bored and indifferent," "sad and broken targets of ridicule," and that they wanted to drop out of school and leave home.[58] Scholars thus criticized certain kinds of class-related behavior through (related) indictments of women as mothers and consumers.

Even when "moms" and "matriarchs" appeared to be very similar, however, race shaped the indictment of the "bad" mother. Female sexuality, for example, was crucial to assessments of both white and black mothers. Indeed, this biracial discourse reformulated normative female sexuality by linking it to motherhood.[59] Nevertheless, even as scholars depicted both white and black "bad" mothers as sexually insatiable or sexually repressed, they were more likely to associate white women with frigidity and black women with promiscuity. "Good" mothers had to achieve a balance between stereotypes that historically had been racially specific: between the frigidity still associated with white women and the promiscuity still associated with black women.[60]

Further, there was one type of maternal failure that was specific to black women, and this was identifying with whiteness. Experts argued that black women who overidentified with white standards rejected or criticized both sons and husbands; as a result, sons and husbands themselves had feelings of racial self-hatred. In *The Mark of Oppression*, Kardiner and Ovesey found middle-class women particularly likely to emulate white women and want their sons to be like white men. One such subject rejected her son when his behavior fit "prejudicial anti-Negro stereotypes"; her maternal rejection reflected an attempt "to deny her Negro identification."[61] Erik Erikson observed that black mothers of all classes who used "sudden correctives . . . to approach the vague but pervasive Anglo-Saxon ideal" created "violent discontinuities" that harmed their children. The "Negro's unavoidable identification with the dominant race" was damaging, said Erikson, because it caused self-hatred to intrude on a child's development out of the oral phase—a trauma that reverberated for years. Maternal behavior prevented children from developing a "lasting ego identity," so necessary for full participation in American life.[62]

It is, of course, more than ironic that studies of racism's effects directly and indirectly evaluated African Americans against a "white control group" at the very same time that experts indicted black women for being too preoccupied with white standards. In this context, maternal behavior that would otherwise be seen as normative (i.e., wanting children to behave) was rendered pathological when it manifested in middle-class black women. This contradictory logic indicates the degree to which black women were in a double bind and how difficult it was for them to escape charges that they had failed as mothers and as women.

In sum, although race and gender intersected in images of all women, gender remained the lens through which experts saw white maternal failure, while race remained the lens through which they saw black maternal failure. If "momism" produced what was in part a racial problem (prejudice) as a result of gender disorders in white women, then "matriarchy" produced what was in part a gender problem (unmanly black men) as a result of racial disorders in black women.

At the time, turning to the family and to psychological categories for an explanation of race relations made sense in the context of both disciplinary paradigm shifts and international events. Using these frameworks did not transform progressive intellectuals who resisted and condemned segregation into reactionary misogynists. The underlying logic in these frameworks, however, suggested that to be a good American man one needed a strong ego; to develop a strong ego, one required a good mother. This logic made mothers central to racism's harmful personal and political effects; it gave the "bad" mother widespread credibility and applicability as a way of explaining the sources of racism in whites and the effects of racism on blacks. It was within this gendered logic that race became a more legitimate concern for mainstream postwar liberalism, and interracial harmony became associated with Americanism. Representations of motherhood implicitly and explicitly shaped widespread debates about who was a healthy citizen, what was a healthy democracy, and how racial prejudice interfered with personal and national health.

The women who populated the literature condemning racial inequities in the 1940s and 50s demonstrate how and why the "bad" mother—white and black—became a common figure in liberal discourse specifically. Her failures provided the basis for social and cultural critiques that included denunciations of racism. Ultimately, mother-blaming was one way through which liberal intellectuals envisioned social change.

NOTES

For comments on earlier versions of this essay, my thanks to Gail Bederman, Mari Jo Buhle, Carolyn Dean, Michael Ermarth, Elizabeth Francis, Jane Gerhard, Michael Geyer, Jacqueline Jones, Uli Linke, Melani McAlister, Uta Poiger, John L. Thomas, and audiences at the annual meeting of the American Historical Association, January 1996, and the Berkshire Conference on Women's History, June 1996.

1. With the help of the psychiatrist, Moss discovers that he is paralyzed by guilt over the death of a white soldier on the mission. The man had been a childhood friend and defends Moss from racist white soldiers—until he too (right before his death) calls Moss "nigger." In order to recover, Moss must learn that his guilt is "universal," the guilt of the soldier who survives his buddy's death. The racial power dynamics between him and his friend, he must conclude,

are irrelevant. For more on *Home of the Brave*, see Michael Rogin, *Blackface, White Noise: Jewish Immigrants in the Hollywood Melting Pot* (Berkeley: University of California Press, 1996), 232–50; and Thomas Pauly, "Black Images and White Culture during the Decade before the Civil Rights Movement," *American Studies* 31 (Fall 1990): 101–19.

2. For the cultural and political texts that helped to produce the idea of racism as un-American, see, for example, Pauly, "Black Images and White Culture"; Mary L. Dudziak, "Desegregation as a Cold War Imperative," *Stanford Law Review* 41 (November 1988): 61–120; Ruth Feldstein, *Making "Moms" and "Matriarchs": Dangerous Women, Race, and American Liberalism, 1930–1965* (Cornell University Press, forthcoming); and Philip Gleason, "Americans All: World War II and the Shaping of American Identity," *Review of Politics* 93 (October 1981): 483–518, especially 495–500. Although this discussion centers on the work of public intellectuals and prominent social scientists, the notion of racism as "un-American," and the related focus on the psychological damage racism inflicted cut across disciplines and genres, permeating popular and political discourse.

3. I have come to think of this discourse in terms of "codes of masculinity" under the influence of Hazel Carby, "Policing the Black Woman's Body in an Urban Context," *Critical Inquiry* 18 (Summer 1992): 738–55. While this literature did suggest that "bad" mothers could harm daughters as well as sons, ultimately, because scholars' primary concerns were with citizens in a democracy, their primary concern was with sons. In other words, this discourse equated healthy and strong citizens with healthy and strong men *through* discussions of women as mothers.

4. Philip Wylie, *Generation of Vipers* (New York: Holt, Rinehart and Winston, 1955; orig. pub. 1942), 201, 208, 206, 213, 216. Marynia Farnham and Ferdinand Lundberg, *Modern Woman: The Lost Sex* (New York: Harper and Brothers, 1947), 298, 23.

5. Discussions which situate these texts in narratives about postwar sexual conservatism include John P. Diggins, *The Proud Decades: America in War and Peace, 1941–1960* (New York: Norton, 1988), 227; Sara Evans, *Born for Liberty: A History of Women in America* (New York: Free Press, 1988), 238–39; Cynthia Harrison, *On Account of Sex: The Politics of Women's Issues, 1945–1968* (Berkeley: University of California Press, 1988), 24–25; Elaine Tyler May, *Homeward Bound: American Families in the Cold War Era* (New York: Basic Books, 1988); and Sonya Michel, "Danger on the Home Front: Motherhood, Sexuality, and Disabled Veterans in American Postwar Films," *Journal of the History of Sexuality* 3 (July 1992): 109–28. For primary texts through which ideas about maternal overprotection and rejection developed, see David M. Levy, *Maternal Overprotection* (New York: Columbia University Press, 1943); and Margaret Ribble, *The Rights of Infants* (New York: Columbia University Press, 1943).

6. It is also worth noting the liberal aspects of these texts: Farnham and

Lundberg supported a "federal department of welfare" that would include subsidies to families (*Modern Woman*, 359, 364), and in later editions, Wylie criticized McCarthyism as "the rule of unreason . . . one with momism" (*Generation of Vipers*, 196).

7. E. Franklin Frazier, *The Negro Family in the United States* (Chicago: University of Chicago Press, 1939). See Patricia Morton, *Disfigured Images: The Historical Assault on Afro-American Women* (New York: Praeger Press, 1991).

8. "Crackpot" in Julie Weiss, *Womanhood and Psychoanalysis: A Study of Mutual Construction in Popular Culture* (Ph.D. diss., Brown University, 1990), 170; "conservative margin" in Joanne Meyerowitz, "Beyond The Feminine Mystique: A Reassessment of Postwar Mass Culture, 1946–1958," in Meyerowitz, ed., *Not June Cleaver: Women and Gender in Postwar America, 1945–1960* (Philadelphia: Temple University Press, 1994), 247. The concept of the "bad" mother was closely related to that of the "good" mother, celebrated as quintessentially American in this same period. Images of "good" mothers constantly invoked—and in fact depended upon—the opposite: images of women as "bad" mothers.

9. For disciplinary changes, see George Stocking, Jr., ed., *Malinowski, Rivers, Benedict and Others: Essays on Culture and Personality*, vol. 4 of *History of Anthropology* (Madison: University of Wisconsin Press, 1986); and Gerald Platt, "The Sociological Endeavor and Psychoanalytic Thought," *American Quarterly* 28 (1976): 343–59.

10. John Dollard, Leonard W. Doob, Neal E. Miller, O. H. Mower, Robert R. Sears, in collaboration with Clellan S. Ford, Carl Iver Hovland, and Richard T. Sollenberger, *Frustration and Aggression* (New Haven: Yale University Press, 1974; orig. pub. 1939), 1, emphasis in original. Dollard and his collaborators worked out of Yale's Institute of Human Relations. For their influence, see Fred Matthews, "The Utopia of Human Relations: The Conflict-Free Family in American Social Thought, 1930–1960," *Journal of the History of the Behavioral Sciences* 24 (October 1988): 343–62; J. G. Morawski, "Organizing Knowledge and Behavior at Yale's Institute of Human Relations," *Isis* 77 (1986): 219–42; and Ellen Herman, *The Romance of American Psychology: Political Culture in the Age of Experts* (Berkeley: University of California Press, 1995).

11. Dollard et al., *Frustration and Aggression*, 1.

12. For early links between racism, frustration, and aggression, see John Dollard, *Caste and Class in a Southern Town* (Madison: University of Wisconsin Press, 1988; orig. pub. 1937). Race relations became more central to progressive scholarly research for domestic reasons as well: as thousands of African Americans migrated from the South to northern and western cities.

13. The war also generated fears about insufficiently aggressive men, particularly American soldiers. For arguments that faulty mothering accounted for insufficiently aggressive soldiers, see, for example, Edward Strecker, *Their Mothers' Sons: The Psychiatrist Examines an American Problem* (Philadelphia: J. B.

Lippincott Co., 1946); and Herbert Kupper, *Back to Life: The Emotional Adjustment of Our Veterans* (New York: American Book-Stratford Press, 1945).

14. See Elazar Barkan, *The Retreat of Scientific Racism: Changing Concepts of Race in Britain and the United States between the World Wars* (Cambridge: Cambridge University Press, 1992), 345.

15. Betsy Emmons, "The Psychiatrists Look at Race Hate," *Negro Digest* (July 1948), 25, emphasis in original.

16. T. W. Adorno, Else Frenkel-Brunswick, Daniel J. Levinson, R. Nevitt Sanford, in collaboration with Betty Aron, Maria Hertz Levinson, and William Morrow, *The Authoritarian Personality,* American Jewish Committee Social Studies Series, Publication no. 3 (New York: Harper and Brothers, 1950); Wilhelm Reich, *The Mass Psychology of Fascism,* trans. by Vincent R. Carfango (New York: Simon and Schuster, 1970; orig. pub. 1933); Erich Fromm, *Escape from Freedom* (New York: Avon, 1969; orig. pub. 1941); and Bruno Bettelheim and Morriss Janowitz, *Dynamics of Prejudice* (New York: Harper, 1950). For the Frankfurt School theorists, see Martin Jay, *The Dialectical Imagination: A History of the Frankfurt School and the Institute of Social Research, 1923–1950* (Boston: Little, Brown, 1973); and Jay, *Permanent Exiles: Essays on Intellectual Migration from Germany to America* (New York: Columbia University Press, 1985). For a critique of the relationship between anti-Semitism and race in this period, see Elisabeth Young-Bruehl, *The Anatomy Of Prejudices* (Cambridge: Harvard University Press, 1996).

17. Gunnar Myrdal, *An American Dilemma,* 2 vols. (New York: Harper Brothers, 1944); Lillian Smith, *Killers of the Dream* (Garden City, N.Y.: Anchor Books, 1963; orig. pub. 1949); Gordon Allport, *The Nature of Prejudice,* 25th anniversary ed. (Reading, Mass.: Addison-Wesley, 1979; orig. pub. 1954); Charles Johnson, *Growing Up in the Black Belt: Negro Youth in the Rural South* (New York: Schocken Books, 1967; orig. pub. 1941); Horace Cayton and St. Clair Drake, *Black Metropolis: A Study of Negro Life in a Northern City* (New York: Harper and Row, 1962; orig. pub. 1945); Abram Kardiner and Lionel Ovesey, *The Mark of Oppression: Explorations in the Personality of the American Negro* (Cleveland and New York: Meridian Books, 1962; orig. pub. 1951).

18. This discussion is based on areas of overlap; on the basis of these overlaps I locate the Marxist cultural critic T. W. Adorno on a liberal spectrum. For differences among those who opposed prejudice, see Walter Jackson, *Gunnar Myrdal and America's Social Conscience: Social Engineering and American Liberalism, 1938–1987* (Chapel Hill: University of North Carolina Press, 1987); Morton Sosna, *In Search of the Silent South: Southern Liberals and the Race Issue* (New York: Columbia University Press, 1977); and Young-Bruehl, *The Anatomy Of Prejudices.*

19. My thanks to Steven Biel for helping me to think of this shift in these terms.

20. Emmons, "The Psychiatrists Look at Race Hate," 25.

21. Gunnar Myrdal, *An American Dilemma*, 1022, emphasis in original. For positive reviews of *An American Dilemma*, see Robert Lynd, "Prison for American Genius," *Saturday Review*, April 22, 1944, 5–7, 27; and E. Franklin Frazier, "Race: An American Dilemma," *Crisis* 51 (1944): 105–6, 129.

22. Walter Jackson, "The Making of a Social Science Classic: Gunnar Myrdal's *An American Dilemma*," *Perspectives in American History*, n.s., 2 (1985): 221–67, quote on 221. For the "Negro Problem" as a paradigm, see Morton, *Disfigured Images*, especially chap. 5. The "Negro problem" did persist. See, for example, Charles Glicksberg, "Science and the Race Problem," *Phylon* 12 (1951): 319–27.

23. Myrdal, *An American Dilemma*, 1003.

24. Young-Bruehl, *The Anatomy of Prejudices*, 36; Adorno et al., *The Authoritarian Personality*, 367. For debates about *The Authoritarian Personality*, see, for example, Richard Christie and Marie Jahoda, eds., *Studies in the Scope and Method of "The Authoritarian Personality"* (Glencoe, Ill.: Free Press, 1954).

25. Allport, *The Nature of Prejudice*, 298, emphasis in original. See also R. Blake and W. Dennis, "The Development of Stereotypes Concerning the Negro," *Journal of Abnormal and Social Psychology* 38 (1943): 525–31.

26. Adorno et al., *The Authoritarian Personality*, 366, 359, 365.

27. Adorno et al., *The Authoritarian Personality*, 367, 371.

28. Benjamin Spock, *Baby and Child Care* (New York: Hawthorn Books, 1968; orig. pub. 1946), 7. In this period, Spock was not much concerned with race relations specifically but was concerned with the damage that overprotective or rejecting mothers did and with the need for appropriately aggressive citizens. For other literature that gave mother-blaming legitimacy, see Erik Erikson, *Childhood and Society* (New York: W. W. Norton, 1963; orig. pub. 1950); Geoffrey Gorer, *The American People: A Study in National Character* (New York: W. W. Norton, 1948); and Margaret Mead, *And Keep Your Powder Dry* (New York: William Morrow, 1965; orig. pub. 1942), especially 80–99. Of course, these discussions of American citizens and American "character" were in fact preoccupied with whites.

29. Adorno et al., *The Authoritarian Personality*, 366, 359, 365.

30. Allport, *The Nature of Prejudice*, 361; see also, Arnold Rose, "Intergroup Anxieties in a Mass Society," *Phylon* 12 (1951): 305–18.

31. Allport, *The Nature of Prejudice*, 361; "outward submissiveness" and "inward aggressiveness" from Rose, "Intergroup Anxieties in a Mass Society," 313.

32. For attempts to regulate homosexuality in this period, see Allan Bérubé, *Coming Out under Fire: The History of Gay Men and Women in World War II* (New York: Free Press, 1990); and John D'Emilio, "The Homosexual Menace: The Politics of Sexuality in Cold War America," in Kathy Peiss and Christina Simmons, eds., *Passion and Power: Sexuality in History* (Philadelphia: Temple University Press, 1989), 226–40.

33. Smith, *Killers of the Dream*, 128. Smith dealt with similar themes in her

novel about a doomed interracial romance, *Strange Fruit* (New York: Reynal and Hitchcock, 1944). For similar themes, see James W. Largen, "White Boy in Georgia," *Negro Digest* 9 (June 1951): 67–75.

34. Lillian Smith, "Addressed to White Liberals," *New Republic*, September 18, 1944, 331–33. For Smith's work and life, see Anne C. Loveland, *Lillian Smith, A Southerner Confronting the South: A Biography* (Baton Rouge: Louisiana State University Press, 1986); Roseanne V. Camacho, "Race, Region, and Gender in a Reassessment of Lillian Smith," in Virginia Bernhard et al., eds., *Southern Women: History and Identities* (Columbia: University of Missouri Press, 1992), 157–76; and Margaret Rose Gladney, ed., *How Am I to Be Heard? Letters of Lillian Smith* (Chapel Hill: University of North Carolina Press, 1993).

35. Smith, *Killers of the Dream*, 17, 73, 100, 132–33, 70, 69, 102. Smith noted that this was not the only type of white mother. In some passages, her descriptions of white southern mothers veered more toward images of overprotectiveness and indulgence: "We were petted children. . . . Sugar-tit words and sugar-tit experiences too often made of our minds and manners a fatty tissue that hid the sharp rickety bones of our souls" (76).

36. Smith, *Killers of the Dream*, 102, 104.

37. Smith, *Killers of the Dream*, 122. For Farnham and Lundberg, see *Modern Woman*, 140–67.

38. Smith, *Killers of the Dream*, 134. In this effort to distance herself from the concept of "momism" even as she reinscribed it, Smith also resembled Erikson, *Childhood and Society*, 289–91.

39. It also produced an unusual awareness of her own privileges as an upper class white woman. See Gladney, *How Am I to Be Heard?* Further, in contrast to some of her more vituperative peers, she showed compassion for southern white women suffering a double loss: they "take the husk of a love which her son in his earliest years had given to another woman," and then faced the withdrawal of their husbands (*Killers of the Dream*, 120). Smith's compassion for black women is also evident but is far more problematic, based as it was on stereotypes about nurturing "mammies."

40. Jackson, *Gunnar Myrdal and America's Conscience*, 290. Consequently, funding was less available for scholars studying African Americans.

41. Kardiner and Ovesey, *The Mark of Oppression*, 11, 20.

42. Kardiner and Ovesey, *The Mark of Oppression*, 95; Johnson, *Growing Up in the Black Belt*, 19, 99.

43. Johnson, *Growing Up in the Black Belt*, 99. Johnson did qualify this assessment of "disorganized" families, commenting that "this does not mean, however, that all members of this group are morally disorganized."

44. Kardiner and Ovesey, *The Mark of Oppression*, 381–87. For the feminization of black men, see also Drake and Cayton, *Black Metropolis*, 517, 603, 587.

45. Kardiner and Ovesey, *The Mark of Oppression*, 97.

46. Drake and Cayton, *Black Metropolis,* 583. See also Johnson, *Growing Up in the Black Belt,* 58; Myrdal, *An American Dilemma,* 933.

47. For building blocks from earlier in the century, see Morton, *Disfigured Images,* 27–65; Carby, "Policing the Black Woman's Body," 738–40. Footnotes and acknowledgments in these texts underscore this scholarly tradition, and the important role that Frazier played in giving black family "disorganization" and maternal domination widespread credibility.

48. Kardiner and Ovesey, *The Mark of Oppression,* 198–99; see also 251, 142.

49. Drake and Cayton, *Black Metropolis,* 584. For earlier expressions of black women as uniquely or "naturally" maternal, see, W. E. B. Du Bois, *The Negro American Family* (Westport, Conn.: Negro Universities Press, 1970; orig. pub. 1908); and U. B. Phillips, *Life and Labor in the Old South* (Boston: Little, Brown, 1963; orig. pub. 1929). For representations of black women as "mammies," see Morton, *Disfigured Images;* Deborah Gray White, *Ar'n't I a Woman? Female Slaves in the Ante-Bellum South* (New York: Norton, 1985), 27–61; and Patricia Hill Collins, *Black Feminist Thought: Knowledge, Consciousness, and the Politics of Empowerment* (Boston: Unwin Hyman, 1990), 67–90.

50. Drake and Cayton, *Black Metropolis,* 608; Kardiner and Ovesey, *The Mark of Oppression,* 161; see also Allport, *The Nature of Prejudice,* 157. For more positive assessments of leisure and consumption, see Drake and Cayton, *Black Metropolis,* 387.

51. Johnson, *Growing Up in the Black Belt,* 79; Kardiner and Ovesey, *The Mark of Oppression,* 129–38.

52. Kardiner and Ovesey, *The Mark of Oppression,* 304; Erikson, *Childhood and Society,* 242.

53. Johnson, *Growing Up in the Black Belt,* 58; see also 63–64, 73–75, 80–98; Kardiner and Ovesey, *The Mark of Oppression,* 314; and Myrdal, *An American Dilemma,* 931.

54. Drake and Cayton, *Black Metropolis,* 389, emphasis in original.

55. Kardiner and Ovesey, *The Mark of Oppression,* 69–70; see also Allport, *The Nature of Prejudice,* 381.

56. See Carby, "Policing the Black Woman's Body," 739–41.

57. See Michael Rogin, "'Democracy and Burnt Cork': The End of Blackface, the Beginning of Civil Rights," *Representations* 46 (Spring 1994): 1–34, especially 9.

58. Kardiner and Ovesey, *The Mark of Oppression,* 214–23; Johnson, *Growing Up in the Black Belt,* 88–90. For other critiques of middle-class blacks through an indictment of the middle-class black mother, see Drake and Cayton, *Black Metropolis,* 564–70, 667–68. In *The Mark of Oppression,* a study written in 1951 and in the context of growing anxieties about the effects of affluence in a consumer-oriented society, "bad" mothers were likely to be middle class as well as working class.

59. Jane Gerhard, *Politicizing Pleasure: Discourses on Womanhood, Female Sexuality, and Feminism in Modern America, 1920–1982* (Ph.D. diss., Brown University, 1996), chap. 1.

60. For a similar argument with regard to questions of dependence and independence, see Nancy Fraser and Linda Gordon, "A Genealogy of *Dependency:* Tracing a Keyword of the U.S. Welfare State," *Signs* 19 (Winter 1994): 309–36. "The problem was that women were supposed to be just dependent enough, and it was easy to tip over into excess in either direction. The norm, moreover, was racially marked, as white women were usually portrayed as erring on the side of excessive dependence, while black women were typically charged with excessive independence" (325).

61. Kardiner and Ovesey, *The Mark of Oppression,* 214–23, 252–54. For self-hatred and color consciousness in women, see also Johnson, *Growing Up in the Black Belt,* 97.

62. Erikson, *Childhood and Society,* 241–46. In other cases, "the children themselves learn to disavow their sensual and overprotective mothers as temptations and a hindrance to the formation of a more American personality." Erikson noted that historically this "oral sensory treasure" contributed to the development of "mild, submissive, dependent" identities in slaves, but suggested that relative to the sexual repression many whites experienced, blacks and other immigrant groups were "privileged in the enjoyment of a more sensual early childhood" (245). See too Johnson, *Growing Up in the Black Belt,* 225; and Smith, *Killers of the Dream,* 100, for positive assessments of "unrepressed" blacks.

Chapter 8

"Momism" and the Making of Treasonous Homosexuals

Jennifer Terry

Nearly a hundred years ago, Dr. William Lee Howard, commenting on the dangerous prominence of feminist activism in the United States, wrote in the *New York Medical Journal* that "emancipated" women were responsible for creating effeminate boys and masculine girls, a most undesirable outcome which, the doctor suggested, was tantamount to the nation's decay.[1] Teddy Roosevelt voiced similar sentiments in 1917, on the eve of America's entry into World War I, when he launched an attack on the women-led peace and antidraft movements by singling out the image of the pacifist mother whose pathological attachment to her son was turning him into an emasculated coward, thus hastening moral disintegration and heading the nation into ruin.[2] But "mom"-bashing gained industrial strength during the decade following World War II, as bad mothers became powerful career vehicles for a host of sexist columnists, legislators, movie directors, and, most notably, psychiatrists who heaped upon mothers culpability for everything from juvenile delinquency to totalitarianism.[3]

The history of blaming mothers for American political problems reveals how norms of gender and sexuality, far from being isolated in "private" realms of the individual personality or the family, are very much public matters. For although fathers were occasionally implicated in the making of properly gendered citizens, again and again throughout the twentieth century, mothers have been held primarily responsible for producing psychologically sound Americans. Within a binary and hierarchical construction of gender, individuals are directed to take their places as proper citizens, behaving appropriately according to their identity as either men or women and maturing into healthy, adjusted heterosexuals, whose social and biological reproduction is deemed essential to the integrity of the self and, metonymically, the nation. Mother's job is to make boys into sufficiently masculine men and girls into feminine women. In America during the twentieth century, one can find striking correlations between moments when cultural norms of gender and sexuality are destabilized and waves of political anxiety that manifest in mother-blaming.

While historians have analyzed the relationship between Cold War rhetoric, sexism, and the "mom"-bashing that emerged in the 1940s, few have considered the specifically homophobic dimensions of this triumvirate. This essay examines how the popularized resurgence of mother-blaming was fueled by a misogynist and homophobic backlash against a perceived erosion of gender distinctions occurring during the war. Reactionary critics especially cited women's increased participation in the public spheres of employment, politics, and culture as evidence of this troubling erosion. In this context, lesbians and gay men, imagined primarily as gender inverts, signified the breakdown of clearly delineated gender roles, and their purported prevalence in American society was blamed on the errant behavior of the nation's "moms." Following the war, gay and lesbian communities in major U.S. cities expanded dramatically as many homosexual veterans opted to take up residence in places like San Francisco, New York, Chicago, and Los Angeles, rather than return to the smaller towns of their origin. The growing political visibility of gay men and lesbians, which increased in the 1950s with the formation of homophile political organizations, contributed to a climate of Cold War anxiety among those who saw homosexuality, like communism, as inimical to American society.[4] As part of a sweeping backlash, the figure of the demonic "mom" functioned not only to generate prescriptive norms of motherhood but to unleash homophobic stereotypes, in the service of an expressly misogynist national agenda premised on compulsory heterosexuality and the hierarchical organization of masculinity and femininity that underpinned it. The stereotypes of the seditious gay man and the treasonous lesbian reveal the complex ideological maneuvers that tied the psychological domains of the individual and family to a nationalist zeal for American global supremacy.

Besides the notorious communist, during the early years of the Cold War, another figure was singled out and characterized as demonic, treasonous, and fundamentally antithetical to the welfare and security of the United States. The so-called "sex pervert" threatened to weaken the nation through his sexual indiscretions and effeminate predilections.[5] In showcased congressional hearings and highly publicized internal security campaigns, the typical "sex pervert" brought under this hostile national spotlight was the white, middle-class, college-educated homosexual man who was most likely an FDR Democrat, employed either in the State Department or some other office of foreign service. The loyalty and national security programs, implemented first by Truman in 1946 and then elaborated by Eisenhower in the 1950s, used the term "sex perversion" virtually interchangeably with male homosexuality. Initially, they targeted gay men as "bad security risks," likely to succumb, like love-starved women, to the advances of a hunky Soviet spy or to give away secrets out of fear of blackmail. As the security programs expanded by successive executive orders, "sex perverts" came to be seen not merely as bad security risks but as fundamentally disloyal, with behaviors, practices, and lives that were contrary to the American way of life.[6] Like the Reds, whose allegiance was to international communism, and the Jews who were believed to put Zionism before all else, male homosexuals answered to an internationalist anti-American authority—that of perverse desire itself—that had infiltrated the heart of American society, threatening to cause its decay from within. In the words of Countess R. G. Wadek, whose passionate treatise *The Homosexual International*, appeared in the Congressional Record in 1952,

[B]y the very nature of their vice, [homosexuals] belong to a sinister, mysterious and efficient international. Welded together by the identity of their forbidden desires, of their strange, sad needs, habits, dangers, not to mention their fatuous vocabulary, members of this international constitute a worldwide conspiracy against society.... Without being necessarily Marxist, [homosexuals] serve the ends of the Communist International in the name of their rebellion against the prejudices, standards, and ideals of the bourgeois world.[7]

The accusation of homosexual disloyalty reflected a broader strategy for controlling behavior and choices contrary to the system of compulsory heterosexuality and male dominance that structured the nuclear family. But the nuclear family itself, and particularly mothers' neurotic behavior toward their sons, were seen as causing the character weakness of male homosexuality.

The executive orders and congressional hearings on loyalty and security rarely mentioned lesbianism, with the notable exception of the Washington, D.C. vice squad leader who expressed an unfulfilled desire to set up a special "Lesbian Squad" to hunt down and arrest female sex perverts.[8] Official purges of lesbians from the military immediately following World War II offer the clearest manifestation of the Cold War antihomosexual panic targeting women, as the military sought to establish and police new standards of femininity in the armed forces.[9] But lesbians, while seldom the focus of official Cold War congressional theatrics, were nonetheless increasingly characterized in popular psychiatric writing as treasonous precisely because of their rejection of wifely and maternal duties at a time when the nation's women were being urged to assume the self-sacrificing role of full-time unpaid domestic service. The dramatic retrenchment to sharply delineated gender roles in the wake of World War II relied upon constructing the figures of the bad mom and her perverse children as perilous germs infecting the heart and soul of the nation.

Discussions about the fundamentally treasonous nature of homosexuality in the postwar period proliferated in the increasingly influential world of psychiatry. During the war, psychiatrists had begun to generate alarmist and contemptuous opinions about both female and male homosexuality.[10] When the war ended, they contributed to a Cold War discourse which assumed as its principal tenet that the personal was political, that is, that the nation's strengths and weaknesses were based upon the personal behavior and psychological qualities of individual citizens. Previous waves of antihomosexual backlash in urban American contexts had resulted in the ascendancy of physicians and scientists as purveyors of information about sex "inversion" and "perversion." These experts responded to conservative concerns about the increase of homosexuality from the rapid urbanization of the 1880s through the hedonism and feminism of the "Roaring Twenties" and into the devastating Great Depression.[11] But following a number of studies from the 1930s and 1940s that were inconclusive as to the biological or hereditary causes of homosexuality, psychoanalytically inclined psychiatrists asserted their authority by stressing psychogenic theories that identified parent-child relationships within the family as the primary cause of gender deviance, homosexuality, and national weakness.[12] By the 1950s, the other site of inquisition, which both bolstered and relied upon the concurrent congressional witch-hunts of the House Un-American Activities Committee, was the psychiatric profession. One need only turn to the psychoanalytic literature of the period to find lively and rather vitriolic constructions of the most treasonous sissies and gay-girls. And there too we will find the origin of their evil and perversion: the specter of the ruinous mom!

Strikingly, ideologues of the 1940s and 1950s elevated the domestic sphere to a highly privileged domain in their formulations about the health and welfare of the nation.[13] Since the American Revolution, the long-standing tradition of Republican Motherhood had emphasized womanly civic virtue and the importance of separating public and domestic spheres to ensure the moral education of American children.[14] And, significantly, during World War I, patriots deployed the figure of the self-sacrificing mother to inspire military discipline and devotion to the nation.[15] However, the ideological valorization of the domestic sphere immediately following World War II was pronounced in its intensity. Indeed, this postwar "family boom" was part and parcel of a multifaceted and highly orchestrated ideological campaign to move women back into a position of subordination to men, as loyal wives and mothers. It was fueled, in part, by a backlash against the relative degree of economic self-sufficiency and social mobility women achieved as a result of well-paid employment in wartime industrial production. To make room for returning veterans, women were encouraged to return to the home, marry, and have children, thus helping to restore American society and ensure the status of the United States as an international economic and political power.

This conservative agenda cast the normal and robust American family in decidedly white, middle-class, and nucleated terms, with a breadwinning father, a housewife mother, and two or three gender-appropriate children. Extended families, families headed by women, and families including mothers who had to work outside the home to make ends meet, particularly common among working-class communities of African Americans and first- and second-generation European and Asian immigrants, were seen as inferior—if sometimes quaint—in comparison to the idealized patriarchal middle-class family. In this postwar articulation of what the Right now calls "family values," the home figured once again, as it had in nineteenth-century bourgeois ideology, as a haven in a heartless world. Its twentieth-century version was an architecturally discrete and psychologically sound site in which to cultivate the moral strength of the nation.[16] But what most distinguished the postwar cult of domesticity from earlier versions was its palpable paranoia, manifesting in anxieties over unsavory influences that threatened the home not only from without but from within.[17]

Psychiatrists associated with the mental hygiene movement founded in the second decade of the century, had long devoted their energies to defining and promoting the country's health and psychological welfare.[18] They saw the family as central to maintaining mental hygiene, but no more so than schools, churches, communities, and workplaces. As World War II came to a close, many of the same professionally credentialed men who had been involved in mental hygiene campaigns and military psychiatry, intensified their focus specifically on the family, approaching it as a unit requiring careful monitoring and expert intervention to ensure the integrity of the nation's future citizens. The maternal role involved the greatest responsibility and elicited the most professional advice. Conferring enormous ideological power upon the middle-class nuclear family, these experts placed women of all classes in a particular kind of double bind: as wives they were to stand dutifully and submissively by their husbands, while at the same time, as mothers, they were to exert power, preeminently by instilling standards of virtue and patriotic self-sufficiency in their children. Assigned the task of ensuring biological, psychological, and social reproduction in the home, a mother needed to center her life around others. Without her family she was nothing. Women who by choice or necessity did not marry or have children, and those who worked outside of the home, were regarded as fundamentally selfish and neglectful. In return for her efforts, the self-sacrificing mother could either receive honorific, if patronizing, credit, or have blame heaped upon her for any character weaknesses among the citizenry. The most complicated of her tasks consisted of exercising the proper measure of discipline and attentiveness to produce a healthy child: she was to be neither smothering nor neglectful. A vast number of advice books, geared to middle-class mothers, brought the most minute gestures and habits into the realm of "childrearing." These texts encouraged mothers to be self-monitoring in their every move.[19] Psychiatrist George Henry, for example, suggested that mothers take an active role in preventing homosexuality by first setting good examples of femininity and then making sure their children engaged in gender-appropriate activities: "There is no adequate substitute for well-adjusted mothers. . . . A girl should not only have knowledge of domestic activities but should engage in these activities until she feels secure in actually performing them and in supervising their performance. Likewise a boy should be trained in the mechanics and the responsibilities of maintaining a home."[20] According to the psychoanalytic perspective framing advice of this sort, even those behaviors not seemingly related to a woman's maternal role made a difference in children's development, for the child's most crucial figure for constituting identity was the mother. Her every move had an impact on her children's psychological health, and, of course, her femininity was the foundation for developing properly gendered citizens.

Endowing the middle-class family with the power to ensure or destroy the nation put middle-class mothers in a politically significant role, but one which was implicitly meant to contain them in a domain outside the public sphere of lawmaking and commerce. Meanwhile their working-class counterparts, laboring inside and outside the home, were increasingly blamed for raising rebellious juvenile delinquents incapable of discerning right from wrong. While fortifying a separation between public and private domains, the marriage of "family values" and Cold War ideology made the suburban split-level home a key staging ground for proper citizenship, even as suburbanites increasingly complained of the malaise, loneliness, and alienation brought on by the isolation and cultural homogenization of their neighborhoods.[21] According to Cold War family values, mothers and fathers assumed highly differentiated roles, with gender-specific criteria for what counted as loyalty or treason. Deviation from one's proper gender role suggested anti-Americanism, as effeminacy in men and masculinity in women increasingly came to be seen as threats to domestic and national security. In psychiatric and popular writing of the time, gender and sexual disorder both signified and caused national disorder. For women in particular, politically dangerous neurotic behavior was most powerfully exemplified either in their flawed, narcissistic, and brutal methods of childrearing, or in their total dissent from the roles of wife and mother.

The tendency to blame mothers that intensified during this period actually started as the Second World War was still raging, when a man of audaciously woman-hating opinions, wholly untrained in psychiatry, offered his thoughts on the subject of motherhood. In his 1942 bestseller, *Generation of Vipers,* popular columnist Philip Wylie, coined the term "momism" to describe the destructive tendency among the overwhelming majority of American mothers to stifle, dominate, and manipulate their children—particularly sons—into submission and crippling weakness.[22] Wylie, a self-described "motherless" man, stressed the importance of American military might in earlier magazine columns warning of the

threats of communism and fascism. But in *Vipers,* Wylie tied this milita-
rist zeal to a vitriolic critique of mothers, by drawing the character of the
sexually frustrated, self-righteous, manipulative "mom," who dominated
her husband, cultivated her son's dependence, and brought the nation's
enemy, totalitarianism, literally home to roost. In Wylie's text, the family
became the pit of hell for men and boys under the tyrannical dominion
of pathological mothers. Mom's destructive power, for Wylie, was a horrid
by-product of civilization, brought on by women's pillage of men's
money, their right to vote, and their subsequent capacity to "rape the
men, not sexually, unfortunately, but morally." Women's voting patterns
were to blame for an "all-time low in political scurviness, hoodlumism,
. . . moral degeneration, civic corruption, . . . homosexuality, drunkenness, financial depression, chaos and war." [23] Besides causing internal
decay, this disdained character, "mom," encompassing women of all social
classes, hastened the nation's vulnerability to outside forces by way of
destroying independent-minded men.

As cultural historian Michael Rogin has noted, Wylie's second edition
of *Vipers,* published during the apex of McCarthyism in 1955, described
both motherhood and communism as deceptive forces against which the
individual man must defend himself.[24] Wylie, like other American Cold
Warriors, made use of American antifascist ideology dating from wartime
to equate Nazism and communism as totalitarian systems that destroyed
individualism and promoted mindless conformity. Moms were the secret
agents of totalitarianism, displacing or uprooting the traditional paternal
power that had previously ensured healthy individuality and prosperity.
By violating the son's boundaries between self and other, moms created a
window of opportunity, or to borrow Cold War parlance, ripped a seam
in the Iron Curtain, through which a dangerous and disguised enemy
could maneuver. Thus moms recruited effectively for both fascism and
communism, since, once infected by momism, sons were unable to make
independent decisions and were drawn in by totalitarian theories. Totalitarianism benefited from the mother's narcissism and voracious appetite
for power. Through her, it commandeered the psychical apparatus of the
domestic sphere and took control of men.[25]

Several years after Wylie published *Vipers,* military psychiatrist Edward
Strecker elaborated on the horrors of momism, this time giving the
concept the luster of scientific truth. From the early years of his career,
Strecker had been affiliated with the mental hygiene movement, which
focused on preventing mental disturbances and encouraged individuals

to "adjust" to the psychological demands of modern society. His early research, undertaken while a major in the U.S. Army Medical Corps during World War I, focused on shell shock, as well as the prevention of alcoholism and sex crimes. As professor of psychiatry at the University of Pennsylvania and psychiatric consultant to the surgeon general of the navy, Strecker authored textbooks and a number of popular books dealing with child psychiatry, morale, psychiatry and war, and the psychological perils of mass society, subjects that appealed to middle-class audiences.[26] His tangential interest in the problem of homosexuality grew when, in 1935, he joined the interdisciplinary Committee for the Study of Sex Variants, which was conducting extensive research on homosexuality in New York City in an effort to determine the cause and prevalence of "sex variance," as well as to recommend ways of preventing it and thus to stem the purported increase of this "maladjustment" in modern urban America.

In 1941 the Committee published its findings, which stressed the importance of parental guidance in ensuring that girls are adequately feminine and boys adequately masculine.[27] Following this, Strecker became a tireless critic of mothers, initially offering his wisdom on the subject in public lectures and a regular column in *The Ladies' Home Journal*.[28] These ventures led to two popular books on the menace of moms, *Their Mothers' Sons*, published in 1946, which focused on the damage done to sons, and its companion volume *Their Mothers' Daughters*, published ten years later with coauthor Vincent Lathbury.[29] Both books are condescending and pompous, based not on any empirical research but simply on Strecker's impressions, spurred by his startling realization, while working as a military psychiatrist during the war, that 20 percent of potential recruits were rejected for neuropsychiatric reasons. Ostensibly the books are manuals advising mothers on childrearing, but throughout, Strecker used psychiatric anecdotes to launch political commentary, arguing that the nation's weakness was due to bad mothering. To perform this commentary, Strecker distinguished between *mothers*, who were good, and *moms*, who were bad (something Wylie hadn't bothered to do), leaving the role of fathers in childrearing unanalyzed, except to occasionally disparage Mom's counterpart, "Pop," an immature man lacking the masculine strength necessary to be a good citizen or effective parent.[30]

In Strecker's view, mothers "brought into the world the sturdy flesh, blood and sinew and activated it with the spirit of indominatable [*sic*] morale." They contributed good genes and good training and were not overbearing but "quiet in their diplomatic interventions," encouraging their children to make independent decisions. Moms, by contrast, prevented their children from maturing by keeping a tight hold on the "silver cord," the "emotional umbilical cord." Mom's sons never matured adequately. Many became feminine and homosexual as a result of their mother's desire to have a daughter or her untoward affections, which caused sons to take flight from heterosexuality.[31] Some of mom's most immature and cowardly sons were those who went so far as to wear women's clothing to get out of military service.[32] The daughters of moms were deeply damaged psychologically, as manifested in symptoms of resistance to marriage and childbirth, as well as sympathy with feminism and often sexual desire for other women.

In Strecker's scheme, moms were both throwbacks to a previous stage of evolution when violence and cruelty were common human expressions, and distinctly modern. They manifested psychological, if not biological, degeneracy due to conflicts between their maternal instinct and their ambitions in the business world and other domains previously limited to men.[33] Under the general category Strecker delineated many types of moms, including the narcissistic mom, the self-sacrificing mom, the pollyanna mom, the ailing mom, and the humorless "pseudointellectual," who took courses and attended lectures but was nothing more than a dilettante. Mom, whatever her specific type, had a primary pathological tendency: "the emotional satisfaction, almost repletion, she derives from keeping the children paddling about in a kind of psychological amniotic fluid rather than letting them swim away with the bold and decisive strokes of maturity away from the emotional maternal womb."[34]

Moms, of course, were generally women. But Strecker used the monstrous figure of mom as a sign under which all evil and corruption could be placed. In his words, "not all substitute moms are flesh and blood." "Moms in a bottle" referred to alcoholism. Other "mom surrogates" included not only overbearing grandmothers and other female relatives but also things as far flung as psychoneuroses, mental hospitals, religion, social movements, collective mob consciousness, national isolationism, labor unions, and even the army. All of them encouraged dependence and escape. Strecker, like Wylie, was horrified by the "mass man," that pitiful creature who lost any ability to think for himself and was incapable of asserting his individual character in the face of the mediocre crowd or the slavishly devoted mob. He described America's wartime enemies as stripped of individual will and self-determination by the ravages of momism writ large. In Strecker's view, Nazism was a "Momarchy," "a mom surrogate with a swastika for a heart," and Hitler's mania was all the more pathological because of its tendency toward feminine irrationality:

> The Fuehrer had all the qualities and ingredients which go into the making of a super-mom. He even had the feminine note of hysteria which may be heard in the voices of moms when they are battling for their children and, if need be, are willing to give their lives for them.... Here indeed was a mom who never forgot his children.[35]

Intensifying the horrific specter of the violent mom, Strecker continued, saying that for those who did not comply, the Nazi mom "wielded a bloody whip of torture and death."[36] The Japanese, too, suffered from the totalitarian effects of momism, and it was their social immaturity that led to their defeat. Callously brushing off the U.S. military's decimation of Hiroshima, Strecker added, "I doubt if even the atomic bomb had sufficient explosive force to dis-womb the Japanese people."[37]

Strecker's metaphorical and literal use of the term mom reveals the link between political and psychological discourse typical of much Cold War–era psychiatric theory on child development. Mom invited both the external and internal threats to run their calamitous course in the psyche, the family, the nation, and the world. And it was particularly her ability to thwart American individualism among her children that made mom, like communism and fascism, an inimical force threatening to level all distinctions between people and render the world's population an undifferentiated mob.

To avoid such a catastrophe, Strecker offered his sage advice to mothers. He allowed that "the Mother's Dilemma" of having to care for children while also encouraging them to grow independent required mothers to maintain a delicate balance. A thin line separated proper and improper parenting. It was a mother's responsibility to understand the difference in order to ensure her child's success and maturity. Maturity and immaturity figured as key measures of adjustment, health, and citizenship in Strecker's framework, which valorized traditional Yankee values of industriousness and individualism. The mature individual was reliable, cooperative, tolerant, patient, respectful of authority, pliable, and persevering. An ability to fit in tempered the mature individual's will. Immaturity, on the other hand, manifested in uncooperative behavior, resistance, insubordination, and the inability or unwillingness to be self-sufficient. It caused most human failures, and worsened with each generation since immature moms gave rise to immature adults who would surely wreak the same havoc on their children. Not surprisingly, moms were to blame for lesbianism and male homosexuality, which Strecker, following a basic tenet of psychoanalytic thinking, saw as particularly glaring expressions of immaturity.

In *Their Mothers' Sons*, Strecker opened with dire statistics supposedly signifying the terrible impact on the nation's military caused by women who refused to allow their sons to grow up. He positioned mom as an internal force of evil, responsible for the millions of men who were unfit to fight for their country in World War II. Those men who appeared to be lacking in manliness most exasperated him. He made his opinions on this matter clear in a chapter on homosexuality, where he cautioned mothers to loosen the stifling grip of maternal love and allow sons to overcome the Oedipal crisis in order to become healthy, masculine heterosexuals. Mothers who tried to make their sons into daughters, those who spoke negatively about heterosexuality, and those who treated their sons as potential lovers thwarted the complex achievement of heterosexual normalcy upon which American democracy was based. The degree to which a son's masculinity was fostered determined not only his ability to become a mature husband and father but, even more importantly, to achieve honor in civic and military duties. Strecker reminded his readers that effeminacy, which signified male homosexuality, barred many men from wartime service and made them both a national burden and potential agents of sedition.[38]

While most other psychiatrists and commentators believed sons were the main victims of mom's tyranny, Strecker stressed the devastating effects momism had on daughters. Since mothers were primarily responsible for turning children into citizens, Strecker argued that rearing daughters to be good wives and mothers was a necessary first step to strengthening the family and, consequently, the nation. He lamented that he had not written the volume on daughters first, stating that, above all else, the nation needed proper mothers to turn boys into proper men who would be the leaders of tomorrow. Daughters distorted by demonic mothers would most certainly either become wicked moms to a new generation or be so traumatized as to forego the basic instinct of motherhood in favor of the corrupt and "counterfeit" sexuality of lesbianism.

One of the most serious dangers daughters faced was feminism, Strecker opined in a chapter-long diatribe in *Their Mothers' Daughters*. In "Feminism—the Biological Rejection," Strecker qualified his equation of maturity with independence, noting that women who seek total autonomy were pathological and lacking in femininity, the necessary biological motivation and psychological art of being a woman. Feminism itself, he noted, was a rejection of femininity, resulting from a girl's unhealthy response to the Oedipus complex, whereby she refused to separate from her mother and developed a competitive and envious attitude toward her father, whom the girl perceived as stealing her mother's love. The daughter's inability to have all of her mother's love led to ongoing frustration and envy. The pathological mom, who fostered a daughter's prolonged attachment, contributed to the daughter's disturbed sentiments. This, commonly coupled with the mother's rejection of her own femininity, prevented the daughter from becoming a healthy and happy heterosexual woman, locking the girl forever in a form of latent lesbianism that manifested in an affinity for feminism.

Strecker and his coauthor, Lathbury, saw this rejection of femininity as tragic, noting that many women who aspired to success in business and professions were fundamentally unhappy, having renounced femininity, heterosexuality, and motherhood. This led the authors to claim that feminism was a pathological symptom posing as a political sensibility, brought on by the frustration or denial of essential maternal instincts, and

> the deep wish to compete with men not because it may be necessary or the circumstances of life demand it, but prompted by the desire to prove the male is inferior to the female. . . . Feminism is a defense reaction against the repressed and intolerably painful feelings of inadequacy and worthlessness as women. . . . If for a minute they stop thinking and proving to one and all that women are better than men, then from childhood memories might emerge the unbearable thought that really women are not worth anything.[39]

Renouncing feminism, not femininity, would restore a woman to health and happiness. Dedication to marriage and motherhood could allay her suffering and strengthen the nation. Clearly, the authors had a gender-specific scheme: independence was a necessary asset for male citizens, while for female citizens, wifely dependence and maternal attentiveness were key.

In a chapter entitled "Lesbianism—the Biological and Psychological Treason," Strecker and Lathbury continued their attack on women's independence from men, echoing a Spencerian notion that homosexuality was "enervating and devitalizing," and arguing that tolerance of this "social threat" would lead to the destruction of civilization. Lesbianism was an extreme manifestation of a daughter's Oedipal frustration that manifested initially in resentment toward men and then in choosing women lovers who symbolized the original mother figure. Thus lesbianism signaled immaturity resulting from a grave pathological interruption in the female's normal development process toward becoming a wife and mother.

Moms produced lesbians in a number of ways, according to Strecker and Lathbury. Some poisoned their daughters against heterosexuality by describing it as repulsive. In addition, moms often expressed either too much or not enough affection toward their daughters, thus either thwarting the process of maturation or triggering the daughters' neurotic quest to make up for a lack of love. But moms not only induced lesbianism in their daughters; their own pathological behaviors were construed by Strecker and Lathbury as indications of latent lesbianism. Among the pronounced signs of this latency were a mother's bitterness about her maternal role and her resentment toward her husband or men in general. So not only did moms *make* lesbians; they *were* lesbians within a broad psychoanalytic construction of the term. Moreover, the most destructive moms were described as masculine, domineering, envious of men, and castrating, qualities they shared with the stereotypical bull dagger. The "treason" they committed was against normative codes of gender and sexuality, and, by implication, against the family and nation.

In much of the Cold War–era psychiatric literature, standards of maturity were different for men and women. In Strecker's own view, maturity for boys and men connoted freedom from maternal entanglements and was defined by separateness. For girls, freedom and separateness were desirable only to a degree. They quickly became signs of pathological selfishness if, for example, a woman did not have a child. Women who did not have children were aberrant and likely to unleash their frustrated maternal desires on society. For Strecker, the instinct of motherhood was universal and primordial. However, in modern American society it had gone afoul. The situation was worsening because the preponderance of immature women meant the problem would be reproduced exponentially in future generations. The threat of a Sapphic population explosion loomed large. For women and especially for lesbians, "biological treason" against childbirth became, in Strecker's view, a form of political sedition.

After logging and detailing all of the damage that moms could do,

Strecker went on to endow mothers with the important responsibility of teaching democracy in the home, where they transformed children into citizens. Warning that civilization was held in the balance of this fine art of motherhood, Strecker spilled forth an apocalyptic rhapsody:

> Again the time will come when world combat will threaten. If it should come to another world war, the result might very well be the annihilation of our civilization and cultures and the final plunge into the abyss of barbarism. When that danger comes, those adults who, in their childhoods, were taught to take at least a few steps along the road of the brotherhood of man will be the human dikes holding back the deluge. . . . [T]here is nothing of which Psychiatry can speak with more confidence and assurance than the danger to our democratic civilizations and cultures from keeping children enwombed psychologically and socially. Here is our gravest menace.[40]

To solve the problem of momism, Strecker suggested a revamping of the entire social system, since in its present form it encouraged dependence and immaturity. First and foremost, the social prestige moms enjoyed must be taken away. Rather than being valorized through movies and popular media, moms should be condemned for the damage they do. As a matter of national security, they must be prevented from destroying the future citizenry. Second, expert knowledge was crucial. Classes should be developed to prepare boys for fatherhood and girls for motherhood. Parents should be systematically educated on how to be good citizens and responsible role models. If parents—and especially mothers—failed to act appropriately for their sex, homosexuality would surely increase, for children of such parents would be deranged in their own sexual development. Furthermore, the government should be on guard for "mothers' groups" that are fronts for breeding national disunity through their pacifist propaganda. By simultaneously arguing that childrearing was the cornerstone of government and that certain women were not good mothers, Strecker positioned psychiatrists as crucial experts for ensuring national security.

As anxiety about the proliferation of internal enemies intensified during the Cold War, psychiatrists focused heavily on the role of mothers in preventing the political subversion with which gender variance and homosexuality had become aligned. Strecker's texts, like other popular psychiatric tracts written during the Cold War, counseled that to prevent lesbianism and male homosexuality, as well as other character weaknesses that made an individual vulnerable to subversive political movements, a woman needed to present her children with a role model of the cheerful, dedicated, and feminine mother. As Edward Strecker put it: "Do not become a feminist. Children recoil from masculinity in a mother, in dress and attitude. . . . You may have to be cool and brisk in the business world, but in the home with the youngsters, let your temperature go up and resume the natural psychological curves of your sex." [41]

Other psychiatrists writing during this period chimed in. If a girl became a lesbian, her mother was largely to blame. Either she had failed to provide a proper model of femininity (by not keeping a clean house, for example, or not showing adoration for her husband), or else she was excessively controlling, domineering, or dependent upon her daughter. [42] In addition, a host of psychoanalytic theories attributed male homosexuality to the so-called "CBI mother"—close, binding, and intimate— whose extraordinary and perverse intimacy interfered with her son's normal heterosexual pursuits and emasculated him through debilitating guilt. [43] In addition to her own possible tendency toward politically subversive causes, the destructive CBI mother cultivated, wittingly or unwittingly, the seeds of disloyalty and treason in her children.

After Alfred Kinsey's best-selling sex surveys from this period reported high rates of homosexual behavior among normal men and women, psychiatrists, who were among Kinsey's most vociferous opponents, maintained that homosexuality was fundamentally pathological. [44] To counter Kinsey's claim that homosexuality was not only widespread but perhaps even normal, they argued, among other things, that the future survival of the nation depended on the prevention and elimination of homosexuality. [45] To this end, they developed utterly labyrinthine theories of the aetiology of both male and female homosexuality, speculating that almost anything in the mother, from overbearing tendencies to hostility to excessive affection to indifferent detachment, could cause not only sexual perversion but a proclivity toward political *sub*version. [46]

During what historian Elaine Tyler May has called the "family boom" of the late 1940s and 1950s, the suburban home came to symbolize security against all kinds of foreign invasions. [47] Its occupants, the nuclear family, figured as a kind of prophylactic against the internal decay of cultural values and external threats of communism and totalitarianism. But as May points out, the wholesome suburban home, rather than staving off the decadence of bureaucratic conformity and consumerism, furtively fostered such decadence through its regimens of parental surveillance over children and its orgies of home furnishing. According to popular psychiatric writing of the time, Mom hastened moral corruption, surrounded as she was by modern appliances, trapped, frustrated, and neurotic, behind the double doors of her ranch-style dream home, suffering from the "problem that has no name" Betty Friedan later identified in more sympathetic terms in *The Feminine Mystique*.[48] Mom was the agent of internal decay, browbeating her children and husband, succumbing, in bitterness, to agoraphobia, or worse, feminism and communism. Through her treachery, Mom undermined the home as a bastion of security, and planted the seeds of cultural ruin in the very garden where she was to be cultivating the next generation to become productive and dutiful citizens. Her queer children were the signifiers of cultural decay and national impotence. Her treason and that of her homosexual sons and lesbian daughters threatened the nation from its deepest interiors: the female body, the psyche, the home.

NOTES

This essay benefited immensely from the comments and suggestions of Mary Louise Adams, Angus MacLaren, Andrea Slane, Jacqueline Urla, and the editors of this volume.

1. William Lee Howard, "Effeminate Men and Masculine Women," *New York Medical Journal* 71 (May 5, 1900): 686–87; reprinted in *Root of Bitterness: Documents of the Social History of Women*, 2d ed., ed. Nancy F. Cott, Jeanne Boydston, Ann Braude, Lori Ginzberg, and Molly Ladd-Taylor (Boston: Northeastern University Press, 1996), 338–40.

2. Susan Zeiger, "She Didn't Raise Her Boy to Be a Slacker: Motherhood, Conscription, and the Culture of the First World War," *Feminist Studies* 22, no. 1 (Spring 1996): 7–39, 18.

3. For an overview of Cold War movies that dovetailed with the general trend toward mom-bashing see Michael Rogin, "Kiss Me Deadly: Communism, Motherhood, and Cold War Movies," in *Ronald Reagan, the Movie and Other Episodes in Political Demonology* (Berkeley: University of California Press, 1987), 236–71.

4. Allan Bérubé, *Coming Out under Fire: The History of Gay Men and Women in World War Two* (New York: Free Press, 1990); John D'Emilio, *Sexual Politics, Sexual Communities: The Making of a Homosexual Minority in the United States, 1940–1970* (Chicago: University of Chicago Press, 1983).

5. See John D'Emilio, "The Homosexual Menace: The Politics of Sexuality in Cold War America," in *Passion and Power: Sexuality in History*, ed. Kathy Peiss and Christina Simmons (Philadelphia: Temple University Press, 1989), 226–40; Geoffrey S. Smith, "National Security and Personal Isolation: Sex, Gender, and Disease in the Cold-War United States," *International History Review* 14, no. 2 (May 1992): 307–37. For an analysis of similar phenomena in Canada, see Gary Kinsman, " 'Character Weaknesses' and 'Fruit Machines': Towards An Analysis of the Anti-Homosexual Security Campaign in the Canadian Civil Service," *Labour/ Le Travail* 35 (Spring 1995): 133–61.

6. For historical analyses of the McCarthyite witch-hunts see, Ralph S. Brown, *Loyalty and Security: Employment Tests in the United States* (New Haven: Yale University Press, 1958); David Caute, *The Great Fear: The Anti-Communist Purge under Truman and Eisenhower* (New York: Simon and Schuster, 1978); Richard M. Freeland, *The Truman Doctrine and the Origins of McCarthyism: Foreign Policy, Domestic Politics, and Internal Security, 1946–1948*, 3d ed. (New York: New York University Press, 1985); Athan G. Theoharris, *Spying on Americans: Political Surveillance from Hoover to the Huston Plan* (Philadelphia: Temple University Press, 1978).

7. R. G. Wadeck, "The Homosexual International," in *Congressional Record*, vol. 98 (May 1, 1952): A2652.

8. In the committee transcripts the only kind of woman to whom explicit reference is made is either the sultry dame alleged to be on the Kremlin's payroll and charged with the task of using her seductive powers to draw state secrets out of vulnerable and unwitting men, or the infamous adulteress whose excessive sexual desires and fundamentally treasonous nature compromise not only the security of the home but of the nation.

9. Allan Bérubé and John D'Emilio, "The Military and the Lesbians during the McCarthy Years," *Signs* 9, no. 4 (Summer 1984): 759–75.

10. A masterful survey of wartime psychiatric studies of homosexuality is presented in Allan Bérubé, *Coming Out under Fire*, chaps. 1 and 6.

11. For analyses of antihomosexual backlashes in the early twentieth century, see George Chauncey, *Gay New York: Gender, Urban Culture, and the Making of the Gay Male World, 1890–1940* (New York: Basic Books, 1994); George Chauncey, "From Sexual Inversion to Homosexuality: Medicine and the Changing Conceptualization of Female 'Deviance,' " in *Passion and Power: Sexuality in History*, ed. Kathy Peiss and Christina Simmons (Philadelphia: Temple University Press, 1989), 87–117; Lillian Faderman, *Odd Girls and Twilight Lovers: A History of Lesbian Life in Twentieth-Century America* (New York: Columbia University Press, 1991); Jonathan Ned Katz, *Gay American History* (New York: Crowell, 1976); Christina Simmons, "Companionate Marriage and the Lesbian Threat," *Frontiers* 4, no. 3 (Fall 1979): 54–59; Lisa Duggan, "The Social Enforcement of Heterosexuality and Lesbian Resistance in the 1920s," in *Class, Race and Sex: The Dynamics of Control*, ed. Amy Swerdlow and Hanna Lessinger (Boston: G. K. Hall, 1983), 75–92.

12. See, for example, George W. Henry, *Sex Variants: A Study of Homosexual Patterns,* 2 vols. (New York: Paul Hoeber and Sons, 1941); George W. Henry, *All the Sexes: A Study of Masculinity and Femininity* (New York: Rinehart and Company, 1955); Benjamin Karpman, *The Sex Offender and His Offenses: Etiology, Pathology, Psychodynamics and Treatment* (New York: Julian Press, 1954); Robert Lindner, "Homosexuality and the Contemporary Scene," in *Must You Conform?* (New York: Holt, Rinehart and Winston, 1956), 31–76.

13. For example, see Ferdinand Lundberg and Marynia F. Farnham, *Modern Woman: The Lost Sex* (New York: Harper, 1947).

14. Linda Kerber, *Women of the Republic: Intellect and Ideology in Revolutionary America* (Chapel Hill: University of North Carolina Press, 1980); Mary Beth Norton, *Liberty's Daughters: The Revolutionary Experience of American Women, 1750–1800* (Boston: Little, Brown and Company, 1980).

15. Zeiger, "She Didn't Raise Her Boy to Be a Slacker," 27–28.

16. For histories of the gender politics of suburban home design, see Gwendolyn Wright, *Building the American Dream: A Social History of Housing in America* (New York: Pantheon Books, 1981); and Dolores Hayden, *Redesigning the American Dream: The Future of Housing, Work, and Family Life* (New York: W. W. Norton, 1984).

17. For historical analyses of the postwar cult of domesticity, see Elaine Tyler May, *Homeward Bound: American Families in Cold War America* (New York: Basic Books, 1988); Stephanie Coontz, *The Way We Never Were: American Families and the Nostalgia Trap* (New York: Basic Books, 1992); Eugenia Kaledin, *Mothers and More: American Women in the 1950s* (Boston: Twayne Publishers, 1984); Wini Breines, *Young, White, and Miserable: Growing Up Female in the Fifties* (Boston: Beacon Press, 1992); Brett Harvey, *The Fifties: A Women's Oral History* (New York: HarperCollins, 1993).

18. For historical background on the mental hygiene movement, see Walter Bromberg, *Psychiatry between the Wars, 1918–1945: A Recollection* (Westport, Conn.: Greenwood Press, 1982); and Elizabeth Lunbeck, *The Psychiatric Persuasion: Knowledge, Gender, and Power in Modern America* (Princeton: Princeton University Press, 1994).

19. For example, see Henry, *Sex Variants* and *All the Sexes;* Benjamin Spock, *The Common Sense Book of Baby and Child Care* (New York: Duell, Sloan and Pearce, 1946).

20. Henry, *Sex Variants: A Study of Homosexual Patterns,* 2d ed. (New York: Paul Hoeber and Sons, 1948), 1025, 1027.

21. Films like *The Man in the Gray Flannel Suit* (1956) highlight the general dissatisfaction and alienation of life in the suburbs. For a popular exposé of suburban cultural malaise from that era see Richard E. Gordon, Katherine K. Gordon, and Max Gunther, *The Split-Level Trap* (New York: Dell Publishing, 1960).

22. Philip Wylie, *Generation of Vipers* (New York: Farrar and Rinehart, 1942).

23. Wylie, *Generation of Vipers*, 188–89.

24. Rogin, "Kiss Me Deadly," 242–43. Wylie, *Generation of Vipers*, 2d ed. (New York: Rinehart, 1955). Other works by Wylie along these lines include *Smoke across the Moon*, a serialized novel published during the 1940s in the *Saturday Evening Post*, which warned about the evils of communism; *When Worlds Collide*, written with Edwin Balmer (New York: Frederick A. Stokes, 1933), a science fiction novel, which was turned into a Hollywood movie in 1951, about the destruction of the earth and the escape of a group of white Americans to a new and virgin planet; and *Tomorrow* (New York: Rinehart, 1954), a novel warning of the dangers of communism and momism, and promoting rearmament for a nuclear war to save the United States.

25. Marvelous cinematic depictions of mothers who use their sons' pathological attachments to them as a way of undermining American political order and inviting communism to take over are presented in *My Son John* (1952) and *The Manchurian Candidate* (1962). For analyses see Rogin, "Kiss Me Deadly," 250–60.

26. Select publications include Edward A. Strecker, "Everyday Psychology of the Normal Child," *Mental Hygiene* 17, no. 1 (January 1933): 65–81; "The Challenge of the Sex Offender," *Mental Hygiene* 22, no. 1 (January 1938): 1–3; *Beyond the Clinical Frontiers: A Psychiatrist Views Crowd Behavior* (New York: W. W. Norton and Company, 1940); "The Man and the Mob," *Mental Hygiene* 24, no. 4 (October 1940): 529–51; "Mental Hygiene and Mass Man," *Mental Hygiene* 25, no. 1 (January 1941): 3–5; *Fundamentals of Psychiatry* (Philadelphia: Lippincott, 1942); "Military Psychiatry: World War I," in *One Hundred Years of American Psychiatry*, ed. J. K. Hall (New York: Columbia University Press, 1944); "The Contribution of Psychiatry to Democratic Morals," *Rhode Island Journal of Medicine* 27 (1944): 383–84; "Psychiatry Speaks to Democracy," *Mental Hygiene* 29, no. 4 (October 1945): 591–605; Edward A. Strecker and Kenneth E. Appel, "Morale," *American Journal of Psychiatry* 99 (September 1942): 163, and *Psychiatry in Modern Warfare* (New York: Macmillan, 1945); Edward A. Strecker and Francis T. Chambers, Jr., *Alcohol: One Man's Meat* (New York: Macmillan, 1938).

27. The Committee for the Study of Sex Variants first reported its findings in Henry, *Sex Variants* (1941).

28. For news coverage of Strecker's lectures against "momism," see "'Moms' Denounced as Peril to Nation," *New York Times*, April 28, 1945.

29. Edward A. Strecker, *Their Mothers' Sons: The Psychiatrist Examines an American Problem* (New York and Philadelphia: J. B. Lippincott, 1946); and Edward A. Strecker and Vincent T. Lathbury, *Their Mothers' Daughters* (Philadelphia: J. B. Lippincott, 1956).

30. Strecker, *Sons*, 131.

31. Strecker, *Sons*, 128–31.

32. Strecker, *Sons*, 18.

33. Strecker and Lathbury, *Daughters*, 40.

34. Strecker, *Sons*, 31, 54–69.

35. Strecker, *Sons*, 104, 122, 133, 134.

36. Strecker, *Sons*, 136.

37. Strecker, *Sons*, 139.

38. Strecker, *Sons*, 128–32.

39. Strecker and Lathbury, *Daughters*, 153.

40. Strecker, *Sons*, 159, 219.

41. Strecker and Lathbury, *Daughters*, 71.

42. See, for example, Henry, *All the Sexes*, 585; Morris W. Brody, "An Analysis of the Psychosexual Development of a Female," *Psychoanalytic Review* (1943), reprinted in *The Homosexuals: As Seen by Themselves and Thirty Authorities*, ed. A. M. Krich (New York: Citadel Press, 1954), 312–24; Frank Caprio, *Female Homosexuality: A Psychodynamic Study of Lesbianism* (New York: Citadel, 1954); Louis S. London, *Sexual Deviations in the Male and Female* (New York: Bell Publishing Company, 1957); Richard C. Robertiello, *Voyage from Lesbos: The Psychoanalysis of a Female Homosexual* (New York: Citadel, 1959). For later examples, see Cornelia B. Wilbur, "Clinical Aspects of Female Homosexuality," in *Sexual Inversion: The Multiple Roots of Homosexuality*, ed. Judd Marmor (New York: Basic Books, 1965), 268–81; Charles W. Socarides, "Female Homosexuality," in *Sexual Behavior and the Law*, ed. Ralph Slovenko (Springfield, Ill.: Charles C. Thomas, 1965), 462–77.

43. "CBI mother" was a term coined by psychiatrist Irving Bieber in Society of Medical Psychoanalysts, *Homosexuality: A Psychoanalytic Study of Male Homosexuals* (New York: Vintage Books, 1962).

44. Alfred Kinsey, Wardell B. Pomeroy, Clyde E. Martin, Paul H. Gebhard, *Sexual Behavior in the Human Male* (Philadelphia: W. B. Saunders, 1948) and *Sexual Behavior in the Human Female* (Philadelphia: W. B. Saunders, 1953).

45. For psychiatrists' commentary on the Kinsey reports, see Edmund Bergler, "The Myth of a National Disease: Homosexuality and the Kinsey Report," *Psychiatric Quarterly* 22 (1948): 66–88, reprinted in *The Homosexuals: As Seen by Themselves and Thirty Authorities*, 226–50; Edmund Bergler and William S. Kroger, *Kinsey's Myth of Female Sexuality: The Medical Facts* (New York: Grune and Stratton, 1954); Albert Deutsch, ed., *Sex Habits of American Men: A Symposium on the Kinsey Report* (New York: Grosset and Dunlap, 1948); Lawrence Kubie, "Psychiatric Implications of the Kinsey Report," *Psychosomatic Medicine* 10 (1948): 95–106; Karl A. Menninger, "One View of the Kinsey Report," *General Practitioner* 8 (1953): 61–72; Benjamin Wortis, "The Kinsey Report and Related Fields: Psychiatry," *Saturday Review of Literature* 31 (1948): 19, 32–34. For an example of religious opposition to Kinsey's report on women's sexuality, see E. J. Daniels and Billy Graham, *I Accuse: Startling Exposé of Kinsey's Sex Reports* (Orlando, Fla.: Christ for the World Publishers, 1954).

46. For example, see Edmund Bergler, *Neurotic Counterfeit-Sex: Impotence, Frigidity, "Mechanical" and Pseudosexuality, Homosexuality* (New York: Grune and Stratton, 1951); *Counterfeit Sex: Homosexuality, Impotence, Frigidity* (New York: Grune and Stratton, 1958); Edmund Bergler, *Homosexuality: Disease or Way of Life* (New York: Hill and Wang, 1956); Edmund Bergler, *One Thousand Homosexuals: Conspiracy of Silence, or Curing and Deglamorizing Homosexuals?* (Paterson, N.J.: Pageant Books, 1959); Caprio, *Female Homosexuality*; Louis S. London, *Sexual Deviations in the Female: Case Histories of Frustrated Women* (New York: Bell Publishing Company, 1956); Richard C. Robertiello, "Clinical Notes: Results of Separation from Iposexual Parents during the Oedipal Period, [and] A Female Homosexual Panic," *Psychoanalytic Review* 51, no. 4 (1964–65): 670–72; Robertiello, *Voyage from Lesbos*. For later examples, see Charles W. Socarides, *The Overt Homosexual* (New York: Grune and Stratton, 1968) and *Homosexuality* (New York: Jason Aronson, 1978).

47. May, *Homeward Bound*.

48. Betty Friedan, *The Feminine Mystique* (New York: Norton, 1963).

Chapter 9

Bad/Good, Good/Bad
Birth Mothers and Adoptive Mothers

Betty Jean Lifton

Everyone has two mothers, according to Freud: the good mother and the bad mother. The psychological task is to bring them together as two parts of the same woman.

I never knew quite what to do with this Freudian insight, for, as an adoptee, I literally had two mothers: my birth mother[1] and my adoptive mother. Both of them were good, and both of them were bad. Which meant I had four mothers.

But—and this is important—they were each good and bad in their own way.

My adoptive mother existed for me in the real here and now. She was always there for me. In that, she was a good mother. My birth mother existed in the shadowy there and then. She disappeared on me. In that, she was a bad mother.

My birth mother gave me life. Good mother. My adoptive mother couldn't give me life. Bad mother.

Good mother/bad mother. Which is which? What is good? What is bad? It is all in the eyes of the perceiver.

In the eyes of society, the married adoptive mother is good and the unmarried birth mother is bad. The adoptive mother is the virtuous woman who rescues an abandoned child and saves her from the orphanage, or the gutter, by making the child her own. She may tell her daughter (or son) the stock story that Mother loved you so much that she gave you up, but children are not fools. The adopted child senses that she was bad, or that maybe her mother was bad: perhaps a prostitute or a drug addict. Why else has she not been invited to birthday parties or to Thanksgiving dinner?

Even today, when society has relaxed its sexual mores, the birth mother remains cast in the role of the bad mother. She is a loose woman, who not only had a baby out of wedlock but gave that baby away. Yet, here is the devil's bargain: in return for her baby, the "bad" birth mother is allowed to go back into society and pass as a "good" woman. No scarlet letter for her, at least not where it shows. She can pass. Should you meet her in church, in the office, or at the club, you wouldn't be able to tell what she's been through. Unless you happen to catch the sadness that crosses her face in an unguarded moment.

The Psychology of the Bad/Good Birth Mother

I've known many birth mothers over the years. Some of my best friends are birth mothers.

My own mother was a birth mother.

"You will never know my pain," my mother said in our first meeting after I'd found her.

At the time, I was just learning my own pain, which until then I had effectively split off from consciousness. How could I possibly have the emotional strength to know and hold hers, too?

She did not struggle to articulate her pain. She had become the pain. It was as much a part of her as any vital organ.

I was to learn years later, after her death, that she had tried to keep me against her mother's wishes. My twenty-year-old father was out of there when he learned of her pregnancy, and, having just turned seventeen, she couldn't raise me on her own. She went temporarily blind after signing my relinquishment paper. Fell onto the subway tracks one day. Fell or jumped, who is to say? Someone pulled her out in time.

When she could see again, she, like so many birth mothers, split me off in order to survive: shut me out of her conscious mind. Went psychologically blind. Dissociated. Left me to fester in her unconscious. She kept me a secret from both her husbands, and from the one child she had after me—her *only* child, in society's eyes.

I saw her just twice. I was the one who disappeared this time. I could not handle my guilt toward my adoptive parents. I could not handle the chaos I felt inside. I did not contact her again for many years.

We were never to meet again. Toward the end of her life, we spoke on the telephone, its wires reuniting mother and daughter like an electrified umbilical cord. She was widowed, living with my unmarried half-brother, dependent on him for everything because she had Meniere's disease, which affected her middle ear. It made her dizzy, unable to venture out alone. Mother and son, inseparable. She was determined from the beginning not to lose this one: her second/first child. She wouldn't tell him about me. She wasn't about to say, "Oh, by the way, there's something I forgot to mention. You have a sister out there."

She just couldn't do it. "Your brother wouldn't understand," she told me repeatedly. Who could? Even Oedipus didn't understand the dire consequences of the secrecy in adoption—until it was too late.

Over the years, I learned to know my mother's pain—not through her words, but through the pain inside of me when I thought of her. It was all so long ago. And yet, I, like all adoptees, still carry within me the child's trauma of losing its mother; of learning it is adopted, rather then born to the people it calls Mom and Dad; of living like a genetic stranger in some other clan; of having to repress the grief, pain, and yearning for that missing bad mother.

The Psychology of the Bad/Good Adoptive Mother

My adoptive mother was a good mother. Or, like most mothers, she was, to use Donald Winnicott's term, "a good enough mother." She did all the things that mothers do: she got up in the middle of the night, she fed me, clothed me, worried about me, and loved me—or at least (perhaps like most mothers) she loved the daughter she wanted me to be and the one she thought I was.

But it could be said that she, like so many adoptive mothers of her time, was a bad mother. She never questioned the wisdom of the so-called adoption experts who told her to take me home and live as if I were born to her. She was glad to hear that I did not need to know anything about my antecedents. She allowed herself to believe that I would feel a natural part of my new family and never feel sorrow for the biological kin I had lost. In allowing herself to become psychologically blind, she dissociated her shameful infertility, just as my birth mother had dissociated her shameful fertility.

I don't know if the experts advised my adoptive mother to tell me my parents were dead, but she, again like so many adoptive parents, did. First, she married them off, then she finished them off. She mumbled something about my mother dying of a broken heart after my father's death. Being a child, I believed her. I secretly grieved for my lost parents who, like Romeo and Juliet, died so young. I imagined they were watching over me. It never occurred to me that dead people have names, identities, and family members they have left behind. That's because I didn't let it enter my mind. I did what the adopted child does in order to survive, in order not to lose the only parents she has: I, also, dissociated. I shut them out of my conscious mind.

Like mother, like child. All of us swimming in what Lewis Carroll might have called The Sea of Dissociation.

I would learn that my parents were not married and were very much alive at the time of my adoption. "Your mother lied to you," my husband said when we discovered the truth. I didn't want to think that my adoptive mother lied; that would make her a bad mother. I preferred to think she had confabulated, made up her own fable in order to shape the truth closer to her heart's desire.

The Adoptee's Dilemma

Adoptees do not think of their birth mother as good or bad, but rather as good *and* bad. Good, because she did not abort them at conception: bad, because she, in effect, aborted them at birth. The adoptee's inner baby rages, convinced that a good mother does not abandon her child no matter what the circumstances. The adult adoptee tries to understand the circumstances and even forgive the abandoner.

When the adoptee gets in touch with her need for the mother who gave her life—the need that she had to deny for most of her childhood—there is an overwhelming yearning to see her mother's face, touch her hand, be enfolded in her arms. At such moments the adoptee allows herself to believe that her birth mother has never forgotten her. Her birth mother will offer unconditional love when her child finds her. She will have endless patience for endless questions. She will tell her husband and other children about her child. She will tell her child who her father is. She will get on well with her child's adoptive parents.

For the adoptee, the bad birth mother is the one who "rejects" her, doesn't want contact. Who keeps her a secret from her husband and other children. Who refuses to tell her child who her father is. Who does not ask about her life with her adoptive parents.

I believe—and here is one of the many paradoxes in adoption—that when an adoptee finds her birth mother, she also finds her adoptive mother. She is free to attach more fully to her. Until then, the unknown birth mother has stood like a ghost between them, demanding half her loyalty and all of her fantasy life. When that ghostly birth mother emerges from what I call the "Ghost Kingdom"—located in the adoptee's psychic reality—when she materializes and becomes a real person, with all her virtues and faults, the adoptee can appreciate how good the adoptive mother was, and is. There is no longer the barrier of secrecy that separated adoptive mother and child. The adoptee's feeling of being in psychological bondage is replaced by a real bond.

The Politics of Bad/Good

Adoption is no longer just about parents and children. In recent years, it has been usurped by the political right, which uses it for its own "moral" purposes. The bad birth mother can only become good if she remains missing in action. If she accepts the "confidentiality" that organizations like the Christian Coalition and the National Council for Adoption, a conservative lobby group, call for in her name. As I write this they have slapped a lawsuit on the state of Tennessee for voting to open its records to adult adoptees on July 1, 1996.[2] If Tennessee wins the case, it will be the third state, after Kansas and Alaska, to open adoption records—and the first in almost half a century.

The Christian Coalition and the NCFA are against adoption reform. They claim that open records will make pregnant women choose abortion rather than risk being found some day by the child they put up for adoption. (The truth is just the opposite: pregnant women will abort rather than give a baby up to the closed adoption system.)[3] They also claim that open records violate the "confidentiality" of the birth mother— a woman whom they alternately demonize and protect, depending on the circumstances. (Think of the wolf claiming to protect the constitutional rights of Little Red Riding Hood.)

Birth mothers who change their minds about relinquishment within a few weeks and go to court to try to get their babies back before the adoption is finalized are demonized. We've all heard of the bad birth mothers of Baby Jessica and Baby Richard, who stayed the legal course with the birth fathers for years rather than let other people raise their children. Such mothers are not seen as good mothers, but as spoilsports, stalkers—even terrorists.

While the good birth mother—by the Big Bad Wolf's definition—would never want to see her child again, the bad birth mother cannot forget the child she relinquished in her younger, more vulnerable years. This bad birth mother doesn't want her confidentiality protected. In truth, she was never promised confidentiality;[4] she was never promised anything, not even notification if or when her child was placed in an adoptive home. (Some birth mothers have found that their children languished in foster care throughout their childhood, or were placed in foster care after a failed adoption.)

The bad birth mother has no shame, in the eyes of the anti–adoption reform groups. She's out of the closet. She worries that her son may have been killed in Korea, in Vietnam, in the Gulf War, in Bosnia. She writes articles and books describing how she searched for her child and found him. She is reunited with him on TV. At support groups and on the Internet, she helps other birth mothers who are searching for their children. She redefines herself as *good*.

The Future of Bad/Good Mothers

As long as adoption reformers come up against the same political conservatism that blocks other social reforms in this country, the closed adoption system, with its secrets and lies, will continue to make potential good mothers into potential bad ones. It can prevent an adoptive mother from giving her beloved child one of the crucial nutrients the child needs in order to feel grounded and whole: access to her birthright. It can close off the open and honest communication that would make her and her child close.

So, too, even today, the secrecy in the closed system keeps many birth mothers in the closet. It discourages them from thinking of themselves as good. It reinforces their shame. It makes them unable to communicate candidly with their family, friends, and subsequent children.

Adoptees must balance everything on their own moral scale when they evaluate the "good" and the "bad" in both their mothers. Many come to see their mothers as neither good nor bad, but as innocent victims, just as they were, of a closed system that they are now working to open for future generations.

I dedicated my book *Journey of the Adopted Self: A Quest For Wholeness* to my two mothers:

> who might have known
> and even liked each other
> in another life
> and another adoption system.[5]

NOTES

1. Adoption has become as much a battle of terminology as of ideology. Historically, the woman who gave birth to a child was known as the "natural" mother. Adoptive parents argued that the use of this term implied that they themselves were "unnatural." They favored "biological mother." However, the mothers who relinquished their children felt that this made them sound as if they were mere biological creatures with no maternal feelings. They favored "birth mother," the term I have used in this article.

2. The new Tennessee legislation to open adoption records on July 1, 1996 allows adopted adults to receive copies of their adoption records and their original birth certificate. If the birth parent does not want to be contacted, he or she can file a "contact veto."

The law was challenged by a class action suit (*Doe v. Sundquist*) filed on June 25, 1996 by the American Center for Law and Justice (founded by Pat Robertson in 1990 "to defend the rights of believers") against the state of Tennessee on behalf of two birth mothers, an adoptive couple, and an adoption agency affiliated with the National Council For Adoption. The plaintiffs are alleging that it is unconstitutional for any state to open adoption records to adoptees. They claim that opening records to adoptees invades the privacy of both birth parents and adoptive parents.

The trial will be held in the District Court in Nashville in the spring of 1997. The decision is expected to be appealed by one side or the other all the way to the Supreme Court. This is a landmark case: if the state of Tennessee wins, it will set a legal precedent for other states to open their records.

3. Research material compiled by the American Adoption Congress from England, Kansas, and Alaska, where adoption records are open, shows that there is no correlation between the confidentiality of adoption and the rate of abortion. Reunion statistics gathered by the American Adoption Congress from six states— Arizona, New Jersey, New Mexico, North Carolina, Washington, and Tennessee— show that in 8,698 reunions, 95 percent of the birth mothers welcomed contact by the adoptee.

4. There were no written promises of confidentiality in the official adoption surrender papers that birth mothers throughout the country were given to sign.

5. *Journey of the Adopted Self: A Quest for Wholeness* (Basic Books, 1994).

Chapter 10

Nonmothers as Bad Mothers
Infertility and the "Maternal Instinct"

Elaine Tyler May

For conception to take place a woman must be a
woman. Not only must she have the physical structure
and hormones of a woman but she must feel she is a
woman and accept it. A girl child becomes and feels
herself a developing woman if she has made a proper
identification with her own mother and has also
learned to accept her femininity and also masculinity as
represented by her father and later, by her husband.
Being a woman means acceptance of her primary role,
that of conceiving and bearing a child. Every woman
has a basic urge and need to produce a child. Being a
woman means a complete readiness to look forward to
the delivery of that child when it is sufficiently nourished by her to take its place as an infant in the outside
world. Being a woman means her feeling of her own
readiness and capability to rear that child and aid in its
physical, emotional and mental development.[1]
— Abraham Stone, medical director of the
Margaret Sanger Research Foundation, 1950

[handwritten margin note: "'basic urge'"]

In the years following World War II, as the baby boom exploded and a
powerful ideology of domesticity gripped the nation, the definition of
womanhood articulated by Dr. Abraham Stone gained widespread acceptance. Some medical experts, particularly specialists in the growing field
of infertility, frequently based their diagnoses and treatments on the

psychological origin (handwritten margin note)

theory that women often caused their own infertility by a subconscious
rejection of their maternal instinct. Unless they could be restored to
psychological health—which meant a full and eager acceptance of motherhood—such women were not considered to be good candidates for
infertility treatment. According to these neo-Freudian theorists, if such
women were helped to conceive, they would become bad mothers. The
first step in treating them was to help them become psychologically ready
for motherhood.

Margaret Valen encountered this theory when she consulted a physician in 1945 to discover why she was not getting pregnant. She was
twenty-five and her husband was twenty-seven, and they had been married only a year, but since they married "late" by 1945 standards, most of
her friends no doubt had children already. Medical experts encouraged
childless couples to seek help early, warning that "the longer sterility has
existed, the harder it is to correct. Only a qualified physician can answer
for each man and wife the question of when they should undergo examination." Margaret went through the usual infertility workup and tried
"everything kookie," but nothing worked. The physicians could find no
physiological cause for the Valens' childlessness.

The Valens were among the 50 percent of infertile couples at the time
who could not be diagnosed.[2] But that did not prevent her physician
from suggesting treatment. When no physiological cause could be found,
some physicians looked for psychological explanations. As a working
woman in the postwar era, Margaret was not behaving in an appropriately
feminine way. Perhaps, the theory went, she was inhibiting her own
fertility because she held a job—an unwomanly thing to do and evidence
that maybe she did not *really* want a child. Particular warnings were
directed toward employed women, who allegedly put their fertility at risk.
"The pressures of modern living and the strains of occupations in which
women have been engaging are . . . significant causes" of infertility, cautioned a leading expert. "The same can be said of men, but to a lesser
extent."[3] In keeping with such theories, Margaret's physician told her she
should quit her job, so she did. Like most infertile women who sought
medical advice, she did whatever her physician told her to do, even if she
thought it was "kookie." But Margaret never got pregnant. Quitting her
job did not do the trick.

working woman (handwritten margin note)

Advising a woman to quit her job was not a standard treatment for
infertility, but it was one approach to a problem that was still difficult to
diagnose and treat. Researchers had found that stress could be a factor in

infertility, by causing fallopian tubes to contract or by affecting the motility of sperm. If employment was a cause of stress, it was not entirely "kookie" for physicians to suggest quitting a job to relieve stress. The problem, however, is that there was no way to be certain that job-related stress caused a woman's tubes to contract. It was just as likely that stress at work affected a man's fertility. But it was unthinkable to suggest that a male breadwinner should quit his job. The woman's job during these years appeared to be expendable. Moreover, in most cases it was the woman, not the man, who sought treatment. . . .

Most infertility practitioners were specialists in female reproductive medicine. The vast majority of the members of the American Society for the Study of Sterility, for example, were in the field of obstetrics and gynecology, followed by urology, with a few in related fields, such as internal medicine, endocrinology, general practice, and pathology.[4] At its annual meeting in 1963, Herbert H. Thomas, the president of the society, justified the continued focus on the female patient: "This does not indicate that we are unaware of the responsibility of the male in the problem of infertility, but the incidence of primary male infertility is variable but relatively low and, in our culture, it is usually the women who initiate the request for assistance." Surely, the president of the society knew the widely published statistics by its own members indicating that approximately half the infertility cases involved a problem with the man. Yet he remained focused on the woman as the patient:

> In seeking counsel with us, she . . . admits to frustration and failure . . . as we endeavor to probe and explore the innermost secrets of her life in order to alleviate her barrenness. As she bares her personal life before us and submits to many indignities and both painful and somewhat hazardous diagnostic procedures . . . we must not betray this trust. . . . The responsibility to our frustrated patient and her husband is a great one.[5]

The definition of the patient as female extended into medical language itself, which cast the female body as inherently flawed. Medical texts, as well as physicians and their patients, routinely described infertility in terms of "failure," "blame," and "fault." One woman, for example, who wrote to a noted specialist about her repeated miscarriages, wondered whether he agreed with her local physician that surgery might correct her "defective cervix." The specialist agreed that surgery might solve the difficulty, but referred to the condition not as a "defective cervix," as the woman's letter had, but as an "incompetent cervix."[6] Medical terminology was filled with metaphors of the "incompetent" female body, while presenting the male reproductive system as robust. This cultural casting of biological phenomena not only described women's physiology as weak and flawed, it also disadvantaged men, whose reproductive systems might need attention and repair.

The anthropologist Emily Martin analyzed the language of reproduction in standard twentieth-century medical textbooks that have been used routinely in medical schools. She found such statements as these: Ovaries "shed" eggs but testicles "produce" sperm, unfertilized eggs "degenerate" and are "wasted," and "menstruation is the uterus crying for lack of a baby." In contrast, although millions of sperm that do not fertilize eggs die within a few hours, the textbooks never called them "wasted," "failed," or "degenerating"; rather, they described the male reproductive physiology as a "remarkable cellular transformation . . . amazing characteristic of spermatogenesis is its sheer magnitude." Descriptions of fertilization in these textbooks reflect cultural ideas about male aggressiveness and female passivity. Although research documented the active role of the egg in traveling through the tube and showed that the process of fertilization involves mechanisms in both the sperm and the egg that make them "mutually active partners," the loaded language persisted. As if cast as a villain in a film noir, the advancing egg "captures and tethers" the sperm and "clasps" the sperm to its nucleus. The egg has become the femme fatale or the overbearing Mom, devouring its male victim.[7]

Psychological Diagnoses

Infertility treatment was frequently unsuccessful, because half the cases eluded diagnosis. Clinical research continued to focus on the development of more precise diagnostic methods and more effective treatments. Practitioners did not all agree about the basic underlying causes of infertility. Some staunchly believed that if a physiological cause could not be identified, it simply had not been discovered yet. Most, however, agreed that emotional factors could be involved. Researchers had already established that stress could affect hormonal secretions, tubal contractions, and even sperm motility. But the causes of the emotional stresses that led to these physiological outcomes, as well as the prescriptions for reducing these stresses, were a subject of considerable debate. Some leading physicians downplayed the psychological factor. "It is easy to overestimate its importance," said the medical director of the Planned Parenthood Center of Los Angeles. "Admittedly, emotional disturbances can play a part in infertility, but physical conditions are a more frequent cause.[8] Others, however, emphasized psychological causes.

At the extreme end of this debate in the 1940s and 1950s were the psychoanalytically oriented practitioners. If they could find no physiological cause for a couple's childlessness, they often looked for evidence of their patients' unconscious desires to avoid parenthood. This psychological scrutiny was generally directed toward women. Although men were more likely than women to resist treatment, physicians rarely considered the possibility that reluctant men had a psychological difficulty that contributed to their impaired fertility or that they "subconsciously" did not really want children. Stress caused by pressure at work was the only psychological factor mentioned in the medical literature on the evaluation of male patients. Experts in the field never suggested that men thwarted their own potential for parenthood by "unconscious wishes" or "a rejection of their masculinity." On the contrary, specialists frequently reassured

 men that infertility did not mean they were lacking in masculinity. Clearly, most physicians believed that masculinity was not something that men were likely to avoid. But psychoanalytically oriented physicians claimed that some women contributed to their own infertility by their reluctance, consciously or unconsciously, to "accept their femininity." According to these practitioners, even the most eager and cooperative female patient might "subconsciously" wish to avoid motherhood.

As infertility continued to gain attention from the popular media, as well as the scientific community, these psychoanalytic perspectives began to infuse the discussion of childlessness. The postwar years witnessed a romance with all forms of psychology, especially Freudian and neo-Freudian theories. Psychoanalytic jargon appeared everywhere, from scientific journals to popular articles, and even in casual conversations. Some neo-Freudian theorists breathed new life into prescriptions that were first voiced by their Victorian forebears about the importance of women attending to their proper role. Old notions that education and careers hindered women's reproductive potential resurfaced, as did exhortations about women's sexual behavior. Although many infertility experts were skeptical of psychoanalytic explanations, neo-Freudian practitioners received a remarkable amount of attention in both the medical and popular literature.[9]

One example of this approach was a 1951 article by a sociologist, a psychologist, and a gynecologist that was published in the *Journal of the American Medical Association.* The authors began with the premise that normal, healthy adults naturally desire children. "Most people who do not truly want them probably have personality defects—for example, infantilism. . . . Women totally lacking the desire for children are so rare that they may be considered as deviants from the normal." Infertile women, they reasoned, might subconsciously thwart their own fertility by rejecting their femininity. They described three "types" of such women:

> The masculine-aggressive woman insists on having a child of her own body, cost what it may. She is a ready, though rarely ideal, candidate for donor insemination, sometimes obtaining her husband's reluctant consent by a species of emotional blackmail. Second, there is the wife who accepts childlessness and lives on good terms with her sterile husband but demands from him constant proofs of his masculinity in the way of achievement and material success. And, third, the truly motherly woman compensates for her lack of children by directing her motherliness toward other persons or objects, real or symbolic.

The three male authors asserted that whatever intrusive procedures were required to enable a woman to get pregnant, including artificial insemination with the sperm of an anonymous donor, the women did not mind. In fact, they argued, the women may even enjoy it.

> The patients are seldom troubled by any notion of violation of their bodies; indeed, some of them derive a peculiar satisfaction from the coldly scientific nature of the operation. Successful results create a feeling of superiority and triumph over the male, as well as a sense of fulfillment.[10]

Some specialists who agreed with these psychological theories warned other practitioners not to treat "neurotic" women for infertility. One advised: "The wise physician will be able to ascertain the psychic health of his patients. He will then be in an enviable position to determine whether or not attempts should be made to relieve sterility." It was important to do so, he argued, for "allowing an emotional [*sic*] immature woman to become fertile may open up the proverbial hornet's nest. The repercussions may result in neurotic children, broken homes, and divorce."[11] Some gynecologists, as well as psychologists and psychiatrists, pointed to "personality" factors in infertility. "The emotional maturity of the patient, that is, her ability adequately to meet the demands of pregnancy as well as motherhood, should always be considered in the treatment of sterility," argued W. S. Kroger, director of Psychosomatic Gyne-

cology at Mount Sinai Hospital in Chicago and one of the leading voices
in the application of psychoanalytic theories to infertility treatment. Kroger urged his fellow practitioners to take note of "those unhealthy attitudes and personality factors likely to complicate or contraindicate pregnancy." To determine if a woman should be treated for infertility, the
physician should "seek answers to the following questions":

1) Is the patient a cold, selfish, demanding person, or is she a warm, giving
   woman?
2) What is her motivation for becoming pregnant?
3) Could the absence of so-called "motherliness" be due to environmental
   factors, permanent or temporary, and does this account for her sterility?
4) How much does her emotional past . . . influence her attitudes toward
   motherhood?
5) What are the deeper meanings underlying her surface attitudes toward
   pregnancy, motherhood, and sterility?

Those who should be rejected for treatment included "the aggressive
and masculine women who are competitive, strong, ambitious, and dominating. They 'wear the pants in the family' and are usually successful
career women, possessing considerable executive ability." The greatest
exemplar of the maladjusted female was the career woman. "We have all
seen a long-desired pregnancy follow the renunciation of a career. This
may be the result of the development of 'motherliness' and the consequent hormonal changes." Kroger concluded that "it should not be necessary for every physician to have training in psychoanalysis" to understand
these basic principles. In other words, physicians who were not trained in
psychology should make a psychological diagnosis that would determine
whether the personality of the patient disqualified her for motherhood,
in which case the physician should refuse treatment.[12] Kroger ended with
a word of caution to the physician who might unwittingly treat a woman
who was emotionally unqualified to become a mother: "If such a woman
finally does conceive, the same psychological difficulties which once prevented conception, may adversely affect the child's psychic development,
and . . . another individual is added to an endless procession of neu-
rotics."[13] . . .

Psychoanalytic ideas moved easily from the medical journals to the
popular press. An article in *Coronet* magazine in 1953, entitled "Sterility
Can Be a State of Mind," asserted that emotional states—hatred, fear,
anxiety, poor adjustment to marriage—could inhibit fertility in from

one-fourth to one-third of all cases of involuntary childlessness. According to the author, infertility often resulted from "high-strung women"; "strong parental prohibitions against sex"; and other psychological inhibitions, such as unresolved Oedipal conflicts. "Some specialists point out that to many persons, the doctor has become the highest authority in the conduct of their personal lives. . . . [He] has taken the place of the father of their childhood." Sometimes a visit to such a physician "may be reassuring to the wife and lead to a relaxation of her Fallopian tubes." The author also argued for the importance of sexual adjustment. " 'The act of love' must, in truth, *be* an act of love, rather than just an act of sex, if fruitful union is to ensue." Repeating a common refrain, the article concluded, "If the wife is working, perhaps she can take a leave of absence for a while, or quit her job and stay at home. Rest and relax, and just forget all about doctors for a while. And see what happens." [14]

Some experts claimed that mere association with children would bring out a woman's "maternal instinct," which could stimulate fertility. *American Magazine* suggested a "plan that sometimes does wonders for childless couples. This is to go out babysitting. . . . [A] woman's maternal instincts are tremendously stimulated when there are children around." This was also the argument frequently given for the alleged "cure" of infertility by adoption. "Sometimes the adoption of a child is the secret," wrote an observer. "In the sunlight of a new happiness, the adoptive mother bears a child of her own." In one case, a psychoanalyst argued that the reason pregnancy followed adoption was because the wife quit her job after adopting a baby.

> Her conflict . . . resolved [sic] around the fact that if she became pregnant, she would have to stop working outside the home and abandon the masculine role. The decision to adopt a baby solved this unconscious conflict by making it absolutely necessary for her to give up her job. This, in some strange way, added to her femininity, and allowed her to conceive. Cases in which pregnancy follows the adoption of a baby are by no means rare. Everyone knows of similar instances. [15]

Some physicians were skeptical of these explanations. One cautioned those who believed that adoption often leads to biological parenting. "This popular belief has no justification. Some couples adopt a child, then subsequently have children of their own, and when this occurs, there's a lot of comment. But we don't hear about the many more couples who do not have children subsequent to adoption." This physician was also cautious about placing too much emphasis on emotional factors in infertility. He noted that emotional tension was as likely to be a *result* of infertility as a cause, since trying to conceive a child and seeking medical help in the effort were stressful activities in themselves: "Many childless couples are emotionally upset because of their failure to have children, but often the tensions have been built up as a result of years of frustration and hence may be an effect rather than a cause of the problem."[16]

Stress   This physician had a point. Infertile couples in the postwar years faced tremendous stresses. First, there was the stigma of childlessness at a time when having many children, at a young age, was the norm. Next was the suggestion, reinforced by psychoanalytic theories and echoed in the popular press, that infertile women were to blame for their own condition. Women were labeled abnormal if they were ambivalent about having children, they were suspected of not *really* wanting children even if they truly believed that they did, they were accused of unconscious wishes to remain childless, they were chastised for holding jobs or aspiring to careers, and they were admonished if they were not adequately passive and submissive. They were made to feel guilty if they had an abortion, held a job or pursued a career, or found sexual satisfaction in any way other than through a vaginal orgasm resulting from male penetration.

Since researchers had determined that stress might affect fertility, some of these pressures may have had the ironic effect of contributing to infertility. Women who were accused of being "abnormal," "selfish," "neurotic," or "immature" as a result of normal and healthy ambivalence toward or resistance to the accepted female role of full-time wife and mother may indeed have suffered enough stress to cause their fallopian tubes to contract. Meanwhile, in spite of the efforts of many specialists to improve the treatment of male infertility and the recognition that most infertility cases involved some problem with the male partner, infertility remained defined as a female complaint.

The New Pronatalism

According to feminist author Susan Faludi, the renewed push toward parenthood in the 1980s took the form of a media blitz aimed at educated career women, warning them that if they delayed childbearing, they were likely to find themselves infertile. Few of the alarmists who pointed to a new "infertility epidemic" took note of studies showing a troubling trend in male fertility: the decline in the average sperm count by more than half in the past thirty years. Nor did they mention the fact that less-educated poor women were more likely than professional women to be infertile, as a result of pelvic inflammatory disease, caused frequently by sexually transmitted diseases. Rather, many articles claimed that the alleged increase in infertility resulted from women postponing motherhood until they were in their thirties, when it might be too late to conceive.[17]

In 1987, NBC correspondent Maria Shriver called childlessness "the curse of the career woman." In the same year, *Life* published a special report entitled "Baby Craving." Headlines warned against "Having It All: Postponing Parenthood Exacts a Price" and bemoaned "The Quiet Pain of Infertility: For the Success-Oriented, It's a Bitter Pill." A columnist for the *New York Times* described the infertile woman as "a walking cliché" of the feminist generation, "a woman on the cusp of forty who put work ahead of motherhood." *Newsweek* noted the "trend of childlessness," and *Mademoiselle* warned, "Caution: You Are Now Entering the Age of Infertility."[18] . . .

Many observers assume that infertility is on the rise. But there is no evidence that the proportion of infertile Americans has increased. There is evidence, however, that the number of people who are seeking treatment has risen dramatically. The number of visits to physicians for infertility treatment rose from 600,000 in 1968 to 1.6 million in 1984. The increase has been due, in part, to the huge baby-boom generation; the infertile among them are a large and visible group. But there are other reasons as well. Even if the chances for successful treatment are not much better than they were a half-century ago, dramatic new technological interventions are now available. High-tech approaches, such as in-vitro fertilization (IVF, fertilization of the egg in a laboratory petri dish and then its insertion directly into the uterus), first successfully used in the birth of Louise Brown in England in 1978, appear to offer "miracle babies" to the childless. Treatments using assisted reproduction techniques jumped 30 percent from 1990 to 1991, even though the chance of ending up with a "take-home baby" from these procedures was only about 15 percent.[19]

The promise of a technological fix, combined with a faith in medical progress, led many Americans to believe that they could triumph over most physical limitations. Physicians have responded to the demand.

Studies have shown that American physicians are more likely than British practitioners to resort to heroic measures for treating infertility, probably because their patients request such intervention.[20] But reproductive medicine, despite its many advances over the past century, remains an imperfect art, available only to those who can afford it. Nor does it guarantee success. Infertility treatment is a high-stakes gamble: It is possible to lose all the money, time, and effort invested and gain nothing in return. If all the efforts of modern science, human struggle, and economic sacrifice do not result in the desired child, the rage, desperation, and anguish can be overwhelming.

Because birth control and reproductive choice are widely taken for granted, the infertile experience extreme frustration. Reproductive choice is much easier to achieve if the goal is to avoid pregnancy. Contraceptive technologies offer a success rate of nearly 100 percent, and legal abortion provides a backup when birth control methods fail. But infertile couples who seek treatment have only a 50 percent chance for success in the 1990s, odds that have not dramatically improved since the 1950s.[21] The inability to "control" one's reproductive fate is among the most exasperating experiences of infertility, especially for those who have put so much effort into the struggle. As the reporter Susan Sward wrote of her struggle with infertility, "As an organized, energetic person, I was used to getting what I wanted in life most of the time. To a major extent, I was also used to feeling in control of my life and knowing what I did would produce results if I tried hard enough. When it came to making babies, I found I had a lot to learn."[22]

Those who become pregnant while using birth control tend to blame the technology. But infertility patients who do not conceive often blame themselves. They feel unable to control their bodies or their destinies, even with medical intervention. For Roberta O'Leary, "It gets more and more difficult to pick up the pieces after each failure. I also don't like the feeling of having no control over what happens." Amanda Talley "felt like a freak of nature ... embarrassed and shameful. ... I felt as though my body betrayed me." Dierdre Kearney explained, "My feelings of helplessness have been hard to handle. We humans like to have control over our own lives and the one thing we think we can control is our body." She has done everything to have a baby and

> still my body betrays me and deprives me of one of the things I want most in life. I cannot make my body do what I want. ... I've heard some women

say that being infertile makes them feel less like a woman. I've never really felt this. I guess, this has made me feel all too much like a woman because it's what makes me a woman that has caused my problem—PERIODS and HORMONES! I just feel helpless in determining my own future. Sometimes I feel like a ship at sea and just when I am close to land, a huge wave washes me out to sea again.[23]

The inability to control one's reproductive functions often leads to feelings of shame and worthlessness, especially for women. Maureen Wendell explained, "I began to feel defective, ashamed. I can't do a 'normal' biological function that most anyone else could do. I had to reevaluate my life, my hopes, my dreams and my identity as a woman. I am blessed to have a very supportive husband but even with that I felt inadequate as a wife." Feelings of inadequacy were magnified by the association of fertility with sexuality. In a taped message, Patricia Painter used the language of sexual potency when describing her husband's healthy sperm. "My husband has this, you know, magnificent, I guess he's extremely virile. He has like super sperm. . . . Everybody from the lab technicians to the receptionist at the doctor's office was always so amazed at the amount and the virility of this sperm. It's like super-human sperm." When they accidentally spilled some of the semen sample, a physician replied,

"It doesn't matter. He could impregnate the whole block with what's left in here. It's amazing." Which made me feel absolutely horrible because he couldn't impregnate me. Well, it was real obvious who had the problem in this relationship, as far as who was the one responsible for us not getting pregnant, and that was me. So I felt extremely terrible about that. This resulted in my being very embarrassed around people. I felt very defective. . . . It was just really such a blow. . . . I would get physically ill . . . 'cause I felt so defective and so embarrassed.

Laura Lerner also felt "abnormal," even though she was not infertile. But she was single, and her singleness deprived her of the opportunity to become a mother. "I am a woman. I am supposed to have children, right? What am I if I don't produce children?" She considered adopting as a single parent or trying donor insemination. But she could not bring herself to do it: "Withdrawing some sperm from the sperm bank sounds so cold and mechanical." Without children, she felt "unnatural. . . . I have had these damn menstrual cycles since age 11 and I have nothing to show for it. . . . I get so I hate the cycle when it comes. . . . I have the most trouble trying to determine why I am here. I feel very incomplete, and very abnormal."

Before she discovered she was infertile, Leila Ember felt that "Life was good! Most importantly I was in control of it!" When she did not get pregnant, however, she began treatment, even though she recoiled at the invasive procedures: "For a person who had never had so much as a band-aid applied to any part of their body I found it quite difficult to endure the poking and prodding and exploratory procedures which were both financially and emotionally expensive." But her body remained uncooperative. Infertility destroyed her peace of mind and self-confidence: "I remember sitting on the floor of my bathroom for what seemed like hours and sobbing. I'd look at my husband and begin to scream how sorry I was that I 'messed up again!' " Blaming herself, she wrote, "My biological clock isn't ticking; it isn't working at all!"

Many childless women who wanted children questioned their own womanhood. Suzanna Drew felt "less of a woman—somehow not complete." Kate Foley felt "barren." Paula Kranz described feelings of "failure . . . it's like an empty space within yourself that you cannot fill." Marie Gutierrez blamed herself when her husband's semen analysis

> came back ok, then O Boy! All fingers pointed to me, *wow* was I ever so unhappy, people don't know what it is like to try and try and never succeed. . . . I told no one . . . we were both embarrassed, marked, hurt. My husband is a very supportive husband, a good man and tells me that he accepts whatever happens, but . . . I can't accept the fact that I feel like some sort of alien, all women who are "normal" have children.

Along with at least four other women and men who wrote me, Marie offered to release her spouse from the marriage so that he could find a fertile partner and have children. . . .

One reason why infertility is so wrenching is that treatment holds out the possibility of a "miracle cure," making it difficult to give up, grieve, and find acceptance. To pursue medical intervention means to hold out hope and experience disappointment month after month, while the possibility of pregnancy still exists.[24] Many infertility patients described the experience as an "emotional roller coaster." Marie Gutierrez explained, "After each surgery and taking the fertility drug Clomid still trying and holding onto every good word from the Doctor that it could possibly happen this time, what a real drop in my Soul and a real letdown for my husband's ego, every test, every pill still no hope."

Amelia Monterey described the cycles of hope and disappointment. A

thirty-three-year-old medical secretary married fifteen years to a construction worker, she lives in a trailer house in rural Minnesota. Like
many others, she and her husband planned, dreamed, worked hard, saved,
and assumed that they would achieve their goals. "We're poor," she wrote,
but they pursued every possible treatment available before they finally
gave up, heartbroken. Amelia wrote: "I've always been a caretaker. . . . I
had no plans for college or even a career. . . . My whole childhood was
built on the dream of becoming a wife and more—a Mother. I had no
other life goals." When she did not become pregnant,

> I tried EVERYTHING! I took Clomid, got [hormone] shots, took my
> [temperature] every morning for years and even put an experimental drug
> up my nose. . . . I even had major surgery. They removed part of my
> ovaries. . . . What I want to get across is the feelings and the heartbreak of
> all these years of poking and probing that I went through. Looking at that
> thermometer *every* morning and not seeing it rise. . . . I went through that
> hurt, ache and devastation EVERY month. . . . [It] was like killing a small
> part of my womanhood.

In a similar cycle of hope and devastation, Susan Delmont had eight
miscarriages and one failed adoption attempt. "I feel like a failure," she
wrote. The experience destroyed her self-confidence; she quit her job,
because she did not have "time enough to cry." She doubts her ability to
raise a child. "I can't seem to apply for adoption. I don't know if I'm fit
to be a mother or not, and I can't just say that I am. If God or whoever
won't let me have my babies, why should an adoption agency?" Still,
depressed as she was, she knew when she was getting the wrong advice
from experts. One psychiatrist told her "just having 8 miscarriages
couldn't make me as sad as I was. He was sure that my father sexually
abused me as a child, and that my subconscious covered it up. Needless
to say, I dumped him." But she was still left with her anguish. "I don't
feel like I've had miscarriages, I feel like I've lost children. . . . I have
'phantom' children—you know, like an amputee has a phantom limb."

Rage

Along with pain and frustration, many infertile respondents expressed
almost bottomless rage—at themselves, their bodies, and the fertile
world. Carey Van Camp described feeling "almost hateful" and feeling "a
burning rage inside me," especially toward pregnant women or infants.
Lydia Sommer said infertility

came as a shock to us—like being punched in the stomach and not being able to catch your breath. . . . The world turns and we stand still. . . . I detest all pregnant women—whether they are my friends or not. They carry their pregnancy like a badge of honor, when they did nothing special to achieve it. Honestly, they make me sick. Sounds pretty bad, doesn't it? I'm becoming more cynical about it as I get older and my clock ticks away.

For many, the sight of their desired goal did not bring out warm feelings toward children. Rather, they felt hateful—even murderous. As Patricia Painter explained,

It was *so* painful to see anybody that was pregnant or had a baby. . . . I was the proverbial woman that was leaving the fertility doctor's office and saw the pregnant lady with two kids, a baby and a, you know, a toddler, in the crosswalks, and wanted to run over them all. God I felt *so* guilty for feeling that way until I got involved with Resolve. I really thought I was a horrible person. I thought God was punishing me or something. . . . I really wanted to run them over very badly with my car. . . . And I knew that every pregnant woman, every woman that had a new baby . . . got pregnant just to hurt my feelings. And God knows they did!

Patricia realized that her initial motivation for pursuing infertility treatment, her "love for children," virtually vanished. "I had a point where I could not see children at all. It was so painful." One friend, to protect her feelings when her toddler ran to the door, "looked around in her house, grabbed a newspaper, and put it in front of his face. Wasn't that nice? So I didn't have to see the kid. I thought that was nice. I'm sure my friends thought I was nuts." She even began to question her own sanity. "My values got real distorted and screwed up. . . . It felt very weird. . . . I had the ability to stand back and say, 'You're getting real strange, Patricia.' . . . And yet I couldn't seem to stop it. Kind of like trying to stop an avalanche, I think. The flood of emotion was so difficult."

Many of the desperately infertile expressed their most intense rage and disdain toward those who they believed neither wanted nor deserved their children, especially the young and the poor. Sonia Everly wrote, "It just doesn't seem fair . . . that young girls are getting pregnant when they have no desire to be parents." Daisy Posner's hatred went in all directions. As a nurse, she worked in labor and delivery. "I hated all the patients, even more so the ones with 3–4 kids who were on cocaine. I was sick with envy and hated God for being so unfair to me." In 1990, after infertility treatment, Daisy had a healthy daughter. But having one child isn't enough. . . . I still feel like a failure for all the miscarriages. I hate my body—it has felt empty and useless ever since my daughter was born. I hate reading about all the pregnant teenagers in the paper. . . . All my friends here are pregnant with their second child. It is all I can do to stay friendly with them—I hate them so much. . . . I pray all the time for another baby but God must hate me. He gives lots of babies to poor drug addicts and only one to me. . . . And I still hated my labor and delivery patients for having more kids. Needless to say I work elsewhere now . . . but I am still stuck in anger and despair.

Some infertile women expressed anger at women who had abortions. Paula Kranz felt "anger, bitterness and jealousy. . . . And then there are women out there being blessed with babies, and they are killing them with abortions." Dierdre Kearney wrote, "Each time I read of a child abuse case or of a woman having a third abortion, I cannot help but question, 'Why?' " But many infertile women saw abortion as a choice, much like infertility treatment. Karen Pasmore found it ironic that "so many women become pregnant without even thinking about it, many when they'd rather not," but she was nevertheless "strongly pro-choice. Many of my friends don't understand my position but if another woman becomes pregnant against her wishes, my infertility is not affected. I guess the grass is always greener."

Infertile women who had abortions themselves often felt guilty for years. Sue Kott got pregnant when she was twenty-five. Although she wanted to have the baby, her boyfriend wanted her to have an abortion. Two years later they married, and she has not been able to conceive again. She never forgave herself for the abortion. After years of infertility treatment, she is still childless, and her husband "refuses to adopt." Sonia Everly, on the other hand, has forgiven herself. Between her two marriages, she became pregnant while in graduate school and had an abortion.

> The abortion was traumatic, as it always is; never an easy decision, but the right one for me, and my partner, at the time. I obviously did not know that would be my only pregnancy. Would my choice have been different had I known? I think so, but I made my decision based on what I knew at that time. I still assumed I could become pregnant when I wanted to, when I was ready.

If abortion was difficult for some infertile women to accept, others found the fecundity of the poor unbearable. Some who believed that they had earned their right to reproductive self-determination were quick to deny the same right to others. Several shared the sentiments of Lisa Brown, who wrote, "I don't appreciate females having more kids than they can provide for and go on welfare. . . . I think there should be a law of 2 kids on welfare only. I think there should be sterilization inforced after the 2nd child."

Lisa's fury was directed toward the wrong target. Poor women on welfare were not responsible for her infertility, but she blamed them, rather than the real villains. In her case, as in many others, there were real villains. She was one of several respondents whose infertility resulted from severe damage to their bodies caused by sexual abuse when they were children. These respondents well understood the source of their problem, but did not express anger directly toward the men who raped them. None, in fact, mentioned whether their molesters had been apprehended. Thirty-one respondents, including two men, specifically mentioned abuse as a direct cause of their childlessness, ranging from emotional abuse to physical and sexual abuse.[25] The most horrifying were the stories of women like Lisa whose reproductive organs were damaged because they were raped when they were young children.

Lisa did not mention the rapes until the end of her letter. She began without a standard salutation, asking "if your some weirdo, getting off on others pain." She described years of infertility treatment, including several reconstructive surgeries, tubal pregnancies, and miscarriages. She and her husband tried to adopt, but they learned that it would take approximately ten years, because they wanted a child under age two. At age forty-three, Lisa had lost her struggle to have a child and lost her marriage as well. She explained,

> When your husband goes out and gets a bar whore pregnate after 12 years of marriage and 4 miscarriages and 2 tubal pregnancies and the loss of 7 children, your mom says, "what do you expect? He wants kids, you can't give him any." So the marriage is gone and death looks good! What good am I to anyone? . . . Bitter? VERY! Being a female has not been fun for me. . . . Why did God see fit to take my kids but lets whores, child beaters and molesters have kids? And hurt or kill them?

Lisa was on the list for IVF when her husband "got a bar whore pregnant" and the marriage ended. "That was the hardest phone call I had to make in my life—calling and cancelling my only sure promise of a child." Although it was certainly far from a "sure promise," she was prepared to pay the $4,500 to try it. It was not until a brief postscript added after she signed her letter that she revealed the source of her difficulty: She was repeatedly raped by her step-grandfather and half-uncle from ages four through seven. "And by the way the rapes were performed (on the top of the bathroom toilet tank lid with my legs drawn up like I was squatting). It tilted my uterus so severely it caused all my future female problems."

Trudy Mayer, a white married factory worker, was also a victim of incest as a child and cannot carry a baby. She wrote three letters explaining her experience and her anguish, expressing anger not toward her molester but toward herself.

> When I first found out that I may never have a child I tryed to kill myself because I was raised to believe that women are to reproduce so that made me feel like if I can't do what God intend women to do then I didn't belong. After that I felt very angry I was angry at me, at God at my Mother for having Me I was looking for some one to hate or blame I still have these feelings.

But the true villain remained unnamed.

> Doctors and friends and family say oh just keep trying it will happen even my husband says we will just keep trying. Me I'm tired of it I want a baby but I don't want to keep going throw the hurt I have been pregnant seven times and each one I have lost and everyone says oh I understand but there is no way that they can understand what I go throu. I read the paper and see where some parents kill there kids or leave them in a trash can or something and stop and say to myself why would someone do such a thing to their own child but how can I understand I have never been in there shoes the same as you, you could never understand no matter how much you would like to.

She has seen specialists and had many surgeries, "so many that my stomach looks like a war zone." It was not until the end of her letter that she gave the reason for her misery: "I was molested very young . . . but it did not stop there it continued until I was 10 years old because I did not know that this was wrong."

Trudy did not name her abuser until her second letter: "I was molested when I was five years old by my father and it went on for years and I thought of suicide many of times through the years." She lived with her husband seven years before she finally married him because if he can handle all these things we have been throu then I would be dum not to marrie him. . . . he has been at every doctors appointment been write there with every miscarriage he has cryed throu them with me he has been my clown but even with all this he new that he could leave and be with some one who can have children but he wanted to be with me even thou being with me hurts him a little of him dies every day because of are childless problem we have a specialist we go to and even with insurance it hurts the pocket book and we have looked in to adoption but they want you to be millionaire just to adopt a child this is what kills us every day a little to a time but what can you do.

In cases of sexual violence, the cause of infertility was grimly evident. But brutality surfaced in the letters of only a minority of respondents. In other cases, the very technologies that were developed to improve individual control over reproduction led to infertility. Ironically, many infertile individuals turned to medical experts to cure a problem that medical technology had created. Vivian Johnson discovered that her tubes were scarred from her previous use of an intrauterine device (IUD), and surgery did not correct the problem. Ultimately, high-tech reproductive medicine overcame the problem created by high-tech contraception. She had twins from her first IVF attempt. Karen Pasmore had a problem shared by tens of thousands of her peers; she was infertile because her mother was treated with diethylstilbestrol, or DES, during pregnancy. The drug was used widely in the 1940s and 1950s to prevent miscarriages.[26] In college, "DES became the specter in my life that it remains today." She turned to invasive high-tech infertility treatment, with no luck. Lorraine Pascasio was luckier. She, too, was a DES daughter. Initially she felt, "I'm defective' . . . Damaged goods." But she finally had a "miracle baby" and wrote her story for the *Ladies Home Journal*.[27]

It is now nearly fifty years since Dr. Abraham Stone offered his definition of a woman as one who accepts "her primary role, that of conceiving and bearing a child." Today most physicians, as well as most women, know that infertility can result from a wide range of factors, affecting both male and female. But the power of that psychological and behavioral definition of womanhood has persisted long after its scientific validity has been questioned. Articles in the popular press still blame career women for an "infertility epidemic," even though infertility continues to affect poor people to a much greater extent than the affluent. This fact should be obvious, since infertility, like other health problems, is more likely to plague those with fewer resources and less access to good medical care.

Nevertheless, in spite of all evidence to the contrary, infertility still carries a stigma suggesting that women are to blame for their own inability to conceive.

NOTES

This essay is excerpted from Elaine Tyler May, *Barren in the Promised Land: Childless Americans and the Pursuit of Happiness* (New York: Basic Books, 1995), chaps. 5 and 7.

1. "Psychological Aspects of Fertility," manuscript draft, dated November 8, 1950, *New York Times*, Stone File, Countway Library of Medicine, Rare Books and Manuscripts, Harvard University, Boston (hereafter Stone File, Countway Library).

2. By 1990, only 20 percent of infertility remained unexplained, yet only half of all infertile couples undergoing medical treatment would achieve pregnancies. See Margarete J. Sandelowski, "Failures of Volition: Female Agency and Infertility in Historical Perspective," *Signs: Journal of Women in Culture and Society* 15 (1990): 475–99.

3. I. C. Rubin, M.D., as told to Margaret Albrecht, "Childlessness and What Can Be Done about It," *Parents*, March 1957, 46ff.

4. Herbert H. Thomas, M.D., "Thirty-Two Years of Fertility Progress," Presidential Address, *Fertility and Sterility* 27 (October 1976): 1125–31.

5. Edward T. Tyler, M.D., as told to Roland H. Berg, "Childless Couples Can Have Babies," *Look*, September 17, 1957, 41–50; and Willis E. Brown, M.D., "Privilege and Responsibility: Presidential Address," *Fertility and Sterility* 14 (1963): 475–81.

6. Mrs. Gary B., Hurst, Texas, January 14, 1964, to Dr. Rock; reply from Robert E. Wheatley, M.D., March 23, 1964, Rock Papers, Countway Library.

7. Emily Martin, "The Egg and the Sperm: How Science Has Constructed a Romance Based on Stereotypical Male-Female Roles," *Signs: Journal of Women in Culture and Society* 16 (1991): 485–501; see also Emily Martin, *The Woman in the Body: A Cultural Analysis of Reproduction* (Boston: Beacon Press, 1987), 45–48.

8. Tyler, "Childless Couples Can Have Babies."

9. For an excellent study of the transformation of psychiatry during the early twentieth century and its cultural significance, see Elizabeth Lunbeck, *The Psychiatric Persuasion: Knowledge, Gender, and Power in Modern America* (Princeton: Princeton University Press, 1994).

10. Herbert D. Lamson, Willem J. Pinard, and Samuel R. Meaker, "Sociologic and Psychological Aspects of Artificial Insemination with Donor Semen," *Journal of the American Medical Association* 145 (April 7, 1951): 1062–63.

11. "Program: American Society for the Study of Sterility, Eighth Annual Conference," June 7 and 8, 1952, Chicago, 10 and 11; and descriptions of papers by Therese Benedek, M.D., "Infertility as a Psychosomatic Defense," and W. S. Kroger, M.D., "The Evaluation of Personality Factors in the Treatment of Infertility," in Tyler Clinic Archives, Los Angeles.

12. Sandelowski, "Failures of Volition," 475–99.

13. W. S. Kroger, M.D., "Evaluation of Personality Factors in the Treatment of Infertility," *Fertility and Sterility* 3 (November–December 1952): 542–51.

14. Vera G. Kinsler, "Sterility Can Be a State of Mind," *Coronet,* April 1953, 109–12.

15. "Family Problems," *American Magazine,* August 1951, 108; William Engle, "Maybe You *Can* Have a Baby," *American Weekly,* November 8, 1953, 8; J. D. Ratcliff, "Clinics for the Childless," *Hygeia* 19 (October 1941): 854; Joseph D. Wassersug, "More Help for Childless Couples," *Hygeia* 25 (November 1947): 384–85.

16. Tyler, "Childless Couples Can Have Babies."

17. Susan Faludi, *Backlash: The Undeclared War against American Women* (New York: Crown, 1991), 24–27. On the declining sperm count, see Amy Linn, "Male Infertility: From Taboo to Treatment," *Philadelphia Inquirer,* May 31, 1987, A1, cited in Faludi, *Backlash,* 31–32. On the new pronatalism, see also Margarete J. Sandelowski, *With Child in Mind: Studies of the Personal Encounter with Infertility* (Philadelphia: University of Pennsylvania Press, 1993), 9.

18. Articles cited in Faludi, *Backlash,* 104–10.

19. On the proportion of the infertile, see Arthur L. Greil, *Not Yet Pregnant: Infertile Couples in Contemporary America* (New Brunswick, N.J.: Rutgers University Press, 1991), 27–28; data on physicians visits from Office of Technology Assessment, in Philip Elmer-Dewitt, "Making Babies," *Time,* September 30, 1991, 56–63; see also David Perlman, "The Art and Science of Conception: Brave New Babies," *San Francisco Chronicle,* March 3, 1990, B3; on the success of IVF, see Nancy Wartik, "Making Babies," *Los Angeles Times Magazine,* March 6, 1994, 18ff.

20. Study cited in Greil, *Not Yet Pregnant,* 11.

21. Most estimates gave infertile couples a 50 percent chance, as they did in the 1950s and 1960s, although some physicians were more conservative. One physician in 1962, for example, gave infertile couples a 40 percent chance of a cure, saying that "more could be helped if husbands would cooperate completely with medical examination and treatment." See Grace Naismith, "Good News for Childless Couples," *Today's Health* 40 (January 1962): 24ff. For 1990 data, see Greil, *Not Yet Pregnant,* 11.

22. Susan Sward, "I Thought Having a Baby Would Be Easy," *San Francisco Chronicle,* March 5, 1990, B4. See also Miriam D. Mazor, "Barren Couples," *Psychology Today,* May 1979, 101–12.

23. The quotations from infertile women, unless otherwise indicated, were

gathered using an author's query sent to newspapers and journals across the country. The query letter, addressed to the editors, asked individuals who had experienced childlessness at some point in their lives to write to me about their experiences and feelings. We had no way of knowing which journals published the query, but more than five hundred people wrote back from all over the country. None of the respondents is identified by his or her real name. For a more detailed discussion of the sample, see "Appendix: A Note on the Sample of Letters," in May, *Barren in the Promised Land*, 261–65.

24. See Greil, *Not Yet Pregnant*, esp. chap. 4.

25. The abuse mentioned included psychological or physical abuse that the respondents did not wish to perpetuate or made them feel they would be bad parents. Some said that they had only recently "discovered" their childhood sexual abuse in therapy, by retrieving repressed memories. Although these approaches are highly controversial in the professional therapeutic community, it is noteworthy that several childless people mentioned these "repressed memories" in relation to their childlessness. Other cases, however, like those quoted in this chapter, were not repressed memories. They were well-remembered rapes that continued for years.

26. See Philip Elmer Dewitt, "Making Babies," *Time*, September 30, 1991, 56–62. DES Action and other groups have been formed by and on behalf of women who have been harmed by DES, the Dalkon Shield, and other medical products. See Karen M. Hicks, *Surviving the Dalkon Shield IUD: Women v. The Pharmaceutical Industry* (New York: Teachers College Press, 1994).

27. Lorraine Pascasio, "A Christmas Baby," *Ladies Home Journal*, December 1991, 14–17.

Chapter 11

On Being the "Bad" Mother of an Autistic Child

Jane Taylor McDonnell

I remember I was standing with a young teacher on the playground of a London nursery school, watching my son Paul, then three. He had already been given every medical and psychological test known at the time but was not yet diagnosed as autistic.

"He doesn't look anyone in the eye, does he?" the teacher remarked.

"No, well . . . ," I began. "But he does with me . . . most of the time." Why did I bristle at this comment? Partly it was because I thought it was so unfair. His father and I had always known Paul to be an affectionate, alert, intelligent child; his was a happy temperament, we had always thought, an "easy" child, but not too easy. He was healthy, well grown, loved us and his wonderful college babysitters, was passionately interested in his books and demanded to be read to for hours each day. Furthermore, he had always been appropriate in the expression of his feelings (sadness, joy, frustration, fear).

But now in London these things were beginning to seem less important than the fact that he was having so much trouble speaking and was obviously getting more and more frustrated as a result. Slowly, a deepening anxiety was crowding out our earlier feelings of pride and joy in this wonderfully "original" child. I was almost desperate to get some kind of diagnosis for Paul and some help for his delays in learning, and I was especially vulnerable now to any implied criticism.

I thought of all this, as we watched Paul together, this teacher and I. And then she asked: "How many hours do you spend in the library every day?"

I was startled—then stunned and angry. When Paul was enrolled in the school at the beginning of the fall, I had offered some information about all of us. We were an academic family, living for a year in London. I taught women's studies and my husband taught English at the same college. I was writing a book (trying to), and spent three or four hours in the London Library every day reading Victorian novels written by women: Harriet Martineau, Margaret Oliphant, Lady Blessington.

This teacher's questions had now gone beyond friendly interest; they seemed intrusive and unwarranted. They also seemed to be of a piece with other questions and comments made by the headmistress. Everyone in the school appeared to be preoccupied with the fact that I was leaving my child in a nursery school as I went off to a library to research a book, and with the fact that the child's father or a babysitter sometimes dropped him off at the school or picked him up after his three hours there. Did they think that because I was an English teacher, I was putting undue pressure on my child to speak, or that because I spent several hours a day in the library, I was neglecting my child?

Could I have been imagining all this? Imagining also the pursed lip, the head turned aside, the glance away from me to Paul, then uneasily back to me again? But I knew they never asked these same questions of Paul's father.

It was true, on the other hand, that Paul had several odd behaviors at this time. He was fascinated with a couple of little balls colored blue and green, part of a construction set, which he recognized as similar to two large marbles he had lost a few months before. His high-pitched delight at rediscovering "boo bah, bee bah" (blue ball, green ball) did seem to be out of all proportion to any possible importance they might have to any normal child.

Paul's other nursery school fascination was with the toilets. As soon as he arrived in school each day, he ran off to the bathrooms and started flushing each of the little toilets. He then hung his head almost down into the bowl as he listened to the sounds of the rushing water, perhaps checking for minute differences in pitch and motion. This, needless to say, was considered extremely odd behavior by all the teachers at the school.

His quirks made me anxious and confused. I wanted to defend him, to let these teachers know how wonderful he really was. At the same time I couldn't deny his developmental delays or pretend that he was learning in the same way other children did. I had a whole set of contradictory feelings about myself as well. I wanted to be reassured that I was doing a great job, but at the same time I wanted my doubts and fears for him to be acknowledged. I wanted it both ways.

But more than anything else, of course, I wanted to be recognized as a *good mother*. And as a good mother, I wanted to be acknowledged as smart and well informed about children, as well as self-aware, kind, generous, energetic, resourceful, relaxed, and funny! I wanted desperately to believe that all my years in graduate school and in the classroom teaching had prepared me to be a better mother, not a crippled one. I did not want to think that the sensitivity and awareness developed through literature was in any way different from that used directly with people. In my great plans for myself it was all supposed to be of one piece: raising children, writing books, and teaching students. I wanted my life to be full of all these riches, and I had always been deeply resentful of any attempts to make women choose between children and work.

So now, in this London nursery school, I felt that my deepest self was being attacked. I thought of the time when the headmistress suggested I talk to the mother of a little boy who was deaf. "She's such a *sensible* Mum," she had pointed out to me. "She has really devoted herself to that child." This mother had spent the first three months at the nursery school with her child. She came every morning with him and stayed the whole time, I was told, "until he was completely used to the school."

I resisted the headmistress and the other teachers in the school, but still the niggling doubts were there, the tiny pinpricks of poisonous anxiety. And in the meantime, Paul was getting worse, much worse, in his school behavior, becoming more and more wild. I tried sitting with him in the circle of the children on the floor as they sang songs or played clapping games. He twisted sharply away from them now, something he had not done before. If another child approached, he simply ran away. More and more he was locked into his obsessions: flushing toilets, arranging little colored balls, flicking light switches, searching for a screwdriver to take things apart.

Six months before this, we had gone to Paul's pediatrician in Minneapolis and asked that he be tested because of his speech delay. The doctor had been alarmed. Here was a beautiful, healthy child who *seemed* so normal in every way—except for a puzzling lack of speech and a certain withdrawal from human contact.

The doctor suggested that I read *Dibs in Search of Self*,[1] the story of a bright but speechless child who had been rejected by his surgeon mother, and who had withdrawn into his own little world until a loving teacher rescued him. I had already read the book and was stunned by the doctor's suggestion that there was a message for me in those pages. The book had suggested that mothers (otherwise well-meaning, intelligent, kind women) had the power to deprive their children of a sense of self, to destroy them at their very core, to kill their "souls," as people a generation or two ago might have put it. It attributed an awesome power to the mother, and it was a power to harm, but not to heal. It seemed that professional help was called for in restoring children to a healthy sense of self.

My reading of *Dibs* had led me to other books about disturbed children, and I had discovered that the worst mother in twentieth-century psychological literature is quite possibly the mother of the autistic or schizophrenic child. These two conditions, now widely accepted as neurological (autism) or biochemical (schizophrenia) in origin, were once conflated, and both were thought to be psychogenic, caused by bad mothers. Possibly the most extreme case made against such mothers, but also one of the most widely read and highly influential, was Bruno Bettelheim's *The Empty Fortress: Infantile Autism and the Birth of the Self,*[2] where the author argued that autism was caused by the cruelly rejecting mother. This mother, in fact, was similar—in her complete disregard for the welfare and even the humanity of her child—to the SS guards of concentration camps. Here is a passage from the beginning of the book:

> In the German concentration camps I witnessed with utter disbelief the nonreacting of certain prisoners to this most cruel experience. I did not know and would not have believed that I would observe similar behavior in the most benign of therapeutic environments [Bettelheim's Orthogenic School in Chicago], because of what children had experienced in the past [at home with their mothers].[3]

Bettelheim, who had himself suffered imprisonment in Dachau and Buchenwald, goes on to draw a sustained analogy between the behaviors of the kind of prisoner who became mentally ill under those conditions and the well-known behaviors of the autistic child.[4] He notes that the prisoners often expressed a sense of rage at any change in their immediate environment, just as autistic children rigidly insist on sameness. Mutism in the prisoner and in the autistic child are both traced to pervasive feelings of helplessness and hopelessness, in the child's case to the mother's withdrawal of the breast. The prisoner's "nearly continuous daydreaming was a close parallel to the self-stimulation of autistic children.

... The purpose, in each case, was to blot out recognition of an immediate threatening reality."[5] Both often show a strange insensitivity to pain. Both carry their bodies in a similar way and often have a shuffling gait. They might both be emotionally depleted to the point of "catatonia," "melancholic depression," complete "loss of memory," or "disregard of reality."[6]

Gaze avoidance is similar in both the autistic child and the prisoner. Bettelheim argues that "the averted gaze of autistic children, their looking vaguely in the distance without seeming to see, and their concentration on things close at hand when there is nothing to see but their own twiddling fingers ... is essentially the same phenomenon as the prisoner's averted gaze.... Both behaviors result from the conviction that it is not safe to let others see one observing."[7]

Finally, even the mental skills which autistic children often show are discredited, labeled as essentially disturbed behavior. "If another parallel were needed, the often remarked-upon autistic repetition of 'empty' rote learning, lists of names or dates, and the like seems to include some of the same reasons why prisoners favored similar activities: to prove to themselves that they had not lost their minds ... even though they could not use (them) to better their fate."[8]

Bettelheim concludes this introductory passage to *The Empty Fortress* by disavowing any further analogy between the SS guards and mothers of autistic children, but he does so in a very surprising way:

> Here I wish to stress again the essential difference between the plight of these prisoners and the conditions that lead to autism and schizophrenia in children: namely that the children never had a chance to develop much of a personality. Thus, to develop childhood schizophrenia it is enough that the infant be convinced that his life is run by insensitive, irrational powers that have absolute control of his life and death.[9]

In other words, the only real difference between the SS guard and the mother of the autistic child is that the mother gets to the child much earlier in life. She is in the unique position of being able to damage him (I say "him" because autism is much more common in boys than in girls) before he has even had a chance to develop a personality. Some prisoners, as Bettelheim well knew, were able to resist the destructive forces on their personalities and to carry on later in life, after liberation, with a traumatized, but essentially intact, mind and spirit. The autistic child never will have such a chance.

One of the most interesting things about Bettelheim's argument is that the autistic child's behavior is taken as proof of etiology; in other words, the fact that autistic children show some of the same behaviors as traumatized concentration camp prisoners suggests that they have been hurt by comparable circumstances in their own lives. And these circumstances, according to his argument, have to have been created by their parents, specifically by their mothers.

Now, three decades after Bettelheim's book was published, this analogy between autistic children and the inmates of concentration camps, between SS guards and the mothers of autistic children, seems preposterous. But we must remember also that Bettelheim's is only the most extreme statement of a view still widely held. Many other writers were convinced that autism was psychogenic,[10] and introductory textbooks used in college psychology classes still sometimes repeat this view. Leo Kanner, who first used the term autistic to describe these children, also claimed that they were treated to "coldness, obsessiveness, and a mechanical type of attention" by their mothers. He argues that the children's "withdrawal seems to be an act of turning away from such a situation."[11] These women he called "refrigerator mothers," a term that stuck and came to be repeated for many years after he first used it.

But perhaps more important than these egregious examples of mother-blaming in the professional literature is the "trickle-down" effect of such views on both the general populace and, even more, on public school teachers, social workers, family doctors and pediatricians, school psychologists, and the like—the people who are most likely to have contact with autistic children and their parents. It seemed pretty obvious to me that Paul's teachers in London, as well as his doctor in the United States, had been trained to view this kind of disability as psychogenic in nature, and specifically as caused by some flaw in the mother.

Such notions have been very resistant to change, in spite of the fact that autism is now widely understood as a neurologically based developmental disorder that affects not just the rate at which skills are learned but also the way in which they are learned. Overwhelming evidence now exists for sensory dysfunction in autism, and it is interesting to see how an alternative explanation to Bettelheim's is now emerging for each of the behaviors he interpreted as caused by trauma similar to that experienced in the concentration camps.[12] Now we know that autistic children have disturbances in one or all of the senses: sight (accounting for the famous gaze avoidance, the use of peripheral vision, and such strange fixations as the "twiddling" fingers Bettelheim mentions); hearing (hypersensitivity, especially to loud or abrasive noises, which accounts for much of their withdrawal); taste and smell (possibly explaining the eating oddities and the "anorexia" that Bettelheim believed to be a self-imposed starvation to escape a threatening world); touch (the "tactile defensiveness" which a baby may show when picked up and cuddled by a parent and which many psychologists cited as the child's learned response to a mother's ambivalence); and proprioception or the sense of the body in space (toe walking or shuffling gait).

Difficulty in coordinating shifts of attention (for example from a person's voice to his or her face and eyes) and in integrating information from several senses at once are now recognized as neurologically based, rather than a defense against a rejecting mother. This probably accounts for the autistic person's problems with complex and rapid social interactions, as well as for his narrowly focused learning—the rote learning that Bettelheim named as neurotic. Finally, and maybe most importantly, a problem with regulation of the nervous system and the enormous stress which autistic people typically feel causes their withdrawal, tantrums, or self-stimulation, all ways of reacting to or blocking out an overload of sense impressions.

Why were professionals so ready to blame mothers for a childhood disorder such as autism? I think there are several reasons, and I have elsewhere offered possible answers to this question.[13] For one thing, because these children often "look" so normal and frequently have very good health, many experts on autism have resisted looking for an organic or medical explanation. And of course there has been a general tendency of twentieth-century environmentalists, as well as Freudians, to trace aberrant behavior in children back to parents.

There is another possible reason for this readiness to blame mothers for a child's autism, however, and that is the frustration that many well-intentioned professionals feel when confronted by these children, who so often seem not to get better even with heroic efforts at treatment. Eric Schopler, himself one of the leading professionals in the field of autism, has written persuasively of the temptation to scapegoat parents.[14] Among the reasons given are the professionals' own "confusion and lack of knowledge" about the causes and optimum treatment of autism, their fear and anxiety, and the projection onto the child of their own guilt at not being able adequately to treat him:

The clinician confronted with an autistic child has the additional burden of coping with the child's difficult interpersonal behavior. The child may be negativistic and irritable. . . . This interpersonal avoidance and disorganization is often communicated to the clinician. He feels . . . insignificant to the child. The resulting sense of helplessness in the adult is not easily expressed against the child, and considerable pressure develops to explain the child's impossible behavior in terms of his parents.[15]

Schopler also suggests that "feelings of inferiority may lead to scapegoating . . . and when the progress in treatment is uneven, the clinician's role as an authoritative expert is seriously threatened."[16] "Conformity" may be another reason for blaming parents. "When the predominant orientation of a clinic is the psychoanalytic framework, then the emphasis on parental pathology for explaining children's difficulties is a shared belief among the staff."[17] And finally, when there are so many possible causes of the child's behavior to consider (perceptual and sensory dysfunction, dietary and metabolic problems, neurological involvement, genetic flaws, as well as the possibility of traumatic experiences), simplification is a real temptation, since it "provides for economy and energy in directing aggression."[18]

In addition, Schopler identifies ways in which parents can play into the hands of scapegoating professionals. I would suggest that what he says about "parents" applies particularly to mothers. Mothers are already "embarrassed by their child's peculiarities," and as targets of blame they have "little possibility for retaliation because the scapegoater is stronger . . . in terms of prestige." The mother is already so used to being attacked that her resulting demoralization makes it harder for her to fight back. And finally, "the victim is accessible." "In their desperate search for help," and after exhausting all other possible avenues of help, parents may seek out a diagnosis from the very professionals who are likely to offer psychogenic explanations of their child's disorder.[19]

So what does all of this add up to? If the subtle hints dropped in the London nursery school constituted the only time I encountered blame as a mother, or if the frustration of an otherwise kindly pediatrician who suggested I read a book about a cured child was the only time someone suggested my child was withdrawing because I had rejected him—then probably not much. But this kind of blame, which was usually indirect and often appeared as much in what was not said as in what was said, happened over and over as Paul was growing up. It's true I was especially sensitive, all the more so because I was relatively well informed, relatively well-read in the literature. But one more event, which happened when Paul was in middle school, deserves mention. It shows again how widespread this belief in the psychogenesis of autism was, and it happened not so many years ago.

Paul was not happy in his neighborhood middle school, and a couple of concerned teachers, as well as a friend who was an activist on behalf of children, suggested that we visit schools in Minneapolis, some forty miles away from our home. One of these schools looked particularly promising. It had been set up to address the problems of children with various learning disabilities. It boasted very small classes, dedicated teachers, and a lot of attention paid to the individual learning styles of children. The teachers obviously worked very hard and seemed to have been very successful in building self-esteem among these children, who quickly learned to take a lot of responsibility for their own education.

For all these reasons, this school seemed perfect for Paul. Even though he had the diagnosis of autism, his learning difficulties as well as his remarkable strengths (as shown on test scores and in other ways) seemed to qualify him as an obvious fit for their program. After touring the school and becoming more and more convinced it was the right place for Paul, we sat down for the interview with the principal. I felt very hopeful that at last Paul could get a really superior education and one suited to his particular learning style.

The principal, however, listened to us for about forty-five seconds. As soon as he heard that Paul was diagnosed with "high functioning autism," he stopped us.

"I can't take him," he said.

We were stunned and wanted to know why not.

"He's autistic," he continued. "And I am one of those people who really does believe that autism is caused in the home. It's psychological in origin. That means we simply can't do anything for him here."

And with that, he closed the interview.

NOTES

1. Virginia Axline, *Dibs in Search of Self* (New York: Ballantine, 1964).

2. Bruno Bettelheim, *The Empty Fortress: Infantile Autism and the Birth of the Self* (New York: Free Press, 1967).

3. Bettelheim, 57.

4. Bettelheim, 63–85.

5. Bettelheim, 67.

6. Bettelheim, 64.

7. Bettelheim, 67.

8. Bettelheim, 67–68.

9. Bettelheim, 68.

10. See review by J. N. Hintgen and C. Q. Bryson, "Recent Developments in the Study of Early Childhood Psychoses: Infantile Autism, Childhood Schizophrenia, and Related Disorders" *Schizophrenia Bulletin* 5 (1972): 8–54.

11. Leo Kanner, "Problems of Nosology and Psychodynamics in Early Infantile Autism," *American Journal of Orthopsychiatry* 19 (1949): 416–26.

12. See, for example, Christopher Gillberg and Mary Coleman, *The Biology of Autistic Syndromes,* 2d ed. (New York: Cambridge University Press, 1992).

13. Jane Taylor McDonnell, *News from the Border: A Mother's Memoir of Her Autistic Son* (New York: Houghton Mifflin, 1993); and Jane Taylor McDonnell, "Mothering the Autistic Child," in *Narrating Mothers: Theorizing Maternal Subjectivities,* ed. Brenda Daly and Maureen Reddy (Nashville: University of Tennessee Press, 1991).

14. Eric Schopler, "Parents of Psychotic Children as Scapegoats," in *Classic Readings in Autism,* ed. Anne M. Donnellan (New York: Teacher's College Press, 1985), 236–41.

15. Schopler, 238.

16. Schopler, 238–39.

17. Schopler, 239.

18. Schopler, 239.

19. Schopler, 240

Chapter 12

"Immoral Conduct"

White Women, Racial Transgressions, and Custody Disputes

Renee Romano

In August 1950, Bernice Beckman, a white New York woman, divorced her white husband Eugene and was granted full custody of their five-year-old son, Eric. A little over a year later, she remarried and her ex-husband immediately kidnapped Eric and secured an ex parte order from a New York judge granting him full custody of the child. Why was Eugene Beckman so upset about his ex-wife's second marriage? Because Bernice Beckman's new husband was black. Beckman sued for custody on the grounds that his ex-wife had engaged in "immoral conduct," and the sympathetic judge not only took Eric away but in order to "protect" the child from his mother, denied Bernice all visitation privileges and issued a restraining order preventing her from ever seeing her son again. Eight years later, Bernice Beckman Riggins was still fighting to regain the right to see her son, if not to be his custodial parent.[1]

The judgment against Bernice Beckman, while severe, was not unique. In the forty years after World War II, white women who married black men were repeatedly labeled as "unfit" mothers for their white children and were sometimes punished by the courts by having custody of these children revoked. Between 1945 and 1985, approximately twenty-five child custody disputes arose on the state appeals court level after local trial courts had denied white women who had married black men custody of their white children from previous marriages. In making these custody dispositions, courts pondered whether white children should be removed from their mother's care because she had married a black man, or whether a mother's special relationship with her children should override the desire to keep white children in an all-white environment. In short, courts weighed a woman's racial transgressions against their traditional preference for maternal custody.[2]

These cases demonstrate, first, that local trial courts throughout this forty-year period proved willing to remove white children from the custody of their interracially married white mothers. Although state appeals courts sometimes overruled these decisions, it was not uncommon for a woman who married a black man to lose custody of her white children, particularly in the period from 1945 to 1965. Second, the cases illustrate the construction of both racial and gender identities. Courts and the white relatives who sued for a change in custody feared that children forced to live in interracial homes would be stigmatized; white mothers were expected to protect and maintain their white children's racial identity. Courts in many instances linked a woman's racial transgression to a gender transgression. Thus, women were denied custody not just because they had married black men but because, by marrying black men, they had demonstrated that they were not good mothers. By marrying interracially, these white women "selfishly" placed their own personal gratification over concern for their children's future welfare as white people in America. A woman's willingness to transgress America's racial boundary, moreover, was often viewed by her relatives and by the courts as a moral fault which called her fitness as mother into question. Many women suffered at least the threat of losing their children after they married interracially. Many, like Bernice Beckman, found the courts willing to do whatever necessary to "protect" white children from their "immoral," racially transgressive mothers.

Finally, the regional variations in these decisions demonstrate the use of the custody issue to punish white women who intermarried. In 1945, thirty states had laws criminalizing interracial marriage, and thus the custody cases from the early period nearly all took place in a limited number of northern and midwestern states.[3] In 1967, when the Supreme Court finally declared all antimiscegenation laws to be unconstitutional in *Loving v. Virginia,* seventeen states (almost all of them in the South) still forbade interracial marriage. Many of the custody cases after 1967 occurred in the southern states which had outlawed interracial marriage before *Loving.* While lower courts in both the North and the South throughout this period proved reluctant to allow white children to grow up in interracial homes with black stepfathers, after 1967 northern appeals courts were far less likely to uphold these rulings than southern appeals courts were. Furthermore, courts in both the North and the South would deny custody to women they considered immoral, but courts in states that had criminalized interracial marriage prior to 1967 were likely to define immorality very broadly. Thus, even though interracial marriage had been decriminalized, southern courts still managed to punish white women who dared to cross the color line, by taking away their white children.[4]

Lower Courts and the Removal of White Children

Throughout the period from 1945 to 1985, lower courts proved sympathetic to relatives who were seeking to have a child removed from the care of an interracially married white mother. Even when courts claimed that their decisions were based on "nonracial issues," they often ignored evidence that white ex-husbands and grandparents were motivated to seek custody primarily because of a woman's relationship with a black man. Most of these cases, for example, were filed immediately after the woman remarried, and even though plaintiffs might cite a variety of reasons to justify a change in custody, their racial concerns were often clearly expressed.

By challenging a woman's right to care for her children, relatives could try to deter a woman from marrying a black man, could punish the mother for her racial transgression, and could reassert their authority over her. The 1952 case of *Portnoy v. Strasser* clearly illustrates this point.[5] On February 2, 1951, a New York county court ordered that the custody of five-year-old Robin Strasser be transferred from her mother to her maternal grandmother. Ann Strasser divorced her white husband in 1945, when their daughter was only a year old. In May 1949, she married a black man. Ann's mother, Mollie Portnoy, sued for custody on the grounds that Ann was a communist who was unconcerned with the child's religious upbringing and that her second husband was of a different race and religion from herself. The referee of the court awarded custody to the grandmother on nonracial grounds.[6] The Appellate Division upheld the decision.

In their appeal to the Supreme Court of New York, Strasser's lawyers emphasized that Portnoy's reasons for seeking custody were all pretenses; the only reason she wanted custody was because Ann's husband was black. Portnoy did not institute custody proceedings until her efforts to break up the marriage had failed, and she threatened her daughter, telling her that, "I want you to leave him . . . or I shall take your children away from you." The lower court, Portnoy's lawyers argued, had practiced a "subtle and serious social prejudice" in awarding the child to the grandmother; they were biased against the child living in a racially mixed neighborhood and receiving paternal care from a black stepfather. Portnoy was obviously using the custody issue as a way to punish her daughter for her interracial marriage. In an amicus curiae brief in the case, the National Lawyers Guild concurred that Portnoy's attempt to take the child away was calculated to serve both "the purpose of chastisement" and "as a weapon to compel her daughter to leave the husband she loves." In this case, the grandmother's efforts to control her daughter were unsuccessful. The Court of Appeals of New York ultimately reversed the custody ruling and gave the child back to her mother.[7]

Other courts also revoked a woman's custody for what were purportedly nonracial issues. A Connecticut court in 1965 took away a white woman's child after her marriage to a black man on the grounds that she had made no provision for the boy's religious education: she had been excommunicated from the Catholic church after remarrying, and since her relationship with a black man had alienated her parents, the boy would no longer see his grandparents.[8] Other courts revoked custody after a subsequent interracial marriage for vague "social and economic reasons," because a mother was "immature," or on even more questionable grounds. In a 1975 Pennsylvania case, a local court ruled that while both parents seemed fit, custody of the children should be changed to the father because he lived in a rural area rather than a suburban one, as the mother did. In another Pennsylvania case, a judge transferred custody of two little girls from their mother to their white father because he wanted to give the mother and her black fiancée time to get acquainted with each other without being "distracted by other obligations."[9]

These legal arguments seem even weaker when compared to those employed in custody cases where race was not a factor. While a court might claim that children were removed from their interracially married mother's care because she no longer provided them with a proper religious upbringing, interreligious marriages did not seem to generate similar custody battles on the state appeals court level. In a 1944 case, for example, the ex-husband of a Christian woman remarried to a Jewish man argued that his ex-wife's marriage to a Jew rendered her "unfit or unsuitable" for the care and custody of their child. The Alabama Supreme

Court, however, ruled that there was no grounds for removing the daughter from her mother. Marriages which were not "forbidden by statute, or violative of social morality" could not in and of themselves render a parent unfit for custody, the Alabama Court declared. "In our opinion," they ruled, "no greater calamity can befall an infant daughter than to deprive her of a mother's care, vigilance and understanding."[10]

The willingness of local courts to remove young children from their mother's care is particularly striking given that interracial marriages were not forbidden by statute in the states where these cases were heard, and that, as the Alabama ruling suggested, legal precedent held that a child should only be removed from its mother's care under exceptional circumstances.[11] Most courts in the 1940s, 50s, 60s, and 70s awarded custody of minor children to their mother after a divorce unless there was extensive evidence that the mother was an unfit parent. The standard rule in custody cases, to do what was in the "best interests of the child," was almost always taken to mean that children of "tender years" should be awarded to their mothers. As a Pennsylvania court explained, this philosophy was "supported by the wisdom of the ages": "It has long been the rule that in the absence of compelling reasons to the contrary, a mother has the right to custody of her children over any other persons, particularly so where the children are of tender years."[12]

The presumption in favor of the mother, however, did not automatically apply when a white mother chose a black man as her second husband. In these cases, concerns about race and gender clearly came into conflict. And despite the common belief that mothers should raise their own children, a subsequent interracial marriage often generated successful suits to change custody dispositions, particularly in the lower courts. Thus lower courts, even when they claimed to be acting in the child's "best interest," cooperated with plaintiffs' attempts to punish white women for their racial transgressions.

Issues of Racial and Gender Identity

Punishment, however, was not the only motivation for taking away the white children of interracially married white women. These cases also reveal the ways in which both the white public and the courts constructed and understood race. During these custody battles, litigants frequently invoked the desire to "protect" white children from the "stigma" of growing up in an interracial home. In doing so, they pointed to the importance, and ultimately, though inadvertently, to the fluidity of "whiteness."[13]

The experience of white women who intermarried in the postwar era demonstrates the fluidity of white racial identity. White women in the 1940s, 50s, and 60s who associated with blacks were often forced down to the status of blacks. Whites who married blacks were "symbolically unwhitened" in the larger white community.[14] First, white women who married blacks usually moved into the black world. As a black photographer married to a white woman told *Ebony* magazine, "When a colored man marries a white woman, she comes to him. He doesn't go to her."[15] Nearly all studies done of interracial marriage before the 1970s found that the white wives in these marriages assumed the status of their black husbands. "In every instance of intermarriage with the Negro," Sister Annella Lynn concluded in her 1953 study, "the conjugal pair have the social status of the Negro." White spouses in interracial marriages, especially white women, "became Negroes socially."[16] According to a 1955 *Ebony* exposé on where mixed couples lived, white women who married blacks frequently found themselves "for the first time denied the right to live in a white neighborhood." Interracial couples, like blacks, were often forced to pay higher prices for inferior living quarters. And having the "wrong address" could affect other aspects of living as well. Michelle Ross, an Atlantic City woman who married a black man in the early 1950s, lost several jobs once her employers realized her address was in the black section of town. In order to get a job at a black business, she pretended to be black. Tellingly, when four American women tried to dissuade Hazel Byrne Simpkins, an Englishwoman, from coming to the States to marry her black fiancé, their final argument was, "But my dear, you'll have to live with them all your life!"[17]

Since becoming romantically involved with a black man could compromise a white woman's racial identity, families often worried that interracial marriage would ruin their daughters' lives. Hettie Cohen, a white Jewish woman who married the black beat poet Leroi Jones, remembered her mother telling her that she would "suffer and pay every minute of [her] life" for her choice of spouse.[18] These parental objections reflected the serious negative consequences of losing the privileges of whiteness. Parents feared, moreover, that this loss of status would be permanent.[19]

If an interracial marriage could ruin a white woman's life, relatives were particularly concerned that her white children would be permanently harmed by being raised in an interracial home. White children with black stepfathers might face social stigmatization, they might be shunned at school, and worst of all, they might lose their own status as white from their close association with blacks. In many of these cases, both the relatives who sued for custody and the courts who made the custody dispositions expressed concern that living with a black parent would have a negative effect on a white child's racial identity.

In the 1962 battle between Sandra Potter Baugh and her ex-husband for custody of their daughter, the father stated his concerns clearly. If his daughter were brought up in an interracial home, she "will not grow up and mature as a normal white child should but rather will be rejected, shunned and avoided by children of both races and as a result her entire life could, and unavoidably would, be adversely affected." No white child who was forced to grow up in an interracial home could be "normal," the father claimed. While the judge in the case admitted that there was no evidence that a happy interracial home would hurt a white child, he ruled for the father. "None of us can anticipate what problems, if any, would develop as the child became older, particularly during puberty, when she, in school and other activities, becomes aware of the opposite sex." By focusing on the daughter's sexual development, the judge's reasoning suggested that an anomaly in the racial order might repeat itself in the next generation; Sandra Baugh's white child would be more likely to marry interracially if she were brought up in an interracial home.[20]

Other courts also cited racial reasons for changing custody. In 1971, the Illinois Circuit Court refused to give a white mother who had married a black man custody of her three children because it feared the children would be traumatized if they had to move to a strange place and live in a racially mixed family.[21] Similarly, a district court in New Mexico advocated a change in custody on the grounds that the children involved would be "better reared with members of their own race."[22]

White children forced to live in interracial homes, courts and relatives feared, might lose their position in the community as white. Thus the U.S. Court for the District of Columbia denied a black stepfather's petition to adopt the illegitimate white son of his wife, even though the courts normally encouraged the adoption of children born out of wedlock. In this case, however, the fact that the boy and his mother were white and his stepfather black, created a "difficult social problem," the court ruled. "The boy when he grows up might lose the social status of a white man by reason of the fact that by record his father will be a negro if this adoption is approved. . . . I feel the court should not fashion the child's future in this manner."[23] In another case, a white father won custody of his two young daughters after his ex-wife moved in with her black boyfriend. The father told the court that while he was away from home, "My children were very seldom around white people at all. The only time I even see them they was all around black people and they have no confirmation of what white is, really, I don't think."[24] In other words, white children raised in interracial homes would not understand the meanings of whiteness and the privileges accorded to whites. In the racial landscape of American society, not understanding what it meant to be white, or being associated with blacks, was viewed as potentially stifling and harmful to a child's development.

If, as many argued, being raised in an interracial home could be permanently damaging to a white child, then mothers who decided to subject their children to the potential harm of living among blacks could only be described as selfish and as more interested in their own personal and sexual gratification than in the well-being of their children. Both relatives and courts in the postwar period suggested that "good" white mothers would not force their children to live among blacks. Thus women who sought to keep their white children after they intermarried were stereotypical "bad" mothers in that they were perceived as unwilling to sacrifice their own desires in order to protect their children.

By "forcing" their children to live with their black husbands, these mothers essentially proved that they did not have the best interests of their children at heart. When, in 1949, Poppy Cannon, an upper-class food editor, married Walter White, the black head of the NAACP, her ex-husband asked for full custody of their daughter. Charles Claudius Philippe had originally agreed that their daughter, Claudia, should live with her mother. When Cannon remarried, however, Philippe objected on the grounds that there had never been "the slightest hint that you would marry a negro" and that Claudia would be forced to "live in a household with a negro step-father." Philippe asked Cannon to put aside "any personal feelings or selfish considerations" and to give up Claudia "before irreparable damage is done her." He was certain that their daughter would be the target of insults and nasty gossip once other children found out that her mother had married a black man, and he could not believe that Cannon "would thrust this terrible onus upon her."[25] An innocent white child, Philippe argued, should not be made to suffer for the sins of her mother.

Sometimes a court even ruled that while race should not be considered a factor in custody cases, a mother's decision to subject her children to an interracial relationship was evidence that she was not concerned about their welfare and should therefore forfeit custody. In 1980, the Supreme Court in Iowa simultaneously declared that they could not consider the fact that a white mother's boyfriend was black in making their custody decision while maintaining that "the subjecting [of] the children to a bi-racial relationship and allowing such a relationship to exist in the pres-ence of the children is not in their best interest and is going to make their lives in the future more difficult." Thus, the Supreme Court of Iowa affirmed a decision changing custody from Sandra Ann Kramer to her ex-husband, despite the fact that he had devoted more attention to gambling, bowling, golf, and poker than to his children during their marriage, that he had gambled away the three thousand dollars set aside for the downpayment on the family's new home, and that he continued to have a gambling problem. The district court, and later the Iowa Supreme Court, decided that Sandra was emotionally unstable, that she had behaved immorally in the presence of her children, and that she seemed to want a more "carefree life-style" than was consistent with the proper care of children. All of these terms, of course, were a coded means of condemning Sandra's choice to have an interracial sexual relationship.[26]

Regional Variations

The connections between transgressing racial mores and being considered a "bad" mother are even clearer in southern court decisions after 1967. In the 1967 decision of *Loving v. Virginia,* the United States Supreme Court decriminalized interracial marriage. Couples could no longer be punished for marrying across the color line. The *Loving* case reflected the larger changes in the Supreme Court's rulings on race. Beginning with the 1954 school desegregation decision *Brown v. Board of Education,* the Supreme Court began to articulate the doctrine of "strict scrutiny" of any racial classifications. In a series of cases which dismantled legal segregation in the South, the Supreme Court ruled that any law which made a classifica-tion based on race was subject to the most stringent judicial scrutiny. The *Loving* decision applied this rule to the arena of marriage, finding that state antimiscegenation laws violated the Fourteenth Amendment and were therefore unconstitutional.[27]

The *Loving* decision created a new legal context for these custody cases. After 1967, most state appeals courts recognized that the rule of strict scrutiny of racial classifications made it more difficult to deny a woman custody solely because of the race of her husband or lover. In the North, as a result, most appeals courts overturned local custody decisions that seemed to punish a white mother for intermarrying. In states where interracial marriage had been illegal before 1967, however, appeals courts continued to find ways to deny white women custody of their children even after *Loving.*

Given the new legal context, courts had to cloak their custody decisions in "nonracial" terms. Southern courts effectively denied white women who crossed the racial line custody of their children in two ways. First, while northern courts often carefully scrutinized lower court decisions for racial bias, southern courts often refused to question a local court's decision. Second, southern courts often focused on a woman's alleged immorality rather than her racial transgression. In other words, southern courts drew on the established belief that white women who intermarried were "bad" mothers to deny these women custody of their children without focusing on the racial issues.

Most appeals courts in the North after *Loving* agreed that race could not be the determinative or, in some states, even an evaluative issue in child custody disputes. Northern courts even proved willing to challenge what seemed to be "nonracial" decisions that removed white children from their interracially married white mothers.[28] Some also explicitly recognized that taking a woman's children away from her because of a subsequent interracial marriage would undermine the *Loving* decision by infringing upon the right of white women to marry an individual of another race.[29] As a Pennsylvania judge argued in a 1972 case, a judicial policy of removing the white children of interracially married white women would serve to deter women from marrying outside their race.[30] Northern appeals courts like these thus proved willing to overturn lower court custody placements when it seemed that the lower court had put too much emphasis on race.[31]

In states where interracial marriage had been illegal prior to *Loving,* however, the situation was often more complex. Southern courts, like northern ones, had to operate within a legal context that made it more difficult for courts to openly base their decisions on racial grounds. In child custody cases, southern courts tried to walk a fine line: they aimed to protect the racial status of white children and punish women who transgressed the color line, while denying that their custody decisions were racially motivated. Southern courts developed two methods for denying white women custody of their children. First, by deferring to local trial courts' expertise, southern appeals courts tacitly upheld rulings based on race. Second, southern courts often justified their rulings by claiming that the white women who intermarried were immoral, and that they placed their own gratification ahead of concerns for their children; in short, that they were "bad" mothers.

Southern appeals courts were far less concerned than their northern counterparts about examining trial court decisions for racial bias. *Ethridge v. Ethridge,* a 1978 Alabama case, illustrates this deference to the trial court. Carolyn Sue Ethridge gained custody of her three children after she and Emmitt Ethridge were divorced in 1972. Emmitt failed to pay child support and was convicted of assaulting his ex-wife with a gun. Furthermore, Carolyn Sue lost her job because her ex-husband harassed her at work and she was forced to leave the state to find employment. In 1974, she took her children to Ohio, and in 1976, she married a black dentist. When her ex-husband took her to court, he was awarded full custody of the children. Carolyn Ethridge charged that the court only transferred custody because of her interracial marriage, but the appeals court found no "overt evidence" that the charge was true. While the ex-husband had exhibited racial bias during the trial, the trial court had treated the black husband "courteously." The appeals court felt that the question of whether the trial court would have denied the mother custody if she had married a white dentist rather than a black one could only be answered through "surmise and speculation": "For this court to speculate affirmatively would be contrary to our duty of review and dishonor the trial court without specific proof. . . . This court is not at liberty to set aside the judgment of the trial court merely because we might have decided differently had we been sitting as the trial judge."[32] The appeals court in Alabama thus refused to question the trial court's decision for fear of "dishonoring" the trial court judge.[33]

Southern appeals courts also decided these cases on "nonracial" grounds by questioning the morality and respectability of the white mother. In both the North and South, courts were willing to deny custody to women they considered "immoral." But southern appeals courts defined immorality very broadly, often characterizing having sex with a black man as a moral lapse that in itself called a woman's fitness as a mother into question, as the 1978 Louisiana case *Schexnayder v. Schex-*

nayder suggests. Sheila Schexnayder had an affair with a black man that lasted for five months. When her ex-husband sought custody of the couple's two young children, the lower courts in Louisiana reluctantly awarded custody to Sheila because of a State Supreme Court precedent that a brief affair was not due cause to deny a mother custody. Although the court found that "the mother's conduct here was particularly scandalous and offensive to the sensibilities of the local community in that her lover was of another race," they felt that they had to uphold the maternal preference rule since Louisiana's antimiscegenation laws had been ruled unconstitutional.[34] The Supreme Court of Louisiana, however, decided that Sheila should lose custody of her children, because in the words of one judge, her behavior during the affair had been "flagrant, even open and notorious." By having an affair with a black man, Schexnayder had shown a "lack of love and consideration for her children," as well as a disregard for generally accepted moral principles. The Supreme Court argued that Sheila's insensitivity to the pain her affair would inflict on her children was grounds for revoking her custody privileges.[35] Thus, she lost custody not because she had an affair with a black man but because her willingness to have an affair with a black man without thinking about how it would affect her children made her qualifications as a mother suspect.

In another Alabama case, *White v. Appleton* (1974), custody of the white child of a young white woman was awarded to her parents after she married a black man on the grounds that the mother was too "immature" to raise her child. Loretta Appleton White had dropped out of high school to get married, given birth at age seventeen, and then divorced her husband that same year. White moved back into the home of her mother and stepfather, who cared for her child while she worked. She held a steady job, however, and always made an effort to care for her son. In August 1973, White found a job in Houston and left her child in the care of her mother, sending for her son in November. But when her mother and stepfather found out that White planned to marry a black man and was living in an apartment with her black fiancée, they sued for permanent custody of the child. The trial court in Alabama, and later the appeals court, upheld the change in custody on the ground that Loretta had not demonstrated that she was responsible and mature enough to care for her child. The appeals court discounted the possibility that the ruling was based on racial considerations. As the appeals court judge ruled,

The conduct of Loretta in first cohabiting with a negro without marriage and subsequently marrying him probably entered into the consideration of the court. Such consideration does not require a conclusion that the decree of the court was founded upon a racial prejudice. To remove a three-year-old child from the only home it has known, place it in a home far removed with a mother who has spent little time with it and with a strange male and stepfather of a different race, could prove to be a traumatic experience indeed.[36]

White allegedly lost custody of her child because she was "immature," but the court based its determination of her maturity on the fact that she had lived with, and then married, a black man.

The actions of southern courts, particularly their desire to punish interracially married white women, calls into question the traditional historical view of southern attitudes about interracial sex. For the most part, historians have focused on the black-rapist myth, a myth which suggested that southerners viewed all interracial sex as coercive. Any act of interracial sex became a rape, even if the woman had supposedly consented.[37] As Martha Hodes has demonstrated, however, this racial ideology was never completely dominant or monolithic. Some white women, particularly those in the lower classes, were held responsible for their relationships with black men. The belief in black male bestiality did not absolve all white women of their sexual transgressions.[38] In these cases, furthermore, white women actually decided to *marry* black men, which further undermined the belief that their interracial relationships were coerced. By choosing to marry interracially, a white woman demonstrated her own immorality.

The ability of southern courts to punish white women who married black men by taking away their children finally drew the attention of the Supreme Court in 1984 in the case of *Palmore v. Sidoti*. In this Florida case, both the trial court and the Florida appeals court held that Anthony Sidoti should be awarded sole custody of his young white daughter. Anthony Sidoti and Linda Sidoti Palmore divorced in 1980, and Linda was awarded custody of the child. But when she began living with, and then married, a black man, her ex-husband sued for custody. While the court ruled that the father's openly stated prejudice against his ex-wife's interracial relationship was not sufficient cause to remove the child from her mother's custody, they drew on both moral and racial arguments to support their decision. The court found it significant that the mother saw fit "to bring a man into her home and carry on a sexual relationship with him without being married to him. Such action tended to place gratification of her own desires ahead of her concern for the child's future welfare." Even though she and Clarence Palmore eventually married, the court reasoned that their premarital sexual relationship was adequate grounds on which to deny her custody. Furthermore, the Florida court ruled that if the child were raised in an interracial home, she would inevitably face future prejudice and bias, and thus it was in the best interest of the child to remove her from this situation.[39]

This case, with its flagrant recourse to racial reasoning, eventually compelled the Supreme Court of the United States to regulate the custody decisions of state courts. In 1984 the Supreme Court overturned the *Palmore* decision, ruling that "the reality of private biases and the possible injury that they might inflict were not permissible considerations for removing an infant child from its natural mother."[40] In other words, judges could not consider the potential effects of racial prejudice in making their custody decisions. The Supreme Court's ruling in *Palmore v. Sidoti*, however, was quite narrow: the Court did not preclude the consideration of *actual* effects of racial prejudice in deciding custody. Furthermore, their decision was made easier because the Florida court had been "candid" and had made "no effort to place its holding on any ground other than race." If the Florida court had focused solely on Linda Palmore's qualifications as a mother and her supposed immorality in living with her black boyfriend rather than on what her child might suffer from being reared in an interracial household, the case would probably never have reached the Supreme Court. While the case thus limited the ability of state courts to make custody decisions openly based on race, it did not call into question the indirect devices southern courts had used to deny custody to mothers who had married black men.[41] Courts could still identify women who intermarried as bad mothers and rule against them on that basis.

The unique interaction of race and gender in these cases becomes even clearer when compared with custody disputes involving children of black-white couples. While associating with blacks could call a white woman's fitness as a mother of white children into question, courts have consistently upheld the right of white mothers to raise their own biracial children. Presumably, if it was considered "dangerous" for white children to be raised in interracial homes, then courts might have viewed it as equally damaging for children born of interracial couples to be raised exclusively by their white mothers following the dissolution of an interracial marriage. This reasoning, for example, was evident in the earliest case of this sort, a 1950 case in Washington state, in which the court decided that it was in the best interests of the children of James and Marylynn Ward to be awarded to their black father rather than their white mother. "They will have a much better opportunity to take their rightful place in society if they are brought up among their own people," the judge ruled, although he was conscious enough of gender norms that he decided the children should be raised in the home of their paternal grandmother rather than in their father's home.[42] Yet while black fathers since 1950 have repeatedly tried to win custody of their biracial children on the basis of the logic in *Ward*, no court since has upheld this reasoning. Six years later, in 1956, an Illinois man claimed that he should be awarded custody of his two biracial children because they had the "outstanding basic racial characteristics of the Negro race." The children would be healthier and better adjusted if allowed to remain "identified, reared and educated with" blacks, he asserted. The appeals court, however, awarded custody to the white mother, ruling that the trial court had placed too much consideration on race. Likewise, when a trial court in Nevada awarded custody of an interracial couple's two children to the black father because the children clearly showed "Negroid physical characteristics," the state supreme court overturned the ruling on the grounds that it denied the white mother equal protection of the laws under the Fourteenth Amendment. Thus the courts implied that, while white children needed to be protected from growing up among blacks, a biracial child would not be harmed by living with its white mother, even if she had subsequently married a white man and reentered the white community. In these cases, the traditional view that children should be raised by their mothers overrode racial considerations.[43]

Decisions allowing white mothers to retain custody of their biracial children might also have reflected the assumption that raising biracial children could in itself serve as punishment for a white woman who had dared to cross the color line. While a woman might be able to redeem herself from an interracial marriage by divorcing her black husband, the presence of a biracial child in her life could permanently mark her as associated with the black community. Thus, one woman who left her black husband after a short marriage in the 1940s expressed relief that their daughter had been born light-skinned. If she had been born with a dark skin, "[S]he would then have been regarded by everyone as a negro and would have to live under the handicaps that confront all Negroes.

Suppose I had left my husband with a dark-skinned child. What would have happened? Would my parents and friends have accepted her? Would they have accepted me? Frankly, I think not." Similarly, a poem written by a white supremacist in the 1960s described the birth of a biracial child as a permanent tragedy for a white woman. As the poem's protagonist laments, "[A]ll my prayers can never clear my baby's mongrel skin, nor make him white as driven snow, nor cleanse my soul of sin."[44]

The custody disputes that arose when white mothers married black men reveal the race and gender ideologies prevalent in post–World War II America. Courts in the postwar period held that growing up among blacks could harm a white child, and that the racial identity of children of interracially remarried white mothers had to be protected. Since subjection to an interracial home so endangered white children, women who intermarried were viewed as selfish and self-centered. Especially after 1967, when courts could no longer be as open about the racial basis for their rulings, women who married interracially were said to have acted immorally, without open reference to the racial component of their transgression. Seeking nonracial grounds on which to decide these custody cases, courts explained their decisions with reference to the prevailing gender ideology: These women lost custody, not because they married black men, but because they were "bad" mothers.

NOTES

1. "White Woman Marries Negro, Loses Her Child," *Jet*, 10 April 1952, 22; "A Lonely Mother Waits and Waits," *Pittsburgh Courier*, 11 July 1959, 9.

2. I would like to thank Rachel Moran of the New York University School of Law and Peter Bardaglio of Goucher College for their comments on an earlier version of this work presented at the 1996 Berkshire Conference on the History of Women.

3. Some states, like California, had laws that forbade interracial marriage within their own borders but recognized marriages that had taken place elsewhere. Thus, conceivably a woman from California could travel to another state to wed and then return to California to find her custody challenged in that state. However, all of the early cases that reached the state appeals court level occurred in states where interracial marriage was legal.

4. While these state court decisions provide a wealth of information to the historian, they are not without their limitations. Most cases never reach the

appeals court level, and state appeals courts selectively choose which cases to hear. Mothers who did not expect the state appeals court to be sympathetic might not bother with an appeal. Court decisions, moreover, do not send a consistent or monolithic message. A single ruling might be overturned by a higher court; rulings often contain more than opinion. Nevertheless, these twenty-five appeals court cases reveal important patterns which are historically significant.

5. *People ex rel. Portnoy v. Strasser*, 104 N.E. 2d 895 (New York, 1952); *People ex rel. Portnoy v. Strasser*, 195 N.Y.S. 2d 905 (New York, 1951). In the case of *Potter v. Potter*, for example, Sandra Baugh, who married a black surgeon, was denied custody of her children on the grounds that she was "a picture of a young woman who has been in serious rebellion." The appeals court upheld the ruling, saying that the circuit court had not been influenced by the race issue and had not considered racial differences in its decision. *Potter v. Potter*, 127 N.W. 2d 320 (Michigan, 1964).

6. The referee based his decision on the grounds that the mother was engaged in communist activities (an allegation she denied) and that she worked and put her little girl in day care.

7. *People ex rel. Portnoy v. Strasser*, 104 N.E. 2d 895 (New York 1952); "Brief for Defendant-Appellant, Court of Appeals of the State of New York," and "Brief of the New York City Chapter of the National Lawyers Guild as Amicus Curiae," National Association for the Advancement of Colored People Papers, group 2, Legal Files (1940–55), box B82, folder: Intermarriage, *People of New York ex rel. Mollie Portnoy v. Ann Strasser*, Court of Appeals, 1951–52, Manuscript Division, Library of Congress, Washington, D.C.; William Hopper, "Void Ruling Taking Girl from Mother in Mixed Marriage," *New York Daily Compass*, 14 March 1952.

8. *Murphy v. Murphy*, 124 A. 2d 891 (Connecticut, 1956).

9. *Commonwealth ex rel. Lucas v. Kreischer*, 209 A. 2d 243 (Pennsylvania, 1973); *Commonwealth ex rel. Myers v. Myers*, 360 A. 2d 587 (Pennsylvania, 1975).

10. *Goldman v. Hicks*, 1 So. 2d 18 (Alabama, 1941).

11. For more on the general issue of child custody, see Mary Ann Mason, *From Father's Property to Children's Rights: The History of Child Custody in the United States* (New York: Columbia University Press, 1994). For a legal view of custody cases involving interracial couples, see Susan Grossman, "A Child of a Different Color: Race as a Factor in Adoption and Custody Proceedings," *Buffalo Law Review* 17 (1967–68): 303–47.

12. *Commonwealth ex rel. Lucas v. Kreischer*, 209 A. 2d 243 (Pennsylvania, 1973), 245.

13. A growing historical literature addresses the cultural and societal significance of whiteness in the United States. David Roediger has described how the benefit of being white served as a symbolic "wage" for the white working class, while Ruth Frankenberg has described whiteness as an unmarked location of

structural advantage. Although many whites remain unaware and unconscious of the privileges they gain solely because of the color of their skin, historians have now begun to explore how those privileges have operated. For works on whiteness, see David Roediger, *Wages of Whiteness* (London: Verso Press, 1991); Ruth Frankenberg, *White Women, Race Matters: The Social Construction of Whiteness* (Minneapolis: University of Minnesota Press, 1993). See also Ian Haney Lopez, "The Social Construction of Race: Some Observations on Illusion, Fabrication and Choice," *Harvard Civil Rights–Civil Liberties Law Review* 29 (Winter 1994): 1–62; Cheryl I. Harris, "Whiteness as Property," *Harvard Law Review* 196 (June 1993): 1709–91. Furthermore, the social definition of blackness in American society, that anyone with any black ancestry is black, is an indicator of the importance of whiteness. This construction of black racial identity was necessary to the functioning of a biracial caste system. Historian Joel Williamson and sociologist F. James Davis have detailed the development of this "one-drop rule" in the United States. Joel Williamson, *New People: Miscegenation and Mulattoes in the United States* (New York: Free Press, 1980); F. James Davis, *Who Is Black?* (University Park: Pennsylvania State University Press, 1991).

14. It seems that associating with blacks was more threatening to a white woman's racial status than it was to a white man's. There are several reasons for this difference. First, women more than men achieve social status through marriage. Thus it is more damaging for a woman to "marry down" than for a man. Second, white women had long been given the primary responsibility for preserving the purity of the white race. While white men could father biracial children without serious social stigma, white women who gave birth to biracial children were degrading their race and themselves. For more on this issue, see Renee Romano, "Crossing the Line: Black-White Interracial Marriage in the United States, 1945–1990" (Ph.D. diss., Stanford University, 1996), chap. 2.

15. "Where Mixed Couples Live: Finding a Home is Trying Problem for Bi-Racial Families throughout the Entire Country," *Ebony*, May 1955, 61.

16. Sister Annella Lynn, "Interracial Marriages in Washington, D.C., 1940–1947" (Ph.D. diss., Catholic University, 1953), 70. Joseph Golden, "Patterns of Negro-White Intermarriage," *American Sociological Review* 19 (April 1954): 14. Other sociologists have reached the same conclusion. Ernest Porterfield found that the gender of the white partner determined where the couple lived; if the husband was white, the couple lived in a white neighborhood; if black, they lived in a black neighborhood. Porterfield, "Mixed Marriage," *Psychology Today*, January 1973, 71–78. Todd Pavela found that particularly in intermarriages at the lower economic and cultural levels, "the white wife became a Negro socially." Todd Pavela, "An Exploratory Study of Negro-White Intermarriage in Indiana," *Journal of Marriage and the Family* 26 (May 1964): 210.

17. "Where Mixed Couples Live," 62; Michelle Ross, "Is Mixed Marriage Jinxed?" *Ebony*, August 1953, 34–42; Hazel Byrne Simpkins, "I Married a Tan

Yank," *Tan Magazine,* March 1951, reprinted in Cloyte M. Larsson, ed., *Marriage across the Color Line* (Chicago: Johnsons Publishing Co., 1965), 104.

18. Hettie Jones, *How I Became Hettie Jones* (New York: E.P. Dutton, 1990), 190.

19. Parents sometimes claimed that their children and grandchildren would be lost to them forever if they married interracially. When one white woman with a small child married a black man, her mother asked the black husband, "Why do you do it like this? Why do you take away by me two children? There is plenty of colored people; why you took away, two children from one mother?" Mollie Portnoy in "Brief for Defendant-Appellant, Court of Appeals of the State of New York."

20. "Are Interracial Homes Bad for Children?" *Ebony,* March 1963, 135. The fear that children in interracial homes would be more likely to transgress the racial order was also expressed in a 1954 policy statement of a Georgia adoption agency, which forbade parents of one race to adopt children of another. "Our laws prohibit interracial marriage," the agency stated. "A child reared in a home with parents of a different race will be apt to meet and want to marry a person of his or her parents' background, not his own." Quoted in *In the Matter of the Petition of R.M.G. and E.M.G.,* 454 A. 2d 766 (D.C. App., 1982).

21. *Stingley v. Wesch,* 222 N.E. 2d 505 (Illinois, 1966); *Langin v. Langin,* 276 N.E. 2d 822 (Illinois, 1971).

22. *Boone v. Boone,* 565 P. 2d 337 (New Mexico, 1977), 338.

23. This decision was eventually reversed by a higher court. *In re Adoption of a Minor,* 228 F. 2d 446 (Washington, D.C., 1955). The appeals court ruled that it was clear that the boy was going to continue living with his white mother and black stepfather whether he was adopted or not, so denying adoption "could only serve the harsh and unjust end of depriving the child of a legitimized status in that home."

24. *Commonwealth ex rel. Myers v. Myers,* 360 A. 2d 587 (Pennsylvania, 1975).

25. Charles Claudius Philippe to Poppy Cannon, 28 July 1949, Walter White-Poppy Cannon White Papers, sec. 2, ser. 1, box 11, folder 77, Beinecke Library, Yale University, New Haven, Conn. Cannon was clearly worried about the possibility that Philippe would sue for custody, although there is no evidence that he ever actually did. Her lawyer wrote the law firm that handled her divorce to find out how her remarriage to a black man could affect child custody proceedings. The firm replied that custody would not be determined solely on the basis of the stepfather's race but also on evidence of his character, education, and ability to provide. Curtin, Brinckerhoff, and Barrett to H. Lee Lurie, Esq., 12 April 1949, Walter White-Poppy Cannon White Papers, sec. 2, ser. 1, box 11, folder 77.

26. *In re the Marriage of Sandra Ann Kramer and Gerald Kramer,* 297 N.W. 2d 359 (Iowa, 1980).

27. The best and most comprehensive study of the *Brown* decision is Richard

Kluger's *Simple Justice* (New York: Vintage Books, 1975). For more on the antimiscegenation rulings, see Walter Wadlington, "The Loving Case: Virginia's Anti-Miscegenation Statute in Historical Perspective," *Virginia Law Review* 52 (October 1966): 1189–223; "Anti-Miscegenation Statutes Repugnant Indeed," *Time*, 23 June 1967, 45–46; Andrew D. Weinberger, "A Reappraisal of the Constitutionality of Miscegenation Statutes," *Journal of Negro Education* 26 (Fall 1957): 438–39; Harvey Applebaum, "Miscegenation Statutes: A Constitutional and Social Problem," *Georgetown Law Journal* 53 (Fall 1964): 70; Anthony Lewis, "Race, Sex and the Supreme Court," *New York Times Magazine*, 22 November 1964, 132; Robert Sickels, *Race, Marriage and the Law* (Albuquerque: University of New Mexico Press, 1972); *Loving v. Virginia*, 388 U.S. 1 (1967).

28. In the 1973 Ohio case *In re Matter of Brenda H.*, for example, the appeals court addressed the issue of race when it could easily have sidestepped it. The case involved a dispute over Brenda, the illegitimate child of Carol and Clifford. Brenda had lived with her mother, Carol, for most of her life, but when Carol's parents threw her out of their house because she had begun dating a black man, she temporarily gave Brenda to Clifford to care for. Clifford, with the encouragement of Carol's parents, sued for permanent custody of Brenda after Carol married her black boyfriend. Although Clifford's counsel never directly raised the issue of the interracial marriage, Carol's lawyers insisted that her interracial marriage was the only motivation for the custody suit. Despite the lack of overt evidence, the court was "completely persuaded that had Carol married a white man there would have been no rallying point for Clifford and Carol's parents for this action of custody would never have been initiated." *In re Matter of Brenda H.*, 305 N.E. 2d 815 (Ohio, 1973).

29. *Langin v. Langin*, 276 N.E. 2d 822 (Illinois, 1971).

30. See *Lucas v. Kreischer*, 289 A. 2d 202 (Pa. Super, 1972); and *Lucas v. Kreischer*, 209 A. 2d 243 (Pennsylvania, 1973). In *Kreischer*, both a trial court and the Pennsylvania superior court awarded custody of three children to Zane Kreischer after his ex-wife married a black man. The trial court openly based its decision on race, ruling that although both parents were suitable and had similar economic circumstances, the mother's interracial marriage put the children at risk of future harm. "[T]he almost universal prejudice and intolerance of interracial marriage is real and undeniable," the superior court agreed. In 1973, however, the Supreme Court of Pennsylvania ruled that there was no compelling reason to deny custody to the mother in this case and awarded her custody of her three children. "The real issue posed by the appeal," the Pennsylvania Supreme Court contended, "is whether a subsequent interracial marriage by the mother, in and of itself, is such a compelling reason as will warrant a court in denying her the custody of her children. We rule it is not."

31. For other instances of this, see *Edel v. Edel*, 293 N.W. 2d 792 (Michigan, 1980), in which the Michigan Court of Appeals remanded a decision where a

judge had taken a white child away from her mother because he felt that the mother and her black fiancée would face societal problems. The appeals court held that "the trial judge committed a 'clear legal error on a major issue' in considering a parent's association with another race" and remanded the case for a rehearing with a different judge.

32. *Ethridge v. Ethridge*, 360 So. 2d 1005 (Alabama, 1978), 1008.

33. Likewise, in the 1974 Florida case, *Niles v. Niles*, the appeals court ruled that the trial judge had "broad discretion" in making child custody placement decisions. In *Niles*, the trial court denied a white mother custody of her children because she had "chosen for herself, and therefore for herself and children, a life style unacceptable to the father of the children and the society in which we live." Yet despite this language, the appeals court refused to explore the mother's charge that she had been denied custody because of her impending marriage to a black man. *Niles v. Niles*, 299 So. 2d 162 (Florida, 1974).

34. *Schexnayder v. Schexnayder*, 364 So. 2d 1318 (Louisiana, 1978), 1318.

35. These were the words of a dissenting opinion by Judge C. J. Samuel in the state appeals court case, but the Supreme Court followed similar reasoning. See *Schexnayder v. Schexnayder*, 364 So. 2d 1318, p. 1321; *Schexnayder v. Schexnayder*, 371 So. 2d 769 (Supreme Court of Louisiana, 1979).

36. *White v. Appleton*, 304 So. 2d 206 (Alabama, 1974), 209. For another case of this type, see *Niles v. Niles*.

37. For more on the myth of the black rapist, see Jacquelyn Dowd Hall, *Revolt against Chivalry* (New York: Columbia University Press, 1979); Joel Williamson, *A Rage for Order* (New York: Oxford University Press, 1986); Gail Bederman, *Manliness and Civilization: A Cultural History of Gender and Race in the United States, 1880–1917* (Chicago: University of Chicago Press, 1995); Stephen Whitfield, *A Death in the Delta: The Story of Emmett Till* (New York: Free Press, 1988).

38. Martha Hodes, "Sex across the Color Line: White Women and Black Men in the Nineteenth Century American South" (Ph.D. diss., Princeton University, 1991).

39. *Palmore v. Sidoti*, 426 So. 2d (Florida, 1981); *Palmore v. Sidoti*, 472 So. 2d 843 (Florida, 1982).

40. *Palmore v. Sidoti*, 104 Sup. Ct. 1879 (1984).

41. For more on this case see, Eileen Blackwood, "Race as a Factor in Custody and Adoption Disputes: *Palmore v. Sidoti*," *Cornell Law Review* 71 (November 1985): 209–26; Robert Weinstock, "*Palmore v. Sidoti*: Color-Blind Custody," *American University Law Review* 34 (Fall 1984): 245–69.

42. *Ward v. Ward*, 216 P. 2d 755 (Washington, 1950).

43. *Fountaine v. Fountaine*, 133 N.E. 2d 532 (Illinois, 1956); *Beazley v. Davis*, 545 P. 2d 206 (Nevada, 1976). For other cases of this type, see *Tucker v. Tucker*, 542 P. 2d 789 (Washington, 1975); *Farmer v. Farmer*, 329 N.Y.S. 2d 584 (1981). Interestingly, courts drew the distinction between a biracial child being raised by a white

biological mother and being raised by white foster or adoptive parents. Since the mid-1970s, there has been an intense debate about whether it is harmful for a black child to be adopted by a white couple and raised in an all-white environment. Yet while transracial adoption is seen as harmful to a black child, courts regularly allowed biracial children to be raised by a white biological parent.

44. Ruth, quoted in Albert Gordon, "Negro-Jewish Marriages," *Judaism* 3 (Spring 1964): 184; poem reprinted in David Harrell, *White Sects and Black Men in the Recent South* (Nashville: Vanderbilt University Press, 1971), 64–65.

Chapter 13

The Making of a "Bad" Mother
A Lesbian Mother and Her Daughters

Christine J. Allison

The United States currently is witnessing a lesbian baby boom.[1] Nonetheless, the term "lesbian mother" continues to sound like an oxymoron to many Americans. In child custody trials judges still deny custody—and even visitation rights—to lesbians who would otherwise be considered ideal parents.[2] Such custody rulings and their underlying equating of lesbian mothers with bad mothers harm both lesbian mothers and their children. The experience of Nancy and her daughters, Marie and Ellen, is a case in point.[3]

In 1977, in a small town in the western United States, Nancy came out as a lesbian and went through a divorce. She fought for custody of her daughters, and lost. Marie was seven, Ellen eleven, when their father gained custody of them. As the transcript of the trial makes clear, Nancy (who had been the primary caretaker of the girls during her marriage) lost custody because of her sexual orientation.[4] The court order reads, "The active practice of a homosexual life style is so antithetical to a heterosexual one that the introduction of the children into its actual practice will inevitably cause severe conflicts and turmoil within the children."

Ultimately, the court's decision produced a set of conditions which compounded, rather than reduced, the pain and prejudice that these children and their mother experienced. By stipulating that the mother was "not to exercise her rights of visitation in the presence of anyone of homosexual orientation," the court set up a problematic situation in which Nancy felt she needed to deceive her children. Moreover, the vitriol of the custody trial so harmed Nancy psychologically that she felt unable to talk to her daughters openly about her sexual orientation, much less give them emotional support to combat the homophobia they encountered.

The girls spent the remainder of their growing-up years with their father, the parent with whom neither wanted to live[5] (according to a report submitted by Social Services at the time of the trial). Rather than moving to a new and larger community, as they would have done with their mother, they stayed with their father in the small, gossipy town where they had been reared. There, peers shunned the girls, both because they lived with their father instead of their mother *and* because their mother was a lesbian. This stigmatization from peers, coupled with the fact that they received almost no help from either parent in understanding homosexuality and homophobia, created ongoing confusion and difficulty for the girls.[6]

If single fathers are an anomaly today, they were even more so in the 1970s. Peers considered Marie and Ellen's family peculiar because of the custody arrangement. Ellen explains that in the divorces she knew of, "it was always the mother who had custody. And it was always very odd for people. . . . 'Oh your father has custody of you? Why is that?'"

However, Marie and Ellen knew that people called their family "weird" not solely because they lived with their father. Many in town knew of their mother's sexual orientation and disapproved of it.[7] People in town found lesbianism strange, Marie says, "not to mention gross and obscene." When people asked why her father had custody, Ellen would say, without elaboration, "That's just what the court said." She learned a code of silence early on: "I had to be careful in a small town of what I said. I could have really set myself up to get hurt if I'd exposed too much information."

Beyond feeling stigmatized, Marie and Ellen felt isolated and confused. Their conservative town had no visible lesbian and gay community. In the late seventies and early eighties—before, or just at the very beginning of, the current lesbian baby boom—they probably did not see lesbian mothers represented anywhere. They certainly did not know any other children whose mothers had lost custody because of their sexual orientation.

Before the custody trial, Nancy went to a couple of psychologists to see if one of them would testify on her behalf. Perhaps because they were not willing to tarnish their reputations through involvement in such a "controversial" case, not one agreed to testify for her. Nancy took the girls to see one psychologist, who later refused to testify, and when he met with Ellen he said reassuringly to her, "I want you to know that your mother is not sick. And your father is not sick either." This consolation, offered without context to an eleven-year-old, raised more questions and fears than it quelled.

The girls' father scarcely helped his children to deal with negative messages regarding their mother's sexual orientation. Soon after the custody trial, Ellen heard rumors circulating at school that Nancy was "gay." She did not know what the term meant. She asked her father if, in fact, her mother was "gay." "No," he said, "I don't think so." Although the word swirled around her, Ellen did not learn its meaning until she was fourteen or fifteen years old. "Nobody told me," she says. "But I knew it was something bad from the community's reactions."

Sadly, the person who could have helped the girls the most had been silenced. Homophobia, from the court and from the wider society, stymied Nancy's efforts to give support to her daughters.[8] She could not demonstrate to them the positive aspects, or the day-to-day normalcy, of a lesbian relationship because she did not have custody of her children and her visitation rights were severely restricted. By stipulating in his custody order that Nancy was "not to exercise her rights of visitation in the presence of anyone of homosexual orientation," the judge by fiat banished Nancy's partner, Ann, from their home when the children visited.[9] (They visited her every other weekend.) Nancy feared that if Ann were there when the children visited, they might tell their father, who would take her to court to have her visitation rights revoked. So Nancy lied to her daughters. Too young to grasp the necessity of the deception, Ellen and Marie felt bewildered and betrayed when they discovered that Ann was staying next door, and not in another city, as Nancy had told them. Meanwhile, in this siege of disapproval, Nancy's self-confidence withered. She doubted the acceptability of her sexual orientation and had difficulty discussing the issue with her children.

Marie and Ellen learned not to talk about their mother's lesbianism from both parents, as from their small community. They might not have known the word "homophobia," but its effects suffused their lives. The judge, in determining custody, failed to consider which parent would be better able to help the children combat the stigma they faced because of their mother's sexual orientation: the lesbian mother or the homophobic father. Denial failed as a childrearing strategy. Being labeled a "bad" mother actually undermined Nancy's ability to be a truly good one.

NOTES

1. Advances in reproductive technologies, some liberalization of adoption and foster parenting policies, and an increasing acceptance (within lesbian communities and in mainstream society) of lesbians' being mothers have facilitated this surge in the number of lesbians becoming parents. See, for example, William B. Rubenstein, ed., *Lesbians, Gay Men, and the Law* (New York: New Press, 1993), and Kath Weston, *Families We Choose* (New York: Columbia University Press, 1991).

2. Two recent and well-publicized cases involving lesbian mothers are Sharon Bottoms's loss of custody of her son in the Virginia Supreme Court in 1995 and Mary Ward's loss of custody of her daughter in a Florida appeals court in 1996. In the Ward case, the father who was granted custody had previously served eight years in prison for killing his first wife, indicating that the judge seemed to view murderers as less "bad" than lesbian mothers. See Cynthia Frazier, "Keeping the Kids," *Lesbian News* 21 (April 1996): 37, and Gady A. Epstein, "Judges Rule against Lesbian Mom," *Tampa Tribune*, August 31, 1996.

3. Data for this case study were gathered from in-depth interviews with Marie, Ellen, Nancy, and her partner, Ann, (not their real names), as well as from transcripts of the custody trial, lawyers' briefs, and supporting legal documents. All quotations are taken from these sources unless otherwise noted. Further information on references is available from the author.

I interviewed Marie, Ellen, Nancy, and Ann separately. The interviews lasted between two and three hours and took place in the winter of 1990–91. I subsequently sent each respondent a transcript of her interview and offered her the opportunity to provide written comments or additions. I received additional information in this manner from Marie and Ellen.

The custody trial took place in September 1977 in a small town in the western United States. After Nancy lost custody of her children, the ACLU took the case and initial legal briefs were filed for an appeal. However, Nancy opted not to appeal the case; after her devastating initial custody trial she felt that she did not have a chance of winning an appeal and that another legal battle like the one she and her partner had just experienced would be too painful and damaging to her partner, her children, and herself.

4. Her sexual preference was *the* focus of the trial. All other factors, including an examination of who had been and would be the best custodian for the children became secondary issues. Of the 360 exhibits admitted in the trial, 356 were specifically relevant to Nancy's sexual orientation. During the trial her husband, his lawyer and the psychologists who testified against her repeatedly referred to her homosexuality as a "sickness"—even though Nancy's custody case took place four years after the American Psychiatric Association had officially removed homosexuality from the list of mental disorders in its official diagnostic

manual (Barry D. Adam, *The Rise of a Gay and Lesbian Movement* [Boston: Twayne Publishers, 1987], 81). Even Nancy's own lawyer constructed her lesbianism as a problem by basing many of his arguments on the idea that it was something she could "overcome."

5. Marie: "I needed my mom . . . and never once did I feel that it was the best interest to live with my dad. . . . *[I]t's been really harmful to live with my dad and extremely painful . . . there's no way that he was the best parent.* . . . If the custody trial had been decided on the best interests of us kids, we would have lived with our mom."

6. This point emerged from my interviews with both Marie and Ellen. For example, Ellen says: "At the time [of her mother's loss of custody] I was eleven or twelve, and no adult told me what was going on. . . . I knew that Mom was with Ann, but I didn't see that there was anything wrong with that. It wasn't explained to me until I was older what it meant or what it was all about or what the court thought it was all about, or what my friends and their parents thought it was all about."

7. Nancy recalls that around the time of the custody trial townspeople who knew about the case and her relationship with Ann reacted to her in ways that made her "feel like I had the plague; I mean, you know, like I had some kind of a disease. . . . Friends, you know, lifetime friends, all of a sudden either they felt sorry for me, which was the absolute worst . . . felt sorry for me 'cause I had this 'condition.' . . . Or there was just this, 'How could you?' . . . [they would] leave the room when I'd enter. . . . They didn't want to associate with me."

8. In a 1980 study, Karen Gail Lewis interviewed twenty-one children with lesbian mothers and found a "glaring absence of any support system for the children" (Karen Gail Lewis, "Children of Lesbians: Their Point of View," *Social Work* 25 [May 1980]: 202). She concluded that antigay social stigma may often leave children of lesbian and gay parents without larger social support systems in which they can talk about feelings and concerns related to their parent's sexual orientation. Psychologists agree that social support, particularly from parents, is tremendously important for children of lesbians and gay men. As psychologist and researcher Charlotte Patterson explains, "'In terms of the long-term welfare of the child, far more important than whether one is teased by one's peers is whether one has the support of loving parents in dealing with it'" (Kathryn Baron, "The 'Gaybie' Boom," *Los Angeles Times*, March 1, 1995).

9. The court found "that the exercise of visitation by the respondent in the presence of anyone of homosexual orientation would significantly impair the children's emotional development."

Chapter 14

Mothering to Death

Su Epstein

The only thing worse than killing is killing intentionally and repeatedly. For most people, the serial murderer is the quintessential criminal offender. But what makes him kill?[1] Criminologists and lay commentators alike tend to blame his psychological makeup and his upbringing. Almost invariably, the relationship between the killer and his mother receives immediate and intensive scrutiny. When the son becomes a killer, the mother becomes a suspect. In fact, in both academic case studies and popular film, mothers are blamed for their sons' murderous deeds.[2]

American films repeatedly represent serial killers as the product of "evil" mothers. In film, the "evil" mother might be domineering, promiscuous, indecent, abusive, or neglectful. Then again, the killer in the film might just *feel* that his mother embodies these traits. Sometimes, the mother sins simply by being strong-willed, unmarried, or minimally devoted to her husband. Whatever the alleged maternal failure, the films suggest that the son lashes out at others as a direct response to it. These sons, as their mothers' "products," generalize their mother hatred, killing other women to prevent potential harm to themselves or others by "evil women." Despite the fact that the sons are doing the killing, the crimes become the fault of the killers' mothers.

Often, the mother's sexuality troubles her killer son. These mothers seem to have too much sex, with the wrong people, in the wrong places. Sometimes the mother's sexuality becomes a form of child abuse, as when she places self-gratification above the essential tasks of mothering. Some films fault the mother for having *any* intimate relationship.

In many cases the mother's sexual behavior accompanies and compounds horrific acts of abuse. In the film *Henry: Portrait of a Serial Killer*

(1989), for example, Henry's mother engages in prostitution in front of her children and her disabled husband. The killer states, "She was a whore, my mama was a whore, but I don't fault her for that. It ain't what she done, it's how she done it." Henry then describes his mother as forcing her husband to watch her, beating him if he does not, and, at times, forcing both the husband and son to wear a dress while they watch. In *The Eyes of Laura Mars* (1978), the killer's mother leaves her child in soiled diapers for days, only to then force him to witness her acts of prostitution. The prostitute mother in *Maniac* (1990) burns her son with a cigarette for refusing to hide quietly in the closet for hours, observing her while she sleeps with strange men.

Not all of the malicious, selfish, abusive mothers engage in prostitution. Some repress their overt sexuality, only to use that drive underhandedly to bind their sons to them in sick ways. In *The Strangler* (1964), the son visits his bedridden mother in a nursing home at least every other day. At each visit she berates him that he doesn't care about her, even though she gave up her life for him. Clearly threatened by any sexual relationship he might have, she laments that maybe he has a girl he loves more than her. When the killer attempts to reassure his mother of his love and devotion, she yells at him that no other woman *would* love him: "You're not good-looking; you are fat. Even as a little boy no one liked you." In *Fade to Black* (1980), the mother nags, insults, and criticizes her son, attacking his appearance, manner, and interests. She obstructs his education, work, and social life. In one scene, this irrepressibly self-centered mother barges into her son's bedroom demanding a back rub. When he requests an additional minute to finish watching a movie, she thrashes about, breaking his prized video equipment. Not surprisingly, this killer son has difficulty dealing with other women.

In other serial-killer films, it is not clear what the mother did to deserve the blame she receives. The son's perception of her as a "bad" mother is what counts. If the son feels he got a raw deal from his mother, it is assumed that he did. In this way, mothers are doubly stomped on: they are blamed for their sons' behavior *and* their own perspective is silenced.

In *Double Exposure* (1982), the mother is "bad" simply because she goes on with her life after divorce. Her son, believing he once heard his mother and stepfather having sex, and feeling that his "evil" mother thereby dishonored his father, transfers his anger to all women by killing a series of sexually attractive fashion models. In *Criminal Law* (1989), the young son accidentally witnesses an abortion performed by his gynecologist mother. Moreover, during a divorce argument, he overhears his father accusing his mother of never having wanted a child. The killer son feels rejected and blames his mother for his parents' divorce, despite her declarations of love for him and explanations of her marital problems. As an adult, he kills his mother's patients to avenge unborn fetuses and to purge society of these "diseased" women who reject motherhood. Both of these films privilege the killer sons' feelings over the mothers' actual behaviors.

Some films just throw in mother-blaming for the sake of it, offering no clue to the mothers' alleged faults. The killer's mother in *I Dismember Mama* (1974), a well-to-do, older woman, does community service, is nice to the people around her, and does not engage in *any* socially inappropriate behavior. Hospitalized for a near-fatal attack on her, her son blames his mother for everything and calls her "unclean and a depraved whore." The film never explains this mother's culpability, yet all characters accept her as being at fault.

Other films legitimize mother-blaming by allowing mothers to blame themselves for producing murderous children.[3] Still others allow an authoritative character, such as a physician, psychologist, lawyer, or judge, to point the accusing finger, making the accusation seem all the more legitimate. All in all, films about serial killers overflow with mother-blaming.

But after all, this is only Hollywood, catering to the fantasies of the American adolescent male. Why take these films' garish twist on criminological explanation seriously? *Serious* analysis of serial killing would not engage in such simplistic finger pointing. Or would it?

Academic case studies of actual serial killers read like only slightly subdued versions of the Hollywood screenplays. Here, too, mothers create sons who kill. As in the films, fathers, boyfriends, stepfathers, and lovers appear only as shadow figures, if at all.

When serial killers narrate their own lives, they often present themselves as victims of inadequate or abusive mothers.[4] Richard Chase, "the vampire killer," speaks of a schizophrenic mother incapable of rearing and socializing him properly.[5] Ted Bundy claimed he grew up thinking his young mother was actually his sister; discovery of the truth caused great distress, he said, and contributed to his murderous tendency.[6] Other serial killers report sexual acts with their mothers or attempted rape by their stepmothers.[7]

The experts' narratives sound strikingly similar to those constructed by the killers. Mother-blaming suffuses the academic literature on serial killers. Psychologist Joel Norris, a noted researcher in the field, lists an array of factors that he believes can shape a future serial killer. If the pregnancy is unwanted or the gestation period difficult for the mother; if the child suffers injuries at birth or head injuries later; if the parents abuse drugs or alcohol or are physically or emotionally abusive—a serial killer may be in the making. While several items on this list could point to either parent, some are mother specific. Further, Norris's discussion of particular cases often focuses on the mother. For example, in the case of Henry Lee Lucas, Norris notes the presence and socially inappropriate behavior of both parents, but focuses on the killer's view that "he was beaten, knocked unconscious, and repeatedly injured by his mother and her pimp."[8]

Frequently the case histories focus on the mother and credit the killer's perception of the mother as bad. Norris writes that "[T]he passively cruel *parent* who imposes a rigid set of conflicting beliefs upon the child can create a monster." He goes on to discuss the case of Bobby Joe Long.

> Long describes *his mother* as cruel in her disregard for his needs. After he had reached adolescence he claims he was *manipulated* into conflict with *one of her boyfriends* on at least one occasion during which he had to beat the man up just to protect himself. On another occasion he was so angry at the attention his mother showered upon her little dog, in contrast to the neglect that he perceived, that he shoved a .22 caliber bullet into the dog's vagina.[9]

Speaking in more general terms about the mother who is "emotionally conflicted" during her pregnancy, Norris notes, "Even if the child is not damaged at birth, the mother's anxieties may result in a colicky, unhappy baby who becomes the object of mistreatment and abuse by a mother who was unhappy about being pregnant. Such mistreatment is also a factor in the development of a violence-prone individual."[10] Again, it is the bad mother who damages her child; the father or other male influence eludes consideration. The serial killer remains a mother's burden.

Another leading researcher in the area of serial killing, Robert Holmes, in discussing serial rapists notes that, "[t]he mother is usually described as being rejecting, excessively controlling, dominant, punitive, overprotective, and seductive. The father is usually described as uninvolved, aloof, distant, absent or passive, but occasionally punitive and cruel."[11] From this assessment, neither parent appears to display appropriate parenting skills. However, Holmes concludes that the mother-rapist relationship is meaningful, while "the relationship with the father appears to be less significant."[12]

Clearly, academics and film producers are reading from the same cultural script when they seek to explain serial killers' behavior. That script places the mother in the nursery, intensely connected to the infant emotionally and practically. Whatever goes right in the child's development reflects the ability of good *parents*; whatever goes wrong reverts solely to the mother. The erasures from the script fade in importance after a while; absent fathers, crushing poverty, substance abuse, and the myriad of other problems a family might face move toward invisibility, as the bad mother of the murderous son takes center stage. And why not? In a psychologically oriented culture that traces the patterns of a lifetime to the first stages of life, a culture in which mother-blaming is as familiar as apple pie, she is an easy target.

NOTES

1. Criminological and law enforcement definitions and statistics suggest that most murderers who get the label "serial killer" are males who systematically kill women or boys.

2. The material presented here is based on several years of secondary and original research on serial killing. Information regarding serial killer films is based on the analysis of 172 American films produced between 1932 and 1992.

3. See *The Bad Seed* (1956), *Berserk* (1967) or *Straight-Jacket* (1964) for examples of this phenomenon.

4. Eric Hickey, *Serial Murderers and Their Victims* (Pacific Grove: Brooks/Cole, 1991); Jack Levin and James Alan Fox, *Mass Murder: America's Growing Menace* (New York: Plenum, 1985); Elliott Leyton, *Hunting Humans: Inside the Minds of Mass Murderers* (New York: Simon and Schuster, 1986); Joel Norris, *Serial Killers: The Growing Menace* (New York: Doubleday, 1988); Robert K. Ressler and Tom Shachtman, *Whoever Fights Monsters* (New York: St Martin's, 1992); Kerry Segrave, *Women Serial and Mass Murderers* (Jefferson, N.C.: McFarland, 1992).

5. Brian Lane and Wilfred Gregg, *The Encyclopedia of Serial Killers* (New York: Berkeley Books, 1992), 89–90.

6. Hickey, *Serial Murders*, 96–98; Ann Rule, *The Stranger beside Me* (New York: New American Library, 1980), 27; S. Winn and D. Merrill, *Ted Bundy: The Killer Next Door* (New York: Bantam, 1980), 107.

7. Ressler and Shachtman, *Whoever Fights Monsters*, 83–103.

8. Norris, *Serial Killers*, 234–35.

9. Ibid., 235, emphasis mine.

10. Ibid., 236–37.

11. Ronald Holmes, *Profiling Violent Crimes* (Newbury Park, Calif.: Sage, 1989), 101.

12. Ibid., 101.

Part III

"Bad" Mothers in Print
A Selection

"Bad" mothers have long been a mainstay of the American media. The five selections that follow offer a glimpse of twentieth-century mother-blaming in print. They represent neither the most egregious nor the best-known examples of "mom"-bashing. Nevertheless, these pieces are typical in their views. They show the range and adaptability of the bad mother label.

In a 1938 *Newsweek* article, "On a Hickory Limb," Burton Rascoe derided the "stage mother," whose unfulfilled ego rapacity led her to push her progeny into the spotlight—a familiar stereotype. Similarly, the *Ladies Home Journal* in 1950 published "The Overprotective Mother," by Dr. Herman N. Bundesen, president of the Chicago Board of Health, warning of the mother who failed to cut the cord of connection between herself and her child. And by the 1960s, Dan Greenburg's caricature of the Jewish mother, who twisted guilt like a virtual garrote around her children's necks, entered mainstream humor.

While too much mothering of the wrong sort has garnered criticism throughout the century, too little mothering has also been a source of alarm. A 1965 *Ladies Home Journal* article about slain civil rights worker Viola Liuzzo reveals the depth of American women's conviction that a mother belongs with her children; no cause, say the housewives interviewed, should have taken a mother of five into danger far from home. In 1990, syndicated columnist George Will charged in a *Newsweek* column titled "Mothers Who Don't Know How" that the young, unmarried mothers of America's many "ghettos" replicated the emotionally and intellectually vacant mothering they had experienced in childhood; their "failure to thrive" children signal the decay of American society.

These articles illustrate the powerful ways in which the "bad" mother label has been deployed to define gender, class, and political norms in America.

Chapter 15

On a Hickory Limb

Burton Rascoe

There is no female in the world more dreadful than the determined mother who has ambitions for her son or daughter. There is no greater social menace. Iron-willed, frustrated, self-sacrificing mothers, trying to live a dream life through their progeny, have wrecked more lives than has syphilis. They have killed the initiative in their sons and daughters, stifled their souls, and made of their husbands mere plugging, resigned creatures who often wonder why they work so hard to make a fortune—or to make a living—when in life they get so little out of their effort.

Hollywood is pestilential with these awful maternal creatures, who are worse than the female mantis. The female mantis merely devours her mate. She lets the progeny escape. And they all bear the sacred name of "Mother"—blast Al Jolson and all his derivatives and those from whom such hokum as Jolson's derives!—and they drag around with them, from casting office to casting office, fine and beautiful, normal kids or strikingly lovely, not-very-bright, but wholesome girls who, if they could ever escape from their ambitious mothers, might find love, a place in the world compatible with their gifts and virtues, a sort of domestic bliss and happiness.

Their mothers want to be movie stars and yet they still have that one grain of common sense left which tells them that, being fat, fulminic, and fifty, they haven't a chance with the current vicarious sweethearts of the movie-going public, the drugstore cowboys and the pocket-pool sharks. . . But many people in the home town have remarked that Mame is so pretty she ought to be in the movies and that being just where Mama wants to be herself, she "sacrifices everything" so that "Mame will have her chance

Reprinted from *Newsweek* 12 (July 25, 1938): 30.

to get where she ought to be and become what she was destined to become — an Eleanora Duse of the movies" . . . And sweet, pretty, wholesome Mame lands up rassling the chinaware and cutlery in a Hollywood beanery (to support herself and Mama) with other girls just as pretty as Mame, who also have determined mothers who have ambitions for their daughters.

And there is the mother who has ambitions for her son. Her vitality and her determination are so great — for her son — that the son never gets even half a chance to formulate any ambition for himself. Mother is always attending to that for him — or thinks she is. She is always directing him, pulling strings for him, fixing it up so that he will one day have a debut in Carnegie Hall as a concert pianist when, as a matter of fact, the poor lad is tone-deaf and couldn't play a roll on a pianola but has admirable talents in geodesy or dentistry and would like to develop them, but can't because he has a mother who has ambitions for him.

Ambitions, my eye! She doesn't want to wean him, even when he is middle-aged. In her own eyes she is a Mother, however, and she will "scrub floors and work her fingers to the bone," to see to it that her son achieves the ambition she has worked out for him. Which means, of course, (although she is not consciously aware of it) that she will go to any lengths to keep her son from achieving anything whatever, even a $15 a week living in a hash house, rather than wean him . . .

Chapter 16

The Overprotective Mother

Herman N. Bundesen

When his parents first came to me for help, Ronnie, who was then nine years old, showed every sign of being what we used to call a "spoiled brat." A little tyrant at home, selfish and demanding of his parents, he responded to any denial or disciplinary measure with an outburst of temper. He was aggressive and bossy with other children, with the result that he had few friends and spent most of his afternoons at home, reading or talking or playing with his mother, who was known as an unselfish, devoted parent, a model to her friends and neighbors.

"She gives her whole life to that boy," was a frequent observation made about Ronnie's mother.

Ronnie had a good record at school. He was bright and interested in his studies, though his teachers had noted his tendency to interrupt others and dominate the class. Ronnie could be good when he wanted to. Why should he be such a demon outside of school?

I am a subscriber to the truism that the problem child is almost invariably the product of problem parents, and have said it many times. But it is important to realize that by no means all parents of psychologically difficult children are ignorant or unloving. In many cases the parent is as much a victim as the child. It is circumstances that are to blame.

This is frequently the case with the oversolicitous or overprotective mother—a common cause of abnormal, antisocial behavior on the part of the child. In this drama the mother plays an unconscious role. Moved by forces of whose existence she is unaware, she responds by dominating or indulging her child to a point which can interfere with normal adjustment and development.

Reprinted from the *Ladies' Home Journal* 67 (March 1950): 250.

I didn't have to find out many of the details of Ronnie's case before I began to suspect this was the trouble here. The "model mother" reports were a tip-off; it is typical of the overprotective mother that she denies herself many normal interests and relationships in order to devote herself unstintingly to her child. The fact is that, unconsciously, she may be encouraging him to stay at home in order to avoid the hurts and hazards of normal play with children his own age.

Further study confirmed these early suspicions. Ronnie's mother made him so completely the center of the universe that he never had a chance to learn what children ought to know about the rights of others, or to do things for himself and thus develop as an independent personality. Long after it was natural for her to do so, for example, she had continued to bathe and dress Ronnie, and she still insisted on driving him to and from school.

Characteristic of the overprotective attitude was her unreasonable exaggeration of the dangers of letting him cross streets by himself. Actually, the few suburban blocks between their home and the school were perfectly safe, even for children much younger than Ronnie. Roaming and exploring a little on the way home from school are normal ways for children to learn and grow. His mother's anxiety thus deprived Ronnie of these and many other childhood experiences that have a proper, necessary place in the business of growing up.

As frequently happens in these cases, Ronnie's father was pushed into the background. Finding that any attempt on his part to discipline the child met with resistance from the mother, he had long since given up, in the interests of peace, and accepted the passive position assigned him. Though he had to put up with a son who was often ill-tempered and more critical of him than a small boy should ever be of his father, I found their relationship fairly pleasant on the whole. Apparently the worst in the child was brought out by his mother, and the abnormally close bond he had with her.

The cause of the abnormal affinity of mother and son was not hard to find as I studied this interesting family more closely. An only child, Ronnie had been born, after five or six childless years, to parents who were in their thirties when they were married. Thus he became the sole object of maternal feelings that had been pent up for years. Ronnie had one or two severe illnesses when he was a baby—experiences which no doubt added to his mother's anxieties, realizing as she did that she would have no more children.

I could find no evidence that Ronnie's mother had been deprived of normal love during her own childhood and was compensating for this lack by excessive feelings about her son—a fairly common cause of overprotectiveness. Neither was there evidence that her relations with her husband failed to gratify her craving for love, another common cause. It was a simple case of "too little, too late" to satisfy the maternal drive, which in Ronnie's mother was strong, and rather to her credit than otherwise.

The fact that Ronnie's parents had sought advice about his temper tantrums and aggressiveness was a sign that they knew something was wrong.

The first and most important step toward correcting the situation was to get both parents to realize what was happening, and how it was hurting their child. Since they were intelligent and truly loved their son, this was not hard to do.

Recognition alone, however, did not solve the problem in Ronnie's case and will not in most cases of overprotectiveness. The habits of thinking and doing that have developed over a period of several years cannot be wished out of existence overnight. Often it is desirable to send the too-protected child away to camp or even to boarding school, so that he will be physically beyond reach of the mother's overpowering impulse to shelter or indulge him and thus dominate his life.

When this is unnecessary or impossible, a systematic effort must be made to keep the youngster busy at school and neighborhood activities and away from home. This is hard on the mother at first, but when she understands that the problem is as much hers as her child's, she is usually equal to the discipline that is required.

It is important, however, for the child to realize that he is loved as much as he ever was. The new attitude, while firm, should be kindly and objective, else confusion and rebellion may result.

Serious as it may become, the problem of overprotectiveness arises from a mother's love of her offspring. To correct it, her love must be directed into the proper channels, but not in any way diminished or destroyed. Overindulged boys and girls are usually not happy themselves in antisocial behavior, and often express a wish that "somebody would make them behave the way they ought to." That is the way to help them do so.

Chapter 17

How to Be a Jewish Mother
A Very Lovely Training Manual

Dan Greenburg

The Basic Theory

There is more to being a Jewish Mother than being Jewish and a mother.[1]
Properly practiced, Jewish motherhood is an art—a complex network of
subtle and highly sophisticated techniques.

Master these techniques and you will be an unqualified success—the
envy of your friends and the backbone of your family.

Fail to master these techniques and you hasten the black day you
discover your children can get along without you.

Basic Philosophizing

You will be called upon to function as a philosopher on two distinct types
of occasions:

(1) Whenever anything bad happens.
(2) Whenever anything good happens.

Whenever anything bad happens, you must point out the fortunate aspects of the situation:

"Ma! Ma!"
"What's the commotion?"

Reprinted from Dan Greenburg, *How to Be a Jewish Mother: A Very Lovely Training Manual*
(Los Angeles: Price Stern Sloan, 1964; 1975): 11–13.

"The bad boys ran off with my hat."

"The bad boys ran off with your hat? You should be glad they didn't also cut your throat."

Also point out that Bad Experience is the best teacher:

"Maybe next time you'll know better than to fool with roughnecks. It's the best thing that could have happened to you, believe me."

Whenever anything good happens, you must, of course, point out the *unfortunate* aspects of the situation. (This is necessary in order that The Evil Eye should not suspect that things are going too well):

"Ma! Ma!"

"So what's the trouble now?"

"The Youth Group Raffle! I won a Pontiac convertible!"

"You won a Pontiac automobile in the Youth Group Raffle? Very nice. The insurance alone is going to send us to the poorhouse."

Making Guilt Work

Underlying all techniques of Jewish Motherhood is the ability to plant, cultivate and harvest guilt. Control guilt and you control the child.

An old folk saw says "Beat a child every day: if you don't know what he's done to deserve the beating, *he* will." A slight modification gives us the Jewish Mother's cardinal rule: Let your child hear you sigh every day; if you don't know what he's done to make you suffer, *he* will.

NOTES

1. On the other hand, you don't have to be either Jewish or a mother to be a Jewish mother. An Irish waitress or an Italian barber could also be a Jewish mother.

Chapter 18

Murder in Alabama
American Wives Think Viola Liuzzo Should Have Stayed Home

Lyn Tornabene

On the night of March 25, 1965, Mrs. Viola Gregg Liuzzo, age 39, white, was murdered on U.S. Highway 80 in Alabama. She had left her home, husband and five young children in Detroit, Mich., to join a civil-rights protest march from Selma to Montgomery. Outrage rippled across the nation. President Johnson went on television to voice his anger. Michigan's Governor Romney spoke for the public conscience: "This shocking murder can stand for us all as an ironic symbol for the need to battle for the cause for which she died—and to ultimately insure that her death was not in vain."

A few weeks later, a group of 18 young white housewives gathered for a club meeting in the living room of a middle-class development home in the suburb of a medium-sized Northern city to discuss the same Viola Liuzzo, a woman none of them had ever met, the first white woman to die fighting for the cause of Negro civil rights.

"She was wrong in leaving her home and going down there and meddling into something," said one. "I feel sorry for what happened. It was a shame, but I feel she should have stayed home and minded her own business."

Another reflected: "In her mind she probably did exactly what she felt was right. But how *could* she do it, knowing the situation, and knowing there was a chance of her not coming back, with children at home?"

A third club member agreed: "She had no right being down there,

Reprinted from the *Ladies' Home Journal* 82 (July 1965): 42–44.

whatever her feelings were. It wasn't her situation. If it were something that happened in Detroit, then yes."

The group had been called together by *Ladies' Home Journal* to discuss a question raised by the startling results of a national survey. It was a question that transcends even the appalling fate of Mrs. Liuzzo: Did she— indeed, does any mother—have the right to leave her family to fight, perhaps to die, for a cause beyond her own home and family? In their talk these 18 average-income suburban housewives would also, it was hoped, cast some revealing light on the question of how American women really feel about the cause of civil rights.

The women in this comfortable room were in no way extraordinary. Their club activities included projects involving CARE, retarded children and hospital volunteer work. This night, instead, the moderator read a news account of the murder of Viola Liuzzo, then paused, and asked, "Did she, as a mother of five, have a right to leave home and risk her life for a social cause?"

A sudden tautness, almost tangible, gripped the women in the room. There was an explosion of noes.

"I want to know who was taking care of her children," demanded an angry voice.

"Do you know how old they are?" asked the moderator. (The Liuzzo children range from six to 18.) It didn't matter. A mother's place is in the home, said the women, almost in chorus. "What if she has capable help?" No matter. One of the participants put it this way: "I would never leave home and travel any distance to get into something that I'm not familiar with, no matter how strongly I felt about it."

And another chimed in: "I don't feel I have the right to endanger myself and leave my children motherless. The sorrow they would feel at the loss of a mother is greater than any cause. Children can't understand the cause. Their sorrow can turn to resentment. Mrs. Liuzzo may have died in vain after all, if her ideals are not carried on in her children. If they resent her being killed, she hasn't gained a thing—in her family, anyway."

A few dissenting voices:

"She probably felt so strongly, she couldn't have lived with herself if she didn't go. Since her husband was going to be home, and she did have a capable daughter, I think she did the right thing."

And another said: "I don't feel this way, but I'm talking about *her:* If you feel strongly about something, you should do something about it."

Several nodded agreement with the woman who said, "I personally don't feel that anyone from any other area ought to travel to get involved in these demonstrations. If they're in your area and you feel very strongly about the issue, I can see getting involved, but I feel that anyone traveling from one state to another to get involved just gives himself a lot more trouble than is already there."

The stay-at-home forces elaborated:

"There's more to civil rights than demonstrations. You can do so much more by sitting side by side with people, doing things for them, than by marching up and down some street you've never been on in your life. Demonstrations are nothing but publicity and the urge to get in with the mob."

"If you can stand up against the criticism in your own community, I think you've accomplished much more than you could if you go to another city."

"I don't think any woman should neglect her family—her children or her husband—to go out and fight for a cause. There are enough causes in her backyard that she can fight for."

At least one woman in the room was indeed already working in her backyard: "This is what I do. I have a friend who's on the Urban League and another active in civil rights near here. I take their families during the week and then they take mine."

The moderator asked how many had seen any of the march on television. Fifteen had. She asked, "Did this leave anybody with the impression, 'Perhaps I should be there?' "

It had not. Said one: "I turned on the TV, but I became so disgusted with the way things were going, I turned it off."

Suddenly the women were hostile. They wanted to know why the questioning was so intensive. They didn't want to talk about civil rights.

The moderator made peace and returned to Mrs. Liuzzo as an example of a woman who got involved in a cause. "There are *other* causes," she said. "Let's get to the question of how involved a woman can get in *any* cause. Up to what point of taking time away from her family."

There was considerable discussion, and the conclusion was voiced by the mother who said: "I'd march in the street to campaign for a traffic light, because I'd rather take a chance on my getting hit than my child getting hit on the way to school. But if my children weren't involved—no."

Another mother added: "I don't think a mother should go away and leave her children with anyone else no matter what the cause."

From across the room came a thoughtful voice: "You have to define the cause and the word neglect. I was president of this club and it sent me out of town and I went for three days."

Moderator: "How did you get to the other city?"

"We flew." Silence. "There was a danger, yes. I did truthfully think about the flight, but I also think the same way when I leave in an evening and drive the car." Silence. "This is a big question you're asking us."

The moderator smiled. Everyone took a breather—shuffled around, opened windows to clear out the smoke. Then they settled down to think some more.

Would they feel differently about a woman without children? Well, the women said, she would have to have her husband's permission, but perhaps if she felt strongly. . . . Perhaps.

"I was just wondering something," said the woman who had flown out of town, "As I was saying, I could not go and put myself into danger, but what if I was colored? What if all of us were colored, would we be willing to go out and fight for our right to vote? As mothers? I don't think we've thought of that. Would you, if you were colored, go out and fight for this cause?"

"If this were for my children, you mean?" asked a woman. "Definitely."

Silence.

Moderator: "Suppose a man and a woman in a family were equally emotionally involved in a cause, and he said, 'I have to go because I think it is right.' Do you think he would have more of a right to go than she?"

No one said yes.

"The children would be losing a mother or a father either way. I can't see where a cause could be so great as to bring harm to your family." Silence. "Short of war."

Moderator: "*Any* cause?"

"No. In a war you don't have a choice. If we were invaded, then I think we'd fight—all of us. But that's not a voluntary thing, and it would mean getting killed for protecting our families, not for someone to vote or things like that. I wouldn't want my husband to go out and fight for a cause that is indirect—I mean, involving other people."

Moderator: "Do you think it could be possible that a man could think it more important for his children to live under a government that guarantees the right to vote to all people than it is for them to have him home?"

"I think we all like to think we feel that, but no one on this earth really feels that way."

Silence.

A woman raised her hand. She said that she "would not hold her husband responsible if he had been a doctor during the Nazi crimes, refused to do something horrible to someone, and was shot."

When she stopped talking, there was an awful quiet. She had said "Nazi."

From the floor: "You know, I'm thinking now that it's a risk to be president. And yet what would we do without a leader? We just can't all sit back and say, well, that's going to be dangerous, so we can't take the chance. We would be nowhere."

Muttering in the room: "Listen, Johnson's been working for that all his life."

Another voice: "Well, I'm sure those people in the civil-rights movement think the way they live is a slow death, and that's why they're fighting."

Now thoughts began to pop out of every corner of the room:

"When you say that, I think of that girl in New York City who was killed and no one helped her. By helping someone, you endanger your life, but I certainly hope someone would help if it were me or my children or anyone I know . . . or anyone."

"Americans have turned their backs on humanity and love for one another, and I just don't think this is right."

"There's a great difference between finding yourself where help is needed and going out to look for it."

"I was just thinking . . . women, especially mothers, have such a *cozy* place right in their home; I'm one of them. I'm a lazy mother when it comes to any kind of outside crisis—politics, anything. I imagine if there were something I really cared about, I could do something about it, even if it were just making phone calls. I think a lot of women sit back with the attitude, 'Oh, Jane next door will do it, or my husband, or John.' I mean, women fall back on men for things like that."

Silence.

Moderator: "Have any of you ever been moved to any kind of action by newspaper or television pictures of clubbings or other brutalities?"

A woman raised her hand and said she had canceled her newspaper subscription.

Moderator: "Anyone else? Anyone ever disagree with something or been moved enough to do something about a situation . . . any situation?"

"I've canceled magazine subscriptions."

Moderator: "Anyone else? Anything?" Silence. "Well, can any of you think of anything that exists or might exist that would be worth risking your life for?"

A quiet girl mumbled, "My country."

Another added, "Its principles. I think if you'll fight for your country you'll fight for its principles, too."

One woman said, "Religion," and when asked if she meant the right to worship as she pleased, answered: "Yes, that, and to be a missionary."

Silence.

Moderator: "Anyone else? Anything else you would risk your life for, or your husband's?"

Silence. Embarrassed laughter. "We're very generous, aren't we?" commented a woman who was knitting. More laughter. More voices:

"I think it all boils down to the defense of your own family, nationwide or right in your own home. I'd take a chance on my life for my family; and each family feels that will hold the nation together. Each guy looking after his own keeps everybody safe."

"I think just the right to defend the way you want to live your life, as long as it is within the laws of man and God—that sums up the whole thing."

"Then, actually, we can't pass judgment on that woman. She might have thought that cause was stronger than her husband going to war."

"I don't think we have the right to judge her for what she did."

The formal meeting ended there. The hostess served coffee and cupcakes, and women who knew one another well formed small cliques. In one corner there was talk of bowling; in another, talk of house-hunting; and in at least one, some distressed conversation. To some of these women the forum had been a frightening revelation, and they were trying to find a way to say so. "We're not really . . ." they'd begin. Then, "I mean, you have to fight for *something*." One said she was amazed and saddened by "how we'd fight for the material good of our immediate families, but not for an idea." The word "ideals" was never used.

Certainly the forum had served its purpose. We had got raw and open answers to the questions we had brought. However, we came away with two more:

"Can this country today afford the luxury of a new form of isolationism—an isolationism of the heart—any more than it could afford international isolationism yesterday?"

"Can women really manage to make their homes tight little, safe little islands in these days and the days to come?"

The Question

A survey conducted for the *Journal* by a leading research organization, Alfred Politz Research, Inc., revealed that American women's feelings about Viola Liuzzo's right to give her life in Alabama were surprisingly and disturbingly mixed—with 55.2 percent of a national sample feeling that she should have stayed home and 18.4 percent offering no opinion.

Specifically, a fully representative national sample of women was asked: "No matter what your own opinions are on the question of voting rights, do you think that Mrs. Viola Liuzzo, the Detroit civil-rights worker who was killed in the Alabama shooting incident, had a right to leave her five children to risk her life for a social cause, or not?" The answers follow:

And the Answers

	Total %	East %	South %	Central %	West %
Yes	26.4	35.5	15.6	27.5	33.7
No	55.2	51.1	61.2	57.3	45.0
No Opinion	18.4	13.4	23.2	15.2	21.3

Chapter 19

Mothers Who Don't Know How

George Will

The almost silent video is short and sweet. And searing. It gives a glimpse of one reason for America's urban regression, the family pathologies that drive the intergenerational transmission of poverty. At first glance the scene the video captures is sweet, a mother feeding her infant. Ten minutes later, at its end, you understand: the mother does not know how to mother.

Jim Egan, a clinical psychologist in Washington, says the video, from a steady camera focused on a twenty-two-year-old woman and her six-month-old baby, was made as part of a study of "failure to thrive." The mother feeds the baby, which sits on her knee, with a spoon from a bowl. The spoon moves steadily, the baby makes no sound and neither does the mother. The only noise, every minute or so, is the soft sound of the baby vomiting. This occurs each time the baby turns with its hands extended, reaching for contact with the mother's warmth. The mother reflexively— not unkindly, but stiffly—holds the baby away. Then the baby regurgi-tates the food swallowed since the last rebuff. Vomiting, says Egan, is the baby's tactic for maintaining at least the attention of feeding.

Egan sees many babies with bald spots on the back of their heads, evidence that the babies are left for long stretches on their backs. A child-care—actually, noncare—product popular in some ghettos is a pillow made to hold a bottle next to an infant so the infant can take nourishment without an adult in attendance. But the baby in the video is more fortunate.

The baby's mother, like most young mothers in Washington and many

Reprinted from *Suddenly: The American Idea Abroad and at Home, 1986–1990* (New York: Free Press, 1990): 187–89.

other inner cities, is unmarried. But she is not a moral failure, not what was once called a "fallen woman." One cannot fall down from where she started. She has an emotionally disturbed mother, under whose care the child suffered dreadful diaper rashes. The study of "failure to thrive" is, for her, a school of mothering.

It is perhaps natural to think that parenting is a natural talent, a spontaneously acquired, unlearned skill. It is not. It is learned, as language is, early, and largely by parental example. Parents generally parent as their parents did. As the woman feeds her baby she gives the sort of verbal stimulation she probably got from her mother: none.

Depressed, unstimulating or unavailable mothers produce in babies "maternal deprivation syndrome," which suppresses infants' development. A mother reared in poverty is apt to have a barren "inner world" of imagination and emotional energy, a consequence of impoverished early experiences. And such a mother nowadays may be the only nurturing adult in an infant's life. A study of turn-of-the-century Massachusetts showed that 90 percent of households included three or more adults— two parents plus perhaps a grandmother, a bachelor uncle, a maiden aunt. Today many homes have but one adult, and infants are handed around to various caretakers. This can be disorienting and developmentally damaging early in life.

Until the 1940s it was widely believed that it did not matter who raised babies, if basic competence was assured. A good orphanage would do. However, subsequent studies documented the bewilderment, withdrawal and depression of infants who begin but do not adequately complete bonding with their mothers. In too many homes today, says Egan, "the lights are on but no one is home." People are there, but not there. Inattentive parents are producing children who are like that: They seem normal but they are not what they should be, what they could have been.

Verbal stimulation of middle-class infants produces in their babble the sounds of the phonetic alphabet much earlier than those sounds occur in the babble of lower-class children. Will children reared in poverty catch up in school? Probably not. They are not just behind; they are, in a sense, crippled. Animals reared in nonstimulative isolation have been shown to have less brain weight than those reared amid the stimulation of company. Those reared in the stimulative environment have a higher ratio of differentiated (specialized functioning) to undifferentiated brain cells. Egan's chilling inference is that an infant can fail to develop some early brain functions as a consequence of social deprivation.

Children, says Egan, are like computers in that what goes in comes out. And each child gets only one floppy disk. He says there is a critical period early in the developmental process of every infant: The merry-go-round goes around only once and the infant does or does not get the brass ring of the full enjoyment of the potential that was his or her birthright. This fact should shock American sensibilities because it refutes the assumption that equality of opportunity is a fact as long as there are no obvious formal, legal, institutional impediments to it. Hence the vast—and increasingly misplaced—faith in schools as the great equalizers of opportunity for upward mobility in a meritocratic society. But studies of early childhood development indicate that school comes too late for many children. Before they cross their first schoolyard, severe damage has been done to their life chances. Even superb schools could not correct the consequences of early deprivation, and superb schools are not frequently found in the neighborhoods where children damaged by their social environment sustain their damages.

Failing families concentrated in a particular class cause urban regression, but Americans recoil from the fact of class. We see our society through ideologically tinted spectacles that filter out unpleasant evidence, such as: 15 percent of IQ points are experientially rather than genetically based, and the preschool experiences of ghetto children can cost them a significant portion of those points.

Studies of "failure to thrive" babies and their mothers suggest a strategy for combating the syndrome, but the studies also indicate that the strategy cannot be a public health policy. Very early intervention, involving close and protracted supervision of young unmarried mothers, can "jump-start" their mothering skills. But there are too many single mothers who need this long, labor-intensive and therefore expensive attention.

As regards incompetent parenting, there also are, Egan emphasizes, gilded ghettos. Their residents include "privileged" children of parents too affluent for their children's good, parents able and eager to give children anything but attention, measuring out what these parents are pleased to call "quality time" in dribs and drabs. There are more ghettos—and more damages to children—than meet the eye.

Part IV

"Bad" Mothering of Late

Chapter 20

"Fetal Rights"
A New Assault on Feminism

Katha Pollitt

Some scenes from the way we live now:

- In New York City, a pregnant woman orders a glass of wine with her restaurant meal. A stranger comes over to her table. "Don't you know you're poisoning your baby?" he says angrily, pointing to a city-mandated sign warning women that drinking during pregnancy can cause birth defects.

- In California, Pamela Rae Stewart is advised by her obstetrician to stay off her feet, to eschew sex and "street drugs," and to go to the hospital immediately if she starts to bleed. She fails to follow this advice and delivers a brain-damaged baby who soon dies. She is charged with failing to deliver support to a child under an old criminal statute that was intended to force men to provide for women they have made pregnant.

- In Washington, D.C., a hospital administration asks a court whether it should intervene and perform a caesarean section on Angela Carder, seriously ill with cancer, against her wishes and those of her husband, her parents and her doctors. Acknowledging that the operation would probably shorten her life without necessarily saving the life of her twenty-five-week-old fetus, the judge nonetheless provides the order. The caesarean is performed immediately, before her lawyers can appeal. Angela Carder dies; so does her unviable fetus. That incident is subsequently dramatized on *L.A. Law*, with postfeminist softy Ann Kelsey arguing for the hospital; on TV the baby lives.

- In the Midwest, the U.S. Court of Appeals for the Seventh Circuit, ruling in *UAW v. Johnson Controls,* upholds an automotive battery plant's seven-year-old "fetal protection policy" barring fertile women (in effect, all women) from jobs that would expose them to lead (see Carolyn Marshall, "An Excuse for Workplace Hazard," April 25, 1987). The court discounts testimony about the individual reproductive lives and plans of female employees (many in their late forties, celibate and/or with completed families), testimony showing that no child born to female employees had shown ill effects traceable to lead exposure and testimony showing that lead poses a comparable danger to male reproductive health. The court accepts testimony that says making the workplace safe would be too expensive.

All over the country, pregnant women who use illegal drugs and/or alcohol are targeted by the criminal justice system. They are "preventively detained" by judges who mete out jail sentences for minor crimes that would ordinarily result in probation or a fine; charged with child abuse or neglect (although by law the fetus is not a child) and threatened with manslaughter charges should they miscarry; and placed under court orders not to drink, although drinking is not a crime and does not invariably (or even usually) result in birth defects. While state legislatures ponder bills that would authorize these questionable practices by criminalizing drug use or "excessive" alcohol use during pregnancy (California senator Pete Wilson is pushing a similar bill at the federal level), mothers are arrested in their hospital beds when their newborns test positive for drugs. Social workers increasingly remove positive-testing babies into foster care on the presumption that even a single use of drugs during pregnancy renders a mother ipso facto an unfit parent.

What's going on here? Right now the hot area in the developing issue of "fetal rights" is the use of drugs and alcohol during pregnancy. We've all seen the nightly news reports of inner-city intensive care units overflowing with crack babies, of Indian reservations where one in four children are said to be born physically and mentally stunted by fetal alcohol syndrome (FAS) or the milder, but still serious, fetal alcohol effect. We've read the front-page stories reporting studies that suggest staggering rates of drug use during pregnancy (11 percent, according to the *New York Times,* or 375,000 women per year) and the dangers of even moderate drinking during pregnancy.

But drugs and alcohol are only the latest focus of a preoccupation with the fetus and its "rights" that has been wandering around the zeitgeist for the past decade. A few years ago, the big issue was forced caesareans. (It was, in fact, largely thanks to the horrific Angela Carder case—one of the few involving a white, middle-class woman—that the American College of Obstetricians and Gynecologists condemned the practice, which nonetheless has not entirely ceased.) If the Supreme Court upholds the *Johnson Controls* decision, the next battleground may be the workplace. The "save the babies" mentality may look like a necessary, if troubling, approach when it's a matter of keeping a drug addict away from a substance that is, after all, illegal. What happens if the same mentality is applied to some 15 million to 20 million highly paid unionized jobs in heavy industry to "protect" fetuses that do not even exist? Or if the list of things women are put on legal notice to avoid expands to match medical findings on the dangers to the fetus posed by junk food, salt, aspirin, air travel, and cigarettes?

Critics of the punitive approach to pregnant drug and alcohol users point out the ironies inherent in treating a public-health concern as a matter for the criminal justice system: the contradiction, for instance, of punishing addicted women when most drug treatment programs refuse to accept pregnant women. Indeed, Jennifer Johnson, a Florida woman who was the first person convicted after giving birth to a baby who tested positive for cocaine, had sought treatment and been turned away. (In her case the charge was delivering drugs to a minor.) The critics point out that threats of jail or the loss of their kids may drive women away from prenatal care and hospital deliveries, and that almost all the women affected so far have been poor and black or Latino, without private doctors to protect them (in Florida, nonwhite women are ten times as likely to be reported for substance abuse as white women, although rates of drug use are actually higher for whites).

These are all important points. But they leave unchallenged the notion of fetal rights itself. What we really ought to be asking is, How have we come to see women as the major threat to the health of their newborns, and the womb as the most dangerous place a child will ever inhabit? Why is our basic model "innocent" fetuses that would be fine if only presumably "guilty" women refrained from indulging their "whims"? The list of dangers to the fetus is after all, very long; the list of dangers to children even longer. Why does maternal behavior, a relatively small piece of the total picture, seem such an urgent matter, while much more important factors—that one in five pregnant women receive no prenatal care at all, for instance—attract so little attention? Here are some of the strands that make up the current tangle that is fetal rights.

The Assault on the Poor

It would be pleasant to report that the aura of crisis surrounding crack and FAS babies—the urge to do *something,* however unconstitutional or cruel, that suddenly pervades society, from judge's bench to chic dinner party to seven o'clock news—was part of a massive national campaign to help women have healthy, wanted pregnancies and healthy babies. But significantly, the current wave of concern is not occurring in that context. Judges order pregnant addicts to jail, but they don't order drug treatment programs to accept them, or Medicaid, which pays for heroin treatment, to cover crack addiction—let alone order landlords not to evict them, or obstetricians to take uninsured women as patients, or the federal government to fund fully the Women, Infants, and Children supplemental feeding program, which reaches only two-thirds of those who are eligible. The policies that have underwritten maternal and infant health in most of the industrialized West since World War II—a national health service, paid maternity leave, direct payments to mothers, government-funded day care, home health visitors for new mothers, welfare payments that reflect the cost of living—are still regarded in the United States by even the most liberal as hopeless causes, and by everyone else as budget-breaking giveaways to the undeserving, pie-in-the-sky items from a mad socialist's wish list.

The focus on maternal behavior allows the government to appear to be concerned about babies without having to spend any money, change any priorities, or challenge any vested interests. As with crime, as with poverty, a complicated, multifaceted problem is construed as a matter of freely chosen individual behavior. We have crime because we have lots of bad people, poverty because we have lots of lazy people (Republican version) or lots of pathological people (Democratic version), and tiny, sickly, impaired babies because we have lots of women who just don't give a damn.

Once the problem has been defined as original sin, coercion and punishment start to look like hardheaded and commonsensical answers. Thus, syndicated columnist and *New Republic* intellectual Charles Krauthammer proposes locking up pregnant drug users en masse. Never mind the impracticality of the notion—suddenly the same Administration that refuses to pay for drug treatment and prenatal care is supposed to finance all that plus nine months of detention for hundreds of thousands of women a year. Or its disregard of real life—what, for example, about the children those women already have? Do they go to jail, too, like Little Dorrit? Or join the rolls of the notorious foster care system? The satisfactions of the punitive mind-set sweep all such considerations aside. (Nor are liberal pundits immune from its spell. Around the same time Krauthammer was calling for mass incarceration, Mary McGrory was suggesting that we stop wasting resources—*what* resources?—on addicted women and simply put their babies in orphanages.)

The New Temperance

While rightly sounding the alarm about the health risks and social costs of drugs, alcohol, and nicotine, the various "just say no" crusades have so upped the moral ante across the board that it is now difficult to distinguish between levels and kinds of substance use and abuse and even rather suspect to try. A joint on the weekend is the moral equivalent of a twenty-four-hour-a-day crack habit; wine with meals is next door to a daily quart of rotgut. The stigmatizing of addicts, casual users, alcoholics, social drinkers, and smokers makes punitive measures against them palatable. It also helps us avoid uncomfortable questions about why we are having all these "substance abuse" epidemics in the first place. Finally, it lets us assume, not always correctly, that drugs and alcohol, all by themselves, cause harm during pregnancy, and ignore the role of malnutrition, violence, chaotic lives, serious maternal health problems, and lack of medical care.

Science Marches On

We know a lot more about fetal development than we did twenty years ago. But how much of what we know will we continue to know in ten years? As recently as the early 1970s, pregnant women were harassed by their doctors to keep their weight down. They were urged to take tranquilizers and other prescription drugs, to drink in moderation (liquor was routinely used to stop premature labor), to deliver under anesthesia, and not bother to breast-feed. Then too, studies examined contemporary wisdom and found it good. Today, those precepts seem the obvious expression of social forces: the wish of doctors to control pregnancy and delivery, a lack of respect for women, and a distaste for female physiological processes. It was not the disinterested progress of science that outmoded these practices. It was another set of social forces: the women's movement, the prepared-childbirth movement, and the natural-health movement.

What about today's precepts? At the very least, the history of scientific research into pregnancy and childbirth ought to make us skeptical. Instead, we leap to embrace tentative findings and outright bad science because they fit current social prejudices. Those who argue for total abstinence during pregnancy have made much, for example, of a recent study in the *New England Journal of Medicine* that claimed women are more vulnerable than men to alcohol because they have less of a stomach enzyme that neutralizes it before it enters the bloodstream. Universally unreported, however, was the fact that the study included alcoholics and patients with gastrointestinal disease. It is a basic rule of medical research that results cannot be generalized from the sick to the healthy.

In a 1989 article in *The Lancet*, "Bias against the Null Hypothesis: The Reproductive Hazards of Cocaine," Canadian researchers reported that studies that found a connection between cocaine use and poor pregnancy outcome had a better than even chance of being accepted for presentation at the annual meeting of the Society for Pediatric Research, while studies that found no connection had a negligible chance—although the latter were better designed. While it's hard to imagine that anyone will ever show that heavy drug use or alcohol consumption is good for fetal development, studies like this one suggest that when the dust settles (because the drug war is officially "won"? because someone finally looks at the newborns of Italy, where everyone drinks moderate amounts of wine with food, and finds them to be perfectly fine?) the current scientific wisdom will look alarmist.

Media Bias

The assumptions that shape the way researchers frame their studies and the questions they choose to investigate are magnified by bias in the news media. Studies that show the bad effects of maternal behavior make the headlines, studies that show no bad effects don't get reported, and studies that show the bad effects of paternal behavior (alcoholic males, and males who drink at conception, have been linked to lower IQ and a propensity to alcoholism in offspring) get two paragraphs in the science section. So did the study, briefly mentioned in a recent issue of the *New York Times,* suggesting that housewives run a higher risk than working women of having premature babies, stillbirths, underweight babies, and babies who die in the first week of life. Imagine the publicity had it come out the other way around! Numbers that back up the feeling of crisis (those 375,000 drug-taking pregnant women) are presented as monolithic, although they cover a wide range of behavior (from daily use of cocaine to marijuana use during delivery, which some midwives recommend, and for which one Long Island woman lost custody of her newborn for eight months), and are illustrated by dire examples of harm that properly apply only to the most hard-core cases.

The 'Pro-Life' Movement

Antichoicers have not succeeded in criminalizing abortion but they have made it inaccessible to millions of women (only sixteen states pay for poor women's abortions, and only 18 percent of counties have even one abortion provider) and made it a badge of sin and failure for millions more. In Sweden, where heavy drinking is common, relatively few FAS babies are born, because alcoholic women have ready access to abortion and it is not a stigmatized choice. In America antichoice sentiment makes it impossible to suggest to a homeless, malnourished, venereally diseased crack addict that her first priority ought to be getting well: Get help, then have a baby. While the possibility of coerced abortions is something to be wary of, the current policy of regulation and punishment in the name of the fetus ironically risks the same end. Faced with criminal charges, pregnant women may seek abortions in order to stay out of jail (a Washington, D.C., woman who "miscarried" a few days before sentencing may have done just that).

As lobbyists, antichoicers have sought to bolster their cause by interjecting the fetus-as-person argument into a wide variety of situations that would seem to have nothing to do with abortion. They have fought to exclude pregnant women from proposed legislation recognizing the validity of "living wills" that reject the use of life support systems (coma baby lives!), and have campaigned to classify as homicides assaults on pregnant women that result in fetal death or miscarriage. Arcane as such proposals may seem, they have the effect of broadening little by little the areas of the law in which the fetus is regarded as a person, and in which the woman is regarded as its container.

At a deeper level, the "pro-life" movement has polluted the way we think about pregnancy. It has promoted a model of pregnancy as a condition that by its very nature pits women and fetuses against each other, with the fetus invariably taking precedence, and a model of women as selfish, confused, potentially violent, and incapable of making responsible choices. As the "rights" of the fetus grow and respect for the capacities and rights of women declines, it becomes harder and harder to explain why drug addiction is a crime if it produces an addicted baby, but not if it produces a miscarriage, and why a woman can choose abortion but not vodka. And that is just what the "pro-lifers" want.

The Privileged Status of the Fetus

Pro-choice activists rightly argue that antiabortion and fetal-rights advocates grant fetuses more rights than women. A point less often made is that they grant fetuses more rights than two-year-olds—the right, for example, to a safe, healthy place to live. No court in this country would ever rule that a parent must undergo a medical procedure in order to benefit a child, even if that procedure is as riskless as a blood donation and the child is sure to die without it. (A Seattle woman is currently suing the father of her leukemic child to force him to donate bone marrow, but she is sure to lose, and her mere attempt roused *Newsday* science writer B. D. Colen to heights of choler unusual even for him.) Nor would a court force someone who had promised to donate a kidney and then changed his mind to keep his date with the organ bank. Yet, as the forced-caesarean issue shows, we seem willing to deny the basic right of bodily integrity to pregnant women and to give the fetus rights we deny children.

Although concern for the fetus may look like a way of helping children, it is actually, in a funny way, a substitute for it. It is an illusion to think that by "protecting" the fetus from its mother's behavior we have insured a healthy birth, a healthy infancy, or a healthy childhood, and that the only insurmountable obstacle for crack babies is prenatal exposure to crack.

It is no coincidence that we are obsessed with pregnant women's behavior at the same time that children's health is declining, by virtually any yardstick one chooses. Take general well-being: In constant dollars, welfare payments are now about two-thirds the 1965 level. Take housing: Thousands of children are now growing up in homeless shelters and welfare hotels. Even desperately alcoholic women bear healthy babies two-thirds of the time. Will two-thirds of today's homeless kids emerge unscathed from their dangerous and lead-permeated environments? Take access to medical care: Inner-city hospitals are closing all over the country, millions of kids have no health insurance, and most doctors refuse uninsured or Medicaid patients. Even immunization rates are down: Whooping cough and measles are on the rise.

The 'Duty of Care'

Not everyone who favors legal intervention to protect the fetus is antichoice. Some pro-choicers support the coercion and punishment of addicts and alcoholics—uneasily, like some of my liberal women friends, or gleefully, like Alan Dershowitz, who dismisses as absurd the "slippery slope" argument (crack today, cigarettes tomorrow) he finds so persuasive when applied to First Amendment issues. For some years now bioethicists have been fascinated by the doctrine of "duty of care," expounded most rigorously by Margery Shaw and John Robertson. In this view, a woman can abort, but once she has decided to bear a child she has a moral, and should have a legal, responsibility to insure a healthy birth. It's an attractive notion because it seems to combine an acceptance of abortion with intuitive feelings shared by just about everyone, including this writer, that pregnancy is a serious undertaking, that society has an interest in the health of babies, that the fetus, although not a person, is also not property.

Whatever its merits as a sentiment, though, the duty of care is a legal disaster. Exactly when, for instance, does the decision to keep a pregnancy take place? For the most desperately addicted—the crack addicts who live on the subway or prostitute themselves for drugs—one may ask if they ever form any idea ordinary people would call a decision, or indeed know they are pregnant until they are practically in labor. Certainly the inaccessibility of abortion denies millions of women the ability to decide.

But for almost all women the decision to carry a pregnancy to term has important, if usually unstated, qualifications. What one owes the fetus is balanced against other considerations, such as serious health risks to oneself (taking chemotherapy or other crucial medication), or the need to feed one's family (keeping a job that may pose risks) or to care for the children one already has (not getting the bed rest the doctor says you need). Why should pregnant women be barred from considering their own interests? It is, after all, what parents do all the time. The model of women's relation to the fetus proposed by the duty of care ethicists is an abstraction that ignores the realities of life even when they affect the fetus itself. In real life, for instance, to quit one's dangerous job means to lose one's health insurance, thus exposing the fetus to another set of risks.

It is also, even as an abstraction, a false picture. Try as she might, a woman cannot insure a healthy newborn; nor can statistical studies of probability (even well-designed ones) be related in an airtight way to individual cases. We know that cigarettes cause lung cancer, but try proving in a court of law that cigarettes and not air pollution, your job, your genes, or causes unknown caused *your* lung cancer.

Yet far from shrinking from the slippery slope, duty of care theorists positively hurl themselves down it. Margery Shaw, for instance, believes that the production of an imperfect newborn should make a woman liable to criminal charges and "wrongful life" suits if she knows, or should have known, the risk involved in her behavior, whether it's drinking when her period is late (she has a duty to keep track of her cycle), delivering at home when her doctor advises her not to (what doctor doesn't?), or failing to abort a genetically damaged fetus (which she has a duty to find out about). So much for that "decision" to bear a child—a woman can't qualify it in her own interests, but the state can revoke it for her on eugenic grounds.

As these examples show, there is no way to limit the duty of care to cases of flagrant or illegal misbehavior—duty is duty, and risk is risk. Thus, there is no way to enshrine duty of care in law without creating the sort of Romania-style fetal-police state whose possibility Dershowitz, among others, pooh-poohs. For there is no way to define the limits of what a pregnant woman must sacrifice for fetal benefit, or what she "should have known," or at what point a trivial risk becomes significant. My aunt advised me to get rid of my cats while I was pregnant because of the risk of toxoplasmosis. My doctor and I thought this rather extreme, and my husband simply took charge of the litter box. What if my doctor had backed up my aunt instead of me? If the worst had happened (and it always does to someone, somewhere), would I have been charged with the crime of not sending my cats to the Bide-A-Wee?

Although duty of care theorists would impose upon women a virtually limitless obligation to put the fetus first, they impose that responsibility *only* on women. Philosophy being what it is, perhaps it should not surprise us that they place no corresponding duty upon society as a whole. But what about Dad? It's his kid too, after all. His drug and alcohol use, his prescription medications, his workplace exposure and general habits of health not only play a part in determining the quality of his sperm but affect the course of pregnancy as well. Cocaine dust and smoke from crack, marijuana, and tobacco present dangers to others who breathe them; his alcoholism often bolsters hers. Does he have a duty of care to make it possible for his pregnant partner to obey those judge's orders and that doctor's advice that now has the force of law? To quit his job to mind the children so that she can get the bed rest without which her fetus may be harmed? Apparently not.

The sexist bias of duty of care has already had alarming legal consequences. In the Pamela Rae Stewart case cited at the beginning of this article, Stewart's husband, who had heard the doctor's advice, ignored it all and beat his wife into the bargain. Everything she did, he did—they had sex together, smoked pot together, delayed getting to the hospital together—but he was not charged with a crime, not even with wife beating, although no one can say that his assaults were not a contributing cause of the infant's injury and death. In Tennessee, a husband succeeded in getting a court order forbidding his wife to drink or take drugs, although he himself had lost his driver's license for driving while intoxicated. In Wyoming, a pregnant woman was arrested for drinking when she presented herself at the hospital for treatment of injuries inflicted by her husband. Those charges were dropped (to be reinstated, should her baby be born with defects), but none were instituted against her spouse.

It is interesting to note in this regard that approximately one in twelve women are beaten during pregnancy, a time when many previously nonviolent men become brutal. We do not know how many miscarriages, stillbirths, and damaged newborns are due, or partly due, to male violence—this is itself a comment on the skewed nature of supposedly objective scientific research. But if it ever does come to be an officially recognized factor in fetal health, the duty of care would probably take yet another ironic twist and hold battered pregnant women liable for their partner's assaults.

The Broken Cord, Michael Dorris's much-praised memoir of his adopted FAS child, Adam, is a textbook example of the way in which all these social trends come together—and the largely uncritical attention the book has received shows how seductive a pattern they make. Dorris has nothing but contempt for Adam's birth mother. Perhaps it is asking too much of human nature to expect him to feel much sympathy for her. He has witnessed, in the most intimate and heartbreaking way, the damage her alcoholism did, and seen the ruin of his every hope for Adam, who is deeply retarded. But why is his anger directed only at her? Here was a seriously alcoholic woman, living on an Indian reservation where heavy drinking is a way of life, along with poverty, squalor, violence, despair, and powerlessness, where, one might even say, a kind of racial suicide is taking place, with liquor as the weapon of choice. Adam's mother, in fact, died two years after his birth from drinking antifreeze.

Dorris dismisses any consideration of these facts as bleeding-heart fuzzy-mindedness. Like Hope on *thirtysomething,* Adam's mother "decides" to have a baby; like the martini-sipping pregnant woman Dorris badgers in an airport bar, she "chooses" to drink out of "weakness" and "self-indulgence."

Dorris proposes preventive detention of alcoholic pregnant women and quotes sympathetically a social worker who thinks the real answer is sterilization. Why do alcoholic Indian women have so many children? To up their government checks. (In fact, Bureau of Indian Affairs hospitals are prohibited by law from performing abortions, even if women can pay for them.) And why, according to Dorris, do they drink so much in the first place? Because of the feminist movement, which has undermined the traditional temperance of reservation women.

The women's movement has had about as much effect on impoverished reservation dwellers as it had on the slum women of eighteenth-century London, whose heavy binge drinking—and stunted babies—appalled contemporary observers. That Dorris pins the blame on such an improbable villain points to what fetal rights is really about: controlling women. It's a reaction to legalized abortion and contraception, which have given women, for the first time in history, real reproductive power. They can have a baby, they can "kill" a baby, they can refuse to conceive at all, without asking permission from anyone. More broadly, it's an index of deep discomfort with the notion of women as self-directed social beings, for whom parenthood is only one aspect of life, as it has always been for men. Never mind that in the real world, women still want children, have children, and take care of children, often under the most discouraging circumstances and at tremendous emotional, economic, and physical cost. There is still a vague but powerful cultural fear that one of these days, women will just walk out on the whole business of motherhood and the large helpings of humble pie we have, as a society, built into that task. And *then* where will we be?

Looked at in this light, the inconsistent and fitful nature of our concern about the health of babies forms a pattern. The threat to newborns is interesting when and only when it can, accurately or fancifully, be laid at women's doorstep. Babies "possibly" impaired by maternal drinking? Front-page stories, a national wave of alarm. A *New England Journal of Medicine* report that 16 percent of American children have been mentally and neurologically damaged because of exposure to lead, mostly from flaking lead paint in substandard housing? Peter Jennings looks mournful and suggests that "all parents can do" is to have their children tested frequently. If the mother isn't to blame, no one is to blame.

In its various aspects "fetal rights" attacks virtually all the gains of the women's movement. Forced medical treatment attacks women's increased control over pregnancy and delivery by putting doctors back in the driver's seat, with judges to back them up. The *Johnson Controls* decision reverses the entry of women into high-paying, unionized, traditionally male jobs. In the female ghetto, where women can hardly be dispensed with, the growing practice of laying off or shifting pregnant women around transforms women, whose rates of labor-force participation are approaching those of men, into casual laborers with reduced access to benefits, pensions, seniority, and promotions. In a particularly vicious twist of the knife, "fetal rights" makes legal abortion—which makes all the other gains possible—the trigger for a loss of human rights. Like the divorce-court judges who tell middle-aged housewives to go out and get a job, or who favor fathers in custody disputes because to recognize the primary-caretaker role of mothers would be "sexist," protectors of the fetus enlist the rhetoric of feminism to punish women.

There are lots of things wrong with the concept of fetal rights. It posits a world in which women will be held accountable, on sketchy or no evidence, for birth defects; in which all fertile women will be treated as potentially pregnant all the time; in which courts, employers, social workers, and doctors—not to mention nosy neighbors and vengeful male partners—will monitor women's behavior. It imposes responsibilities without giving women the wherewithal to fulfill them, and places upon women alone duties that belong to both parents and to the community.

But the worst thing about fetal rights is that it portrays a woman as having only contingent value. Her work, her health, her choices and needs and beliefs can all be set aside in an instant because, next to maternity, they are all perceived as trivial. For the middle class, fetal rights is mostly symbolic, the gateway to a view of motherhood as self-sacrifice and endless guilty soul-searching. It ties in neatly with the currently fashionable suspicion of working mothers, day care, and (now that wives are more likely than husbands to sue for it) divorce. For the poor, for whom it means jail and the loss of custody, it becomes a way of saying that women can't even be mothers. They can only be potting soil.

The plight of addicted and alcohol-impaired babies is indeed a tragedy. Finally, we are forced to look at the results of our harsh neglect of the welfare and working poor, and it's only natural that we don't like what we see. We are indeed in danger of losing a generation. But what about the generation we already have? Why is it so hard for us to see that the tragedy of Adam Dorris is inextricable from the tragedy of his mother? Why is her loss—to society, to herself—so easy to dismiss?

"People are always talking about women's duties to others," said Lynn Paltrow, the ACLU lawyer who successfully led the Pamela Rae Stewart defense, "as though women were not the chief caregivers in this society. But no one talks about women's duty of care to *themselves*. A pregnant addict or alcoholic needs to get help for *herself*. She's not just potentially ruining someone else's life. She's ruining her own life.

"Why isn't her own life important? Why don't we care about her?"

NOTE

This essay originally appeared in the *Nation* 250 (March 26, 1990).

Chapter 21

Breastfeeding in the 1990s

The Karen Carter Case and the Politics of Maternal Sexuality

Lauri Umansky

On a snowy night in January 1991, a twenty-eight-year-old single mother made a frantic phone call to her local crisis center. "Is it normal to feel aroused while nursing?" she asked the volunteer who took the call. Worried about possible child sexual abuse, the volunteer notified the police. It would be a full year before Karen Carter regained custody of her two-year-old daughter.[1]

Carter's case is both more and less unusual than others it resembles. Questions of propriety in breastfeeding seem to trouble Americans. Occasionally the cultural confusion in this realm makes its way into the courts and the legislatures. A few states have passed laws specifying the "right to breastfeed" in public, for example, while intense opposition has stymied such legislation in other states.[2] Nor are the allegations of sexual abuse levied against Carter or the difficulties she experienced in extricating herself from the grip of the Department of Social Services (DSS) unique to her case. The slippery terrain of abuse charges and the inefficient workings of social service systems throughout the nation represent troubling but not novel problems.[3] Moreover, the volunteer's panicked response to the concurrent mention of motherhood and sexuality reflects a well-documented pattern: mothers, especially single or divorced mothers, can risk social opprobrium and possible legal consequences when they lead sexually active lives.[4] These aspects of the Carter story illustrate how multiple definitions of the "bad" mother can cohere in a single case, bringing to bear on one woman's life the weight of a culture fraught with uncertainty about mothering, about female sexuality, and especially about the boundaries where the two meet.

The immediate chain of events began on January 12, 1991. That evening, Carter called a local volunteer hotline in her mid-sized northeastern city with some questions about breastfeeding. An adherent of the La Leche League philosophy, which encourages parents to allow children to wean themselves, Carter had no serious qualms about nursing a child of almost three years.[5] She did feel disturbed by her recent feelings of sexual arousal while nursing. In her worldview, shaped strongly by evangelical, "born again" Christianity, these sexual sensations seemed odd and somehow wrong. Carter decided to seek reassurance. No stranger to the network of social services and hotlines serving parents under stress, she called the central volunteer hotline, which serves as a clearinghouse for all such services in her area, seeking the number of La Leche League. The central hotline forwarded the call, because of its "sexual" nature, to the rape crisis center instead. The rape crisis center "hotlined" her, that is, traced her number and turned her in to the police on suspicion of child sexual abuse. Taken to the police station for five hours of questioning, she was finally read her rights and charged with "sexual abuse in the first degree."[6] Specifically, the charges mentioned "mouth to breast contact" and "hand to breast contact." DSS took Carter's two-year-old daughter, Melissa, into protective custody, where she would remain for the better part of a year.

After a weekend in jail, Carter saw the charges dropped outright by the criminal court on Monday morning. However, DSS kept her daughter and immediately filed charges of abuse and neglect in family court. With Melissa in foster care, the family court handed down a decision nearly three months later. The presiding judge, like the criminal court judge before him, dismissed the case, citing a failure of proof. But DSS, armed with a whole new set of allegations, filed a petition before a second judge. The imminent danger hearing that resulted from these allegations dragged on over a period of five months, until the court released Melissa into the custody of her grandparents in August of 1991. A third judge decided ultimately, in November of 1991, that no abuse had taken place but that Melissa suffered from neglect. After a number of delays, Karen Carter finally regained custody of Melissa in January of 1992, a year from the date of the original accusations, with many conditions attached to her release and with the ultimate right to supervision still residing in DSS.

The foregoing is the barest outline of a complex case. As soon as DSS filed its second petition, the issues inhering in the case mushroomed from philosophical differences over the proper time to wean a child to more robust, all-around attempts to prove the mother unfit.[7] After many rounds of interrogation, Melissa began to name not only her mother, but also her grandparents, her uncles and aunt, and her preschool teacher as perpetrators of sexual abuse against her. The court listened to DSS quoting Melissa's reports of rectal temperature taking as instances of vaginal penetration, only to determine, eventually, that Mother inserted the thermometer into the rectum from a frontal position in order to maintain eye contact and to comfort the child throughout the procedure. In short, these allegations, along with hearsay suggestions of naked orgies involving the extended Carter family and various other charges, were found impossible to prove, even in the relative free-for-all of family court, where hearsay is often admissible as evidence. The child, after months of foster care, multiple physical examinations which produced no physical evidence of abuse, and over thirty interrogations, was judged to be an unreliable reporter.

Horrifying and potentially damaging, these unsubstantiated accusations of abuse did not form the basis of Karen Carter's final "conviction" in family court. Instead, Carter's confidential psychiatric and counseling records were subpoenaed, and her own ambivalent feelings about her sexuality and her mothering ability were used to indict her.

Carter's records revealed that although she had been valedictorian of her high school class and was college-educated, she also had a history of depression, marked by intermittent bouts of emotional crisis since the age of eighteen, including four short psychiatric hospitalizations. In and out of episodes of emotional distress, Carter had learned, long before she gave birth to Melissa, how to gain access to a variety of social service agencies, shelters, and crisis hotlines.[8] This very readiness to seek help, as well as the psychiatric record itself, would later be used against her.

In contrast, a stabilizing force in Carter's life had been her deep-seated religious beliefs and her relationship with her pastor and his family, with whom she had lived for the year prior to the one in which she became pregnant with Melissa.[9] Soon after moving in with this family, Carter located a therapist through a local, private, nondenominational Christian organization. The counselor she obtained through this organization had received training in pastoral counseling through her employers but had no formal training in psychology or counseling outside of that framework.[10] In five years of work with Janet Miller, Carter began to explore her own memories of sexual abuse and her conflicted feelings about sex in general. She found these topics excruciating, because her religious framework taught her to shun any sexual acts outside of marriage, including masturbation. Yet Carter, since the age of twenty-two, had begun to have sex occasionally, so that by the age of twenty-eight, when she was asked in court to tally up her sexual partners, she reported a lifetime total of eight, all adult men. In the context of her therapy, Carter came to see this level of sexual activity as extremely problematic—as a compulsion even. Miller referred her to the self-help, Twelve-Step program Sexaholics Anonymous, modeled after the better-known Alcoholics Anonymous. Carter began to attend Sexaholics Anonymous meetings and to adopt the terminology of the group. In her therapy with Miller, she referred to herself as a "sexual addict," and her therapist adopted the same language.

In court, this "sexual addict" label got tossed about with alacrity. Miller testified that Carter, who had training in practical nursing, had taken out an ad in a local newspaper, reading "'Nurse wants to play doctor.' " When asked by the counsel for the county if Carter had contacted any of the respondents to the ad, Miller replied affirmatively and then, unprompted, added that Carter "was highly active in her sexual addiction." With that fuel, the county probed on: "And at that point that's when she began having sex?" Yes, Miller assented. Thus, according to Miller, the point at which Carter began to have sex marked the onset of an "addiction," which was to last "about 18 months," before Carter "dealt with her addiction" through therapy and involvement in Sexaholics Anonymous. In other words, according to the therapist whose "diagnosis" of sexual addiction would remain unchallenged throughout Carter's various hearings, any sexual activity at all (outside of marriage, one presumes) constituted a pathology.

On direct examination, Carter also spoke of her struggle to deal with what her own attorney called, variously, "sexual promiscuity" or the need to "sexually act out." The attorney, Alexis Allison, was actually at pains to show that Carter had never directed her sexual urges toward children, and that she had sought appropriate help, through therapy and the Sexaholics Anonymous program, for her "problem." But in establishing that nothing in Carter's past pointed toward a propensity to abuse children, Allison also valorized the notion that sexual desire of any sort, in an adult, unmarried woman, constitutes a problem in need of therapeutic amelioration. Allison's questioning led Carter to refer to all of her sexual experiences with men as instances of "sexually acting out." Rather than challenging the idea of sexual addiction, Allison tried to show, first, that Carter had ceased her sexual "acting out." Allison did this by eliciting from her client that Carter had been abstinent, excluding instances of masturbation, since learning of her pregnancy with Melissa. Second, Allison herself referred to "sexual promiscuity" as a "problem" that Sexaholics Anonymous had "helped" Carter to resolve.

Allison was not the only person to follow Miller's and Carter's lead in this damaging process of labeling. Testimony for the county by a volunteer at a local women's shelter referred to a crisis telephone conversation with Karen Carter in which Carter allegedly "talked a lot about her sexual addiction." The volunteer testified that Carter "told me that she was a sexual addict. She talked to me about not knowing who Melissa's father was. She said that . . . it's a wonder we both don't have AIDS." This line of testimony went uninterrupted by objection, and Carter's attorney did not challenge the use of the label "sexual addict" in cross-examination.

The court did not rely solely on the judgment of Janet Miller or the various quasi-professional workers who had spoken to Carter on hotlines or in shelters. Rather, the court allowed the county and the respondent to present professional psychological evaluations, to try to determine whether sexual misconduct had taken place. Ironically, the "expert" evaluation of psychologist Jennifer Sloan, engaged by Carter, weighed heavily in the eventual judicial decision to label Carter a "neglectful" mother. Notably, Sloan, too, used the label of sexual addict, as introduced by Carter herself pursuant to her course of treatment by Janet Miller, as if it were an accepted diagnostic term. With no explanation of the term, Sloan writes in her report that "Ms. Carter's level of sexual addiction is unclear," but that she seemed to be tackling this "addiction" and had "made many gains in this area including abstinence from masturbation, abstinence from inappropriate sexual contacts and from placing her daughter at risk from men." However, Sloan continues, Carter had, at times, demonstrated "secrecy" about her sexual addiction, thus contributing to a "lack of response or of attention by service providers to the issue."[11] Sloan's final recommendation was that "Melissa remain in foster care for a brief period of time in order to give Ms. Carter an opportunity to focus her attentions on her sexual addiction. Just as it would be inappropriate for an alcoholic to work on beginning stages of treatment while remaining in a home with liberal access to alcohol, it would be inappropriate at this time to expect Ms. Carter to provide primary caretaking responsibilities for Melissa while she is at an early stage of treatment for her sexual addiction."

Like Miller, Sloan lauded absolute abstinence from sexual activity, including masturbation. She seemed to assume that a sexual mother, or a sexual single mother, harbored an addiction that would necessarily harm the child. To regain the right to be the custodial parent of her own child, Carter was directed to cease all sexual activity, a redundant request for a woman who had testified in court that she had not had sexual contact with anyone for almost four years.

The court quoted Sloan's report extensively in its third and final decision, which constituted a finding of neglect. Accepting the notion that a sexual addict would allow that preoccupation to infiltrate and dominate all aspects of her life, the court recast many of Carter's mothering decisions as the inevitable sequelae of a pathological confusion about all matters sexual. Judge O'Connor declared that "(c)learly, the respondent has a difficulty in the area of her sexual life and she allows that, whether by fantasies or whatever, to virtually totally occupy her relationship with the child." As evidence of that preoccupation, the judge cites "(h)aving the child being nursed beyond apparently a time when that would be necessary," along with the fact that Carter had shared a bed with her two-year-old daughter at times. Most damaging in the judge's assessment, however, was the fact that Carter had sought counseling for her daughter after Carter and a corroborating witness had seen what looked to them like an incident of sexual molestation of Melissa by some neighborhood children. The rape crisis counselor who handled that matter found no conclusive evidence that Melissa had been molested by these children, and Judge O'Connor therefore concluded that Carter's own hypervigilance about sex had subjected Melissa to an unnecessary course of counseling. Similarly, Carter's "overconcern" about sex had spurred the fateful phone call that sparked the chain of events that resulted in foster care placement, dozens of interviews, and multiple intrusive physical examinations. Said the judge, "I think the child is now confused, if nothing else, and this is the type of activity the State allows the Trial Court to determine is neglect." [12] And the genesis of this neglect, according to the court? The mother's "sexual addiction."

In a clinical sense, the use of the term "sexual addiction" in the Carter case is distinctly unorthodox. The American Psychiatric Association's *Diagnostic and Statistical Manual of Mental Disorders* names sexual addiction only as part of a catchall list of sexual disorders not accounted for by more traditional diagnoses. The diagnosis of "Sexual Disorder Not Otherwise Specified" can include "distress about a pattern of repeated conquests or other forms of nonparaphilic sexual addiction, involving a succession of people who exist only as things to be used."[13] The use of this term in Carter's case seems overly hasty, at best, according to the *DSM* criteria. Carter assumed the label of "sexual addict" after one sexual act, an act which no one characterized as a "conquest," or as particularly loveless, or as symptomatic of a tendency to objectify others or to use them "as things." Moreover, in the court proceedings, no one sought the nuanced inner meanings of Carter's sexual pursuits, although *DSM* bases its diagnosis on the clinician's evaluation of just those types of subjective, affective criteria. Miller and all who followed her lead treated "sexual addiction" as a behavioral disorder, objectively quantifiable; hence the cessation of sexual activity, rather than the lessening of the distress accompanying sexual activity, would signify improvement. The use of the diagnostic label of "sexual addiction" in this case was inappropriate both in its focus on behavioral rather than emotional indicators and in its hyperbolic interpretation of Carter's rather modest sexual history.

More to the point, not even the psychologist who assessed the case cited any established criteria to diagnose Carter as a sexual addict. Rather, the case turned on the use of the *popularly* defined syndrome known as sexual addiction. One of many spin-offs from the Alcoholics Anonymous Twelve-Step Program for self-recovery from addiction, the idea of sexual addiction was first formulated in the late 1970s but began to achieve its widest popularity in the early-to-mid-1980s.[14] Across the nation, self-help groups began to meet under the aegis of the Twelve-Step plan: Sex Addicts Anonymous, Loveaholics Anonymous, Sexaholics Anonymous, and so on.[15] As alcoholics stood before themselves and the world to acknowledge their addiction to alcohol, "sexaholics," too, strove to admit and make amends for their wrongdoings.[16] As "sexaholics" began to reveal themselves, the notion of sexual addiction began to make its way into everyday parlance, with powerful publicity provided by television and the popular press.[17] And as Twelve-Step programs have gained legitimacy among mental health professionals in the past decade, so too, inevitably, have they been drawn into the courts in the "expert" testimony of those professionals. The self-appellation of "sex addict" used by Karen Carter carried no less and no more meaning than the same label when used by pastoral counselor Janet Miller, Dr. Jennifer Sloan, attorney Alexis Allison, or Judge Joseph O'Connor. In each instance, it was a popular psychological term, coated with a new veneer of legitimacy as it was incorporated into the various professional idioms and milieux of its users.

As Carter's case makes clear, the act of "owning up" to a particular behavior, reputedly valuable as a therapeutic step toward recovery from an addiction, carries an entirely different meaning in the courtroom. The confessional mode, no matter how cathartic in therapy or "recovery," is altogether antithetical to the preservation of one's rights in a legal setting.[18] Karen Carter learned that everything she said in court, and all that was subpoenaed into court, could be and was used against her. The "fit" between the Twelve-Step process of proclaiming one's guilt in the name of self-healing and the legal process of affixing guilt wherever reasonable doubt can be eliminated (or, worse, in the family courts, where a preponderance of evidence allows) is poor indeed. The transposition of the Twelve-Step model into legal discourse leaves large cracks and disjunctures. In the Carter case, various cultural and religious prejudices against the expression of female, and especially maternal, sexuality seeped into those cracks.

The Carter case delivers a profoundly disturbing message about maternal sexuality: If a mother has any sex outside of marriage, even prior to the birth of her child, she jeopardizes the health and safety of her child. According to this lexicon of denial, the complex matters of interpersonal intimacy and sexual expression for unmarried women reduce to a simple mandate for abstinence. To wit, the very first time Carter failed to say no to a man, she acquired the label of "sex addict." Her later abstinence from sexual contact did not exonerate her; virginity cannot be recouped. According to the morality script that the family courts allowed to guide the law in this case, because Carter had engaged in an initial act of intercourse outside of marriage, she represented an ever-present threat of unbridled sexuality. That she muddied the line between selfless maternity and female sexuality by mentioning the motherly act of breastfeeding in the same breath as sexual arousal made her a "bad" mother who posed a danger to her child. And if the confessional zeal of the self-help movement impelled her to cast the first stone at herself, who is to question?

NOTES

1. All names and locations have been changed, at "Karen Carter's" request. However, events recounted here occurred as told; the case is not a composite.

2. Charles Mahtesian, "The Politics of Nature's Nurture," *Governing* 8, no. 11 (August 1995): 54. See also the Boston-area case of Brenda Frank, a case with many similarities to Carter's. *Boston Globe*, March 11, 1992 and April 20, 1992.

3. A substantial literature exists about the abuses perpetrated by the Department of Social Services. See, for example, Richard Wexler, *Wounded Innocents: The Real Victims of the War Against Child Abuse* (New York: Prometheus Books, 1991).

4. Phyllis Chesler, *Mothers on Trial: The Battle for Children and Custody* (Seattle: Seal Press, 1986).

5. La Leche League International, *The Womanly Art of Breastfeeding,* rev. ed. (Franklin Park, Ill.: La Leche League International, 1981).

6. My account of this case is based on several sources. First, in 1992 I conducted a series of telephone and in-person interviews with Carter: February 4, March 14, March 15, March 16, August 29, August 30, August 31, and September 27. References contained herein to Carter's emotional state or her assessment of events are based on this interview material. I also interviewed Carter's parents on August 30, 1992, and her pastor, on the same date. In all cases, I substantiated the information obtained through interviews with written materials from the court record and from Carter's own files of legal documents concerning the case. Carter also made available to me her copies of all the psychiatric and psychological evaluations conducted during the case. Additionally, I have viewed all of the documents in Carter's possession concerning the case, including police reports and all communications, orders, and decisions from the courts and from DSS. Finally, Carter's Legal Aid attorney made available to me the full transcripts of Carter's hearings in family court.

There were three family court proceedings in this case. The first hearing, in April 1991, resulted in an order dismissing the county's charges of abuse and neglect. The second proceeding, an "imminent danger" hearing, consisted of numerous sessions over a five-month period. The third proceeding, held in November 1991, resulted in a finding of neglect but returned the child to her mother as of January 6, 1992.

All quotations are taken from these materials unless otherwise noted. For more detailed references, please contact the author.

7. Initially, the new allegations were that Carter had "engaged in acts of sexual contact" with Melissa and that she had inserted "foreign objects in said child's vagina" while breastfeeding as well as on other occasions. During the course of the imminent danger hearing, many other allegations were made, most supported only by hearsay evidence but some citing interrogations of Melissa; these latter allegations included reports of sexual abuse by Melissa's grandparents, her aunt and uncles, and her day care teacher. Going much further afield, one witness for the county referred to an overabundance of toys in Carter's apartment as a sign of a troubled parent/child relationship.

8. This readiness to seek help is discussed in depth, and stated as a positive behavior in the report of the psychiatrist appointed by the county to conduct an evaluation of Karen Carter.

9. In all of the interviews with Carter, she stressed the centrality of her religious beliefs to her self-understanding; she identifies her pastor and his wife as major stabilizing figures in her life.

10. Carter reports that Miller had worked as a hairdresser prior to becoming a counselor, and that, during the long course of therapy, Miller herself had expressed concern over her lack of formal training in psychotherapy.

11. The "secrecy" Sloan refers to is the apparent lack of full candor exercised by Carter in discussing her "sexual addiction" with the various social workers, psychiatrists, and other professionals involved in the case. Sloan takes no note of the fact that the sex addict label is being used against Carter at this point, and that perhaps Carter is demonstrating a rational tactical assessment of the harm that the label has wrought. It hardly seems fair to fault a mother trying to regain custody of her child for trying to present herself in a favorable light, and it certainly seems unfair to generalize from that carefully gauged presentation of self to broader judgments of the mother's personality structure and capacity for truth telling.

12. As throughout this case, the court did not acknowledge the "confusing" or otherwise damaging effects of foster care and the separation from Mother, in and of themselves. The effects of those experiences were rendered invisible by the assumption of earlier wrongdoings by Carter. For example, several witnesses testified that Melissa responded awkwardly to her mother, and vice versa, during supervised visits or psychological evaluation sessions. No consideration was given to the extenuating circumstances, such as separation, foster care, and outside observation!

13. American Psychiatric Association, *Diagnostic Criteria from DSM-III-R*, (Washington, D.C.: American Psychiatric Association, 1987), 168–69.

14. Patrick Carnes, *Out of the Shadows: Understanding Sexual Addiction* (Minneapolis: CompCare Publications, 1983), ii–iii, 134.

15. Ibid., 134–35.

16. Ibid., 137; Carnes lists "The Twelve Steps of Alcoholics Anonymous Adapted for Sexual Addicts." Step 1 is to admit "we were powerless over our sexual addiction—that our lives had become unmanageable." In Step 5, the "addict" "admitted to God, to ourselves, and to another human being the exact nature of our wrongs." In Step 8, the addict "made a list of all persons we had harmed, and became willing to make amends to them all." The confessional nature of this process is clear. It is important, too, that the confession be public, as in the popularly known self-introductory phrase of Alcoholics Anonymous: "My name is Lauri, and I am an alcoholic."

17. The most thorough critique of the Twelve-Step movement that I have seen to date is Wendy Kaminer, *I'm Dysfunctional, You're Dysfunctional* (Boston: Addison-Wesley, 1992). Several recent articles also critique the phenomenal infiltration of Twelve-Step programs and ideology into American life. See, for exam-

ple, Michael Brennan, "Self-Indulgent Self-Help," *Newsweek* 119, no. 3 (January 20, 1992): 8; also, David Reiff, "Victims All? Recovery, Co-Dependency, and the Art of Blaming Somebody Else," *Harper's*, 283, no. 1697 (October 1991): 49. No writing I have seen discusses the legal implications of the Twelve-Step ideology, specifically.

18. This analysis of the perilous transposition of the confessional mode into a new discursive realm owes a heavy debt to Foucault, who writes about the ways in which psychoanalysts became the "priests" of a new social order. See Michel Foucault, *The History of Sexuality* (London: Allen Lane, 1979).

Chapter 22

Rejecting Zoe Baird
Class Resentment and the Working Mother

Diane Sampson

Hardly, it seemed, had the musicians playing the 1993 inaugural balls tuned their instruments before Zoe Baird, Bill Clinton's first nominee for attorney general, was hearing her nomination's swan song. Baird's short letter to Clinton withdrawing her nomination answered a swelling public chorus of outrage and dismay, a chorus led by congressional leaders who only a week before had assured the media that Baird's would be a "smooth confirmation."[1] At the heart of her swift and angry public rejection lay Baird's hiring of an undocumented woman and her husband, Lillian and Victor Cordero, to perform child care and chauffeuring duties. According to the *New York Times* front-page article, not only were the Corderos ineligible to work in the United States, but Baird and her husband, Paul Gewirtz, had neither reported the Corderos' wages nor paid the requisite Social Security taxes.[2] Conservative senator Orrin Hatch sounded the early common chord among the insiders, the pundits, the congressional leaders, and the major media sources when he responded to reporters' questions that it was "no big deal."[3] But almost immediately, Capitol switchboards and talk show phone lines around the country were jammed with callers refusing to support what looked like one set of rules for the "ruling class" and another for the "regular folks."[4]

In retrospect, Baird was never a sure bet. Clinton's clear inclination to nominate a woman was alternately applauded and rebuked in the popular presses and within the Beltway. His eventual choice of Baird puzzled and frustrated many on the political left, who saw her legal work for GE, and later Aetna, as demonstration of strong corporate sympathies—sympathies antithetical to Clinton's stump speeches about "people who play by the rules."[5] Baird was also not generally supported by women's groups, who would not endorse a conservative nominee simply because she was a woman.[6] And although Baird informed Clinton's vetting team that she had hired the Corderos, the team failed to anticipate both the public fury over her violation of immigration law and the need to orchestrate support for her strategically in the case of resistance to her nomination.[7] Thus when the spotlight on Baird's qualifications unexpectedly swung from her conservative stand on tort reform to her "child care situation," there was no constituency prepared to take up her defense.

For her part, Baird insisted that the violation was civil, not criminal. This defense fell flat before an audience riveted by the spectacle of a powerful, wealthy white woman humbled because of her child care arrangements. And, although she assured both the Judiciary Committee and the CNN viewing public at every turn that it was Gewirtz who had mishandled the legalities surrounding the Corderos' employment, this possibility was largely ignored. Gewirtz-as-culprit received noticeable attention only from Rush Limbaugh, who ridiculed the "blame-it-on-the-husband" defense as a "feminazi" ploy.[8] Finally, as Baird's supporters fell silent, her Beltway detractors were left to enact the mood of their constituents: outrage, sympathetic disapproval, and self-righteous disdain.

Most media sources depicted the public response as "easily understood." Commentators unscrambling the public melee of the nomination unself-consciously wielded words like work, child care, and immigration as proof that the surrounding issues were easily accessed and that, by association, the public antagonism was easily explained. The common refusal of Baird as attorney general, they overwhelmingly agreed, was a rejection of class privilege. However, that the terms of the debate—words like immigration, child care, work—are grounded in practical, everyday life does not mean that they are realized, or uncontested. Indeed, these words are fighting words. They represent a welter of varying and conflicting emotions, cultural configurations, and social relations. Thus, rather than seeing Baird's failed nomination as easy to understand, we should see this as a moment when "regular folks" came to the issues raised by Baird's nomination and confirmation hearings well seasoned by battles waged in bedrooms, school rooms, and board rooms. Accordingly, their responses to Baird were contradictory, nuanced, and passionate.

This is no less true of their responses to Baird-as-mother. Although Baird's role as a mother was obviously related to the political fiasco in which she found herself, the mass media primarily ignored it as an issue

in the public response. Rather, there seemed to be a tacit understanding—
as opposed to an explicit investigation—that motherhood constituted
one thread in the larger fabric of Baird's failed nomination. That Baird
was the first female nominee for the office of attorney general, and by
definition the first mother, underscored the likelihood that her role as
woman and mother would emerge as part of the confirmation process.
Baird's inability to pass the litmus test for good mother proves elemental
to understanding the significance of the unprecedented public outcry over
her nomination.

On January 21, 1993, after two long days of questioning before the
Senate Judiciary Committee, Baird faced the unhappy choice of either
withdrawing her nomination or forcing a close confirmation vote—a
vote which would prove costly to Clinton.[9] In the most oft-quoted lines
from the hearings, Baird prefigured the fate of her nomination:

> I have told you that I have made a mistake, that I was wrong, that I did not
> adequately perceive the significance of the matter here, or I allowed myself
> to be more concerned about the difficulty we were having in child care
> than I was concerned about this situation.
>
> Quite honestly, I was acting at that time really more as a mother than as
> someone who would be sitting here designated to be Attorney General.[10]

Although Baird gestured toward the practical concerns of a working
mother, the effect was to render the roles of mother and attorney general
if not mutually exclusive, then hopelessly incongruous. This defense
begged the question of what it means to act "more as a mother" than as
an attorney general. How does a good mother act? Was Baird a good
mother? Presumably, she met the practical qualifications for a good
mother in our culture by providing her son with safe shelter, food, and at
least minimally adequate care. But as Denise Riley, in *War in the Nursery*,
finds, "There's a crucial difference between invoking 'the mother' and
speaking about the practical needs of women with children."[11] Baird
telescoped broad cultural assumptions and prescriptions into a rhetorical
position by suggesting that her role as mother—in fact her role as good
mother—demanded that she transgress the law. In this, she summoned
up powerful codes redolent of hard-held, long-battled emotional and
cultural ideals. And by these codes, Zoe Baird was a bad mother.

In her opening statement, Baird introduced herself to the nation by
recounting the lessons taken from her parents' home: "Their guidance
and teachings centered on love of family, interest in public affairs and an

opportunity to serve."[12] In a manner reminiscent of nineteenth-century suffragists, she simultaneously invoked American nostalgia for patriotic hearth and home and distanced herself from the taint of individualistic achievement, yoking her political ambitions instead to a love of family and community. Continuing in the conventions of this tradition, Baird claimed unique sensitivity to the most vexing social problem facing the attorney general—crime control and prosecution—by virtue of mother-hood:

> As a mother of a 3-year-old, I can particularly appreciate the passion and the anger about the day-to-day terror of crime in America, whether urban, suburban, or even rural. My son cannot play outside our home in New Haven at night, because of fear of crime. There was a drug-related murder just a block from our house not long ago.
>
> Unfortunately, most Americans live in much greater fear of crime than I. I want the single urban mother who fears for her child in school every day, from violent gangs, and the elderly widow who is afraid to go to the supermarket after dark, to know that they have a friend in the Attorney General.[13]

Like the suffragists before her, who brandished arguments about the superior moral rectitude of women in order to negotiate the right to social and political space, Baird constructed the political arena in general, and the office of attorney general in particular, as the right place not only for a woman but for a mother. Although this signpost was subtle, it was unmistakable. Baird made motherhood the site from which she enunciated her qualifications for the job and, as such, motherhood formed the rhetorical binding of both the confirmation hearings and the public responses to those hearings.

Baird's invocation of the authority of motherhood to modify the appearance of ambition might otherwise have gone unnoticed. But, as readers were reminded in nearly every article and editorial and on nearly every radio or television broadcast, Baird's salary from Aetna was half a million dollars. In fact, she earned five times more than Gewirtz, her husband, a law professor at Yale.[14] The fact was inescapable: Baird was an ambitious woman. Inasmuch as she was not traveling the proverbial mommy track, her professional trajectory contradicted our culturally accepted "common core of assumptions" about the labor and the position of the middle-class white mother. It was Senator Joseph Biden, chair of the confirmation hearings, who inadvertently pointed to Baird's prolific career as unnatural—as astonishing—when, attempting to defuse the vilification of Baird, he noted that her hiring of the Corderos "took place in the context of a woman in her mid-thirties taking a job that most men don't get, if they ever get, until they are in their mid-sixties or mid-fifties, and with an 8-month-old baby."[15] Baird, he suggested, had been doing a man's job better than most men.

Biden not only pointed up Baird's career success, he implicitly argued that she crossed well-marked boundaries. She was doing a *job most men don't get.* Her earnings, as well as her corporate position, and their potential to bankrupt "normal" family relations, formed an inescapable subtext in the popular responses to Baird; effectively she was charged with usurping Gewirtz's role, while not adequately attending to her own role as mother. Within these normal family relations, which should be read as a sexual-social contract, the white middle-class mother recognizes work and home as not only separated but often opposed. "Good mother" and "working mother" sit comfortably together insofar as the middle-class woman handles her business at home—which Baird did not do. The dissonance between Baird's rhetorical stance and her lived life was jarring, because she defended herself both by claiming she had acted as a mother and by claiming that she had abdicated this role, giving Gewirtz control over the process of securing child care.[16]

As she framed her defense, Baird was caught between the rock of having mismanaged her affairs by hiring undocumented workers and the hard place of having mismanaged her affairs by abdicating her proper maternal role. As read by the national presses, relegating the details of her son's care to Gewirtz smelled like neglect or naked ambition—both culturally accepted signifiers of a bad mother. But her insistence that the immigration violation was technical and not criminal finally played no better. According to Sydney Blumenthal, writing in the *New Yorker,* Gewirtz believed she should argue that her offense was "a 'technical violation' that had been 'regularized' by disclosure."[17] But this defense suggested a "moral relativism"—tinged with the overtones of class privilege—making odd bedfellows of Senators Biden and Strom Thurmond. Both forbade this reasoning by Baird. Biden, chair of the confirmation process, commandeered her testimony about the Corderos, threatening to oppose Baird if she "insisted on saying she had committed only a 'technical' violation and was not contrite."[18] His attempts to salve popular sentiment through public scoldings—ostensibly believing that if Baird said she was sorry she would get through the process with her nomination intact—

conditioned the viewing audiences to see Baird's violation as a moral lapse. Thurmond went so far as to ask Baird if she had "repented." [19] This public conversation questioning Baird's judgment explicitly called into question her ability to be the moral/legal leader of the United States, and implicitly her ability to be a moral force within her home, her ability to be a good mother.

Forced to abandon her prepared defenses, Baird struggled to articulate the difficulties accompanying the combination of professional life with maternal life.

> I had my first and only child, a then 8-month-old boy. I was beginning the most challenging job of my professional career as the new general counsel of a major company, I believe probably the first time a woman has taken on something like that for a company of that size and complexity. . . .
>
> I had some of the credibility issues that people have referred to here . . . here is a woman coming in who is younger than I am, and she has got a kid and can she really do this job. So I had a major commitment in those early days to try very hard not only to do the job well, but to deal with all the credibility issues that come with that.[20]

Baird's plea for identification with other working mothers was greeted in the editorials and on the air by both angry jeers and genuine frustration. Representative of this response is the editorial by Judy Mann, writing in the *Washington Post,* who evoked the burden most working women feel as they attempt to simultaneously negotiate their professional lives, their domestic responsibilities, and their emotional commitments to their children "on a lot less than $500,000." Mann revealingly tied her gendered class analysis of Baird's defense to a reproach of Baird's mothering:

> In order to support our children, most women have had to work, and many of us have gone out of our minds trying to find child care we can live with that also is child care we can afford. So the resentment . . . is not just a question of resentment against a rich woman. It was resentment against a woman who could afford to go first class on child care and still did it on the cheap.[21]

More often, the indictment of Baird as mother was subtle and wrapped in the language of equity and sacrifice as heard in the response of one working mother quoted in the *New York Times:* "I don't think it's fair. *I raised my kids* while I was working. I worked days. My husband worked nights at the post office. Our in-laws filled in when they had to." [22] The unspoken assumption in these responses to Baird is that class privilege absolved Baird from sacrifice. Class privilege meant Baird did not have to take care of her own kid, and not taking care of her own kid made her a bad mother. With raw and ferocious voices, women responding to Baird both insisted that a good mother buys the best for her child and rejected the possibility that the best was hard to find on $500,000 a year.[23]

On January 21, 1993, only one week after the *Times* broke the story of her violation of immigration law, Baird's run at attorney general was finished. In deference to the opinions of her close friends and mentors, and in an effort to avoid any damage to the new administration, she asked Clinton to withdraw her nomination. Baird pointed out the impossibility of leading an already beleaguered Justice Department amidst the "continuing controversy" which served as an insistent backbeat to her confirmation hearings. Her short letter to Clinton conveyed a sense of bewilderment and frustration as she expressed "surprise at the extent of public reaction" against her nomination.[24]

Baird's vilification illuminates rules broadly accepted in our culture about women's roles and public positions and ultimately lays bare a riot of images, definitions, and constructions of "good" mother that are slippery, but powerful. Because the ideology of the good mother, of what constitutes a good mother, is loaded, many contestants have their hats in the ring vying for the privilege of defining it. The stakes are high. Exploring the overwhelming refusal to see Baird as a good mother lets us look at how, on this occasion notions of good motherhood were employed to question the cultural legitimacy of the professional woman, to restate the importance of normative family relationships, and to pry open broad discontent about class inequalities—all without overtly threatening the status quo. In the end, Baird stated her qualifications and ambitions in terms of motherhood, and then failed the litmus test for good mother. Rather than becoming the first female attorney general in the United States, the first mother to be attorney general, Baird became the first nominee to withdraw her nomination for that post in this century.[25]

NOTES

This chapter is the product of much shared labor and thinking. For their efforts as friends, child care providers, critics, and mentors, I want to thank Kristin Hass, Molly Ladd-Taylor, Marnie Leavitt, Kim Mikita, Sondra Soderborg, Lauri Umansky, Erika Young, and especially Heidi Ardizzone, who helps me keep my mother self in tune with my scholar self. Some ideas in this paper appeared in *Michigan Feminist Studies,* a journal published by graduate students at the University of Michigan. I am grateful for the contributions my editor there, Jennifer Mittelstadt, made to my thinking and writing. Finally, none of this work could have been done without Blake Zenger, who fills my life with love.

1. Clifford Krauss, "A Top GOP Senator Backs Nominee in a Storm," *New York Times,* January 16, 1993, L7.

2. David Johnston, "Clinton's Choice for Justice Dept. Hired Illegal Aliens for Household," *New York Times,* January 14, 1993, A1+.

3. Krauss, "A Top GOP Senator Backs Nominee," L7.

4. See, for example, Lynne Duke and Barbara Vobejda, "On Justice Nominee, Public Delivered the Opinion," *Washington Post,* January 23, 1993, A1+; Robert Reinhold, "Fueled By Radio and TV, Outcry Became Uproar," *New York Times,* January 23, 1993, L9; and Howard Kurtz, "Talk Radio's Early Word on Zoe Baird," *Washington Post,* January 23, 1993, B3.

5. For examples, see Stephen Pizzo, "Dirty Justice," *Mother Jones* (March/April 1993): 19; Jeffrey Rosen, "Danny and Zoe," *New Republic,* February 1, 1993, 28–30; and Terry Eastland, "An Attorney General Quayle Could Love," *Wall Street Journal,* January 13, 1993, A15.

6. Gwen Ifill, "The Baird Appointment: In Trouble from the Start, Then A Firestorm," *New York Times,* January 23, 1993, 8L.

7. See Sydney Blumenthal, "Letter from Washington: Adventures in Babysitting," *New Yorker,* February 15, 1993, 53; Howard Fineman, Mark Miller, Ann McDaniel, and Bob Cohn, "Off the Books, Out of the Chair," *Newsweek,* February 1, 1993, 33; Jill Smolowe, "How It Happened," *Time,* February 1, 1993, 32.

8. See Kurtz, "Talk Radio's Early Word on Zoe Baird," B3.

9. See, for example, Felicity Barringer, "Clinton Cancels Baird Nomination For Justice Department: Much Outrage, Little Sympathy on Main Street," *New York Times,* January 22, 1993, A1+.

10. Senate Committee on the Judiciary, *On the Nomination of Zoe Baird, of Connecticut, to Be Attorney General of the United States,* 103d Cong., 1st sess., January 19 and 21, 1993, 80. Baird's hearings were dominated by questions about the hiring of the Corderos and about her culpability in this civil offense.

11. Denise Riley, *War in the Nursery: Theories of the Child and Mother* (London: Virago, 1983): 174.

12. Senate Committee, *On the Nomination of Zoe Baird,* 21.

13. Senate Committee, *On the Nomination of Zoe Baird,* 22–23.

14. See, for example, Adam Clymer, "Baird Endures Difficult Day Adrift at the Senate Hearing," *New York Times,* January 22, 1993, A14; Blumenthal, 55; Fineman, Miller, McDaniel, and Cohn, 32.

15. Senate Committee, *On the Nomination of Zoe Baird,* 195.

16. As sociologist Evelyn Nakano Glenn forcefully argues, however, this "con-

cept of mothering as universally women's work disguises the fact that it is further subdivided, so that different aspects of caring labor are assigned to different groups of women." Just as early suffragists hired washer women and nursemaids while they "enlarged" women's social influence and position, today it is socially and culturally possible for the mother with some measure of social privilege to assume the role of mother-manager, as she passes off the *physical* labor of child care to another woman. In this way, the position of middle-class women in the work force has been built on the exploitable domestic/reproductive labor of poorer women, such as Lillian Cordero, forestalling the renegotiation of the traditional gender contract. I am relying here on the work of Evelyn Nakano Glenn: "Social Constructions of Mothering," in *Mothering: Ideology, Experience, and Agency,* ed. Evelyn Nakano Glenn, Grace Chang, and Linda Rennie Forcey (New York: Routledge, 1994): 7; and "From Servitude to Service Work: Historical Continuities in the Racial Division of Paid Reproductive Labor," *Signs* 18, no. 1 (Autumn 1992): 1–43. See also Elsa Barkley Brown, "'What Has Happened Here': The Politics of Difference in Women's History and Feminist Politics," *Feminist Studies* 18, no. 2 (Summer 1992): 295–312.

17. Blumenthal, *Adventures in Babysitting,* 59.

18. Blumenthal, *Adventures in Babysitting,* 59.

19. Senate Committee, *On the Nomination of Zoe Baird,* 91.

20. Senate Committee, *On the Nomination of Zoe Baird,* 168.

21. Judy Mann, The Raw Nerve of Child Care," *Washington Post,* January 27, 1993, D26.

22. Quoted by Barringer, "Clinton Cancels Baird Nomination," A1+. Emphasis added.

23. Although I know of no empirical proof that the majority of the phone callers were women, those who reported and commented on the callers categorized them as middle-class women. Further, although many news articles carefully included the words "parents" and "mothers and fathers" when discussing the importance of the child care issue, overwhelmingly they interviewed women, suggesting that this was, finally, of particular importance to women.

24. Zoe Baird, "Text of Letters between Clinton and Baird," *New York Times,* January 23, 1993, 8L.

25. Mark Stence, "Those Who Withdrew," *Washington Post,* January 23, 1993, A10.

Chapter 23

Moms Don't Rock
The Popular Demonization of Courtney Love

Norma Coates

Her rock group did not release an album in 1995. Nor was 1995 the year that her husband, grunge rock idol/icon Kurt Cobain committed suicide. Yet Barbara Walters selected Courtney Love as one of her "10 Most Fascinating People of 1995." In her interview, sandwiched between those with Newt Gingrich and Christopher Reeve, Love looked like the "train wreck" that Walters described. Although clad in beige Armani, with her normally disheveled hair put up in a fairly neat bun, Love presented a vision of disorder and chaos. Her trademark slut-red lipstick looking like a smear across the lower section of her face, Love cried, smoked, managed to make Barbara Walters say "suck," and otherwise acted like a woman out of control. The climax of the interview came when Walters asked the question that everyone was waiting for: "Are you a good mother?" Love answered, "Yes, yes, yes." But we all knew the real answer: a big, resounding NO.

In her introduction Walters brought out a salient fact: there is no way that the "typical" American over the age of thirty should know or care about Courtney Love, but they do. Love is a rock and roll musician, one who works within the generic conventions of alternative rock. Love refused a path to "respectable" notoriety in her refusal to play the role of grieving and tasteful rock widow, à la Yoko Ono, after the suicide of her rock superstar husband, Kurt Cobain.[1] Moreover, Love's nonrespectable notoriety preceded Cobain's suicide by a year and a half. Love burst into mainstream consciousness because of a profile published in the September 1992 edition of *Vanity Fair*. The article was not a cover story; in fact, it was buried toward the back of the magazine, in the section devoted to lesser celebrities. But it was not the photograph of a very pregnant, nearly nude Love, with a cigarette obviously airbrushed out of her left hand, that ignited the firestorm of controversy to follow. It was the revelation, from a source "very close to the couple," that Love used heroin while pregnant with her daughter. Subsequently, as a direct result of the article, infant Frances Bean Cobain was seized from her parents for a period and placed in the custody of Love's sister.

Love remains under the microscope of mainstream scrutiny, aided and abetted by forces she herself unleased as well as factors that are totally out of her control (such as Cobain's suicide). The question of her fitness to mother lurks just beneath the surface, when it does not emerge openly, in mainstream representations of Love; it is the source of the media's fascination with her. Love's antics are frequently chronicled in mass market magazines such as *People, Entertainment Weekly, Newsweek,* and *Time.* Even *Vanity Fair* featured her on its cover, portraying her, perhaps sardonically, as an angel surrounded by towheaded young boys.[2]

The mainstream demonization of Love as a "bad" mother is not surprising. However, her subsequent demonization within rock itself *is* surprising. Rock represents "oppositional" culture in the popular imagination, a space of rampant sexuality, noise, and unruliness that is best conjured up by the triptych "sex, drugs, and rock and roll." Moreover, as Love's maternal travails show, this space is constructed as male and young; it is a place outside of the responsibilities of increased age, responsibilities that include parenting.

The visible history of motherhood in rock is brief. Motherhood has no fixed meaning within the "rock formation," a term coined by cultural critic Lawrence Grossberg to describe the particular post–World War II ideological and cultural configuration within which rock as we know it resides.[3] Mothers may not be visible in rock, but they are one of the mainstream forces that rock allegedly opposes itself to: "[r]ock'n'roll rebellion emerged at roughly the same time as post-war 'mom-ism,' a fashionable critique which singled out the mother as the cause of a hefty proportion of America's ills."[4] Rock'n'roll of the 1950s, then, was part of a rebellion against the so-called feminizing, castrating influence of mom, a way to attribute blame "for the bland conformism of '50s America."[5] By the 1960s, rock was firmly grounded in the opposition between rebel masculinity and "woman as conformism incarnate."[6] Mothers, then, can serve as the primary object of the masculine rebellion performed in rock, but they undermine rock if they show themselves in it.

That is not to say that there are no female rock artists who are also mothers. There have been mothers in rock as long as there have been women in rock. Recent revisionist "herstories" of rock counter the perception that women are latecomers to the rock scene by recuperating female r&b and rockabilly artists as the "rock" artists they truly were.[7] However, mothers, like women in general, have only been "in" rock in ways that are comprehensible within the masculinist contours of the rock formation. Standard rock histories fail to identify performers as either mothers or fathers.[8] Hiding or just ignoring the existence of rockers' kids was, and often still is, standard practice. For example, the fact that John Lennon had a wife and child was suppressed when the Beatles first came to fame in the United States, for fear it would negatively affect his image as an idol of female teenyboppers. But more insidiously, motherhood is perceived as something that somehow softens or weakens a female rock performer.[9] Moreover, in the opinion of some writers and fans, motherhood has led to the ostracism of female performers from the rock community, as this passage about seminal punk rocker Patti Smith, from Lucy O'Brien's *She Bop: The Definitive History of Women in Rock, Pop and Soul,* indicates:

> Now that her rock performance has become legend, a younger generation of female bands cite Smith as an influence without equivocation. Accompanying this, though, is a sense of disappointment about where she disappeared to. One of the greatest rock'n'roll icons this century retiring? to the suburbs? to raise a family? She retained a dignity and mystery by ending Patti Smith, rock star, at her peak. But there is also the sense that, like countless women before her, she opted out to have children. Though a family is important, it disrupts the longevity that women need to prove they can stay the course. . . . When maturity beckoned, she lost her nerve. The warrior retreated.[10]

O'Brien analyzes the exit of Mo Tucker, drummer for the legendary Velvet Underground, from the music scene in a similar way. Like Smith, Tucker returned to rock performance once her children did not require full-time maternal devotion. O'Brien and other rock writers reiterate normative representations of motherhood in the rock formation, because that is one of two ways that motherhood can be rendered acceptable in rock; that is, as treachery against rock.

The other way the rock formation recognizes motherhood is through colonization, that is, through framing motherhood in "macho" terms.

When Chrissie Hynde, the archetypal "tough chick" leader of the punk/ New Wave band The Pretenders, went on tour with her baby during the mid-1980s, *Musician* magazine featured her in a cover story entitled "One Tough Mother & The Pretenders." The article managed to make motherhood sound like a "guy thing," exemplified by this photo caption: "You might consider having a baby, having half your band die and putting together a new one for an LP and tour stressful. For Chrissie Hynde, it's no big deal."[11]

It is easy to ignore parenting in rock. Traditionally, fathers take less responsibility for child care in modern Anglo-European society. Men present no obvious signs, equivalent to pregnancy, that they are about to become parents. Rock sexuality is synonymous with unbridled, unfettered sexuality: sexuality without consequences, and particularly, sexuality without children. The recent influx of "women in rock," particularly younger women, like Courtney Love, who play guitar, scream, and sing from the point of view of female experience and sexuality, trouble not only the meaning of sexuality in rock but the meaning of rock itself. Moreover, rockers who mother unsettle and perhaps subvert not only the meaning of rock but the meaning of motherhood.

Courtney Love's antics, notoriety, and belligerent persona are the stuff of tabloid fascination. Following her exploits can provide a safe way to live out one's "rock and roll fantasy" without having to clean up the wreckage later. The mainstream media construct Love as a figure through whom we are reminded that however much we may fantasize or even desire the "ideal" rock and roll lifestyle, or another "transgressive" life-style, it has effects that we would never want to visit upon our children. The boundaries of "acceptable" motherhood are thereby policed through the demonization of Courtney Love.

For example, some of 1995's extensive media coverage of Love focused on her practice of bringing her young daughter on stage with her during concerts. Karen Schoemer in *Newsweek* uses the opportunity to question the rock press's "lionization" of Love (a questionable interpretation) and to make a number of digs at her:

> But these attempts to lionize Love ring as hollow as the tabloids' attempts to demonize her. On just about every count, Courtney ultimately fails to live up to her myth. She's no feminist: her rabid quest for attention in any form fulfills too many archaic female stereotypes. Whether or not she's a good mother may be no one's business to judge, but who would want to

trade places with little Frances, now 2 and regularly being dragged on-stage?[12]

Love can't seem to win on this one. This interesting excerpt from the *Washington Post* uses Love's bringing Frances on stage to question her "militant feminist" stance, as if mothering and feminism were incompatible:

> She's a "militant feminist," chain-smoking Hole singer-guitarist Courtney Love told the audience at a packed Radio Music Hall Wednesday night, but she doesn't like "girls who complain." The performance of Love and her band was militant enough, but it's hard to credit the feminist part. From the baby-doll dress she wore to the gesture of briefly bringing out her little daughter, Frances Bean Cobain, Love's stance was as incoherent as it was confrontational.[13]

More sympathetic reviews of Love's performances still implicitly, if indirectly, comment upon her "bad" mothering:

> An emotional and defiant Courtney Love jolted alive a heat-stricken Lollapalooza last night by leaving the Shoreline Amphitheater stage twice to challenge members of the audience before she was finally carried away in the arms of a security guard. On her daughter Frances Bean's third birthday, she first went after two men, flipping them off, then jumped off the stage after them, apparently because they were showing insufficient enthusiasm. . . . Love had been in tears for much of her set. Clad in a black leather miniskirt and matching sleeveless vest, with a black fishnet-stockinged leg placed atop a speaker monitor, she strummed an aqua guitar at high voltage. . . . It was four screaming songs before she took a long pull of a cigarette, and addressed the crowd. "Let's hear some respect for Elastica," she exhorted, then "louder, you f—— p——." The crowd responded as much out of fear as appreciation, but the best response of all came to her plea for "respect for Frances Bean Cobain, who's 3-years-old today." Then she led a happy-birthday singalong.[14]

Finally, even authors who do not condemn Love's mothering practices overtly do so covertly through the selection and juxtaposition of pungent events and images:

> Frances Bean Cobain, outfitted in miniature protective earphones and in the arms of her nanny at stage rear, watched her mom Courtney Love and Hole rock out Wednesday night at WUST Radio Music Hall in Washington, D.C.

At the long-awaited concert to promote Hole's latest album, "Live Through This" (released days after Kurt Cobain's April suicide), Love interrupted her hour-and-a-half-long concert twice: to ask "Where's my daughter?" (backstage) and to ask Frances (the child of Love and Cobain) to come back on-stage and give her mommy a hug and a kiss—which the toddler gladly did.

After displaying her maternal side, Courtney playfully responded to a fan's Nirvana request by asking, "In utero? [The title of the last album of her late husband's band, Nirvana] What's that? Let's talk about existentialism." She closed the show with a stage dive.[15]

The authors of all of these snippets, from national magazines, leading newspapers, or wire services agree, despite what they may say explicitly, that Love is a "bad" mother. In all of these excerpts, a thinly veiled subtext inscribes the boundaries of "good" mothering through biased representations of Love's mothering practices.

For example, only one of the excerpted articles makes it clear that young Frances has industrial-strength hearing protectors on her ears. The other articles overlook this piece of information. This may seem like a trivial hook to hang an argument on, but the subtext reveals that it is indeed strong. The idea that Love would expose her child to the decibel level of hard-rock shows, especially from the vantage point of being on or quite near the primary speakers blasting the sound out across a large auditorium, or in the case of Lollapalooza, a large field, implies anything from maternal irresponsibility to abusive neglect. Anyone who has attended a few loud rock shows knows the ringing in the ears that doesn't always go away until the next day. And, for many of us, it was our mothers who warned us that too much of that loud music would make us go deaf. Moreover, these articles represent the rock concert, and especially the rock stage, as a place of danger. To haul a child on stage in front of thousands of screaming, possibly drunken and drug-addled fans, according to the implicit message of these articles, is a potentially traumatizing experience for a young child, one from which she should be protected—by her mother. This image links easily to others in popular memory: "bad" mothers in films, television, sports, and other sources, using their innocent child for personal gain.

These articles posit Love as a poor behavioral model for her daughter, and by extrapolation, all the daughters who come to Love's show to see her, many of whom will become mothers themselves: a mother does not throw temper tantrums in front of her daughter. Certain bourgeois behavioral codes are being reinforced here, codes which reinscribe WASP self-control and grace under pressure. Subtle social hierarchies that valorize emotional restraint over displays of strong feelings, still associated with non-WASP ethnic groups within the United States, are also put into play. At the same time, these articles portray Love, a wealthy rock star from an untraditional yet upper-middle-class background, as "declassed" so as to differentiate and distance her behavior from what is normative for her class. These excerpts also conjure up tired tropes of "ladylike behavior," of which we can assume Love knows nothing. They deploy the demonized figure of Love, not as an anti-role model for middle-class female children, but to draw the boundaries of their—and their mothers'—middle-class behavior.

These excerpts also implicitly critique peripatetic mothers, who wander away from a stable home base with or without their children. The most extreme conclusion one might draw from them is that Mother should stay at home all of the time, providing a stable and safe haven for her child, an embodiment of conservative "family values." Children, it follows, must not be dragged from town to town or have their daily routine disrupted because of the requirements of their mother's job. Nor, these excerpts imply, should children ever be too far from the watchful gaze of their mother. One of the news tidbits circulated in the "bad"-mother discourse about Love is that Frances has had at least fifty nannies in her short life.[16]

Ultimately, these excerpts convey a clear message that mothers do not belong in the masculine and dangerous world of rock. This message serves the agendas of those who would inscribe boundaries around motherhood as well as those who would inscribe boundaries around rock. Perhaps Love's biggest sin is her career choice. On the one hand, Love's presence in rock troubles rock's role as cultural source for role-modeling a mythical but potent "masculinity." On the other hand, since "sex, drugs, and rock and roll" go together, Love's association with rock raises the frightening moral specter of a mother exposing her child to sex and drugs as well. Mothers, bourgeois wisdom would have it, should protect youngsters from rock's dark side, not participate in it themselves.

One "masculine" rock practice that Love participates in is stagediving: leaping into the crowd during concerts. During the summer 1995 Lollapalooza alternative rock festival, Love would excoriate the audience with verbal abuse, dive into the crowd, and often be physically attacked, frequently fighting back. In addition, her clothes would be torn off, exposing her underwear or more. Such behavior is troubling to moral guardians, as it is not behavior associated with responsible mothering. Critics frequently and roundly rebuke Love for her stagediving.

Stagediving is the sort of behavior mothers are supposed to *prevent*. A recent number of severe injuries and deaths have produced public outcry to stop or control it. Mothers of victims are the most vocal opponents of stagediving. A minor moral panic on the pages of "supermarket" publications such as *People* magazine and *Family Circle* added stagediving to the list of things that mothers must protect their children from. A 1995 article in *Family Circle* "When Music Turns to Mayhem: What Every Parent Must Know about Rock Concerts," obviously targeted to mothers of teenage children, offers prescriptive tips from various male experts to mothers. (Of course, the band and performer most singled out in the article are Hole and Courtney Love.) Men, being more knowledgeable about rock and about life in general, make the rules, but leave it to the mothers to enforce them.

Mothers have been called upon to control other aspects of rock practice as well. For example, the success of the Parents' Music Resource Center (PMRC), which lobbied the music industry in the mid-1980s to place warning labels on rock and rap recordings with "questionable" content, relied on mothers' efforts. The PMRC, a group of affluent white women known by their detractors as the "Washington Wives," was founded by Tipper Gore, wife of then Senator and later Vice President Albert Gore. Mrs. Gore was shocked after hearing references to masturbation on a Prince album.[17] Having struck up alliances with other national groups, notably the National Parent-Teacher Association, the PMRC successfully introduced censorship into the recorded music industry through the labeling of "offensive" albums with "Parental Guidance: Explicit Lyrics" labels.[18] Both of Love's recordings with her band Hole, *Pretty on the Inside* and *Live through This,* carry the parental advisory label. Some large national department stores, such as Wal-Mart, do not carry recordings with that label, since to do so, they argue, jeopardizes their image as a "family" store.[19]

Initially, the PMRC targeted primarily recordings by black and heavy-metal artists, thus adding disturbing racial and class elements to this call for rock music censorship.[20] "Good" rock music became that which is sanctioned by white middle-class tastes. The rise of watchdog-cum-censor organizations such as the PMRC and the coalition of groups combating stagediving add to the prescriptive definition of a (white and middle-class) mother's duties. Mothers must take the time to screen their children's music, read reviews, and generally protect their kids from the taint of "morally corrupt" music—like that performed by Courtney Love.

Love herself didn't have this sort of protective mothering, the press tells us over and over. Love's early life reads like a nightmare scenario of the excesses of the 1960s hippie lifestyle As *Newsweek* described it,

> Courtney's background gives major clues to her behavior. Born in 1965 to San Francisco hippie parents, she had a notoriously unstable childhood. Her father was a Grateful Dead scenester; her mother, Linda Carroll, was from a wealthy family and later became a therapist whose clients have included radical '60s fugitive Katherine Ann Power. Courtney's parents split when she was very young, and she moved around a lot as a kid— Oregon, New Zealand, Australia, Oregon again. Her mother remarried several times, and at 12 Courtney landed in an Oregon reformatory for shoplifting a Kiss T-shirt. The rest of her adolescence was spent bouncing in and out of reform schools, working as a stripper, singing in bands.[21]

The above is a rather restrained recitation of the "horrors" of Love's childhood. Her parents divorced when Love was two. Her father might or might not have given her very strong LSD when she was a small child. Born Love Michelle Harrison, she was renamed Courtney Michelle Harrison at age three; then she assumed the last name of each of her mother's two subsequent husbands, sticking finally with Courtney Love. The child, we are led to believe, was left with a rather unstable sense of identity. She followed her mother's peripatetic forays and was occasionally left in the care of others when she proved too hard to handle.[22] After reform school, Love became an emancipated adult at sixteen, living in various places around the world while bankrolled by a trust fund inherited from her mother's side of the family. Love remains estranged from her parents.

A caustic *Washington Post* writer commented that "[w]omen of Love's generation frequently seem, through their mothers, to have inherited the worst of both worlds."[23] The quip refers to Love's supposedly messy sexual politics, characterized as a muddle between Eisenhower-era domesticity and hippie feminism; allegedly, Love and sister Generation Xers reflect the "bad" mothering of the baby boomers who rejected traditional domesticity. As Melissa Rossi, Love's unauthorized biographer, assesses Love's upbringing, "in short, Courtney was a product of a world where the adults were absorbed in getting their heads together."[24] Now, it follows, these monstrous products are becoming bad mothers themselves.

The frequent repetition of the saga of Love's childhood acquires the force to damn all "unconventional" modes of mothering. In particular, the representation of Love as a person, and now a mother, who was warped by her hippie mother's irresponsibility, can be used to validate conservative notions of "family values," promoted as the antidote to the "moral wreckage" of the past three decades.

Much of the mainstream's horrified fascination with Love's behavior centers on her purported on-and-off dalliance with heroin. Even before her husband committed suicide, and before her band released the album which would propel them to rock stardom, Love became notorious through a profile published in *Vanity Fair* magazine. This profile repeated rumors that Love had used heroin while pregnant with her daughter. Upon the baby's birth, the Los Angeles County of Children's Services removed the child from Love and Cobain and placed her with Love's sister for a month, largely because of the innuendo in the *Vanity Fair* article.[25] The child had been born healthy, but Love later admitted that she had indeed used heroin during her pregnancy but stopped as soon as she found out that she was expecting. The stigma of drug use and abuse has stuck with Love ever since, and not without cause. When asked about it in a December 1994 interview with *Rolling Stone,* Love characterized her drug use as follows: "I take Valiums. Percodan. Don't like heroin. It turns me into a cunt. Makes me ugly. Never liked it. Hate needles. When I did do it, it was like [*holds out her arm and turns her head away*]. I have used heroin—after Kurt died."[26]

In addition, Love's references to the "smack-addled prose" of her own "orthographically challenged" Internet and America Online postings do not help her image as a junkie mom. Therefore, when Barbara Walters asked her, point-blank in the middle of her interview, if she was on anything, we were set up to doubt her. When Walters followed that question with "Have you ever used drugs in front of your daughter?" we were led to imagine a sordid scene of candles, spoons, and works interspersed among the baby toys.

Beyond "irresponsible behavior" or even drug abuse, Love's most damaging activity as a mother is her refusal to deny her sexuality. Her physical appearance models that of the stereotypical slatternly woman, or whore. Clad in torn baby-doll dresses a few sizes too small for her full-figured body, Love exaggerates the already sexualized effect by painting her full, sensuous lips bright red. She wears her dyed hair tousled. Bruises from her stagedives into audiences frequently mar her exposed skin.

She does not fit the normative image of a mother as desexualized or asexual.

But physical appearance is not all that marks Love as sexual, and a "bad" form of sexual at that. Love's stagediving has definite sexual connotations. She harangues audiences with sexual gestures. One particularly nasty observer of her stage show circulates the claim that Love positions the stage monitor so that she can raise one leg upon it, exposing her naked crotch to the audience. As dubious as this claim may be, Love's public appearances, whether on stage or not, are distinctly sexualized. In addition, Love has been linked romantically with many other rock artists since her husband's suicide, violating unwritten but forceful rules that dictate an appropriate period of mourning. Love is also alleged to have harassed at least one of her lovers after their breakup.[27] To further upset the moral guardians of the mainstream, Love has flirted with bisexuality, guaranteed to raise the hackles of those who would protect our youth from such influences.

Love's flaunting of her sexual nature rails against normative definitions of mothers' sexuality. The hue and cry against Love for this transgression rings loud. The normative definition of mothers' sexuality is that it is absent or in abeyance. Love exposes that belief for the oppressive fallacy that it is, and for that she is punished. As with her drug use, Love is demonized not only as herself but as a proxy for those supposedly sexually transgressive "welfare mothers," accused by conservatives and other "protectors" of family values of transmitting immoral values while draining the public coffers. Once again, mothers who would retain their sexuality are policed, and class boundaries inscribed, through the figure of Courtney Love.

Many critics within the so-called oppositional culture of rock also use Love's active transgression of the boundaries of normative mothering to marginalize and dismiss her musical work. This includes everyone from academics chattering on the Internet to rock critics to Nirvana fans who continue to spread the rock version of an "urban legend" that Kurt Cobain actually wrote the songs, or at least the melodic bridges, on Hole's *Live through This*. This excerpt from a posting on alt.music.alternative exemplifies the milder sorts of derision tossed at Love from discursive sites within the rock formation:

> She's a pretty bad musician who seems to model herself after Sid Vicious' girlfriend [Nancy Spungen, who was murdered by the ex-Sex Pistol shortly

before his own death by heroin overdose]. She did heroin while she was pregnant. She was married to an extremely talented musician, but she apparently was too caught up in her own addiction to prevent him from killing himself. Then she drops the ball again; her bass player overdoses too. What an impressive resume! She definitely deserves center stage at Lollapalooza. We should have stoned her.[28]

The author of this post stops short of accusing Love of her husband's murder, a charge which has been disseminated widely through the World Wide Web and tabloid television and appeared as the cover story in the April 1996 issue of the pro-drug, countercultural magazine *High Times*.[29] In addition to reciting the litany of sins and deaths for which she is responsible, the author takes pains to point out that Love did heroin while pregnant—never mentioning that her late husband was also a user.

The occasional recuperative article about Love does slip through. However, these articles never manage to escape the negative frame containing Love, especially in regard to her mothering practices. Photo illustrations or information not directly relevant to the story convey the usual negative meanings attached to the figure of Love. For example, in an April 24, 1995 article, roughly a year after Cobain's suicide, *People* published an "Update" about Love. Entitled "Love's Wound," the piece took a kinder tone than most mainstream discourse about Love. However, while labeling her a "unique" mother and giving a nod to Love's attempts to be a "good mother" (signified, in this case, by her ownership of a Volvo, the "family car" of affluent suburbanites), the article still managed to highlight Love's hard-drug abuse, sexual dalliances with celebrities of both sexes, and offstage behavior which "has fueled the kind of rumors that would make even Madonna's press agent blanch."[30] Ultimately, the article reinforces the negative representation of Love's mothering practices by delivering a decidedly ambiguous message about its subject. The article concludes, in fact, by attributing Frances's positive development in large part to her paternal grandmother rather than Love.

Besides offering an implicit instruction guide for "good" motherhood, the article just cited suggests another reason why the moral guardians love to hate Love. She uses her "bad" mother persona in the same way she uses her "bad" girl persona. For example, bringing her daughter on tour with her becomes a complex and contradictory act—and in many ways, a strong sign of Love's contempt for conventional mores and beliefs. On the one hand, despite social changes in recent years, the belief that mothers should be with their children at all times runs deep in the American psyche. This belief underlies much of the new conservatism of the religious right, and even those in Congress who supported and won legislation for the television V-chip: mothers have abdicated their responsibility to protect children from the mass media (and the likes of Courtney Love who appear on it); therefore, we must substitute an electronic device and a censorious rating system for good motherhood. When Love, a denizen of the dread MTV, brings her daughter on tour with her, she provokes the ire of the mainstream and exposes the hypocrisy of its derision.

On the other hand, Love does like to play the "bad" girl. Flaunting her transgressive style of mothering lets her antagonize her mainstream detractors, as well as expose the inherent conservatism and reactionary gender politics which imbue and haunt rock. It is not clear, however, that the latter is always Love's intent. It is difficult for "women in rock" to break free of the masculinized tropes which define rock style, attitude, and "authenticity." Love's persona could just be a gender-bending reiteration of the rock and roll "bad" boy act, with little if any self-consciously feminist politics attached to it. In this way, Love may be interpreted as playing into the hands of those that would keep women on the margins of rock.

However, in the case of Love, and possibly for other women who would practice "transgressive motherhood" in rock or any other site, it is ultimately not that simple. Love does seem vulnerable to the traditional messages and definitions of motherhood. Her public pronouncements in the televised interview with Walters, and in other public fora, including the Internet, indicate that the dominant maternal stereotype has Love under its sway. Love, as of this writing in November 1996, is attempting to project a lower-key, or at least less offensive, public image.[31] This change might indeed issue from maternal concern for her young child's development; or she might be moving away from the "bad" mother act in order to pursue a film career. However, the film role that "broke" Love as an actress is that of the ex-stripper and junkie who became the fourth wife of the publisher of *Hustler* magazine in *The People vs. Larry Flynt*, and the movie includes nude scenes and scenes in which she is shooting up. This indicates that Love is not likely to stop transgressing, and thereby questioning, the artificial boundaries between "good" and "bad" motherhood anytime soon.

NOTES

1. Ironically, until she assumed the mantle of rock widow upon the murder of her husband, John Lennon, in 1980, Ono never received the popular respect she deserved for her many years as an avant-garde artist on both the London and New York scenes in the 1960s and for her pioneering musical work.

2. It took the announcement of Madonna's pregnancy to push Love out of the "bad mother of the moment" spotlight. Upon the birth of Madonna's baby in October 1996, however, the mainstream media softened its views of Madonna's fitness to mother. Unwed mother Madonna apparently made all the right moves, including one of her trademark chameleon-like changes of image, during the pregnancy which may have softened public attitudes toward her. In addition, since her daughter's birth and as of this writing in November 1996, Madonna has been keeping her baby out of the public eye and maintaining an uncharacteristically low profile.

3. Lawrence Grossberg, *"We Gotta Get Out of This Place": Popular Conservatism and Postmodern Culture* (New York: Routledge, 1992), 144–45.

4. Simon Reynolds and Joy Press, *The Sex Revolts: Gender, Rebellion and Rock'n'Roll* (Cambridge: Harvard University Press, 1995), 4.

5. Ibid., 5.

6. Ibid., 6.

7. The first, and still the best, of this new brand of rock "herstory" is Gillian Gaar, *She's a Rebel: The History of Women in Rock & Roll* (Seattle: Seal Press, 1992). A more recent herstory, *She Bop: The Definitive History of Women in Rock, Pop and Soul* (New York: Penguin Books, 1995), by Lucy O'Brien, a British journalist, supplies more commentary than the Gaar book but, despite its title, is less comprehensive.

8. For example, the second edition of the *Rolling Stone History of Rock and Roll*, a canonical volume, albeit published before the recent revisionist attempts to write women into rock history, included profiles of just two female performers.

9. For example, a male respondent on Rocklist, an Internet discussion group, upon learning of Madonna's pregnancy, wondered whether Madonna would now focus on exclusively softer sounds.

10. Lucy O'Brien, *She Bop*, 117.

11. Charles M. Young, "One Tough Mother & The Pretenders," *Musician* 65 (March 1984): 53.

12. Karen Schoemer, "Playing the Game of Love: Courtney Love's Bad-Girl Image Threatens to Overshadow Her Music," *Newsweek*, February 6, 1995, 56.

13. Mark Jenkins, "Courtney Love's Militant Muddle," *Washington Post*, October 1, 1995, H5.

14. Sam Whiting, "Love Loses It at Lollapalooza: Hole's Shoreline Set Cut

Short When Courtney Scuffles with Fans," *San Francisco Chronicle*, August 19, 1995, E1.

15. Gannett News Service, September 29, 1994.

16. Lorna Frame, "Mother of All Rebels," *Daily Record*, October 16, 1996, 10.

17. Dan Hurley, "When Music Turns to Mayhem: What Every Parent Should Know about Rock Concerts," *Family Circle*, August 8, 1995. The other notable "Washington Wives" included Susan Baker, wife of then Treasury Secretary James A. Baker III, Nancy Thurmond, wife of Senator Strom Thurmond, and Georgie Packwood, now ex-wife of the notorious and disgraced ex-Senator Bob Packwood.

18. John Morthland, "Rock'n'Roll Feels the Fire," *High Fidelity*, December 1985, 75+.

19. Neil Strauss, "Wal-Mart's CD Standards Are Changing Pop Music," *New York Times*, November 12, 1996, 1.

20. Morthland, "Rock'n'Roll Feels the Fire," 75.

21. Schoemer, "Playing the Game of Love," 56.

22. Craig Marks, "Endless Love," *Spin* 10, no. 11 (February 1995).

23. Nicole Arthur, "The Hole Truth: What Courtney Love is and What She Isn't," *Washington Post*, May 21, 1995, G01.

24. Melinda Rossi, *Courtney Love: Queen of Noise, A Most Unauthorized Biography* (New York: Pocket Books, 1996), 24.

25. Roger Catlin, "'Vanity Fair' Transforms Love from Addict to Angel," *Austin-American Statesman*, May 30, 1995, E10.

26. Mark Seliger, "Life after Death: Courtney Love," *Rolling Stone*, December 15, 1994, 65.

27. Rossi, *Courtney Love*, 130.

28. anstine@uniblab.sas.upenn.edu (David R. Anstine), August 5, 1994, a posting on alt.music.alternative published in the alt.fan.courtney-love faq.

29. Los Angeles private detective Tom Grant has launched a crusade to prove that Love murdered or otherwise arranged for the murder of Cobain, despite the fact that Cobain's death was ruled a suicide almost immediately. Grant maintains an elaborate World Wide Web site which he constantly updates with more data proving that Love is a murderess. The address of Grant's site is http://home.earthlink.net/tomgrant/

30. Steve Dougherty et al., "Love's Wound: Kurt Cobain's Widow, Courtney Love, Lives with Her Grief and Her Anger," *People*, April 24, 1994, 50.

31. Jeff Giles, "Courtney's Second Coming," *Newsweek*, October 21, 1996, 92.

Chapter 24

Murdering Mothers

Annalee Newitz

I like to read true crime stories about women who kill their children. It's become something of a hobby. Recently, I completed a project about true crime books that chronicle the lives of serial killers,[1] and my fascination with these male murderers (for serial killers are overwhelmingly male) led me to wonder where women fit into the equation. Women who kill, my research initially revealed, are often housewives or domestic workers.[2] Many end up killing the very people who share their domestic spaces: their families. Over half of female murderers kill family members; by contrast, men prefer strangers.[3] Headlines during the early nineties seemed to confirm these statistics and demonstrated that I am not the only person who is fascinated by women who kill. Newspapers and books described how Susan Smith had murdered her children; Kathleen Bush, honored by the Clinton administration for her fortitude in caring for her ill daughter, was reported to have been secretly poisoning her child for years by putting feces into her feeding tube; and everyone has been talking about the live-action remake of Disney's *101 Dalmatians,* featuring Glenn Close as Cruella De Vil, a sadistic mother figure whose lust for puppies merges themes of child abuse with creepy camp.

In 1987, bestselling true-crime author Ann Rule published *Small Sacrifices: A True Story of Passion and Murder,* which detailed the crimes of Diane Downs, a woman who shot her children and tried to blame the crime on "a stranger" attempting to carjack them. That Rule, one of the only bestselling authors in the true-crime genre, had turned her attention to filicide, is itself indicative of what currently arouses our national morbid fascination. Like thousands of others who read Rule's book, and gobbled up column inches about Susan Smith, I have something of a personal investment in these stories. While I cannot account for the individual predilections of every true-crime fan, I *can* offer a few compelling hypotheses about why so many of us in the late twentieth century are reading about mothers who kill. We are, in one way or another, trying to figure out how to live without children; and perhaps more importantly, we are trying to live without motherhood as we have known it.

Mainstream conceptions of motherhood, and feminine identity itself, are undergoing violent transformation. As more women enter the workplace as professionals and skilled laborers, as the days before legal abortion fade into memory, and as new images of dynamic, strong women begin to populate the mass media, we find it increasingly difficult to pinpoint what a "good" mother would be. How to be a mother at all is an even bigger issue. By and large, women who want to have families must work full-time in order to support them; the old ideal of "a man at work and a woman in the home" is not just morally repugnant to many women but often economically impossible. While "nontraditional" single-parent homes, blended families, and queer families have become more common, equally common are the women who put off childbirth until their forties—or indefinitely—so that they can establish their careers. And then there are the women like myself, who simply don't want to have and raise children. Many women and men simply cannot have families in precisely the way their parents did, or choose not to.[4]

Yet traditional ideas about parenting, and mothering in particular, remain with us and generate painful contradictions in our daily lives. Women are "free" to remain childless, and yet the general reaction to a child-free woman in the United States is still one of polite dismay, and even not-so-polite moral judgment. If a woman who has reached a certain age doesn't have children, the logic goes, something must be wrong. Although one never has to explain why one *wants* to have children, I've found that choosing *not* to have them requires justification. And this justification doesn't come easy; generally, it is not enough to assert that I just don't care to have children, or that I am too busy with work. People seem to be waiting for some darker reason, some hidden failure in my character or trauma from my past which makes me incapable of childrearing. It is for this reason that I've turned to true crime. In books about women who kill their children, I find one form of justification. I find good reasons for women not to have children: here, in the paperback section at your local drugstore, are stories about women alarmingly similar to myself, who had children because it was expected of them, and became homicidal.

But why do I need to go to such extremes to dream up a female self-image which involves refusing motherhood? Perhaps because women who do not become mothers are still considered "bad" and even taboo. I often get the feeling that, at least in the estimation of U.S. pop culture and media, women cannot choose to remain childless; they can only choose to be a good mother or a bad one. Images and stories about bad mothers become, for me, a kind of substitute for stories about nonmothers. Frequently, the closest mainstream media can come to imagining a woman without children is to imagine a woman who has somehow destroyed her children through abuse, murder, or neglect. Rejecting motherhood gets recast as rejecting one's actual, living children. This idea is an incredible burden for many women: even as they are trying to strike out into new territory as workers and leaders, they are having to cope with the guilt of being "bad" for not bearing children (or not rearing them in the right way).

One way to deal with this guilt is to discover what it means to be *truly* guilty, and *truly* bad, in stories about women like Diane Downs or Kathleen Bush. Women like myself negotiate our way through narratives about bad mothers in order to begin imagining our own narratives about having no children at all. Reading about women who kill their children is not just a titillating distraction; it's not just about the disturbing pleasures of imagining mothers engaged in the act of murder. These stories are also a way to murder the idea of "mother" itself; they provide an escape route into another female identity entirely, one that does not inevitably head toward pregnancy and childrearing. The murdering mother is more than just a killer of children; she can be understood as an outlaw figure, a romantic antihero. She is a killer of tradition, a woman whose crimes seem to protest the social values which make women into mothers against their wishes, or under conditions not of their own choosing.

Susan Smith's Unnatural Act

Sweet-faced, white Susan Smith told South Carolina police in 1994 that she was desperate to find her young children, who had just been abducted by a black male stranger. Tabloid and mainstream media went wild, casting Smith as an innocent small-town victim of big-time crime. Later, the "Susan Smith Case" became sensational news when it turned out that Smith had been lying, had invented a menacing black stranger to cover up the fact that she had deliberately drowned her children by locking them in her car and letting it roll into a lake. Suddenly, Smith was much more complex than the media had initially thought. She was a traditional southern woman who seemed cut out for the role of mother, yet nevertheless decided to kill her two sons. As Andrea Peyser describes in *Mother Love, Deadly Love: The Susan Smith Murders,* Smith was voted "friendliest" in her high school class—a true honor in the small southern town of Union. But the murders suggested that her "friendliness" was a mask.[5]

What it masked is a source of some debate. Was Smith a suicidally depressed, mentally ill young woman, or a selfish, violent slut? In her murder confession, Smith wrote, "I felt more anxieties coming on me about not wanting to live. I felt I couldn't be a good mom anymore, but I didn't want my children to grow up without a mom. I felt I had to end our lives." Instead, she ended only the lives of her children. As investigators subsequently discovered, Smith had been suicidal for years (she attempted suicide the first time at age thirteen); at one point she went to a high school counselor for help with depression, claiming that she was being sexually molested by her stepfather. After talking with her mother, Smith recanted and never raised the subject publicly again. According to Peyser, most people in Union believed that Smith had invented the abuse story to get attention.[6] While stories of her stepfather's abuse were left unsubstantiated, what remained unquestionable were stories of the rejection and sexual manipulation Smith experienced with other men in her life. David Smith, her husband and the father of her children, had a number of not-so-secret affairs. When the Smiths separated, Susan became involved with a wealthy young man, Tom Findlay, whom she hoped to marry. Findlay had sex with Smith occasionally for several months, then dumped her, claiming that he wasn't ready for marriage and didn't want to be saddled with children.

This last relationship, which ended in a rejection explicitly involving Smith's children, became part of the prosecution's argument that Smith had killed the boys in a malicious, premeditated way, essentially to snare a man. Perhaps more disturbing to the general public was the way that Smith, apparently a happy, competent mother, was able to kill her children and lie about it so well. It would seem that she wore a mask not only of "friendliness" but of "motherhood" too. At one point, Peyser imagines something like a monster lurking under Smith's motherly façade: she describes "a perverse grimace, an expression of pain and rage so great, its only means of survival was to destroy."[7] In another passage,

Peyser implies that Smith's self-interested public statements reveal her true (homicidal) personality.

> Aside from briefly recounting the carjacking, Susan used her first few minutes of fame to discuss the main subject on her mind: Susan. "I can't even describe what I'm going through. I mean, my heart is—it just aches so bad. I can't sleep. I can't eat. I can't do anything but think about them."
> ... There was Susan, dwelling upon her own feelings of inadequacy. Her first five sentences began with the word *I*. This could be understandable, under the circumstances. But many a mother within earshot might wonder why a woman who'd just seen her sons stolen before her eyes would choose to talk mostly about herself.[8]

In Peyser's book, there is a kind of connection established between homicidal "pain and rage" and a woman's desire to express her feelings publicly. Peyser seems suspicious of Smith's "choos[ing] to talk mostly about herself," when, implicitly, Smith should be focusing all her attention on her children. One wonders how Smith might have phrased her statements if she had actually been innocent. Does a good mother never begin sentences with "I"? Does she utterly efface all her selfhood and speak only about her children? If she had, in fact, not been lying, how could Smith have phrased, "I can't do anything but think about them," without sounding like she was talking "mostly about herself"?

Given the signals Peyser claims we can use to identify Smith as a child murderer, one might expect all mothers to kill their children off any day now. Pain and rage, even "perverse" pain and rage, are staples of human emotion, as is a desire to have and project a personal identity. Peyser's suspicions about Smith's feelings and public display of autonomy are deeply bound up with broader fears about women in a culture which has, traditionally, asked them to trade social power for roles as mothers and domestic caretakers. As feminist critic Dorothy Dinnerstein points out, mothers have been mythologized as what she calls the "dirty goddess." This myth, common in patriarchal societies, portrays mothers as selfless, capable of a kind of omnipotent love; yet it simultaneously reviles them as voracious, destructive monsters. Mothers' emotions and selfhood are feared because these women seem to have power over the life and death of their families.[9] Philip Wylie's infamous 1942 manifesto, "Common Women," on the dangers of what he called "momism," exemplifies the kind of mythologizing that Dinnerstein describes. Comparing the power of "mother" to Hitler's dictatorship, Wylie equates a mother's greatest crime with selfishness and a godlike ability to enslave her children. Sounding eerily like Peyser describing Smith, he writes,

> [Mother's] policy of protection, from the beginning, was not love of her boy but of herself, and as she found returns coming in from the disoriented young boy in smiles, pats . . . and all manner of childish representations of the real business, she moved on to possession. Possession of the physical person of a man is slavery; possession of the spirit of a man is slavery also.[10]

Built into the very structure of motherhood, then, is the idea of a "mask" which might be torn away to reveal mother not as a devoted caretaker but as a kind of demon. Wylie rips the mask off mother's "policy of protection" to reveal Hitler, a slavemaster, the genocidal face of the women we call "mom."

Smith's murder of her sons, then, confirms the worst nightmares of a male-dominated society, in which mother turns out to be exactly as horrifying and murderous as we thought she was all along.[11] Given that Smith is so obviously a sexist stereotype waiting to happen, why is it that I find her crimes peculiarly sympathetic? I'm opposed to all forms of killing, including the death penalty, and yet it is precisely the extremity of Smith's action, the sheer brutal magnitude of it, which arouses my identification. Perhaps it would be most accurate to say that my identification is a contextual affair. Only when I look at Smith's life as a narrative of female oppression do I begin to think, "If I lived the way she had in Union, South Carolina, then maybe, just maybe, I would have had to kill someone too." I keep going back in my mind to Smith's attempt at suicide when she was thirteen and her later accusation that her stepfather was molesting her. Sure, she could have made it up. But what if she didn't? What if her "masks" came from years of suppressing the truth about what was happening to her body, to her family, and to her selfhood in a town where her suicide attempts were dismissed as little attention-grabbing stunts? Smith, like millions of women before her, was trying to raise children in a world which told her to be "friendly" even if she was in serious danger or suffering from excruciating self-hatred. Written down like that, Smith's life becomes for me a kind of allegory about the violence generated by the psychological repression and social oppression that go along with gender hierarchy. Smith's crime, and her lies after she committed it, might be understood as a rational response to what she'd been taught as a traditional woman: the truth about your life, no matter how horrible, doesn't matter if you can put a pretty smile on your face.

Smith ripped off her own mask, and in so doing called into question the "naturalness" of a woman's desire to mother. She also violated the most sanctified code of "family values" when she chose to kill her children. Had Smith simply killed her rich ex-boyfriend, or her estranged husband, her crime would hardly have caught anyone's attention outside of her immediate region. "Heat of passion" murders are a staple of both homicide files and pop culture; indeed, these murders tend to confirm a belief in the idea that conflicts between the sexes are inevitable. Smith's filicide undeniably confirms similarly problematic notions about supposedly hysterical, hormonally imbalanced women,[12] but it also undercuts the idea that women's essential identities can be characterized by a need to nurture and protect children. Far from being controlled by "nature," women are constantly making a *choice* to raise their children; that Smith could decide to stop raising her own, indeed to eliminate them from her life, makes this quite clear.

Smith's conduct will not advance the cause of feminism, and if anything it may shore up prejudices against women and mothers who wish to be taken seriously as rational beings. And yet something about her, the combination of sweet housewife and dangerous killer in her personality, serves as a kind of warning against forcing women to don a mask which they do not wish to wear. As journalist Ann Jones puts it, "Women who kill find extreme solutions to problems that thousands of women cope with in more peaceable ways from day to day."[13] One might add that the extremity of Smith's "solution" reveals the unacknowledged extremity of her position as a mother under male domination. Smith is like a terrorist—an unconscious terrorist—whose methods are reprehensible, but whose message is not. In my fantasy reconstruction of her, Smith seems to taunt, "Just try to make me be a mother. Try it and I'll kill you." I'm not advocating what Smith did, just as I would not advocate terrorism. I'm simply confessing that my emotional response to her actions is different from my moral one. For better or worse, Smith's story makes me feel powerful. She proves that not all women should be mothers, and she shows why.

At the same time, the reception of Smith's crime in the news and in books like Peyser's is a reminder that most people still associate female autonomy and childlessness with selfishness and extreme acts of criminal violence. Smith may be calling into question the rightness of "family values" for everyone, but it's just as easy to claim that her lack of these values drove her to filicide. Either way, Smith's story forces people to acknowledge that something about motherhood made one woman want to kill.

The Kinky Shrink and Her Boy

Motherhood can also inspire sadism in women and can even lead female professionals to engage in the sexual harassment of their junior male colleagues. In the case of Margaret Bean-Bayog, we see how the powerful social correlation between female identity and motherhood is destructive for both women and men. Dubbed "the kinky shrink" in the popular press, Bean-Bayog was a respected Freudian psychiatrist in Boston, where she worked at Harvard and in her own private practice. She was a high-ranking female professional in a field dominated by men. Childless, and yet wanting children very badly, Bean-Bayog devoted her time to treating problems associated with dysfunctional families and alcohol abuse. At one point an alcoholic herself, Bean-Bayog seemed committed to her cause for personal, as well as professional, reasons. In 1986, Bean-Bayog began treating Paul Lozano, a suicidally depressed Harvard medical student suffering from, among other things, a sense of alienation from his peers due to his working-class Latino background. After seeing her for several months, Lozano attempted suicide again, and Bean-Bayog began seeing him in therapy four times a week for free (she claimed he had agreed to pay her later). To treat him, she decided on what she called an "experimental technique" in which she would play the role of his mother, and he would play the role of her dependent, needy child.

Bean-Bayog, over a period of years, used their role playing to encourage Lozano to become intensely emotionally involved with her. Calling him "her boy," she sent him cards and notes signed "Love, Mom," and gave him stuffed animals to hug when she wasn't around. Lozano, for his part, played the role of little boy, even writing detailed stories with Bean-Bayog about things he imagined they might do together as mother and son.[14] As their relationship deepened, Bean-Bayog wrote Lozano a set of flash cards which he was supposed to read whenever he was lonely for her, one of which read,

> You can too act and feel like a three-year-old when you're twenty-five. You can curl up with the blanket, the sweater, the pound puppy [a stuffed dog

she gave him], all the notes I've written you and all the books. You can breast-feed and be cozy. No one can take those feelings from you.[15]

Later, Bean-Bayog wrote a set of sadomasochistic sexual fantasies about herself and Lozano, which somehow ended up in Lozano's possession.

> You stand at my feet, staring at my vagina. I am embarrassed and ashamed. I pull to close my legs closed but I can't. You smile. Suddenly, you notice my vagina is shining wet. You can't believe it. You love it. You kneel down between my widely separated knees and stroke it. I writhe, aroused and humiliated. . . . You make some notes. "Enjoys restraints. Manipulative and seductive."[16]

Not surprisingly, Lozano's therapy did nothing to help his condition. He continued to be suicidally depressed, and he began manifesting new symptoms, such as speaking in baby talk and crying on the phone with his sister. Refusing to take his antidepressant medication on a regular basis, he was in and out of hospitals due to his nervous breakdowns and suicidal thoughts.

Bean-Bayog and her husband were in the process of adopting a baby in 1990. Around that time she decided to terminate therapy with Lozano. With her baby, she did not have enough time for him, she said, and could no longer hope to make him well.[17] Nine months after she terminated therapy, in 1991, Lozano committed suicide after saying he heard Bean-Bayog's voice in his head telling him to die. His family discovered a box in his apartment which turned out to contain letters and other gifts from Bean-Bayog, including the sexual fantasies she had written about him. They decided to sue Bean-Bayog for malpractice. At subsequent legal proceedings, it was never proven that Bean-Bayog had actually given the fantasy scenarios to Lozano: she claimed he had stolen them from her office, and that she had merely written them down for herself, in order to deal with feelings of countertransference[18] coming out of the therapy. Although Lozano told another psychiatrist that he and Bean-Bayog had engaged in various sexual acts during therapy sessions, this also was never proven. Ultimately, Bean-Bayog's insurance paid the Lozano family one million dollars in damages, and she gave up her medical license rather than face a malpractice suit.

Bean-Bayog was not Lozano's mother, nor did she kill him. Yet she played the role of his mother, four days a week for nearly four years, and the way she played that role probably strengthened his wish to die. One thing is certainly clear: the mother role she played was incestuous and overpowering. She did not act like a mother who wanted "her boy" to grow up and desire other women. In short, she did not behave like a mother who wanted her child to survive to adulthood.

Bean-Bayog is, in many ways, a caricature of the overwhelming, sexually voracious woman who converts men into children and destroys them. In an ironic twist, she is a Freudian analyst who resembles nothing so much as Freud's "phallic mother,"[19] a woman both powerful and erotic who haunts the male unconscious, a reminder of a time in his life when he was helpless and his mother seemed like one of the strongest people in the world. More ironic yet, the "phallic mother" is a concept that feminist psychoanalysts and cultural theorists have attacked for decades now as a sexist invention attributable more to Freud's nineteenth-century sensibilities than to any kind of universal psychic reality.[20] Interestingly, of the two books written about the Bean-Bayog case, the one which I would argue takes a more "feminist" stance, Eileen McNamara's *Breakdown*, harshly condemns Bean-Bayog's actions.[21] It would seem that, when the phallic mother does happen to appear in real life, and not just in Freud's fantasies, feminism is deeply troubled by her.[22]

McNamara makes it clear that she believes Bean-Bayog turned Lozano into "her boy" for emotional and sexual gratification, in part because she wanted a baby of her own so much. At first glance, McNamara seems to be setting up her account of the case in opposition to "feminism" when she notes that feminists were particularly angered by accusations against Bean-Bayog, and that many of her supporters were feminists who felt she was getting unequal treatment as a professional woman.[23] Yet McNamara's own feminist stance becomes clear when she suggests that a woman might be capable of using her professional and personal power to victimize someone. One of the basic tenets of second-generation feminist analysis—going back to Betty Friedan, Sara Evans, or even French theorist Julia Kristeva[24]—has been that one must use both personal and political analysis in order to explain women's oppression, and indeed the oppression of many other minority groups as well. McNamara makes her case against Bean-Bayog—and for Lozano—by explaining the personal dimensions of both their lives, and how the personal invariably informs the political (in this case, the "political" is represented by the "professional").

Bean-Bayog's background as a highly educated third-generation doctor, and her status as a white middle-class woman who had deeply intimate relationships with men of color, come into play as McNamara sketches out her portrait of an individual who could not distinguish between her personal desires and professional obligations to Lozano.

> For one thing, [Bean-Bayog] had crafted a therapeutic role for herself as a nurturing mother at the very time in her own life when she was in the midst of frustrating and ultimately unsuccessful fertility treatments. . . . How could she expect to keep her personal yearnings for motherhood out of the therapeutic process that cast her in the very role she craved? The handwritten children's stories found among Paul Lozano's belongings, while written by her, were collaborative efforts between patient and therapist, she insists. But the themes read more like a white middle-class woman's idea of an idyllic childhood than those of a Latino male. They make sugar cookies, for instance, not *sopaipillas* or *empañadas*. [25]

Bean-Bayog may have had a personal motivation for arousing Lozano's affections, and yet at the same time could have used her class and racial status—not to mention her clinical relationship with him—to manipulate Lozano into believing that if he did not have her approval and love he would die.

McNamara notes that Bean-Bayog's husband is a Filipino and that the couple ultimately adopted a Hispanic baby boy. While Bean-Bayog doesn't fit the strict definition of a racist, she certainly has a fraught personal history with men of color, and the fact that she turned Lozano, a Hispanic male, into "her boy" before adopting a Hispanic male baby is slightly unsettling. Although Bean-Bayog recorded Lozano telling her in therapy that he had trouble with cultural differences between his family and Anglo families, and that he "[couldn't] understand Anglo culture very well," McNamara says that "there is no indication, in 986 pages of office notes, that issues of class, race, and culture were ever explored in four years of therapy." [26] Bean-Bayog may have confused her personal relationships to men of color with her professional relationship to Lozano; it also seems clear that she may have contributed to the "repression"—and exacerbation—of Lozano's problems regarding cultural assimilation. Having established these possibilities, McNamara speculates about why Lozano displayed classic signs of borderline personality disorder caused by child abuse. "Since Paul Lozano was first diagnosed as borderline in 1987, six months after he began his intense relationship with Dr. Bean-Bayog, is it not possible that he displayed those symptoms as a result of a sexual relationship with his psychiatrist?" [27] Bean-Bayog's treatment of Lozano in therapy could be viewed as tantamount to sexual abuse, not to mention sexual harassment. And, furthermore, Lozano might have also

been "symptomatic" as a result of a therapeutic relationship that repressed his cultural identity.

As McNamara goes on to explain, it is commonly accepted that women
might develop borderline symptoms after being sexually molested or
otherwise mistreated by a male psychiatrist. McNamara's account suggests
one of the basic tenets of feminist practice that feminist supporters of
Bean-Bayog seem to have forgotten: don't blame the victim. While Bean-
Bayog may have been "victimized" by the media, the real victim in this
case would appear to be Lozano, who committed suicide after one of the
most powerful people in his life told him she could no longer help him.
Bean-Bayog was not only Lozano's psychiatrist, not only his "mother,"
but also his high-ranking colleague at Harvard Medical School, where she
was a doctor and Lozano was a student. Bean-Bayog had both personal
and professional power over Lozano, and it is precisely this kind of
ambiguous power—and its particular way of creating victims—that feminists have worked to demystify. A blurred line between personal and
professional power often leads to sexual harassment on the job, or women
hitting the "glass ceiling" due to sexism. Perhaps understandably, however,
feminism as such is largely unwilling to acknowledge that sometimes
women can abuse power in the same way men do. Women can use the
role of "mother" to take power by tapping into our fears of the "dirty
goddess," or the "phallic mother," just as men can use the role of patriarch
to call upon the power of history's unjust ideas about male superiority.
Both roles, "mother" and "patriarch," are personal and political: they are
simultaneously family and public roles.

Unlike Susan Smith, who seems to have acted out of a sense of
powerlessness, Margaret Bean-Bayog *chose* to play the role of a pathological mother, because her professional credentials gave her the power to do
it. Both women engaged in extremely transgressive behavior, illustrating
how the cultural injunction to raise children can elicit female violence
and sadism rather than love. With women like these becoming famous in
our culture, it's clear that there is nothing simple, nothing "pure," about
motherhood.

What's Feminism Got to Do with It?

I am not the only feminist who feels this way—indeed, clearly not the
only feminist who experiences an uneasy identification with women who

destroy their children rather than attempting to destroy a culture which forces them to choose between being "good" mothers or weird, undefined outsiders. The bad mother, and her role as social transgressor, lends herself well to feminist narratives. For instance, one of the most famous child abuse/murder cases of the past two decades, the case of Hedda Nussbaum and Joel Steinberg in New York, is the topic of *Waverly Place*, a work of pseudofiction by Susan Brownmiller. Brownmiller changed the face of feminism in the 1970s with her book on rape, *Against Our Will: Men, Women and Rape*, which explored the way individual acts of coercive sex and sexualized violence are generated by a culture which celebrates war and confuses exploitation with progress. In *Waverly Place*, Brownmiller offers a case history of one battered woman, Judith Winograd (that is, Hedda Nussbaum), who allowed her husband Barry Kantor (Joel Steinberg) to beat their adoptive daughter to death, nearly killing Judith in the process as well. Brownmiller decided to fictionalize the case so that she could depict Nussbaum's state of mind while she lived with Steinberg, who broke her nose and pelvic bone, and scarred her lips and legs beyond recognition in their decade-long relationship.[28] Brownmiller's fictionalized recreation of Nussbaum and Steinberg's relationship also allows her to flesh out their ambiguous motivations and to invite the reader's identification with Nussbaum, the mother who watched with seeming apathy as her beaten daughter died.

The true story behind *Waverly Place* is, at least in broad outline, perfectly reproduced in the novel. In 1987, Joel Steinberg beat the couple's illegally adopted daughter, Lisa, until she passed out. She fell into a coma, and Steinberg left. Nussbaum, alone in their Greenwich Village apartment, allegedly did not alert police about their dying child for nearly a day. When police and paramedics did arrive, they found Nussbaum in what appeared to be a drugged stupor, Lisa nearly dead of head injuries and her baby brother (also adopted) tied to a crib and covered in his own feces. Lisa subsequently died. Originally both Nussbaum and Steinberg were charged with Lisa's murder, but when Nussbaum agreed to testify against Steinberg, charges against her were dropped. The case was New York's first televised murder trial. As a result, media coverage and public reaction were equally intense. While Nussbaum was technically an "innocent," suspicion about her role in Lisa's death lingered. As Richard Cohen put it in the *Washington Post* opinion section,

> A victim can also be an accessory to a crime. Nussbaum's testimony
> suggests that was the case with her. She told a tale of complicity, of a

mother who did nothing as her daughter was brutalized—who put up with the most incredible indignities herself and who, even as Lisa was taken to the hospital in a terminal coma, attempted to provide Steinberg with an alibi: the child had been injured by roller skating.[29]

Nussbaum, in this account, is a bad mother, because she obviously didn't care about her children. She wasn't directly murderous, of course, but she displayed a fascinating "lack of affect," a seeming imperviousness to the feelings of protectiveness we associate with motherhood.

Brownmiller herself is interested in exploring the meaning of the emotional blankness in her Nussbaum character, Judith. What is perhaps most striking about Brownmiller's novel is its attention to detail, the way she relentlessly brings to life Judith's internal state as she is repeatedly beaten and humiliated by Barry: "He grabbed me by the shoulders and shoved. I fell backward, banging my head against a brick wall. . . . The back of my head hurt, but it didn't matter. What mattered was the powerful current flooding between us. I felt so alert, so alive."[30] Later, the beatings grow worse as Judith tries to juggle her job as an editor at Random House with motherhood.

> "I'm hungry. Make me something to eat," he snarled. . . . "Whatsa matter? No ideas? The busy little editor forget to go shopping?" . . . He dragged [Judith] back by her feet, grabbed her neck, and banged her head against the oven. This is it, she thought. He is killing me. She tried to scream, but nothing came out. Somehow, he got the oven door open, and shoved her head and shoulders inside. *Nooooooo, I am going to be burned alive . . .* The heel of his shoe slammed into her crotch. She lay there and took the blows. She was past caring. He was stomping on her pubic bone when she passed out.[31]

Waverly Place is filled with scenes like these. While we can extrapolate, based on Brownmiller's reputation as a feminist, that the novel is intended to demonstrate the horrors of physically abusive relationships, it sometimes reads simply like a thriller. In fact, it sounds very much like the psychological horror novels Stephen King writes, where gore, shocks, and violence are part of the narrative fun.[32] I would argue that Brownmiller's first-person accounts of abuse serve as a confession that feminism itself has something of a romance with the disturbing extremes of female violence and constraint. We are supposed to hate Barry, to hate Judith's abuse, but Brownmiller also wants us to feel the erotic pull of cruelty, and the unsettling, bitter apathy of Judith's parenting.

The poetic license Brownmiller takes allows her to generate a feminist allegory, one that is as much about the failures of feminism as it is about the dangers of male domination. In the narratives that take place around Judith's first-person story, Brownmiller describes the way other characters understand Judith through their knowledge of battered women, often gained from reading feminist analysis like Brownmiller's own. Cindy Owens, her reporter character, talks to her sister Joanne, a friend of Judith's, about a series of articles she's doing on battered women. "It would be ghoulish and in poor taste, wouldn't it, if I called Judith Winograd?" she asks. Then, she adds, "Until I started this series, I never thought of Judith as a syndrome. Did you?"[33] Later, we see Cindy embrace a colleague with delight when she hears Mondale has chosen Geraldine Ferraro as his running-mate in the 1984 elections. Clearly a feminist and a woman with some professional power, Cindy thinks of Judith merely as a "syndrome," and not someone she might try to help. Brownmiller also imagines Judith and a friend attending a consciousness-raising session of the women's liberation movement in 1970. While Judith is definitely a woman who needs the kind of help feminist consciousness could give her, the meeting is alienating for her. "Eight women about their age are sitting in a sparsely furnished living room, talking about their abortions," Brownmiller writes, "Afterward Carol [Judith's friend] asks Judith, 'What did you think?' Judith considers. 'I think they're a bunch of dykes.' "[34]

It's ambiguous as to whether Brownmiller is suggesting that Judith's life is a result of rejecting feminism, or a result of feminism's rejecting her. Either way, we are given a view of two parallel worlds in *Waverly Place:* the world in which feminism and the gay rights movement happen, and the world in which a woman is nearly beaten to death over and over by her sexist lover. Brownmiller seems to ask how, with the close historical proximity between the real-life Nussbaum and the feminist movement, could a child have been beaten to death while her battered mother looked on? That a woman like Hedda Nussbaum could exist points up the failures of feminism in a way that the defeat of the ERA never could: here was a person who should have known better, whose women friends should have known better. Traditional feminism, or what is commonly called second wave feminism, cannot fully account for a woman like Hedda Nussbaum. That is, it cannot cure her apathy, her seeming love of violence, her willingness to sacrifice a child.

And yet Judith/Hedda seems to share something with feminism, too.

She was, for a while, a professional editor at Random House; and she chose to have children with a man she lived with but never married. Without knowing she was battered, one might see Judith as someone who had been profoundly liberated by feminist ideals. Indeed, as Ann Jones explains in *Women Who Kill*, female-authored homicides tend to get associated with periods of feminist organizing—not because feminism makes women kill, but because "the presence of one prompts fear of the other."[35] Indeed, Brownmiller tells Nussbaum's story because she wants to know where feminism went wrong, and what kind of woman it might be that feminism could not reach. With *Waverly Place*, Brownmiller demonstrates that the problem with feminism is that it serves only as an explanation, or a description, of women's suffering; it is not yet the kind of socially transformative tool it might be. Women around Judith see her as a "syndrome," not an ally; and even Brownmiller herself depicts Judith's situation in great detail without ever directly suggesting that there might be a way to change it.

The stories I have told about Susan Smith and Margaret Bean-Bayog are my way of doing what Brownmiller has done with Nussbaum's story, my way of offering case histories that demonstrate both the mistakes and the inroads, made by contemporary feminism.[36] Smith and Bean-Bayog are, like Nussbaum, women whom feminism cannot account for, let alone cure. But I believe their stories should end with solutions, even if those solutions are imperfect. I consider these women's stories an invitation to begin thinking about the kind of woman who does not need violent crime in order to choose childlessness, and who does not think of childlessness as a violent crime in itself. I have found, so far, one kind of feminist identity which does both, and does it with flair: I am speaking, of course, about riot grrl feminists. Not so long ago, I began to think of myself as a riot grrl too.

Riot Grrls

He said, "Get outta here, girlie
I'm just tryin' to have some fun."
So you wanna have some fun?
We'll break out the big guns.
                    —L7, from their album *Bricks Are Heavy*

> Every fucking "feminist" is not the same, every fucking
> girl is not the same, OK???
> —Kathleen Hanna, member of the band Bikini Kill

John Waters recently made a movie called *Serial Mom*, which is about a sweet housewife, someone like Susan Smith perhaps, who joyfully kills hypocritical and annoying people in her neighborhood. With her family she's gentle and loving, but when one of her son's teachers is rude to her she runs him over in a parking lot. Later, she beats a woman to death with a frozen piece of meat for watching smarmy movies like *Little Orphan Annie*. The movie is horrifying, and yet funny. *Serial Mom* has been received by fans and critics as high camp of the very best sort: mean, smart, and unrelentingly ironic. At the film's climax, "Serial Mom" attempts to escape police in a crowded nightclub where riot grrl rockers L7 are performing. L7 gleefully lift Serial Mom up on stage, and the fans cheer for her while she lights a young man on fire. Serial Mom is an icon who speaks to the riot grrl generation of feminists: she is, like her real-life "murdering mother" counterparts, an antihero whose violence contradicts (and parodies) dominant ideas of the female gender role.

The term "riot grrl" was coined in the early 80s to describe an underground movement within the alternative music and punk scenes, in which women fought the sexist stereotypes of the music industry by forming pro-feminist bands, refusing to let men segregate "mosh pits" (stylized combat dance areas) at concerts, and generally making a lot of angry noise. What characterizes the riot grrl movement within music—particularly now that it has gone mainstream with bands like Hole, L7, and even Alanis Morissette—are images and songs which combine aggressive sexuality, knowledge of women's oppression, self-confident mock-macho swagger, and a toughness suggesting that these women *would* riot if they thought they were getting the shaft. This is a group of feminists who have no trouble imagining how a woman might get so angry that she would kill her children, or poison her baby, or semideliberately drive a man to suicide.

In the nineties, riot grrl images and culture have moved beyond the music world.[37] There have been riot grrl movies which celebrate female militancy, strength, and professional competence, like *Thelma and Louise*, *Silence of the Lambs*, *Tank Girl*, *Fried Green Tomatoes*, and the *Alien* series. Riot grrl icons and narratives take for granted that female power will be central to their meaning. Yet they also have an opinion about *how* women should use power, and they grapple with problems that powerful women face as they try to be "good" in a world where having any power at all, no matter how destructive, tends to justify itself. The riot grrl is depicted as an oppositional figure, challenging traditional forms of power *and* traditional forms of subversion. Riot grrl feminism blends the pro-sex ideas of West Coast feminism[38] with the blank anger of anti-porn feminist Andrea Dworkin or Valerie Solanas's *SCUM Manifesto.*[39] Theorists like Judith Butler and Donna Haraway have provided a philosophical backdrop for riot grrl feminism, advocating the strategic use of irony and drag, as well as encouraging people to question scientific ideologies of "gender difference."[40]

Riot grrls are part of a generation which *has* female power and are trying to figure out how to explore and deploy it wisely. This exploration is, finally, what's happening when we read about Susan Smith and Margaret Bean-Bayog: their acts are so "unspeakable" precisely because we are just now inventing the language and symbolism with which to explain how their stories fit into female identity. But exploration is never enough. Just as a more traditional feminism such as Brownmiller's can explain Hedda Nussbaum's masochism but cannot save her from it, riot grrl feminism can explain Margaret Bean-Bayog's sadism but cannot save Paul Lozano from it. Riot grrls know that we live in a culture which can produce not only female servitude but also female power run amok. The lessons of Brownmiller's novel about Nussbaum remain with us, then: we cannot mistake the explanation for the cure, and we cannot become so enthralled by our powers of deduction that we forget to change our everyday lives as women. As long as we simply *describe* the problems of female identity, we are left with the impression that feminism has failed, as it failed to prevent Susan Smith and Joel Steinberg from murdering their children.

I want to argue that riot grrl feminism is so compelling precisely because it dares to ask the question, Now that women are strong, what should they do? Even so-called power feminist Naomi Wolf, who has written an entire book on how to use the "new female power," can't bring herself to ask that question.[41] Instead, she sticks with the old empty injunction to take power where you can and run with it. It is not outlandish to suggest that Wolf's idea of power is precisely what produces a woman like Smith, whose crimes are as horrible as those of the unarguably patriarchal, sexist Joel Steinberg; it also produces a Bean-Bayog, whose sexual molestation of her patient looks like nothing so much as plain old simple sexual harassment. These are women who learned about power from abusive, sexist men, women who took power in exactly the same way it had been taken from them. A riot grrl feminist knows we cannot take power exactly as we find it, because power as it exists in the world now is often destructive.

But I would want, finally, to point out that when I describe riot grrl feminism I'm being unabashedly celebratory, and I'm not offering a prescription for everyone. I do not believe that a macho grrl swagger will save us from gender inequalities and sexism. And I do not believe subversion for subversion's sake is the most useful form of social criticism, either. But being a riot grrl has given me the tools necessary to explain why having children would not make me happy—and, more importantly, it has given me a way to describe why my unhappiness would be no small affair. Because I am well aware of the power I might exert as a mother, and a woman, it is clear that making me or any woman unhappy for long enough might just result in violent retribution.

If I lived in a place where children might be raised communally, with many loving parents instead of just one or two, I would consider child care an honor and a pleasure. If child care were treated as a form of labor, and not some sort of after-work hobby involving "quality time," I would also find parenting more attractive. Parenting as I have known it, however, is unacceptable, a burden which is all too often thrust upon women as a chore they are supposed to "naturally" love and for which they rarely receive any significant social esteem or reward. When men and women of every sexual orientation are raising their children respectfully and communally, I will shed my riot grrl rage, throw away the true-crime books, and help the men change diapers. Until then, I do not want to be a mother.

NOTES

1. See Annalee Newitz, "Serial Killers, True Crime and Economic Performance Anxiety," *CineAction* 38 (October 1995): 38–46.

2. "About 67% of [female serial killers] were reported as having no legitimate employment outside the home," writes Eric Hickey in his *Serial Murderers and Their Victims* (Belmont, Calif.: Brooks-Cole, 1991), 109.

3. Hickey reports that "[male] serial murder involves primarily stranger-to-stranger violence . . . the killing of family and acquaintances by male serial killers all but disappeared in recent years" (Hickey, 139).

4. Changing ideas about childless women, and case studies of them, are documented by Mardy S. Ireland in *Reconceiving Women: Separating Motherhood from Female Identity* (New York: Guilford, 1993). Ireland identifies three groups of childless women: those who wanted to have children but could not, those who "waited too long" and didn't have children by chance, and those who consciously chose not to have them.

5. Andrea Peyser, *Mother Love, Deadly Love: The Susan Smith Murders* (New York: Harper Paperbacks, 1995), 2.

6. Ibid., 6.

7. Ibid., 125.

8. Ibid., 53–54.

9. See Dorothy Dinnerstein, *The Mermaid and the Minotaur: Sexual Arrangements and Human Malaise* (New York: Harper and Row, 1976).

10. Philip Wylie, "Common Women," in *Generation of Vipers* (Normal, Ill.: Dalkey Archive, 1996; orig. pub. 1942), 208–9.

11. No doubt the fact that Smith murdered male children also enhanced her "dirty goddess" status: she was destroying her family and destroying masculinity simultaneously.

12. As Carroll Smith-Rosenberg notes, nineteenth-century doctors warned that "female hormones" from menstruation "could drive some women temporarily insane; menstruating women might go berserk, destroying furniture, attacking family and strangers alike, and even killing their infants." See Carroll Smith-Rosenberg, *Disorderly Conduct: Visions of Gender in Victorian America* (New York: Oxford University Press, 1985), 190–91.

13. Ann Jones, *Women Who Kill*, 2d ed. (Boston: Beacon, 1996; orig. pub. 1980), 14.

14. Because Bean-Bayog took such detailed notes of their sessions, and Lozano saved their correspondence, nearly all of their mother-son fantasies were recorded on paper and later used as evidence at a court hearing.

15. Taken from Eileen McNamara's account of the Bean-Bayog case, *Breakdown: Sex, Suicide, and the Harvard Psychiatrist* (New York: Pocket Books, 1994), 99.

16. Ibid., 104.

17. Ibid., 191.

18. A term which refers to feelings aroused in the therapist by the patient.

19. Freud notes that, in the child's understanding of sexuality, "There was once a time when the male genital was found compatible with the picture of the mother." This is at a time when "[the boy] still holds women at full value," meaning that he still views them as people who possess power equal to that of men. Quotes taken from "Leonardo da Vinci and a Memory of His Childhood," in Peter Gay, ed., *The Freud Reader* (New York and London: Norton, 1989), 460–61.

20. See, for instance, Judith Herman, *Trauma and Recovery: The Aftermath of Violence* (New York: Basic Books, 1992), and Judith Butler, *Gender Trouble: Feminism and the Subversion of Identity* (New York: Routledge, 1990).

21. The other book, *Obsession*, takes the side of Bean-Bayog. See Morris and Gary Chafetz, *Obsession* (New York: Crown, 1994).

22. I would point out that McNamara never calls herself a feminist and that her position on feminism per se is never overtly discussed. Many of her underlying assumptions, however, especially regarding sexual harassment, could be characterized as feminist. Thus, my point is less that she herself is a feminist and more that her argument for Bean-Bayog's guilt implies a feminist analysis.

23. McNamara, 258, 271.

24. Betty Friedan's *The Feminine Mystique* (New York: Dell, 1963) describes how women's personal lives are structured to keep them from achieving social authority; Sara Evans's influential *Personal Politics* (New York: Vintage, 1979) elaborates on this idea, and Julia Kristeva's famous essay "Stabat Mater" combines feminist psychoanalysis with a graphic personal account of giving birth. See Toril Moi, ed., *The Kristeva Reader* (New York: Columbia University Press, 1986), 160–86.

25. McNamara, 68.

26. Ibid., 81.

27. Ibid., 280.

28. Susan Brownmiller, *Waverly Place* (New York: Grove Press, 1989), vii. Brownmiller writes, "I chose to write fiction because I wanted the freedom to invent dialogue, motivations, events, and characters based on my own understanding of battery and abuse, a perspective frequently at variance with the scenarios created by the prosecution or the defense in courts of law."

29. Richard Cohen, "When Weakness Becomes an Alibi," *Washington Post* 112 (December 21, 1988): A19.

30. Brownmiller, 39.

31. Ibid., 129–30.

32. Along these lines, it's interesting to note that horror novelist Stephen King has recently turned to writing novels about battered women; *Dolores Claiborne* and *Rose Madder* are two of these.

33. Brownmiller, 219–20.

34. Ibid., 31–32.

35. Jones, 3.

36. By this I mean that loosely affiliated set of pro-woman ideas that have come to be called "third wave feminism." For a complete and well-considered explanation of the relationship between third and second wave feminists, see Leslie Heywood and Jennifer Drake's introduction to *Third Wave Agenda* (Minneapolis: University of Minnesota Press, 1997).

37. Even a recent issue of *Entertainment Weekly* has a feature story about

rising female stars in the entertainment industry which calls these women—in movies, TV, and music—"grrrls." See Benjamin Svetkey, Chris Willman, Dave Karger, and Dan Snierson, "Women on the Verge," *Entertainment Weekly* 332 (June 21, 1996): 16–28. An up-and-coming actress in this article is called "this year's grrrl," while a singer is referred to as a "riot rocker."

38. While not all the pro-sex feminist advocates hail from the West Coast, it is a distinctive aspect of feminism in this region, where activists like Susie Bright advocate feminist pornography, and critic Constance Penley not only does scholarship on feminism and pornography at UC Santa Barbara but is also helping to create a pornographic film archive there. There is, moreover, a strong connection between the gay/bi/transgendered movement and feminism on the West Coast, which helps place sexual awareness on the front burner, as it were.

39. Dworkin is famous for her angry prose and extreme ideas in controversial books like *Woman Hating* (New York: Dutton, 1974) and *Pornography: Men Possessing Women* (New York: Plume, 1979). Valerie Solanas, now best known as the woman who shot Andy Warhol, founded the half-ironic "Society for Cutting Up Men" (SCUM), devoted to the murder of all men for the good of society. You can read more about SCUM in Valerie Solanas, *SCUM Manifesto* (San Francisco: AK Press, 1996; orig. self-pub. in 1967).

40. For Butler's most popular account of gender identity, see *Gender Trouble*. Indeed, Haraway has herself provided an allegorical figure for the riot grrl: the feminist cyborg. In her widely read "A Cyborg Manifesto," Haraway explores how the cyborg, who is a combination of human, animal, and technological parts, is a figure who breaks down false binaries and encourages respect for all life forms, including those that humans will invent (i.e., artificial intelligences). See Donna Haraway, *Simians, Cyborgs, and Women: The Reinvention of Nature* (New York: Routledge, 1991). Interestingly, many riot grrl movies and books involve cyborgs. *Terminator 2*, with its muscle-bound, military-trained woman and cyborg is one example; Marge Piercy's novel *He, She and It* (New York: Fawcett, 1991), in which a woman warrior has a love affair with a cyborg programmed by her hacker grandmother, is another.

41. I'm referring to Naomi Wolf's book *Fire with Fire: The New Female Power and How to Use It* (New York: Ballantine, 1993).

Chapter 25

On Fixing "Bad" Mothers and Saving Their Children

Annette R. Appell

"Bad" Mothers

They are the mothers of the roughly half million children in foster care in the United States. Courts have removed these children from their homes because their mothers have failed to meet someone's standards of proper mothering. A small minority of bad mothers have physically harmed or intentionally abandoned their children. The rest are guilty of less serious offenses: they use illegal drugs, consume too much alcohol, are abused by husbands or boyfriends, allow their children to be abused by husbands or boyfriends, or leave their children with family or friends without making a "proper" care plan.[1] In the eyes of the world, when it is looking, all of these mothers are the same. They are reviled and dehumanized, and their children must be saved from them. Yet bad mothers are mostly like other mothers. They love their children. They care about how their children are growing up: their clothes, their haircuts, their progress in school. Their children too are like other kids. They need stability and love, but too rarely find both, or either, as state wards.[2]

These "bad" mothers become, and often remain, bad mothers because they have made bad choices, or, due to their poverty or other circumstances, did not have real choices. In either event, these are the mothers who were caught, failed to measure up, and lost their children as a result. These mothers tend to be poor and are disproportionately of color.[3] Their parenting is more visible to government and public agencies than that of their middle-class counterparts. These bad mothers' lives intersect with official entities and bureaucracies on a number of levels: the government pays their medical bills; public hospitals, clinics, and emergency rooms provide their families' health care; the government may well be contributing direct financial support for the care of their children; public building inspectors and police enter their homes. Middle-class mothers are more likely to pay for their health care with private insurance. They use private doctors who protect and advise their clients in ways that preserve confidentiality and autonomy.[4] If these doctors interfere at all, they do so privately and are less likely to call the child abuse hotline. Middle-class mothers hire private contractors if something in their house breaks. The government rarely sees inside their homes. "Bad" mothers use alcohol, crack, or cocaine; their middle-class counterparts use alcohol or prescribed antidepressants. They may use illicit drugs too, but are much more likely to escape detection.[5] Bad mothers are the mothers who get caught.

The Child Welfare System

Once someone such as a doctor, teacher, social worker, or neighbor identifies a bad mother, that person may notify the child abuse hotline. The hotline then assigns a child protection investigator to determine whether the child is at risk. If the investigator finds actual or potential abuse or neglect, the state or county child welfare agency assigns a caseworker to work with the family. In addition to protecting the immediate safety of the child, the child welfare agency's mandate is to try to keep the family together in the first instance and help reunify those families it cannot, for the moment, preserve.[6] The agency caseworkers may or may not have special training in child protection or family systems. Most do not hold degrees of any kind in social work.[7]

If the agency seeks to place the child in foster care, then a juvenile or family court must determine whether the child should be removed from the mother and made a state ward. Most courts will appoint an attorney to defend the mother's maternal rights. The mothers' attorneys often have high caseloads and few resources. Frequently, they have little experience or training in this area.[8] A mother who is fortunate enough to be able to hire her own attorney, one who has adequate resources and specializes in child protection law, will be more successful both in court and with the child welfare agency.

If the court places a child in foster care, the agency writes client service plans, consisting of tasks for the mother to complete in order to have her child returned to her. Ideally, the mother and caseworker establish these plans collaboratively.[9] Too often, however, the caseworker drafts the plans without the input of the mother or other family members and inserts stock tasks for the mother to complete in order to have her children returned. The task sheets may even be pretyped forms into which the caseworker inserts the mother's name. Typical tasks include: submission to a psychological evaluation, participation in counseling, attendance at parenting classes, submission to random drug tests, and parent-child visitation.[10] Caseworkers may also assign tasks to foster parents, children, fathers, and caseworkers. Every six months, the agency or court reviews these plans and the mother's compliance.[11]

In the meantime, the court also oversees the case. It must first determine whether the child was neglected, abused, or otherwise in need of care. If so, then the court makes custodial decisions regarding the child. In many jurisdictions, the court determines whether and when the child can return home, and in some jurisdictions, whether mother and child can have unsupervised visitation, the presumption being that all contact must be supervised. If mother and child cannot be reunited, then the child welfare agency may ask the court to terminate parental rights so that the agency may place the child for adoption.

Four "Bad" Mothers

The following narratives relate the stories of four women who lost their children in the juvenile court system serving Chicago and a large portion of its metropolitan area.[12] The state child welfare agency, the Illinois Department of Children and Family Services (DCFS), along with a host of private agencies contracting with DCFS, provided child welfare services to the mothers and their children. These stories represent four archetypical "bad" mothers: the drug user, the mentally impaired woman,[13] the battered woman, and the teenager. These women's stories are typical of mothers' experiences in the child welfare system.[14] Some mothers are "worse" and some are "better" than these four.

Race and class loom large in these cases, but explicitly identifying these dynamics requires a more analytic account. Suffice it to say that three of the four mothers are African American.[15] None of the mothers has a college degree. They come from working-poor or working-class families.

Generally, the African American mothers had African American case-workers; the judges and children's attorneys were white. The white mother had white caseworkers and a white judge, and her children had white attorneys. The foster mothers were, for the most part, the same race as the mothers. All but two of the caseworkers, judges, and attorneys were women.

Janice: The Drug-Using Mother

It was an afternoon in January 1993, shortly after the Chicago and national media had whipped themselves into a frenzy over the "home alone" story: a white suburban couple had gone off for a vacation in Mexico over the Christmas holiday, leaving their two daughters, aged nine and four, to fend for themselves.[16] Janice was at her stepfather's South Side home, where she and her three younger daughters, Camille (twelve), Denise (seven), and Danielle (six), had been living since Janice's part-ner—the girls' father—John, had been jailed for insurance fraud the previous summer. Janice's stepfather, a trash collector, had previously lived alone in the one-bedroom apartment, which was in disrepair and packed with items he had collected over the years on the job. The addition of Janice, her three daughters, and all of their clothes (with no additional furniture in which to store them) made the already cluttered apartment appear chaotic.

That January afternoon, one of the neighbors came by to tell Janice to tune the television to a nationally syndicated television talk show. Janice obliged. There she saw her oldest daughter Toni, then about nineteen. Next to Toni sat the public official who is regularly appointed as guardian *ad litem* (GAL)[17] and attorney for children in Cook County child protec-tion proceedings. Toni was telling the eager talk show host about how, at the age of eight, she had been left alone by her mother for weeks at a time. Toni claimed she had even been left alone to take care of her newborn sister Camille. The talk show host, his fervor rising, suggested that her plight, unlike that of the suburban white girls who were left home alone, had been ignored because she was black and from the inner city. Toni wanted to tell the viewing public *her* story. So she continued to talk about how her mother had neglected her and was now doing the same to Camille, who Toni claimed had been left with the responsibility for her little sisters, Danielle and Denise. Toni also announced that Danielle and Denise were born addicted to crack cocaine. The Cook

County Public Guardian, providing the analysis the host was seeking, explained that because Toni and her family were members of the "underclass," the public expected no better and the state did not intervene as readily or punitively as it should.

Most of what Toni and the public guardian said was false. Danielle and Denise had not been born with cocaine in their systems. Toni had not been removed from Janice for neglect.[18] Janice did, however, have a longstanding, if not debilitating, drug and alcohol problem. She turned to these substances when in crisis. Although she often found herself in crisis, she had been particularly stressed by John's imprisonment, which had left her family homeless and without John's financial support. As a result, she found herself again drawn to drugs.

Two months before the broadcast, Toni went to Janice's home and found Camille, Danielle, and Denise home alone after school. Toni called the police, who arrested Janice when she returned home shortly after. The police photographed the apartment's disarray and called DCFS. Janice confessed her struggle with drugs and alcohol to the child protection personnel and admitted she needed help. DCFS arranged for her entry into an inpatient drug program and for a babysitter for the girls while their grandfather was at work. DCFS also helped Janice repair and organize the apartment.

Janice benefited from her hospitalization. She was diagnosed not only with substance dependency but also with depression and an anxiety disorder. She left the hospital with an aftercare plan that included substance abuse groups, psychiatric medication, and psychotherapy. She complied with the plan, and her criminal case was eventually dismissed. Her girls were ecstatic. They saw their mom getting better; they in turn flourished. Janice began to volunteer at their school and participated proudly in their extracurricular activities. The family was doing so well that DCFS intended to close the case without seeking juvenile court involvement.

This plan, however, did not fit Toni's or the public guardian's agenda, so the week after the talk show appearance, they filed a child neglect petition "on behalf of" Danielle, Denise, and Camille. The petition alleged that during the previous year Janice had smoked crack cocaine in front of her daughters, that the home was in a state of disrepair, that the girls were dirty, and that Janice had left them alone. The petition did not mention Janice's drug treatment, the improved condition of the apartment, or that a responsible adult, the grandfather, lived in the home.

Despite the lack of any testimony whatsoever that Janice had harmed her children or placed them at imminent risk of harm, the judge awarded DCFS temporary custody of the girls and prohibited Janice from having unsupervised contact with them.

The girls were devastated by their removal from Janice. She and her daughters were very attached to each other. Her children shone in Janice's reflection and also felt protective of her. Janice took care of them, played with them, was involved with their schooling, and was trying to usher them carefully through the various stages of childhood and adolescence. All of above-average intelligence, the girls did well in school and participated in extracurricular activities. Although there were surely dysfunctional aspects to the family and Janice did fail her children at times, overall she was an involved and caring mother.

The ideal home, or even a very good one, eluded the girls while in the state's care. In their first three years in custody, DCFS moved them approximately five times: to several foster homes, a group home, and a shelter. One foster mother terrorized the girls. Another relegated Camille to taking care of her little sisters and the foster mother's own children. In that same home, Camille had sex at the age of fourteen. Later, while Camille lived in a group home for adolescent state wards in one of Chicago's more violent neighborhoods, a gang member raped her. Although the young man was arrested, his fellow gang members continued to threaten her. Because DCFS (her guardian) failed to move her away from the menace, she ran away. Janice found Camille and established a safe place for her with a relative.

Like her daughters, Janice did not fare well after the family was split. After the court took her children, she fought hard to recover them. She kept records of her own and her daughters' achievements and made sure to get letters or notes indicating every time she attended her aftercare program. She was taking medication for her depression and anxiety and attending group meetings, therapy, and parenting classes. Her caseworker was behind Janice. But without custody of the girls, she no longer qualified for public aid. Soon her medical benefits and food stamps were cut and her income reduced to zero. Without her medical benefits, she could no longer pay for therapy. Without income, she no longer had carfare to attend her group sessions or money to pay for her psychotropic medication.

Without money for even her most essential and personal needs, she sought employment. Her caseworker wanted her to focus instead on her recovery and getting her daughters back. She could not do either well. She could not keep a job because of her depression; she could not work on her recovery without money or having her life in better order. Her caseworker insisted that Janice apply for federal disability payments. Janice resisted, because she found it offensive to claim that she had a mental disability, and she worried about how such a claim would reflect on her capacity to parent. She spiraled into a depression that lasted months.

On top of all of these problems, Janice's caseworkers changed repeatedly. Every six months to a year, she had a new one. For months at a time she had none. Each new worker had a different analysis of the case. Some, unable to comprehend why the children were removed in the first place, thought the family should be together. Others considered Janice manipulative and assigned new tasks for her to complete in order to have her children returned; they feared she would run off with the children (although she never did), and that she would expose them to all sorts of undefined horrors. Each new worker required several months to familiarize herself with the case and additional time—usually three to six months—for Janice to prove that she was free from drugs.

The court, personified by a white, middle-class, middle-aged female judge and a younger, white male attorney acting as GAL were forever disapproving of Janice's lifestyle and her long history of drug use. In addition to complying with her service plan, they wanted her to establish a consistent track record of sobriety and a stable home. But because Janice could not hold down a job and could not get public aid, she found it impossible to afford an apartment. Consequently, she moved around frequently, staying with family or friends as long as she was welcome. The GAL wanted at least six consecutive months of clean urine screens, but DCFS never provided her with six consecutive months of drops.

Although Janice eventually applied for disability benefits and was able, therefore, to pay for her service plan requirements of therapy, medication, and parenting classes, she has never been able to prove that she has been drug-free for six months. This failure has either been due to her own relapses or, more frequently, to the state's failure to provide her with six consistent months of services in the three years it has retained custody of her children.

Janice may never get her children back. The few times she comes close, something or someone—including herself—sets her back. She is unable to follow all of DCFS's and the court's rules all of the time, either because she does not know what they are or they do not suit her. Most recently, in a show of self-sabotage, she tested positive for cocaine three times during the month her motion for unsupervised visits was pending. The court will not grant her even five minutes alone with her children, because she uses drugs. Yet the court has heard no evidence that Janice's drug use has ever placed her children in harm's way.

Janice has been defeated by the child protection system. She cannot bring herself to respect it, as it failed utterly to respect her. Janice is Janice. She takes shortcuts; she rationalizes; she still sometimes turns to drugs; she is frequently in crisis; she does not always complete what she starts. But she loves and always cared for her children, however imperfectly. The state was the bad parent, who let her daughter get raped twice, who let her children act as servants to a foster mother, and who failed to give them a stable home. The court and DCFS, however, want Janice to become someone else: someone who is more compliant, more subservient, more consistent, more stable, less passionate, less colorful, and absolutely 100 per cent drug free.

Georgia: The Mentally Impaired Mother

Georgia is not used to being listened to or cared for. She has no close friends and no supportive family connections. Her brother and mother, themselves mentally impaired, have always been cruel or cold to her. Passive and without the sense of entitlement that might make her recognize her rights and fight for them, Georgia has an IQ in the upper seventies, an area referred to by some as the borderline between retardation and normal intelligence. Over the years, a number of mental health professionals have given her a range of diagnoses, from dysthymia (mild, persistent depression) to schizophrenia. Some professionals have prescribed psychotropic medication; others have said she does not need it.

Georgia's mother and brother, with whom she lived, were not supportive when she gave birth to her daughter, Jane. Soon after the birth, DCFS became involved with the family, because Georgia was late in getting vaccinations and allowed her mother, whom DCFS deemed an inappropriate caretaker, to babysit Jane.[19] The juvenile court allowed Georgia to keep Jane but placed Georgia under an order of protection. DCFS provided her with family preservation workers. Although Georgia was emotionally unstable at the time, DCFS did not remove Jane till six months later, and then because Georgia let her mother babysit Jane again.

DCFS's service provision, like that of many bureaucracies, is fragmented according to administrative convenience, not according to client needs. Thus when DCFS removed Jane from her mother, the family preservation workers did not continue to work with Georgia. Instead, they promptly transferred her case to a foster care worker, without giving Georgia any information about what had happened or would happen.

About two weeks after removing Jane, DCFS assigned a foster care worker named Nadine, who did not contact Georgia for nearly two months, and then only because Georgia's brother called DCFS to find out what was going on. At that time, Nadine did not offer Georgia a visit with Jane, nor did she provide a client service plan. Nadine waited another three months to do that. Thus Jane grew from six to eleven months while her case stagnated.

Despite the fact that DCFS became involved due to an inadequate care plan, the family reunification plans neglected to discuss appropriate care plans for Jane. Instead, the plans contained tasks purportedly related to Georgia's mental health and stability, including development of "skills" in the areas of "socialization," "recreational," "self-help," and "independent living," and continued attendance at Georgia's adult day program. Unable to articulate what she meant by the listed skills, what would constitute improvement in those skills, and how such skills were related to Georgia's parenting, Nadine admitted she took the listed skills from a conversation she had with Georgia's adult day program's psychiatric nurse. The plan also confined Georgia to supervised visitation with Jane. So to set up a visit, Georgia, a woman without a telephone, was required to call Nadine, a woman without a secretary, an answering machine, or voice mail. Not surprisingly, this system proved unworkable.

Georgia complied with the first service plan to the best of her ability. Then, shortly before Christmas, her brother kicked her out of the house. She was also pregnant again. Nadine, upon learning that Georgia was homeless, did nothing. In fact, Nadine later claimed that she did not know what assistance or services she could offer Georgia, including, presumably, helping her find shelter or providing a Christmas visit with Jane. Georgia dropped out of her day program and dropped out of sight.

She eventually wound up at a Christian rescue mission, the Home of Truth shelter,[20] right around the time Nadine was "drafting" (i.e., photocopying) a second client service plan. Even though Georgia had completed her day program and was not eligible to participate in it for another six months, Nadine's service plan, identical to the previous one, required Georgia to enroll immediately in the program and to work on the social skills recited above. Nadine had not seen Georgia for months and did not know where she was. Georgia, who did not view Nadine as an ally, did not contact her.

Several months later, Georgia gave birth to Shalaya. Concerned about Georgia's mental stability, DCFS removed Shalaya from Georgia's custody shortly after birth. Nadine got Shalaya's case too. When Nadine and Georgia next met, Georgia stated she wanted *both* Shalaya and Jane returned home. Nadine responded by saying that Jane's foster mother wanted to adopt her. Nadine neglected to mention, however, that DCFS's stated goal at the time was to return Jane to Georgia. Nadine was not opposed to reuniting Georgia and Shalaya.

Nadine then established what can only be described as schizophrenic service plans for Georgia. Although Jane and Shalaya were living in the same foster home, Nadine set up separate parent-child visiting plans for the girls: she scheduled weekly visits for Georgia and Shalaya but permitted only monthly visits for Georgia and Jane. Furthermore, Nadine pre-scheduled the visits with Shalaya but required Georgia to call Nadine each month to set up a visit with Jane. Georgia was required in one plan to stay at the Home of Truth shelter and in another to get her own apartment.

Shalaya was returned to Georgia six months after having been removed as a newborn. But just a few months later, DCFS petitioned the court on behalf of then two-and-a-half-year-old Jane to declare Georgia an unfit mother. DCFS sought authority to place Jane for adoption, thus terminating the legal relationship between Georgia and Jane, and, derivatively, Jane and Shalaya. In the petition, DCFS alleged that Georgia was unfit because she was so mentally impaired that she could not then or in the future parent her child (an odd charge given the fact that Georgia was actively parenting Shalaya with DCFS's and the court's approval); because she had failed to visit Jane, though able to do so for twelve months; because she had failed to show a reasonable degree of interest in or concern for Jane's welfare; because she had failed to make reasonable progress in or efforts toward correcting the conditions which led to the removal of her child; and because she had deserted Jane for the three months preceding the filing of the supplemental petition. Because DCFS's own records showed Georgia's purported desertion and twelve-month failure to visit Jane to be patently false, the state, under pressure, dropped those grounds.

The trial did not begin for thirteen months, primarily due to the state's requests for continuances. Jane was thus three and a half years old when it began. In one highlight of the trial, the shelter director testified that she had observed Georgia trying unsuccessfully to contact Nadine by telephone at least once a week for over a year; she also noted that Nadine rarely returned telephone calls and rarely initiated contact with Georgia.

The trial occupied four full court days but took over four months to complete, due to the court's busy schedule. The judge, though visibly bored and annoyed by Georgia's diligent defense during the trial,[21] held that the state had not proved Georgia to be an unfit parent and therefore denied DCFS's petition to terminate her parental rights. Jane celebrated her third and fourth birthdays during the pendency of DCFS's ill-fated petition.

Fortunately, after the trial, a new caseworker granted Georgia and Jane visits every two weeks. Before and during the trial, DCFS had allowed Georgia to see Jane less than once a month, so the child barely knew her mother. Moreover, Georgia had no idea how to establish a relationship with Jane. DCFS either did not know how to assist her or gave no thought to the problem. Finally, with some help from the shelter director and a gifted social work intern, Georgia began to develop a better connection with Jane. Eventually, they were granted weekly visits. Georgia would like to bring Jane to church with her and Shalaya. Jane would like to have a sleep-over with her mother and little sister. But those activities could not be completed within the one-hour visitation slot, and DCFS does not provide casework services in the evenings or on weekends. Georgia's case has essentially stagnated.

Georgia, however, has not. During the years since Jane was taken from her, Georgia has grown and changed, despite and not because of DCFS's intervention. She has found a home at the shelter and familylike support in its director. She has also become involved with church, where she is an active participant in Bible class. With this support and stability, Georgia has opened up more. She is more friendly and more readily displays her sharp sense of humor. She takes good care of Shalaya, in fact may be a bit overprotective. Shalaya in turn is a happy, secure little girl. Nevertheless, DCFS is always nearby. For Georgia to lose Shalaya, it only takes one caseworker or supervisor to decide that the little girl would be better off in someone else's care. Jane, who loves Georgia, Shalaya, and, undoubtedly, the foster mother, remains in limbo. DCFS continues to establish service plans for Georgia. Georgia wants Jane returned to her, but DCFS has not revealed its long-term plans.

Sarah: The Battered Mother

While Sarah was married to Edwin, they had two children, Celia and Jim. Edwin is Puerto Rican and Sarah is European American. Sarah's family effectively disowned her when she married Edwin. While Sarah, Edwin, and the children were living in Puerto Rico with Edwin's family, Edwin's drinking escalated. He began to hit and then beat Sarah. When the beatings became severe and Sarah began to fear for her children, she fled to a friend in Arizona. She stayed there for awhile and underwent brain and spinal surgery for neurological problems caused either by her husband's beatings or by an earlier car accident.

While in Arizona, Celia, two years old at the time, told Sarah that in Puerto Rico, Edwin's brother Jose had touched or scratched her "pee pee." Sarah contacted the child protection authorities about Celia's statements; she related to them as well her own observations that Celia had regressed in toilet training and had avoided Jose the last time they saw him. The authorities told her that because there was no physical evidence of abuse and Celia was so young, it was impossible to determine if he had touched her inappropriately; he could have simply been tickling her. The state agency took no further action and made no recommendations or referrals.

In the meantime, Edwin attempted to woo Sarah back. He told her that he had changed, had stopped drinking, and would not beat her again; he begged her to come home. Eventually she relented, and the family returned to Puerto Rico. But soon Edwin fell back into his old ways. Later he began hitting the kids, so a couple of years after their reunion, Sarah fled again with the children. They made their way back to Chicago, where they moved from place to place, finally taking refuge with Jose until Sarah could save the bus fare to return to her safe haven in Arizona.

Just a few days before she and the kids were scheduled to leave for Arizona, Celia, then nearly five years old, told Sarah in so many words that Jose had molested her. When Sarah confronted Jose with Celia's accusations, he became enraged and set fire to the flat in which they were all living. Sarah and the children escaped through a window. When the police came, Sarah told them about the molestation. They arrested Jose and called DCFS. The DCFS child protection investigator who met the family at the police station told Sarah to bring the children to a trauma center which assesses children for physical and sexual abuse.[22]

The trauma center found physical evidence of sexual abuse of Celia but not of Jim. Because Sarah had confronted Jose immediately upon Celia's disclosure of abuse, and because he was locked up, it looked as if DCFS would return the children to Sarah at the conclusion of the evaluation. However, during its pendency, the child protection investigator learned about Sarah's earlier call to the Arizona child welfare authorities. Even though the Arizona report was inconclusive and Sarah had been in dire straits after fleeing Edwin, the investigator blamed her for taking refuge with Jose. Sarah's situation as a woman alone with two children, no money, and no home, on the run from an abusive husband, did not move the investigator.[23] Further tipping the scale, the investigator also learned that Sarah had had sex with Jose. That Sarah would sleep with her husband's brother suggested, to the investigator, her character weaknesses. Moreover, during the same interview in which he denied that he had sexually abused Celia, Jose told the investigator that Sarah used cocaine and crack. A police officer also told the investigator that an unidentified man stated that Sarah mixed pills and alcohol. The investigator chose to believe the two men, not Sarah. In addition, the investigator noted Sarah's shaking and unsteady gait. Afraid while in Puerto Rico to leave her children alone with Edwin, Sarah had not kept up with the medical regimen for her neurological condition, and the events of that night had exacerbated the problem. She was planning to continue her treatment in Arizona. The investigator, however, saw her as neglecting her children by neglecting herself. These bits of information, along with Jose's abuse of Celia, became part of Sarah's file and the allegations against her.

The investigator did not offer to assist Sarah in keeping her family together, away from Edwin and Jose. Instead, although Jose was already incarcerated and Sarah was working closely with the state attorney to assist in his prosecution, the investigator submitted her report to juvenile court, requesting that it remove the children. Her report indicated that Celia had been sexually abused and the family had nowhere to go, even though the investigator knew that Sarah had found a safe and appropriate place for the family to stay. The state filed child abuse and neglect petitions "on behalf" of both of the children, even though Jim had not been abused by Jose. The petitions alleged that the children were "being inadequately sheltered due to the parent, caretaker, or responsible person's disregard of his or her responsibilities," that they were at risk of substantial harm due to the parent's failure to stop another from sexually abusing the child, and that Celia had been sexually abused because her parent failed to stop the abuse. The judge ordered both of the children to be placed in foster care and all contact between Sarah and her children to be supervised.

In order to get her children back, Sarah was required to complete a lengthy client service plan that included such tasks as (1) undergoing a substance abuse evaluation, completing a substance abuse treatment program, abstaining from drugs and alcohol, and submitting to random urine screens; (2) seeing a neurologist and following any of his or her recommendations; (3) submitting to a psychological evaluation, following its recommendations, and getting individual counseling to understand why the children came into placement and to deal with domestic violence, the sexual abuse of her children, the physical abuse she had suffered at the hands of Jose and Edwin, drug/alcohol abuse, attempted murder (presumably the arson) by Jose, and child protection and family reunification issues; (4) completing parenting classes; (5) ceasing any relationship in which her partner physically or sexually abused her or her children; (6) maintaining an income for herself and her children; (7) maintaining a safe home for herself and her children, free from sexual and physical abuse.

She was permitted to see her children, who were placed out in the suburbs, once a week for one hour. Sarah lived in the city and had no car, so for each one-hour visit, she traveled two hours in each direction on public transportation. When her counselor, a specialist in domestic violence, recommended that Sarah be permitted to visit her children without supervision, DCFS fired the counselor: in the caseworker's eyes, the counselor must be incompetent or overly identified with Sarah. The caseworker thought it would be at least a year until Sarah should be allowed to have unsupervised visits, and several years before she and the children would be reunited.

Complying with her service plan and visiting her children became Sarah's full-time occupation. In fact, she had to pass up a scholarship to a local college in order to fulfill all of her tasks. She did everything she was supposed to do; she also found many of her own services instead of relying on her caseworker to refer her. In addition, Sarah's primary concern was to engage Celia in counseling regarding the sex abuse. Sarah had to push the caseworker to enroll Celia in counseling: it took months. Sarah called her caseworker practically daily with questions and concerns about her children and her case plan. The caseworker, accustomed to mothers socialized into silence and passivity by the welfare bureaucracies, forbade Sarah to call her more than once a week.

The children missed their mother. Their initial placement with one of Sarah's relatives lasted less than a week. Soon they were placed in a foster home with first-time foster parents. Celia could not understand why her mother had abandoned her to live with these strange people. Both children were angry about being taken from their mother and consequently began acting out. The placement eventually exploded, and DCFS moved the children to another foster home. The previous foster mother had admitted to the caseworker that sometimes she wanted to kill the children. The next foster placement was much better.

Sarah had no money and no place to live. She had to choose between doing all of the things necessary to be reunited with her children and getting a job or going back to school. Because of her neurological problems, she qualified for social security disability payments but did not begin receiving them for many months. In the meantime, she was living with her father. He advised her to abandon her children to the state and get on with her life. He would not let the children stay at his home for more than an hour or two.

Nevertheless, Sarah was moving along on her case plan quickly. In addition, she filed divorce proceedings against Edwin, and Jose pled guilty to arson and the sexual assault of Celia. Although he was sentenced to thirteen years in prison, the children were not returned to Sarah. Fortunately, by then Sarah had been able to replace her public defender with a private attorney, who was able to push the caseworkers to move more quickly toward reunification and challenge them to identify exactly why mother and children were still separated.

Soon after, but nearly eight months after the children were removed, the court granted Sarah unsupervised visits with them for short periods during the day. The court order included more than ten directives for Sarah to follow as a condition of the "privilege" of seeing her children without someone watching over them. Gradually, DCFS allowed the visits to be increased to nearly an entire day.

Next Sarah sought overnight visits. Because her father would not let the kids stay overnight and Sarah could not afford an apartment of her own, she moved into the Home of Truth shelter, which would permit her to have her children overnight. The shelter—the same that had taken Georgia in—frightened Sarah. The women there functioned on a variety of levels. All were extremely poor; some were mentally ill; others were drug addicts; and some were just plain hostile. Sarah did not like having her children there but knew it was the only way she could spend significant amounts of time with them. Because the shelter director assured the court that Sarah was following the shelter's rules, and that the family would never be alone there, the court granted the overnight visitation. The court order again required Sarah to do a multiplicity of tasks, including complying with the shelter's 7:00 p.m. curfew. The day the order was entered, the court commanded her to submit her urine for drug and alcohol screening.

Next Sarah obtained an apartment for her family. Although they were welcome to live at the shelter, Sarah wanted a more homelike setting. Fortunately, due to a class action suit filed by the locally funded legal services corporation, DCFS was required to assist homeless families involved in the child welfare system to obtain housing when return of the children was imminent.[24] Such housing assistance was crucial for Sarah, because obtaining an apartment required, in addition to the basic rent money, a security deposit and the last month's rent. In Chicago, those two items could amount to at least a thousand dollars. Sarah also needed furniture. The state helped her with the money she needed to secure the apartment, while her caseworker and attorney separately solicited donations of furniture and other household goods.

Soon Sarah moved into her own apartment. Although it was not in a particularly safe neighborhood, it was warm, clean, cozy, and rodent-free—much better than most of the public housing stock available to poor families in Chicago, with its cinder block walls, urine-soaked elevators, and gang hegemony. Now Sarah had to go back to the judge to ask permission for her children to sleep over at her house, rather than at the shelter. Three months after the judge awarded overnight visitation at the shelter, and after requiring another urine screen, the court permitted weekend visitation at the apartment.

It took another two months for full reunification. Thus, fourteen months after the initial abuse incident, the family was reunited, though subject to a court order listing over twenty tasks for Sarah and requiring court oversight of the case for at least another year.

Sarah provides a loving, protective home for her children. She is involved in their schooling, has enrolled them in scouts, sports, and a Big

Brother/Big Sister program. She wants them to grow up safely, with structure, and with good role models. But she continues to fear that the child welfare authorities and the police will decide that she is a bad mother and will take her children away. She will do all she can to avoid seeking "official" assistance—even if she is a victim of a crime. No doubt, her children too always will live without the security that most other children feel: that good or bad, home is home and Mom is Mom.

Emily: The Teen Mother

When Emily was seven, her mother was found lying drunk on a sidewalk. The paramedics who came to her aid called DCFS. Emily's mother explained that she had not been feeling well and had passed out from the hot sun. Emily and her four-year-old sister, Keisha, appeared clean and well-dressed and bore no overt signs of abuse or neglect, so DCFS closed the case. The next year, Emily was treated for a severe cut on her forehead. Although initially denying it, eventually she revealed that her mother had hit her. Interviews with neighbors and relatives indicated that Emily's mother was a drinker, that Emily was frequently absent from school, and that Emily and Keisha were often up late at night. In fact, Emily had missed eighty-nine days of school and consequently flunked the first grade. Because of their mother's condition, Emily often fed and clothed herself and Keisha. Apparently, their mother had also been training Emily to steal. DCFS took custody of the girls.

First, DCFS placed them with Keisha's father. He was not Emily's biological father but had played a paternal role in her life. DCFS, however, provided no further assistance to Emily or her stepfather. Four years later, DCFS became involved again when the child protection authorities received a report that he was whipping Emily with an electrical cord. DCFS took custody of her and enlisted a number of Emily's relatives to provide foster care for her. The placements did not last very long: Emily did not like to follow rules, having spent her formative years with little structure or discipline. By the time she was fourteen, she had lived in five different homes, not including her mother's.

Emily gave birth to her first child at the age of fourteen and a half. As might have been predicted from her youth and history, she was not terribly interested in settling down to care for her new child, Manda. Instead, she continued to do as she pleased, leaving Manda with various friends and relatives. Although Manda was never physically harmed or deprived of food, shelter, or clothing, DCFS took the baby away from Emily and gave her to Emily's aunt Beatrice.

DCFS, who had done little for Emily in its capacity as her guardian, now took on the additional role of family reunification agency. DCFS and the two agencies assisting on the case gave Emily a new list of things to do, in addition to her tasks as a teen ward. Her service plans required her to complete parenting classes, maintain stable housing, attend school regularly, obey the rules of her placement, "act in a sexually responsible manner, including the usage of birth control," and maintain proper hygiene and grooming habits.

Unfortunately, despite these service plans, DCFS continued to fail to meet Emily's needs as a ward and an adolescent, let alone as a mother. DCFS did not help Emily and Beatrice to understand their respective roles and duties vis à vis Manda. Hence, Beatrice assumed the mother role for Manda and at the same time treated Emily like a wayward daughter. Aunt and niece each resented the other. Emily's relationship with DCFS was similar. She did not work with her slew of caseworkers and they felt frustrated and impotent with her. Emily still did not stay long in any one place. Her relatives got fed up with her attitude, her refusal to follow rules, and her penchant for spending nights away from home with friends. Sometimes she was kicked out of a relative's home or group home; sometimes she ran away. Like most teenagers, she did not like to follow directives; she was busy exploring her identity, sexuality, and independence.

She gave birth again when she was nearly sixteen, to Priscilla. Although Emily still moved around frequently, she was now slightly more mature and provided good care for Priscilla. Unfortunately, Priscilla was not keeping her food down or gaining weight. Emily brought Priscilla to the hospital, where she was diagnosed with failure to thrive.[25] Even though DCFS knew Priscilla's condition was caused by a defect in her esophagus and not neglectful mothering, they blamed Emily and took away daughter number two. When surgery corrected Priscilla's esophageal problem and she began to gain weight, DCFS attributed the weight gain to the new foster mother and refused to reunite Priscilla and Emily.

Because of Priscilla's special medical needs, DCFS placed her, through a special foster care program, with nonrelative foster parents in the suburbs. Predictably, Emily, a city dweller with no income due to her status as a ward of the state, rarely saw Priscilla thereafter. In addition to her extant list of tasks and bevy of caseworkers, Emily received a new caseworker from the special foster care agency. This woman added her own lists of tasks and referrals.

In the meantime, Beatrice wanted to adopt Manda. None of the caseworkers told her that as a foster mother, she must respect and encourage the parent-child relationship. Emily was angry with Beatrice for usurping Manda. Beatrice, in turn, considered Emily sullen and disrespectful. Moreover, Emily's tendency to come and go to and within Beatrice's home at will discomforted Beatrice. Predictably, Emily did not visit Manda frequently, and their relationship withered.

When Emily was eighteen, she gave birth to Calvin. She managed to keep Calvin from DCFS for ten months. Although she continued to move from place to place, she was very nurturing of Calvin and responsive to him. He was meeting his developmental milestones early and was a happy, healthy, well-adjusted child. Nevertheless, Emily was raising him without the assistance of her numerous caseworkers, without the many services in which they expected her to enroll, and without the mandatory parenting classes "bad" mothers were required to attend. Her caseworkers were furious with her over this. One had even refused to work with Emily anymore. Finally, when Emily missed one in a series of Calvin's immunizations, the DCFS caseworker, who had never seen Calvin, called the child abuse hotline. After meeting with Emily and Calvin, and speaking with Calvin's doctors and Emily's relatives, the DCFS child abuse and neglect investigator saw no reason to take custody. On the contrary, she found Calvin to be especially happy and well adjusted. The DCFS caseworker, who still had not once laid eyes on Calvin, nevertheless requested that the court place him in DCFS custody.

The same judge who heard Emily's case as a neglected child also heard the case against her as a bad mother. In fact, usually her cases as a mother and as a child were heard together. The judge, therefore, was very familiar with Emily. He had heard all about her stubborn and reckless ways over the years. Like the caseworkers, he was very frustrated by Emily's refusal to do what the adults in her life told her to do. Therefore, despite the testimony of the child abuse investigator and the fact that Calvin's GAL advocated keeping him with Emily, the judge took Calvin away from his mother. The judge's stated reason for separating ten-month-old Calvin from his mother was that she came late to court.[26] Although the proceeding was supposed to be about Calvin's best interests and safety, it was clearly about punishing his mother. Unfortunately, Calvin too was punished, by losing a loving and caring mother at an especially vulnerable developmental state.[27]

DCFS placed Calvin with Beatrice, despite the problems between aunt and niece. Emily continued to live from relative to friend to relative. She also spent time with the family of Calvin and Priscilla's father. She stayed as long as she was welcome, or as long as she could tolerate the structure. Soon she was pregnant again. Two months after her nineteenth birthday, she gave birth to Darron. Her DCFS caseworker, confident that the court would take custody of this child as well, took his time bringing the case to court. He waited until Darron was two months old and Emily's cases were already scheduled for court. Emily took excellent care of Darron during that two months.

As a result of the strong advocacy of Calvin's GAL and a couple of social workers experienced in working with teenagers, the judge not only permitted Darron to stay with his mother but also returned Calvin to her on that court date. Yet the judge ordered Emily to comply with no less than eighteen conditions if she wanted to keep her children. These included refraining from the use of corporal punishment; providing urine samples for drug screens; attending a substance abuse assessment and cooperating with all of its recommendations (presumably because Emily admitted to smoking marijuana several years earlier); living at a specified group home for teen mothers; following all of the rules of the group home; and submitting to a psychological evaluation (although there was no indication of any psychopathology).

The staff at the group home were impressed with the quality of care Emily provided for her sons. Unlike many of the girls, Emily never neglected her children or left them alone. She was attentive and loving toward them. Emily did not follow the rules of the home, though. She stayed away more than she was permitted, brought her children to their relatives' homes, and was her usual rebellious self. Her caseworker brought Emily's rule violations to the court's attention. The judge, without a hearing and without notice to Emily or her sons' GAL, took custody of Calvin and Darron, age eighteen months and three months, respectively.

As long as Emily is a bad daughter, she will, in the court's and DCFS's eyes, be a bad mother: she will not get her children back. In the meantime, her service plan is over fifty pages long. She is allowed to visit her children once a week at Chuck E. Cheese or White Castle until they are adopted. She is pregnant again. Although she has never harmed or ne-glected any of her children, her new baby too, without doubt, will become a ward of the state.

Concluding Observations

Each of these four mothers' stories reveals the punitive nature of the child protection system and, as a corollary, the failure of the state to be a "good" parent. In each of the foregoing cases, the courts and caseworkers focused solely on the mothers' weaknesses rather than their strengths. It is not surprising then that these women and their families never received any meaningful assistance. An asset-based approach[28] to these families, one which would have begun by respecting rather than denigrating the mothers (and the mother-child bond), might have recognized their pow-erful love and efforts to care for their children; the solutions might have centered around helping each mother establish family or community ties to bolster her family. Janice and her daughters could have been teamed with relatives to assist the family if Janice was using drugs or drinking too much. Georgia could have been plugged into community mental health services and encouraged to join a play group so that she could develop relationships with other parents. Sarah and her children could have been allowed to go to Arizona, where they had a support system waiting, or could have been referred to a community agency for battered women, where she would have received help with housing, counseling, and her divorce. With the structured support and assistance of relatives, Emily might have been allowed to live in her own apartment.

Instead, the mothers' conduct, psychological makeup, compliance, and drug and alcohol use became the focus. If the mothers are the problem, then it is they who must be fixed. To be fixed, however, they must become different women. From this perspective, failure is usually a foregone conclusion. Although each of the four mothers had problems, those problems were at best tenuously connected to the harm their children suffered or risked suffering, and the "help" they and their children re-ceived was at best tangential and at worst harmful to the children's well-being.

As long as the child welfare system is focused on "fixing" women, it will not be able to save their children. Instead, the children should be at the center, where their needs can be assessed and addressed. Service goals then would be directed at the mother only insofar as they are necessary to meet the child's needs. Making a child wait while a danger to that child is removed from the home or while a mother addresses a serious, acute problem which is clearly interfering with her fundamental care for her children makes sense—anything else does not. Similarly, if a mother needs assistance or supervision, then so be it, as long as this "help" relates to the child's safety and does not revolve around transforming the mother into some ideal maternal figure. But making children linger in foster care is unconscionable when what they are waiting for is so subjective: turning "bad" women into "good" ones.[29]

Mothers all around the country, like the four described above, are infantilized and penalized for their failings.[30] The child welfare establishment too often views their lives through a single lens; the textures and perspectives of each mother and her children become invisible or muted. These four stories illustrate how this myopia disrespects women and results in serious failures to plan for children and meet their needs. While waiting for their "bad" mothers to become "good," children are at risk of growing up without the love, care, and sense of belonging that a parent—even a bad one—can provide.

Afterword

The court closed Sarah's case three months early. The family was thrilled. Emily's judge was transferred right before Darron's trial. The new judge threw out the case at the conclusion of a full trial for lack of proof of neglect, and Darron went home. His siblings remain in foster care. After the shelter hired a new director who was not an advocate for Georgia, DCFS successfully petitioned the court for custody of Shalaya. Shalaya is now in foster care, and Georgia is despondent. The court has decided to initiate proceedings to terminate Janice's parental rights to Danielle and Denise.

NOTES

1. See, for example, Child Welfare League of America, *Child Abuse and Neglect: A Look at the States* (Washington, D.C.: CWLA Press, 1995), 25.

2. See, for example, United States General Accounting Office Report to Con-

gressional Requesters, *Foster Care: Incomplete Implementation of the Reforms and Unknown Effectiveness* (Washington, D.C.: U.S. General Accounting Office, 1989).

3. Peggy Cooper Davis and Gautam Barua, "Custodial Choices for Children at Risk: Bias, Sequentiality, and the Law," *Roundtable* 2 (1995): 150. Others have noted that the child protection law is the poor person's family law. See, for example, Mary Ann Mason, *From Father's Property to Children's Rights* (New York: Columbia University Press, 1994), 189–90.

4. Ira J. Chasnoff, Harvey J. Landress, and Mark E. Barrett, "The Prevalence of Illicit-Drug or Alcohol Use during Pregnancy and Discrepancies in Mandatory Reporting in Pinellas County, Florida," *New England Journal of Medicine* 322, no. 17 (April 26, 1990): 1205.

5. Ibid., 1204.

6. As a condition of receiving matching federal funds for foster care and certain other child welfare programs, states must make reasonable efforts to keep families together and to reunite those who have been separated. Adoption Assistance and Child Welfare Act, 42 U.S.C.A. (1991) §670, et seq. In fact, most components of the child welfare system, including client service planning and the hotline, are mandated by federal law. See ibid. and the Abused and Neglected Child Reporting Act, 42 U.S.C.A. (1995) §§5101–18e.

7. David J. Herring, "Exploring the Political Roles of the Family: Justifications for Permanency Planning for Children," *Loyola University of Chicago Law Journal* 26 (Winter 1995): 205.

8. It is typical for parent defenders to carry caseloads of five hundred in urban jurisdictions. Ibid., n. 142.

9. Linda Katz, "Effective Permanency Planning for Children in Foster Care," *Social Work* 35 (1990): 221.

10. This is the experience of the author, as well as others familiar with the child welfare system. See, for example, Herring, 200–201.

11. 42 U.S.C.A. (1991) §675(5).

12. These, of course, are merely partial accounts of these women's lives, given not by the women themselves but by the author who represented them or their children in child protection proceedings. The names of the individuals and institutions, except DCFS and the court, have been omitted or changed.

13. "Mentally impaired" is used here to refer to mental illness or low intellectual functioning.

14. What is not typical about the mothers is that three of them had an attorney with the expertise and resources to help them navigate the system. That same attorney represented two of the fourth mother's children.

15. In this way also, the women are representative: 78.6 per cent of the families involved in the Cook County Juvenile Court are African American. Children and Family Justice Center of Northwestern University School of Law, *Juvenile Trends*

over a Decade: Cook County Juvenile Court 1983–1993 (Chicago: Children and Family Justice Center, 1994).

16. See Anna Quindlen, "Home Alone—and Lonely—in America," *Chicago Tribune,* January 12, 1993, 7; Lucy Howard, "Close to Home," *Newsweek,* January 11, 1993, 4.

17. The GAL is an adult appointed to represent the interests of the child before the court. Frequently, the GAL is an attorney, who seeks to represent the "best interests of the child." See, "Special Issue on Ethical Issues in the Legal Representation of Children," *Fordham Law Review* 64, no. 4 (March 1996): 1279 et seq.

18. On the contrary, Toni came into the juvenile system as an uncontrollable and eventually delinquent child.

19. Georgia had a difficult time grasping why leaving her daughter with her mother was inappropriate, because Georgia's mother raised Georgia without DCFS intervention.

20. The name of the shelter has been changed to further protect the mothers' anonymity.

21. The judge was heard several times muttering "fly specks" as Georgia's attorney uncovered inconsistencies in Nadine's testimony and the client service plans.

22. One of several such centers in Chicago, it requires the children to stay in the hospital for five days and nights, further traumatizing abused children by removing them from their families and familiar surroundings. A more child-centered method would be to interview and assess the children during the daytime so that they can return to their families or a foster home at night.

23. See generally Bernardine Dohrn, "Bad Mothers, Good Mothers, and the State: Children on the Margins," *Roundtable* 2 (1995): 1.

24. *Norman v. Suter,* No. 89 C 1624, Consent Decree (N.D. Ill. March 28, 1991). Because of the 1996 congressional restrictions prohibiting legal aid programs funded by the Legal Services Corporation from engaging in class action law suits, such litigation may be less likely to occur in the future.

25. "Failure to thrive" describes a child who is not gaining weight appropriately. Such a failure can be caused by organic factors, such as intolerance of certain foods, spitting up, or esophageal problems. Or such a failure can be nonorganic, that is, caused by parental neglect, such as inadequate feeding.

26. The judge stated on the record that he was going to send Calvin home, but because Emily was late to court, he changed his mind. Clearly the judge had failed to focus on the child (and instead was punishing an unruly teenager) or to recognize the experiences of the mothers who come to court. Commonly, parents are summoned to court for a 9:00 a.m. court call, but their cases may not be called until 3:00 p.m., or may be rescheduled for a different date altogether.

Moreover, most parents must use an often unpredictable public transportation system which has no direct lines to the court.

27. Childhood development experts suggest that separating a child from his primary attachment figure between the ages of six months and three years can result in emotional disturbances. See, for example, American Academy of Pediatrics, Committee on Early Childhood, Adoption, and Dependent Care, "Developmental Issues in Foster Care for Children," *American Bar Association Juvenile and Child Welfare Law Reporter* 12 (January 1994): 171.

28. See Margaret Beyer, "Too Little Too Late: Designing Family Support to Succeed," *New York University Review of Law and Social Change* 22, no. 2 (1996): 311.

29. This subjectivity is particularly troubling given the prominence outlined above of race and class in the construction of the "bad" mother.

30. Although well-run child welfare agencies, thoughtful caseworkers, responsive courts, and wise judges exist, many child welfare systems in the United States are in a state of crisis and are unable adequately to protect or serve children and their families. See Robert Pear, "Many States Fail to Meet Mandates on Child Welfare," *New York Times,* March 17, 1996, sec. 1, 1. The four women in this essay fell victim to one of those failed systems.

Chapter 26

Poisonous Choice

Rickie Solinger

Confusing the right to *choose* with the right to *shoes*, he
campaigned only in his pumps, saying, "It's my body
and my decision."
                                    —Kenneth Cole shoe ad, 1996

Who is a mother? What a thoroughly postmodern ring that question has!
Certainly our daily news has put the question before us in recent years in
a daunting array of forms: Marybeth Whitehead's claim that biological
motherhood trumps a surrogacy contract; the war between an adopting
couple, the DeBoers, and birthmother Cara Schmidt, over who would get
to be the parents of Baby Jessica; the ethics involved when an infertile
woman purchases "donor eggs" from a financially strapped young person;
the politics of *Heather Has Two Moms*; the attempts to legislate Norplant
or sterilization for women "unfit" to be mothers. These situations and
numerous others have pushed many Americans to rethink the question,
"Who is a mother?" Who decides, and using what criteria?

As we ponder the contemporary tangles of rights and choice, poverty
and wealth, youth and age, sexuality and race, biology and technology,
nationality and misogyny that make "motherhood" so murky today, it is
worth remembering that the question "Who is a mother?" has burned
across American history. The ways that this question has been answered
in earlier times are instructive, indeed, as we confront the same question
at the end of the century.

Three examples from the past will serve here to illustrate that Americans have been preoccupied with the mother question for a long time. In

the nineteenth century, the motherhood status of a large though unknown number of African American women was effaced as they or their
children were merchandised from the upper to the lower South. For
slaveowners, market imperatives, reinforced by race hatred, eclipsed biology and sentiment. Slaveowners selected which among their female chat-
tel would be used as "breeders" and which would have their children sold
away. Owners, in other words, got to decide which enslaved women were
mothers and which ones were not.[1]

Also in the nineteenth century, and into the twentieth, the motherhood
status of a large but unknown number of white women was discredited
by "child rescue" reformers, who scooped up thousands of "street ur-
chins" and packed them onto "orphan trains" heading out to midwestern
farms and robust Protestant families. These reformers, associated with the
Children's Aid Society and other organizations, got to decide that poor,
Catholic women living in crowded, urban neighborhoods had weak
claims to be the mothers of their children. "Child rescuers" referred to
these children as orphans, even though many had living parents, and
asserted that "innocent if tarnished children [should be saved] from the
tyranny of unredeemable adults."[2]

In *Wake up Little Susie: Single Pregnancy and Race before Roe v. Wade,* I
showed how, in the decades after World War II, hundreds of thousands of
white unmarried girls and women were pressed—even coerced—into
giving their babies to properly married men and women to raise. During
these decades, biology did not constitute maternity for the thousands of
white unwed females who "got themselves pregnant." To be a mother
then required a properly sanctioned, legal relation to a man. Doctors,
lawyers, clergy, teachers, parents, and other adult authorities got to decide
that parturient girls and women who lacked that relation were not the
mothers of the children they bore.[3]

Long before Baby M and donor eggs and lesbian custody claims,
then, the United States had a rich and complex tradition of effacing the
motherhood status of some women. Laws and social mores in the past
justified taking children away from their mothers on many grounds,
including race and condition of bondage, class, religion, and marital
status. Throughout American history, the particular populations of
women whose motherhood status was vulnerable have shifted. But across
time, the girls and women whose motherhood claims were ignored or
denied shared a profound vulnerability, because they were defined as
possessing attributes that counted as social demerits—qualities that

marked them as not-mothers. Denial of their motherhood status was also fundamentally the result of what these females *lacked:* rights.

The enslaved woman, the poor city dweller, the middle-class, white unwed mother, lacked, of course, the *right* to determine for herself if she were mother to the child she bore, the right to live with and raise the child, if she wanted to. Slavery, the urban reform movement, and a cluster of authorities working to forestall the explosion of single mothers in the United States freely canceled women's claims to their children, defining their targets generally as females without the right to mother. Some girls and women in these groups did mother their children, of course, but the point is, they did not have the *right* to do so, even if many did in fact get the opportunity. It would be inaccurate, of course, to claim that the tightly constrained girls and women in these groups lacked *choice,* a human experience that presumes a degree of social latitude or free will to begin with.

Surveying public discussion—including legislative efforts and judicial renderings—about pregnancy and motherhood at the end of the twentieth century, we can see that the American tradition of denying motherhood rights to some women, based on some set of social demerits, remains vibrant. In recent times, government agencies, the courts, and other entities have threatened, enforced, or terminated the motherhood status of certain women and girls, against their stated desires and without evidence of abuse, because, for example, the woman in question was disabled, a political activist, too young, unmarried, comatose (judge denied abortion), divorced and had sex, too old, the wrong race, an atheist, a Native American, deaf, mentally ill, retarded, seeking an abortion, lesbian, reported to speak Spanish to her child, enrolled full-time in college, a drug user, poor. Contemporary political discourse, particularly, challenges the motherhood status of the class of females who are young, poor, and of color—the girls whose pregnancies and births are regularly cited as the source of the largest problems facing our country today.[4]

In the same way that the vulnerable ones lacked rights in the past, so do many girls and women—defined as possessing any of myriad social demerits—today. It is startling how weak the claim to mother rights remains at the end of the century. After all, many residents of the United States have perceived themselves since 1973 as living in a country that is governed, regarding matters of pregnancy and motherhood, by "choice," that is, by a public policy that empowers every woman to do as she wishes in this arena—a public policy that seems to encompass *rights,* but does not.

The primary purpose of this essay is to consider the consequences for millions of women in the United States of the brief flicker, and then the withering away, of "rights" claims in the pregnancy/motherhood arena, and the substitution of "choice" as the governing principle — the principle that girls and women must count on in order to own their own bodies and their destinies. I will argue that the concept of "choice" endangers many women in this country. And the danger is broad and deep, going well beyond the issue of abortion. The concept of "choice" influences public opinion and public policies regarding all aspects of pregnancy and motherhood in this country, and, most fundamentally, shapes answers to the question, "Who is a mother?" in ways that threaten the motherhood status of many women in the United States.

Rights and the Rise of Choice

In the late 1960s and into the 1970s, activists struggling for legal abortion did not talk, generally, in terms of "choice," although the term did crop up. NARAL's first national action, in 1969, a Mothers' Day demonstration held in conjunction with press conferences in eleven cities, was called "Children by Choice."[5] Among most activists in this area, however, including many NARAL organizers, the concepts of women's rights and bodily self-determination were paramount.[6] One feminist of that era explained why legal abortion became such a pressing concern: "In the late 1960s ... the issue of reproductive rights was tied to the awakening concept of feminism, the understanding that the right to control whether you're pregnant or not is indivisible from the right to self-determination."[7] The early reproductive rights movement claimed that all girls and women had the same rights in this arena, whatever their life circumstances or resources. The movement also claimed that these rights depended upon guaranteed access to the resources all girls and women would need in order to have reproductive freedom.

Despite these early rights claims, however, both the language of the court's majority opinion, as expressed by Justice Blackmun in *Roe v. Wade*— in which he referred to abortion as "this choice" a number of times—and the abortion rights movement's determination to develop a respectable, nonconfrontational, single-issue set of institutionalized tactics to secure the *Roe* decision after 1973 encouraged many proponents of legal abortion to adopt the term "choice" rather than "rights" in the early

1970s.[8] These proponents also built a tightly framed association between *choice* and *abortion,* thus cropping the bigger picture that "reproductive rights" envisioned. In a culture weary, after the 1960s and early 1970s, of strident rights claims, "choice" became *the* way liberal and mainstream feminists could talk about abortion without mentioning the "A-word."[9] The term "choice" was attractive for that reason and because it offered American women "rights lite," a package many perceived as less threatening than unadulterated rights, thus easier to sell.

At the point (approximately 1973) when "choice" replaced "rights" as the most common call for the legalized access to abortion, "choice" was perceived as the less threatening slogan for at least four reasons. "Choice" didn't create a new class of prerogatives for all women, an unattractive prospect to many people already uneasy about the expanding number of new sexual and economic prerogatives associated with the women's liberation movement. Nor did "choice" impose rights on women who didn't want them. In addition, "choice" could be perceived as an essentially conservative claim of personal freedom from state intervention, a claim that was consistent, of course with the "privacy" basis of the *Roe v. Wade* decision.[10] And finally, "choice" connotes the private exercise of personal freedom. This usage in the abortion arena, as Rhonda Copelon points out, underwrites "the conservative idea that the personal is separate from the political, and that the larger social structure has no impact on [or responsibility for] private, individual choice."[11]

The adoption of "choice" as the key term and the focus on abortion rather than on the broader array of issues that shaped the pregnancy and motherhood experiences of women, especially those who were *not* white and middle-class, had immediate consequences. Those who paid attention to the language of the dissenters in the *Roe* decision, Justices White and Rehnquist, could have predicted some of the consequences of "choice" that surfaced following the decision and have held on. The dissenters defined "the power of choice" as based on women's "convenience," "whim," "caprice," on women willing to "exterminate" their pregnancies "for no reason at all," or because of their "dislike of children." The dissenters clearly and early associated "choice" with bad women making bad choices.[12]

It is true that in the late 1960s, after several states had liberalized their abortion laws, and certainly after *Roe v. Wade* in 1973, thousands of women began to decide whether or not they wanted to stay pregnant and to seek out abortion as if it were their right.[13] In fact, for women with the resources to obtain abortions (and abortion was more widely available to all women in the early 1970s, before Congress passed the Hyde Amendment that denied Medicaid coverage for the abortions of poor women, before the advent of other legislated restrictions on access, and before the antiabortion forces' campaign of terror against abortion providers and their clinics), "choice" seemed indistinguishable from "reproductive rights."

Unfortunately, however, only a few years after *Roe*, one impact of "choice" was to alienate middle-class women from others—usually poorer and younger women—whose choices, at the same time, were collapsing under the weight of a new generation of constraints, symbolized most dramatically by the Hyde Amendment.[14] Many middle-class women did not notice that what they'd gained—choice—was a profoundly individualistic asset. The concept of reproductive choice presumed that a woman could exercise her new options unconstrained by socioeconomic structures such as sexism or racism or poverty. "Choice" assumed that every woman who sought them would have access to services enabling her to determine whether and when to become a mother. These assumptions did not match the life conditions of many women.[15]

Since the pregnancy and motherhood experiences of adult, white, middle-class women were different from those of other women—the underaged, the poor, and many women of color—the former often did not notice that soon after "choice" was legalized, many Americans, both liberals and conservatives, began drawing from the heart of the concept of choice to condemn large numbers of women in the United Staes for having made the *wrong choice*. If, after 1973, each woman possessed choice, then each pregnancy carried to term now signified a deliberate choice. That included the pregnancies (and babies) of all single mothers, all welfare mothers, all mothers who subsequently relinquished their babies, all teen mothers. Of these women it could now be said, and it was said, that they had made a *bad choice*.[16]

Over the next generation, public opinion and public policy makers increasingly defined these groups of women categorically as females who made bad choices, and rhetorically separated them from other women who exercised reproductive choice legitimately. One could argue that over time this tendency was a crucial factor in legitimating the termination of the federal assistance guarantee embodied for sixty-one years in the Aid to Families with Dependent Children (AFDC) program. As we see at the end of the century, public policy regarding such women has hardened: (poor) mothers-who-make-bad-choices are now defined as having a less compelling right to public aid, or no right at all—because of their bad choices. Many policy analysts argue that such women are so thoroughly undeserving that in addition to being denied cash assistance, their right to control their own mothering-related decisions (choices) in the future should be circumscribed or terminated.[17]

An additional and related quality of "choice" remained obscured in the generation after the adoption of that term: many mainstream feminists and others favoring legal abortion ignored the fact that "choice" is the ultimate consumerist concept in America. Inadvertently, perhaps, pro-choicers had linked the issues of pregnancy and motherhood to the marketplace—to shopping and buying, spending, getting, and owning. Throughout the 1970s and 1980s, and intensifying in the 1990s, "choice" became a ubiquitous term in the advertising arena. Choice was what the consumer was to exercise in selecting toothpaste, cars, furs, a neighborhood, a public or a private school for the children—but only if one had the resources. In a marketplace economy, everyone knows that without resources, the concept of choice is a taunting illusion, for choice cannot be exercised.

Reproductive "choice" implied that women could exercise decisions regarding pregnancy and motherhood within a consumerist framework and justified these decisions as consumerist behaviors. (It is not a coincidence that babies and children also became increasingly commodified in this general era.) What many people did not recognize in the 1970s, at the dawn of the era of choice—and many still don't—is that "choice" may appear to give females dignity as consumers, in the arena of reproduction, but it clearly denies them dignity as women and as mothers. Rights may have secured dignity, but choice could not. The dreadful situation of poor mothers, who have little status as consumers, proves that point.[18]

The Right to Choose and Motherhood

Before the legalization of abortion, of course, massive numbers of women had ignored the law in order to control their fertility.[19] After legalization, those who tried to estimate the actual number of these women often referred confidently to very large numbers; some experts claimed one million or more. One journalist in the early post-*Roe* years, typically gestured toward "statistics showing that almost as many women had abortions before they were legalized as [after]." [20] Even if the number of illegal abortions was similar to the number performed after legalization, as many public health experts claimed in the early seventies, the rightful and open exercise of choice had several huge, immediate, and apparently unforeseen and unintended impacts on the question, Who is a mother?

The most dramatic of the unintended consequences appears to have been that *Roe v. Wade* not only "gave" women the right to choose whether or not to stay pregnant. The Supreme Court ruling also renewed a prerogative for white women that this group had lacked for a generation. Now a white woman, even an unmarried one—who in the 1950s and 1960s would have been sharply pressed to relinquish her "illegitimate" infant—could decide for herself whether to become the mother of the child she bore. (African American women exercised this prerogative before and after *Roe*; they kept their "illegitimate" babies, though from the 1950s onward, in a context in which politicians and others tried to punish them for it.) [21] Whether or not the decriminalization of abortion actually *caused* white women to decide this matter for themselves, statistical records certainly suggest that many of these women were beginning to believe in the late 1960s and early 1970s that having the ability to make such a fundamental decision about motherhood—to choose abortion—gave them permission to exercise the alternate choice: to keep children that they would not have been able to keep during the preceding generation. [22]

Consequently, between 1967 and 1973, the number of families headed by single mothers nearly doubled. [23] In 1971, the number of adoptions fell for the first time since the federal government started keeping records. Unmarried white women were beginning to deny the authority of the experts pressing them to relinquish their "illegitimate" children, the group that had since World War II constituted 90 percent of the infants available for adoption. By 1975, the director of the North American Center on Adoption claimed (incorrectly, but dramatically and meaningfully) that in 1970, 80 percent of all unwed mothers gave their children up for adoption, whereas "now," she said, "eighty percent are deciding to keep their babies." [24] Many commentators at the time cited the legalization of abortion as bound up with liberalized attitudes toward unmarried sexuality, pregnancy, and childbearing, most specifically with the reduced stigma attached to single motherhood. [25]

As larger numbers of white, unmarried girls and women got abortions or—more or less de-stigmatized—began to keep their babies after *Roe*, two more related and unintentional consequences of choice surfaced. First, the decline of adoptable white babies significantly inflated the market value (and commodification) of those infants who were available in the United States. In 1976, an officer at the California Children's Home Society pointed to the "incredible nationwide baby hunger" sweeping the country, and the *New York Times* noted that "Babies are being sold in a fast-growing black market that charges anywhere from $5000 for an illegal adoption to $50,000 for a custom-made child. . . . Healthy white infants have become such a profitable commodity in the United States that law-enforcement officials fear the Mafia will soon become involved."[26]

Second, the decline caused an explosion in foreign adoptions. As the high price attached to white, native babies indicates, there were not, a few years after *Roe,* anywhere near enough of them to go around. So many American couples began to seek babies in other countries. Between 1968 and 1976, the number of foreign adoptions quadrupled.[27] Childless American couples turned to Colombia, Cambodia, Korea, and Mexico. Stories about where to get babies were passed around in the late 1970s, such as the one about the facility near Tijuana where "couples could pick out a child from a room full of babies, sort of like a supermarket."[28]

With so many American women becoming single mothers (a new coinage in the 1970s, replacing the stigmatized expression "unwed mother"), the market demand for white babies created opportunities for unscrupulous baby brokers to prey on *other women*—almost always young and poor, especially in the cases of Mexican, Cambodian, and other Third World women. The public discussion of the burgeoning domestic black market and the market in foreign babies, however, almost never referred to the fact that the babies "for sale" already had mothers. Instead, it focused on the desperation and hope of the mostly white, middle-class American couples seeking a baby: their risks, their disappointments, their joy when they finally succeeded in acquiring a child.[29] The relinquishing mother, foreign or domestic, was every bit as invisible as the white, middle-class birth mother had been in the 1950s and 1960s when it was she who provided the babies for adoption. Probably most Americans did not realize how profoundly the motherhood "choices" of middle-class women—to get abortions, or to become single mothers (both of which choices diminished the pool of babies who might have been available to others), or to become adoptive mothers—indirectly created or directly depended on the definition of other woman as having weak, or coercively transferable, motherhood rights. Nor was it always clear how much motherhood "choices" had to do with money, for both the women who had it and the women who did not.

To complicate the picture still further, in 1978 the first birth via in vitro fertilization occurred in England. That birth set off a wild, exciting, vituperative round of debates, still raging, about the politics and ethics of techno-motherhood.[30] (At the same time, this first in vitro birth promised a miraculous replacement source for all the white babies who'd been removed from the adoption market by the exercise of "choice," that is, by abortion and single motherhood.) One aspect of the new reproductive technologies (NRTs), though, that was not really debatable was that women who chose to combat infertility with NRTs had to be able to afford to do so. This was expensive terrain and clearly, any woman looking to become a mother using these methods needed a lot of money.[31] The advent of NRTs underscored, once again, the fact that women were exercising the right to choose in the marketplace, as consumers, and the fact that the babies they sought or lost or bought had become pretty thoroughly commodified.[32]

In the midst of all this upheaval about the meaning of choice and the privileges of motherhood, thousands of women in the United States who had been previously disqualified from making public motherhood claims for a number of reasons began to form support groups, lobbying organizations, and political action groups dedicated to making the case that in the era of choice, they, too, could be mothers. For example, the National Council of Single Adoptive Parents was formed in 1973, Custody Action for Lesbian Mothers and RESOLVE (an association to address issues of concern to infertile couples) in 1974, and Concerned United Birthparents in 1976. A number of other related organizations were formed in the 1970s and early 1980s. While many women who formed and joined these groups interpreted "choice" as providing them with a strong, new justification for pressing their own claims as mothers or potential mothers, many also felt that, given the miasmic context that "choice" created, it was necessary to assert these claims in terms of rights.[33]

In many ways, these groups became unlikely but sincere and clarified voices for feminism in the 1970s and 1980s, as members of more mainstream groups such as NOW divided against themselves, entangled in bitter disputes about sexuality, race, class, and often the unacknowledged ambiguities of promoting "choice." Sometimes unrecognized or rebuffed by other feminists, the new mothers' rights groups reinterpreted "choice," arguing that it underwrote the *right* of nontraditional mothers to speak up and the *right* to claim motherhood status for themselves. In the 1970s, few women spoke out in political terms, in public, mainstream venues, to claim personal autonomy *through motherhood*.[34] But these new mothers' rights groups created sanctuaries and platforms for "bad" mothers of the 1950s and 1960s—the formerly shamed birth mothers who'd been made to give up their babies; and for "bad" mothers of the 1970s—lesbian mothers, for example, whose ex-husbands tried to terminate their motherhood status through the courts. Ironically, members of these groups spoke up about their rights as mothers at a time when women's rights as mothers were, in a sense, losing definition.

Effacing Motherhood Rights in the Era of Choice

The women who organized Custody Action for Lesbian Mothers in 1974, the Committee for Mothers' and Children's Rights in 1980, and other mothers' rights groups formed in the decade after *Roe v. Wade* grafted the rights claims of the civil rights movement, the early women's movement, and the abortion rights movement onto their own claims about their entitlement to be mothers. At this time, however, as I've noted, the rights claim was becoming the weaker "choice" claim in the arena of reproductive politics. Also undermining the rights claim was a widespread cultural unhappiness with the coupling of motherhood and either rights or choice, a feature of the "backlash" documented by Susan Faludi. In the decade after *Roe v. Wade* this unhappiness took several concrete and sensational forms, including the rise of the antiabortion movement and the Reagan administration's organized attack on teen mothers and demonization of "welfare queens."[35] All of these public focuses on bad-women-making-bad-choices deepened the threat against the association of motherhood with either rights or choice, especially regarding young women, poor women, and women of color. For both liberals and conservatives, the idea of according teen mothers and welfare "abusers" *rights* was increasingly repugnant, since many people, at all points on the political spectrum, began to argue that the behavior of these girls and women was governed by bad choices, or license. Public interest in constraining and punishing women who exercised license, that is, disregarded the rules of personal conduct, grew stronger across the seventies, especially as the rights concepts of the civil rights movement and the women's rights movement were in the process of being transformed by late-century politics and economics.

By the post-*Roe v. Wade* era, the popularity of sanctioning women who made bad choices had weakened the legacy of the civil rights movement and threatened to trump it altogether, despite the fact that this movement's language of human rights had infused the culture at large, stimulating and shaping the rights claims of many groups in the 1970s.

Women of color were especially vulnerable, because the legacy of the civil rights movement was so complex regarding the meaning of their reproductive lives. On the one hand, during the civil rights movement, the bodies and reproductive capacity of African American women became highly visible and intensely politicized. Many leading African American male activists and others spoke out against genocide-promoting birth controllers and abortion rights proponents, in what they defined as efforts to protect their women, their culture, their demographic and political viability.[36] White demographers and racist politicians argued for constraining the fertility of black girls and women in order to contain ghetto unrest; to lower the tax bills of (white) taxpayers, bills inflated by welfare and other costs associated with the births of too many poor, brown children; and generally to forestall the shredding of the prerogatives of white supremacy.[37] (While their bodies and fertility were major focuses of a public discussion that aimed to transform their new reproductive rights into reproductive duty, the voices and interests of African American women, themselves, were scarcely heard, despite the centrality of their lives and their motherhood claims to these discussions.)[38]

On the other hand, ignoring the highly public roles of Rosa Parks and Fannie Lou Hamer and the less public, but nevertheless critical, roles of thousands of other African American women, many Americans perceived the civil rights movement as a male phenomenon.[39] This was especially true for the large number of white Americans who saw their own terrible fears and glorious promise reflected in the black man. Many whites at this time, perhaps particularly those endorsing some version of civil rights for African Americans, ostensibly viewed African American women and the political issues that involved their fertility as *outside of and independent from* the concerns of the movement. As white liberals spoke out in favor of the civil rights of African Americans or quietly, if bitterly, swallowed the inevitable recognition of those rights, some publicly discussed the excessive, expensive reproductive behavior of black women and crafted solutions, including mandated birth control, sterilization, and the legalization of abortion, to constrain their reproduction.[40] In this way, the bodies of black girls and women became the core, if displaced, focus of liberal resistance to the civil rights movement. At the same time, white conservatives explicitly tied their resistance to civil rights to the same bodies.

Both within and outside of the civil rights movement, then, the reproductive capacity of African American women (along with the related image of the burning ghetto) became a central terrain on which the politics of race and the economics of race and poverty, and rage were enacted. Into the mid-1970s, as African American women in large numbers came to use birth control and abortion services in their own interests,[41] much of the most heated rhetoric temporarily quieted down. Nevertheless, black women's bodies and their motherhood status remained intensely politicized.

One factor sustaining this politicization in the nascent "era of choice" was that many Americans measured the media's treatment of the reproductive behavior of African American women against the rhetoric of the emergent, largely white women's pro-choice movement, which advocated that women have few children and have them within a context of economic security.[42] By the end of the 1970s, many white Americans believed that African American women should have been implementing white feminist goals. When African American women didn't meet these goals (or when they were portrayed by the media as having "too many children"), they were judged more harshly than ever.[43] Charges against these women cited civil rights legislation that promised African Americans "equal opportunity." Black women who did not benefit from these "guarantees" were judged victims of their own bad choices. Here again, "excessively" procreating women were marked culprits.[44] Most explicitly, the rights claims of a liberatory movement were employed to demonstrate that bad-women-making-bad-choices were not living up to their new rights. Politicians, policy makers, and many ordinary Americans accused these women of spurning rights while perpetually making bad choices and proving themselves to be bad mothers.

The other great liberatory movement of the 1970s, the women's movement, also became, over time, a source of ideas for those interested in punishing women who exercised reproductive "choice" inappropriately. This movement's two central goals—to discredit the biological imperative and to expand women's employment and economic opportunities—appeared in the 1960s and early 1970s to be self-evidently fundamental to the empowerment of women. But by 1980, both of these tenets were being widely used in ways that endangered many women in the United States, and particularly threatened the motherhood claims of women who were young, poor, and/or of color.

The right to reject the biological imperative, "biology is destiny," was the first and most revolutionary principle of Second Wave feminism and central to the grass-roots feminist struggle for abortion rights.[45] But throughout the 1970s, partly because hundreds of thousands of women obtained abortions, other women, mostly middle class, began to demonstrate that biology was not destiny by pursuing foreign and domestic adoptions, new reproductive technologies, and various routes to single motherhood. Motherhood by choice (rather than as women's destiny) was widely implemented, through an explosion of purchasing power in the arena of motherhood. Any woman could become a mother if she had enough money to purchase a pregnancy, a child, and hence, motherhood.

Those women—poor, young, and especially poor, young, and of color—who appeared to behave reproductively as if biology were (still) destiny and had "too many" children were targeted as retrogressive by population controllers, by politicians interested in stimulating hostility to welfare recipients, and by others: Not only were these females irresponsibly backward, because they were non-users or ineffective users of birth control; they were also violating the first principle of modern womanhood—rational exercise of choice.[46] The attacks marginalized poor women in general as aberrant; they also deepened the alienation between middle-class white women and those with fewer resources. The former were in the process of *defining* their reproductive *right* to choose,[47] as the latter were, often, *being defined* as resisting their alleged *duty* to choose.[48]

The second core feminist goal in the late 1960s and early 1970s—equal rights for women in the areas of employment and economic opportunity—also turned into a threat against poor women and women of color and their "choices" by the mid-1970s. It is a well-known fact that in the 1950s, rather than "returning home" after stints as war workers, a million women a year streamed into the work force. This trend continued and accelerated in subsequent decades, in part the result of feminist claims regarding women's employment rights, in part the result of the growing need for female workers in the newly burgeoning service economy, and in part because families needed two incomes as the purchasing value of paychecks began to decline in the early 1970s.[49]

Most women workers in the United States, however, did not achieve economic self-sufficiency by earning a salary.[50] Most women earned two-thirds what men did, and most women workers were stuck in "pink ghetto" jobs. Decent wages and self-sufficiency (and adequate child care) were particularly elusive for women who entered the work force poor. Women who worked but remained poor or didn't achieve self-sufficiency—especially the growing number of single mothers—were increasingly confronted by these loaded questions: Can you afford to be a mother? Can you afford to exercise choice? Do you have the right to be a mother?

With the fall of the biological imperative, social commentators increasingly defined still-poor, often working mothers as having made the deliberate choice to have children, despite the fact that they couldn't afford motherhood. In the past, these women would have been simply seen as the "irresponsible poor." Now they were defined as more complex failures. They ignored their release from the biological imperative, plus they failed to capitalize on women's new economic opportunities to achieve personal liberation and economic self-sufficiency, the qualities that increasingly defined legitimate motherhood.[51] As it turned out, the escalating rates of women's work force participation became a justification for stigmatizing and disqualifying poor women as mothers. Women who earned enough at work (or who had husbands who did) therefore earned the right to choose motherhood. Those who did not earn enough, or earned nothing at all, were blameworthy, since "economic opportunity" was now women's right. Such women did not earn the right to choose motherhood. By 1980, motherhood was a contingent right that only good earners could choose.[52]

Many poor women and women of color—and others who assumed that the language of rights embodied in legislation and judicial decisions of the 1960s and 70s would justify their motherhood claims and protect them from attack—were hurt by the ways that "rights" were eviscerated by the mid-1970s. Most ironically, other Americans in this era continued to draw brazenly on the language of rights that had animated the civil rights and women's rights struggles of the late 1960s and early 1970s. By the end of the 1970s, in fact, men had rights, children had rights, fetuses had rights. In what was arguably the most profound irony of the decade, while fathers, children, and fetuses had achieved rights, women had achieved merely choice, and even that was increasingly provisional.

Conclusion

At the end of the century, the overlapping politics of abortion and welfare demonstrate exactly how poisonous "choice" has become. Congress and state legislatures across the country are bent on making laws specifically and explicitly designed to block the bad-choices-of-bad-women. The specter of women making bad choices or exercising license has become the wedge for recriminalizing abortion and ending welfare. At the heart of federal and state welfare "reform" and the congressional effort to enact the "D & X ban" that would outlaw a specific method of performing late abortions, for example, is the idea that without laws to constrain them, women make irresponsible choices at best and, more typically, choose to scam the system. This contemporary legislation aims to constrain and punish women whose behavior is shaped by the "caprice," "whim," and "convenience" Rehnquist and White warned against in 1973. Ironically, the dissenting opinion in the *Roe v. Wade* decision has become the majority view.[53]

As with slave women, poor Catholic urban women, and white unwed mothers in the past, many contemporary women are cast as lacking the right to claim motherhood status or to escape sanctions for having made the claim. If the new legal constraints are effective, "choice" will become completely irrelevant to their lives as well. But "choice" has a new trenchant relevancy for public policy, as it provides the antiwelfare constituency with a justification for ending benefits and provides antiabortion proponents with justification for tightening access to abortion.

After a quarter of a century, it is clear that "choice," a term that many people continue to use as if it is interchangeable with "rights," operates in a context quite alienated from women's rights.[54] Choice, like motherhood, has become a class privilege: for most women with economic resources, "choice" signifies the ability to make motherhood decisions. For women without, "choice" equals license and calls for restraints. "Choice" frames an updated set of class-based laws of procreation and provides a class-based guide to answering the question, Who is a mother?

NOTES

1. See, for example, Herbert G. Gutman, *The Black Family in Slavery and Freedom, 1750–1925* (New York: Vintage Books, 1977), 149, 153.

2. See Christine Stansell, "Women, Children, and the Uses of the Streets: Class and Gender Conflict in New York City, 1850–1860," *Feminist Studies* 8 (1982): 309–35.

3. Rickie Solinger, *Wake up Little Susie: Single Pregnancy and Race before* Roe v. Wade (New York: Routledge, 1992).

4. In late 1996, the Supreme Court ruled, 6–3, in *M.L.B. v. S.L.J.*, No. 95-853, that "the parent-child relationship is so fundamental that a state cannot prevent poor people from appealing the termination of their parental rights simply because they lack the money to pay court costs." This case concerned a mother of two in Mississippi who could not afford to pay two thousand dollars to obtain a trial transcript necessary for her to appeal a family court decision that "freed" her children for adoption by her ex-husband's new wife. Writing for the majority, Justice Ruth Bader Ginsburg "noted that the Constitution does not require the Government to compensate for most of the disabilities of poverty." But, she wrote, "we place decrees forever terminating parental rights in the category of cases in which the State may not bolt the door to equal justice." This decision seems very significant, although Justice Ginsburg also made a distinction in her majority opinion between termination of parental rights and loss of custody in a divorce, which, she wrote, "does not sever the parent-child bond." Linda Greenhouse, "Indigent Who Lost Parental Rights Gains in Top Court," *New York Times*, December 17, 1996, 1, 10.

5. Suzanne Staggenborg, *The Pro-Choice Movement: Organization and Activism in the Abortion Conflict* (New York: Oxford University Press, 1991), 51.

6. Ibid., 25.

7. Ninia Baehr, *Abortion without Apology* (Boston: South End Press, 1990), 29.

8. "*Roe v. Wade*, The 1973 Supreme Court Decision on State Abortion Laws," in Robert M. Baird and Stuart E. Rosenbaum, eds., *The Ethics of Abortion: Pro-Life! vs. Pro-Choice!* (Buffalo: Prometheus Books, 1993), 33–40; see also Staggenborg, *The Pro-Choice Movement*.

9. For a related discussion of language concerning abortion in the 1980s, see Will Saletan, "Electoral Politics and Abortion: Narrowing the Message," in Rickie Solinger, ed., *Abortion Wars: Fifty Years of Struggle, 1950–2000* (Berkeley: University of California Press, 1997), chap. 6.

10. "*Roe v. Wade*," in *The Ethics of Abortion*, 36–37.

11. Rhonda Copelon, "From Privacy to Autonomy: The Conditions for Sexual and Reproductive Freedom," in Marlene Gerber Fried, ed., *From Abortion to Reproductive Freedom: Transforming a Movement* (Boston: South End Press, 1990), 33.

12. "*Roe v. Wade*," 40–41.

13. See June Sklar and Beth Berkov, "Abortion, Illegitimacy, and the American Birth Rate," *Science* 185 (September 1974): 909–15.

14. See David Garrow, *Liberty and Sexuality: The Right to Privacy and the*

Making of Roe v. Wade (New York: Macmillan, 1994), 626–35. See also Rosalind Pollack Petchesky, *Abortion and Woman's Choice: The State, Sexuality, and Reproductive Freedom*, rev. ed. (Boston: Northeastern University Press, 1990), 250–52.

15. See, for example, Marlene Gerber Fried, "Abortion in the United States: Legal but Inaccessible," in Solinger, *Abortion Wars*, chap. 9; and Marlene Gerber Fried, "Transforming the Reproductive Rights Movement: The Post-Webster Agenda," in Fried, *From Abortion to Reproductive Freedom*, 1–26.

16. See, most prominently, Charles Murray, *Losing Ground: American Social Policy, 1950–1980* (New York: Basic Books, 1984). For a particularly literal-minded example, see "Parents Who Gave Up Babies Organize to Gain New Rights," *New York Times*, January 23, 1978, 18. Here Maria Bleschner, the secretary of the Adoptive Parents Committee (founded 1955) is quoted as saying, "If a woman wants to visit her child, she has no business placing that child. Either you're a parent, or you're not."

17. In addition to the Personal Responsibility Act, passed by Congress in 1996, the provisions of which define poor mothers as undeserving and manipulative, see Tamar Lewin, "A Plan to Pay Welfare Mothers for Birth Control," *New York Times*, February 9, 1991, 9. See also Christopher Jencks and Kathryn Edin, "Do Poor Women Have a Right to Bear Children?" *American Prospect* (Winter 1995): 43–52.

18. For a good example of the meaning of choice to poor mothers, see U.S. House of Representatives, *Hearings before the Subcommittee on Domestic Marketing, Consumer Relations and Nutrition of the Committee on Agriculture*, Cleveland, February 28, 1983, 98th Congr., 1st sess., 1983 (Washington, D.C.: U.S. Government Printing Office, 1983), 30. Evelyn Carter, a welfare recipient testified as follows before government officials: "My kids don't go hungry because there are so many days that I don't eat or that I eat very little so my kids may eat a few days longer. This is what I would like the Government to know while they talk about the cuts. . . . You talk about cuts. What do you want from us? We don't choose to be poor. What do you want from us?"

19. In Sklar and Berkov, "Abortion, Illegitimacy, and the American Birth Rate," the authors claim that "well over half—most likely between two-thirds and three-quarters—of all legal abortions in the United States in 1971 were replacements for illegal abortions" (915).

20. Roger M. Williams, "The Power of Fetal Politics," *Saturday Review*, June 16, 1979, 15.

21. See Solinger, *Wake up Little Susie.*

22. See, for example, "Why a Sudden Drop in Baby Adoptions?" *U.S. News and World Report*, July 30, 1973, 62. For a pioneering account, see also Jane Harriman, "In Trouble," *Atlantic*, March 1970, 94–98.

23. "Why a Sudden Drop in Baby Adoptions?"

24. "Black Market Babies: $4000 to $40,000," *U.S. News and World Report,* May 19, 1975, 34.

25. See, for example, Lynne McTaggert, "Babies for Sale: The Booming Adoption Rackets," *Saturday Review,* November 10, 1977, 16. The author observes, "The nationwide repeal of the abortion laws in 1973 has contributed to a severe baby shortage . . . [and] with increasingly more liberal attitudes toward illegitimacy, most unwed mothers are deciding to keep their babies."

26. "Price for Babies Rising in Wider Black Market," *New York Times,* April 25, 1976, 50.

27. Wendell Rawls, Jr., "Adoption Abroad Brings Heartache to Some Couples," *New York Times,* June 24, 1978, 1,20.

28. Robert Lindsey, "Childless Couples Adopt in Mexico, Often Illegally," *New York Times,* November 13, 1978, 18.

29. See, for example, Dierdre Levinson, "Hers," *New York Times Magazine,* November 4, 1982, 2; Celestine Bohlen, "The Hurdles are Many, but the Reward Is a Child," *New York Times,* November 15, 1990, 4; Sarah Lyall, "Party on Long Island Celebrates Latin Adoptions," *New York Times,* April 3, 1989, B3.

30. The dozens of publications on this topic include Gena Corea, *The Mother Machine: From Artificial Insemination to Artificial Wombs* (New York: Harper & Row, 1985); Robyn Rowland, *Living Laboratories: Women and Reproductive Technologies* (Bloomington: Indiana University Press, 1992); Ruth Hubbard, *The Politics of Women's Biology* (New Brunswick, N.J.: Rutgers University Press, 1992), part 3; Barbara Katz Rothman, *Recreating Motherhood: Ideology and Technology in a Patriarchal Society* (New York: Norton, 1989).

31. See, for example, *Infertility: Medical and Social Choices Summary* (Washington, D.C.: Congress of the United States, Office of Technology Assessment, 1988), which reported that in 1987 Americans spent one billion dollars on medical care to combat infertility, 7 percent, or $210 million, of that on in vitro fertilization.

32. For statements illuminating the relation between NRTs, infants' "defects," and commodification, see, for example, U.S. House of Representatives, *Hearings before the Subcommittee on Transportation, Tourism and Hazardous Materials of the Committee on Energy and Commerce,* on H.R. 2433, "A Bill to Prohibit Certain Arrangements Commonly Called Surrogate Motherhood, and for Other Purposes," 100th Cong., 1st sess., October 15, 1987 (Washington, D.C.: U.S. Government Printing Office, 1988), 78; and for a statement regarding adoption as the transfer of a commodity between birthmother and adoptive parents, see letter from Kenneth Groves, Forest Hills, New York, to the *New York Times,* May 28, 1977, 18.

33. An early member of Concerned United Birthparents expressed her claim in a manner that strongly suggested she believed in her mother-rights: "I am a mother—and that simply can't be obliterated." "Parents Who Gave Up Babies."

34. See Lauri Umansky, *Motherhood Reconceived: Feminism and the Legacies of the Sixties* (New York: New York University Press, 1996) for a fuller discussion of motherhood discourse among early Second Wave feminists.

35. On the rise of the antiabortion movement, see Petchesky, *Abortion and Woman's Choice*, chap. 7; regarding the attack on teen pregnancy in this era, see Kristen Luker, *Dubious Conceptions: The Politics of Teenage Pregnancy* (Cambridge: Harvard University Press, 1996); for a comprehensive analysis of rising hostility toward welfare recipients beginning in the 1970s, consult Mimi Abramovitz, "The Attack on Women and Welfare," lecture delivered at the Brecht Forum, New York City, October 31, 1996, tape or transcript available from Alternative Radio, P.O. Box 551, Boulder, Colo. 80306, (800) 444-1977.

36. See Joyce Ladner, *Tomorrow's Tomorrow: The Black Woman* (New York: Anchor Books, 1972), 247–63; Robert G. Weisbord, *Genocide? Birth Control and the Black American* (Westport, Conn.: Greenwood Press, 1975).

37. See Solinger, *Wake up Little Susie*, chaps. 2, 6, 7.

38. See, for example, the wide-ranging discussions that exclude African American women in the U.S. Congress on the need to constrain the reproductive behavior of this group, in U.S. Senate, Committee on Government Operation, Subcommittee on Foreign Aid Expenditures, *Population Crisis: Hearings on S.1676, A Bill to Reorganize the Department of State and the Department of Health, Education, and Welfare*, 89th Cong., 1st sess., (Washington, D.C.: Government Printing Office, 1966), August 31, September 8, 15, 22, 1964, parts 1–4.

39. The fact that the *citizenship rights* of African Americans were at issue tended to encourage many white Americans to associate the movement's goals with men.

40. See, most famously, Daniel Patrick Moynihan, *The Negro Family: The Case for National Action* (Washington, D.C.: Government Printing Office, 1965); see also Thomas Littlewood, *The Politics of Population Control* (Notre Dame, Ind.: University of Notre Dame Press, 1977); and Petchesky, *Abortion and Woman's Choice*, 116–25.

41. See Loretta Ross, "African-American Women and Abortion, 1950 to the End of the Century," in Solinger, *Abortion Wars*, chap. 8.

42. See Patricia Hill Collins, "The Meaning of Motherhood in Black Culture and Black Mother/Daughter Relationships," *Sage* 4 (Fall 1987): 4–11.

43. See Manning Marable, *How Capitalism Underdeveloped Black America* (Boston: South End Press, 1983), 279, n. 3, for references to studies indicating that in this era, African American women reported wanting fewer children than white women reported wanting.

44. It is, of course, a profound irony that at approximately the same time that the Hyde Amendment cut off Medicaid funding for poor women's abortions, the federal government began to slash welfare benefits. As a result of these public

policy initiatives, poor women who got pregnant were more likely than ever to become and to stay poor mothers.

45. See Ellen Willis, "Putting Women Back into the Abortion Debate," in Marlene Gerber Fried, *From Abortion to Reproductive Freedom: Transforming a Movement* (Boston: South End Press, 1990): "To me the fight for abortion has always been the cutting edge of feminism, precisely because it denied that anatomy is destiny" (134).

46. See Marlene Gerber Fried and Loretta Ross, "Our Bodies, Our Lives, Our Right to Decide: The Struggle for Abortion Rights and Reproductive Freedom," excerpt from Open Magazine Pamphlet, reprinted in *Radical America* 24 (April–June 1990, pub. July 1992): "[The government] locates the cause and the blame of poverty in women's individual choices—women are poor because they have too many children" (36).

47. Like the copywriter in the Kenneth Cole ad, I find the slogan, "the right to choose" somewhat ridiculous: it impossibly mixes "right," a privilege to which one is justly entitled, and "choice," the privilege to exercise discrimination in the marketplace between a group of options, *if* one has the wherewithal to enter the marketplace to begin with. Our Constitution does not, of course, guarantee anyone the right to enter the marketplace of reproductive (or any other) options. The Supreme Court's decisions regarding the legitimacy of the Hyde Amendment certainly prove that. See *Harris v. McRae,* 448 U.S. 297 (1981). Also see Petchesky, *Abortion and Woman's Choice,* 131.

48. Fried and Ross, in "Our Bodies, Our Lives," note that "individual freedom of choice is a privilege not enjoyed by those whose reproductive lives are shaped primarily by poverty and discrimination" (36).

49. See Abramovitz, "The Attack on Women and Welfare"; and Teresa Amott and Julie Matthaei, *Race, Gender and Work: A Multicultural Economic History of Women in the United States* (Boston: South End Press, 1996), chap. 10.

50. Amott and Matthaei, *Race, Gender and Work,* table 9–6, 310.

51. We have witnessed a fascinating and terribly consequential shift during the past generation from a focus on "illegitimate children" to a focus on *illegitimate mothers.*

52. For a straightforward expression of this conviction, see the oral testimony of William Pierce, executive director of the National Committee for Adoption: "If we had an adoption system that worked in this country, we would have hundreds of thousands of babies that would be placed with capable couples. They wouldn't be raised by young, poorly educated, unemployed young women." U.S. House, Hearings on "A Bill to Prohibit Certain Arrangements Commonly Called Surrogate Motherhood and for Other Purposes," 103.

53. A few additional and extreme examples that demonstrate the widespread expectation that women will abuse choice and make bad choices if they're not

constrained by law and policy include the efforts of Louisiana legislators to deny a rape-exception provision in their already draconian antiabortion legislation. The lawmakers explained that such an exception would pave the way for thousands of false rape reports. *New York Times,* July 8, 1990, 10. See also the account of the New York City Social Services Department's institution of a new policy in 1977 requiring mothers applying for aid to sign the following affidavit: "I had relations with the above-named father at or about the period of conception preceding the birth of said child, and I did not have relations with any other male person during such period of conception." *New York Times,* February 12, 1977, 25.

54. See Petchesky, *Abortion and Women's Choice,* chap. 3.

Contributors

Emily K. Abel is professor of health services and women's studies at UCLA. Her most recent works are *Circles of Care: Work and Identity in Women's Lives*, coedited with Margaret K. Nelson, and *Who Cares for the Elderly? Public Policy and the Experiences of Adult Daughters*. She currently is writing a history of women's care for sick and disabled family members from 1850 to 1940.

Christine J. Allison is a Ph.D. student in sociology at the University of California at Santa Barbara. Her areas of interest include feminist studies, sexuality, and public policy. She is currently working on a master's thesis which examines how children with lesbian mothers manage social stigma.

Annette R. Appell is assistant professor of law at the University of South Carolina Law Center. Previously, she spent eight years representing children and parents in child protection and adoption proceedings in the Juvenile Court of Cook County, Illinois, first as an assistant public guardian, acting as attorney and guardian ad litem for thousands of children, and then as attorney and law teacher at the Children and Family Justice Center of Northwestern University.

Paula J. Caplan is a clinical and research psychologist, author, playwright, and actor. She is a visiting scholar at Brown University's Pembroke Center for Women and a former full professor of applied psychology at the Ontario Institute for Studies in Education. In addition to *Don't Blame Mother*, she is the author of the following books: *Children's Learning and Attention Problems*; *Between Women: Lowering the Barriers*; *The Myth of Women's Masochism*; *Lifting a Ton of Feathers: A Woman's Guide to Surviving in the Academic World*; *Thinking Critically about Research on Sex and Gender*, coauthored with her son, Jeremy B. Caplan; *You're Smarter than They Make You Feel: How the Experts*

Intimidate Us and What We Can Do about It; and *They Say You're Crazy: How the World's Most Powerful Psychiatrists Decide Who's Normal.*

Norma Coates is a feminist media scholar who writes about popular music. She has spent much of her academic career trying to answer the question, "How can a smart chick like me love the Stones and still respect herself in the morning?"

Su Epstein currently teaches sociology, criminology, cultural studies, and women's studies at SUNY College at Oneonta. Her research and academic interests typically are in the areas of cultural criminology and deviance.

Ruth Feldstein teaches in the history and literature program at Harvard University. She has a book forthcoming from Cornell University Press that addresses connections between race and gender in American liberal culture from the 1930s through the 1960s.

Kathleen W. Jones is an assistant professor of history at Virginia Polytechnic Institute and State University. She is currently completing *Taming the Troublesome Child: American Families, Child Guidance, and the Limits of Psychiatric Authority,* to be published by Harvard University Press.

Molly Ladd-Taylor is associate professor of history at York University in Toronto. She is the author of *Mother-Work: Women, Child Welfare and the State, 1890–1930* and editor of *Raising a Baby the Government Way: Mothers' Letters to the Children's Bureau, 1915–1932.* She recently published "Saving Babies and Sterilizing Mothers: Eugenics and Welfare Politics in the Interwar United States" in *Social Politics* (Spring 1997).

Betty Jean Lifton is a writer, psychologist, and adoption counselor. She is the author of *Journey of the Adopted Self: A Quest for Wholeness*; *Lost and Found: The Adoption Experience*; and *Twice Born: Memoirs of an Adopted Daughter*; as well as *The King of Children: The Life and Death of Janusz Korczak, A Place Called Hiroshima* (with the photographer Eikoh Hosoe), and numerous books and plays for children. She has lectured extensively and held workshops in the U.S. and abroad on the psychology of the adopted child, the birth mother, and adoptive parents. She is a founding member of the American Adoption Congress, which works for truth and openness in adoption.

Elaine Tyler May is professor of American studies and history at the University of Minnesota. She is the author of *Barren in the Promised Land: Childless Americans and the Pursuit of Happiness*; *Homeward Bound: American Families in the Cold War Era*; *Pushing the Limits: American Women, 1940–1961*; and *Great Expectations: Marriage and Divorce in Post-Victorian America.*

Jane Taylor McDonnell teaches women's studies at Carleton College, where she has offered a course called "The Politics of Motherhood" and where she directed the concentration in women's Studies for thirteen years. She is the author of *News from the Border: A Mother's Memoir of Her Autistic Son.* Together with her son, she has given many presentations on the subject of autism to radio and television audiences, as well as to college students, parent groups, and teachers' workshops. She is at work on a book concerning personal narratives, *Living to Tell the Tale: A Writer's Guide to the Memoir.*

Annalee Newitz has published articles on U.S. popular culture in journals, books, and newspapers. She is the coeditor of *White Trash: Race and Class in America* and *The Bad Subjects Anthology.* Currently she is completing a book about how the horrors of twentieth-century economic life get represented in pop culture about monsters and psychopaths. She will receive a Ph.D. in English from Berkeley in 1997.

Steven Noll is a visiting assistant professor in the department of history at the University of Florida. He has recently published *Feeble-Minded in Our Midst*, a study of southern institutions for the mentally retarded from 1900 to 1940. He is presently working on a study of deinstitutionalization during the 1920s and 1930s.

Katha Pollitt is associate editor at *The Nation* and author of *Reasonable Creatures: Essays on Women and Feminism.*

Renee Romano is an assistant professor of history and African American Studies at Wesleyan University. She is currently working on a book on black-white interracial marriage in the United States since 1945.

Elizabeth Rose teaches U.S. and women's history at Vanderbilt University. She received her Ph.D. from Rutgers University in 1994 and is the author of *A Mother's Job: The History of Day Care, 1890–1960* (Oxford University Press, forthcoming).

Diane Sampson is a Ph.D. candidate in the American culture department at the University of Michigan. When not writing or teaching about social reproduction and work in the twentieth-century United States, she parents three children with her partner, Blake Zenger. She is working on a dissertation entitled "Zoe Baird and Lillian Cordero: Working Women, Illegal Girls, and the Politics of Social Reproduction in the Late Twentieth Century."

Rickie Solinger is the author of *Wake up Little Susie: Single Pregnancy and Race before Roe v. Wade* and *The Abortionist: A Woman against the Law.* She is the editor of *Abortion Laws: Fifty Years of Struggle, 1950–2000,* and is currently working on a book entitled *Who Is a Mother? And Who Decides?* She lives in Boulder, Colorado, where she is a visiting scholar in women's studies at the University of Colorado.

Jennifer Terry is assistant professor of comparative studies at Ohio State University. She coedited *Deviant Bodies: Critical Perspectives on Difference in Science and Popular Culture* and *Processed Lives: Gender and Technology in Everyday Life.* Her essays on sexuality and science have appeared in *differences, Journal of Sex Research,* and *Socialist Review.* Her forthcoming book is entitled *An American Obsession: Science, Homosexuality, and Defining Norms of Citizenship.*

Karen W. Tice, a social worker and assistant professor of educational policy studies and evaluation at the University of Kentucky, studies women's activism and the professionalization of social work. She is the author of *Tales of Wayward Girls and Immoral Women: Social Case Records and the Construction of Professional Knowledge, 1900–1935* (forthcoming).

Lauri Umansky teaches history and women's studies at Suffolk University. Her writings include *Motherhood Reconceived: Feminism and the Legacies of the 1960s.*

Index